Arts and Ideas II

Fine Arts 106

Student Manual

Revised Printing

Laurinda Dixon

Syracuse University

KENDALL/HUNT PUBLISHING COMPANY
4050 Westmark Drive Dubuque, Iowa 52002

Cover image: Winslow Homers The Country School (detail). The Saint Louis Art Museum.

Revised Printing 2006

ISBN 0-7575-2669-1

Printed in the United States of America
10 9 8 7 6 5 4 3 2

Contents

General Course and Exam Information

The course syllabus and calendar are posted on the web at http://syllabus.syr.edu/FIA/dixon/FIA106

Required Texts and Materials

The following items are required and can be purchased at the Syracuse University Bookstore.

Gloria K. Fiero, *The Humanistic Tradition,* Volume II, Fifth Edition.

Student Manual for Arts & Ideas, FIA 106, Second Edition

Course Requirements

Your grade will be based on your record of attendance and class participation, three non-cumulative examinations, and a take-home essay project.

ATTENDANCE at all lecture and discussion sessions is mandatory.

CLASS PARTICIPATION usually will not be possible in the large lectures, but you are expected to contribute to discussion sections.

THE TAKE-HOME PROJECT will require that you visit an art exhibition specially mounted for this class, and that you write about it. Details will be distributed in discussion sections toward the end of the semester. Worth 25% of the grade.

EXAMINATIONS will test your knowledge of specific historical and visual information about works of art discussed in lectures and illustrated in the Fiero book and on the web. You also will be tested on art historical vocabulary and asked to write short essays comparing and contrasting works of art. Images, essay questions, and terms will be drawn from the lists of terms and study questions that accompany each chapter division in this handbook. The three exams are worth 25% each; total, 75%.

Your individual discussion leader grades your exams and papers. He or she calculates your final grade according to the percentages described above, taking into consideration additional factors such as attendance and participation in discussions. Professor Dixon does not evaluate your performance or assign your grade.

Extra credit is not allowed in this course.

Absence Policy

By remaining in this course, you agree to the terms and conditions stated below.

UNDER NO CIRCUMSTANCES WILL MAKE-UP EXAMINATIONS BE OFFERED IN THIS COURSE. A student may miss an exam for a very serious reason only, such as incapacitating illness or documented death in the immediate family. Medical excuses require a physician's note stating that the student was physically unable to take an exam at the date and time at which it was offered. The form routinely given by the Student Health Service is not sufficient documentation. Death in the immediate family must also be documented by a published obituary or similar document. If you miss an exam for an unacceptable reason, you will receive zero (0) points for the exam, which will be counted like any other grade. Professor Dixon is the only person who has the right to judge what constitutes an acceptable excuse for missing an examination. YOU MUST INFORM YOUR DISCUSSION LEADER (T.A.) OR PROFESSOR DIXON 24 HOURS IN ADVANCE OF ANY ABSENCE FROM AN EXAM. Students with legitimate excuses will be dealt with on an individual basis.

Special Needs

Students who may need special consideration because of any sort of disability must obtain documentation from the Learning Center and make an appointment to speak with their discussion leader during the first week of classes. Special problems may be addressed to Professor Dixon. Final decisions rest with her.

Academic Dishonesty

Academic dishonesty in any form is unacceptable. Anyone caught cheating at any time during the semester will receive an AUTOMATIC "F" for the course.

Department of Fine Arts Policy on Plagiarism

The Department of Fine Arts does not tolerate plagiarism in the work of students enrolled in Fine Arts courses. Plagiarism is defined in the Syracuse University Bulletin, Academic Rules and Regulations, as "the representation of another's words, ideas, programs, formulae, opinions, or other products of work as one's own, either overtly or by failing to attribute them to their true source. Sanctions for violations will be imposed by the dean, faculty, or Student Standards Committee of the appropriate school or college."

The Department of Fine Arts wishes to make clear to students that in all class work—both examinations and papers—information that is indebted to another source must be identified. If the work of someone else is being summarized or paraphrased, that, too, must be acknowledged by a clear reference.

Direct quotations taken from another source must be surrounded by quotation marks and credited by a footnote, endnote, or parenthetical statement. Specific page numbers are essential. Specific citations are also necessary even when you put another author's ideas into your own words. If the idea did not originate with you, give a citation.

Proper citation will not only help you avoid the suspicion of plagiarism, but also adds authority to your statements, gives respectful credit to people who have helped you, and protects you in case your source contains errors.

Students who are unsure as to what procedures to follow are encouraged to discuss the matter with their discussion leaders.

Additional Images on the web at http://syllabus.syr.edu/FIA/dixon/FIA106

For Exam 1

Borromini, Plan of St. Carlo
Copley, *Portrait of Paul Revere*
David, *Portrait of Napoleon*
David, *Intervention of the Sabine Women*
Giovanni da Bologna, *Mercury*
Hogarth, *Marriage à la Mode* (*The Marriage Contract* and *After the Marriage*)
Kauffmann, *Cornelia*
Steen, *Sick Maiden*
Veronese, *Feast in the House of Levi*
Vignola, *Plan of Il Gesù*
Watteau, *Gersaint's Signboard*
West, *Agrippina*

For Exam 2

Cole, *Voyage of Life* (*Youth* and *Manhood*)
Degas, *Bather*
Delacroix, *Portrait of Paganini*
Delacroix, *Death of Sardanapolis*
Eakins, *Gross Clinic*
Fremiét, *Woman Carried Off by a Gorilla*
Friedrich, *Wanderer*
Géricault, *Portrait of a Madwoman*
Millais, *Ophelia*
Millet, *The Gleaners*

For Exam 3

Maya Ying Lin, Vietnam Memorial
Severini, *Armored Train*
Shahn, *Sacco and Vanzetti*
Wood, *American Gothic*

UNIT ONE

Faith, Reason, and Power in the Early Modern World

STUDY GUIDE

The Catholic Reformation and the Baroque Style

Fiero, Chapter 20

Names

Bernini
Borromini
Caravaggio
El Greco
Artemisia Gentileschi
Giovanni da Bologna
Loyola
~~Neri~~
Parmigianino
Pozzo
Teresa of Avila
Tintoretto
~~Veronese~~
Vignola and della Porta

Terms

chiaroscuro
Council of Trent
Counter Reformation
Jesuits
mannerism
Protestants

Music

aria
concertato
Gabrieli
Monteverdi
opera
overture
polychoral
recitative

Study Questions

1. Describe the "theatrical" aspect of Baroque art and music. Consider the art of Bernini and the music of Monteverdi.
2. How do each of the following illustrate the Catholic Reformation emphasis on the immediacy of religious experience: Loyola's *Spiritual Exercise*, Bernini's *Ecstasy of St. Teresa*, and Artemisia's *Judith*?
3. Discuss the effect of the Catholic Reformation on the New World in the 17th century. How is Spanish social and religious colonization still evident in South America?
4. Discuss the alterations in Church architecture which met the challenge of the Catholic Reformation using Il Gesù as an example.

Images from Fiero

20.2, 20.4, 20.5, 20.7, 20.8, 20.9, 20.10, 20.11, 20.12, 20.13, 20.14, 20.15, 20.16, 20.17, 20.19, 20.20, 20.21

Additional Images on the Web

Borromini, Plan of San Carlo; Giovanni da Bologna, *Mercury*; Vignola, plan of Il Gesu; Veronesi, *Feast in the House of Levi*

STUDY GUIDE

Absolute Power and the Aristocratic Style

Fiero, Chapter 21

Names and Places, Europe

absolutism
academy
Claude Lorrain
Girardon
Le Vau
Louis XIV
~~Lully~~
Mansart
Perrault
Poussin
Rigaud
Rubens
Velàzquez
Versailles

Names and Places Beyond Europe

Persia

Ottoman Empire
Sulieman

India

Moguls
Shah Jahan

China

Ming Dynasty
Qing dynasty
cloisonné
porcelain

Japan

haiku
Hakuin Ekaku
kabuki
Ogata Korin
Tokugawa dynasty
Toshusai Sharaku
~~Zen~~

Study Questions

1. Compare the façade of the Louvre to that of San Carlo alle Quattro Fontane. How are classical elements used in each? How does each building affirm an official authoritarian stance?
2. How is French opera as formulated by Lully reflective of the concept of authoritarianism in the arts? Compare Lully's musical strategies with Mansart's architecture.
3. Compare the styles of Rubens and Poussin. How do they both reflect official court concerns?
4. Compare the palace complex at Versailles to the Mogul and Chinese complexes illustrated in this chapter. What differences do you see in the Eastern examples?

Images from Fiero

21.1, 21.2, 21.3, 21.4, 21.5, 21.6, 21.9, 21.10, 21.11, 21.12, 21.13, 21.14, 21.15, 21.17, 21.18, 21.19, 21.20, 21.21, 21.22, 21.24, 21.26, 21.27, 21.28, 21.29, 21.30, 21.31, 21.32, 21.33, 21.34, 21.35

Web Resources

Kabuki sounds and makeup, plus summaries of major plays:
http://www.fix.co.jp/kabuki/kabuki.html

Virtual tour of China's Forbidden City
http://www.chinavista.com/beijing/gugong/!start.html

Virtual tour of the Chateau de Versailles
http://www.chateauversailles.fr/en/

STUDY GUIDE

The Baroque in the Protestant North; The Scientific Revolution and the New Learning

Fiero, Chapters 22 and 23

Names

Descartes
Galileo
Hals /
de Heem /
de Hooch /
Leyster /
~~Newton~~
Oosterwyck /
Rembrandt
Steen /
Ter Borch
Van Dyck /
Vermeer /
Wren /
~~Wright~~

Terms

camera obscura
deism
etching
genre scene
impasto
still life
vanitas

Music

Bach
cantata
fugue
Handel
~~harpsichord~~
organ
oratorio
text painting
Vivaldi

Study Questions

1. Compare the painterly styles of Rembrandt and Vermeer. How do both reflect the bourgeois Baroque aspect of Dutch culture by different means?
2. Compare a landscape by Claude Lorrain (chapter 21) with one by Vermeer. How are they different and why?
3. What effect did Protestantism have on music and art in 17th-century Holland?
4. Describe the relationship between art and science in 17th-century Holland, using specific examples.

Images from Fiero

22.1, 22.2, 22.4, 22.6, 23.2, 23.4, 23.5, 23.6, 23.7, 23.8, 23.9, 23.10, 23.12, 23.13, 23.14, 23.15, 23.16

Additional Image on the Web

Steen, *Lovesick Maiden*

Vivaldi's Four Seasons: The Sonnets

Vivaldi's *Four Seasons* are four concertos for solo violin and strings. Each one is highly programmatic, demonstrating Baroque "text painting." They follow the words of the following sonnets, which describe nature's moods throughout the cycle of the year.

Spring

Spring has come, and the birds greet it with a cheerful song; And with the breath of the gentle breezes, springs trickle with a pleasant murmur. Lightening and thunder, elected to announce it, come and cover the air with a black cloak. After the storm, the birds return to their enchanting song. Then on the pleasant, flowering meadow a goatherd, with his faithful dog at his side, sleeps to the sweet murmur of the foliage and plants. To the festive sound of a rustic bagpipe, nymphs and shepherds dance under the beloved canopy at the brilliant appearance of spring.

Summer

Under the harsh season ignited by the sun, man and flock languish and the pines burn; the cuckoo offers his voice and, soon heard, the young turtledove and goldfinch sing. Zepher (west wind) blows gently, but suddenly Boreas (north wind) offers opposition to his neighbor; and the shepherd boy weeps, because he fears a severe storm in the offing—and his destiny. The repose of his tired limbs is disturbed by the fear of lightning and fiery thunder, and by a furious swarm of flies and wasps. Unfortunately, his fears are justified. The sky thunders and fulminates, and hail flattens the corn and majestic grains.

Autumn

The peasant celebrates the blissful pleasure of a happy harvest with dances and songs, and glowing with the liquor of Bacchus, many complete their enjoyment with sleep. The air tempered by pleasure, makes everyone give up dances and songs. It is this season that invites so many to the great enjoyment of a sweet sleep. At dawn the hunters are off to the hunt with horns, rifles, and dogs. The wild beast flees and they follow its trail. Frightened already, and fatigued by the noise of rifles and dogs, wounded, it threatens languidly to flee, but, overcome, it dies.

Winter

To tremble from the cold in the icy snow, in the harsh breath of a horrid wind; to run, stamping our feet every moment, our teeth chattering in the extreme cold. Before the fire to pass peaceful contented days while the rain outside pours down. To walk on the ice and, at a slow pace for fear of falling, move carefully. To make a bold turn, to slip, to fall down. To go on the ice once more and run hard until the ice breaks up. To hear the sirocco (warm south wind), Boreas, and all the winds at war leave their iron gates; this is winter, but, even so, what joy it brings!

STUDY GUIDE

The Promise of Reason; The Limits of Reason

Fiero, Chapters 24 and 25

Names and Terms

Diderot
Enlightenment
Hobbes
Hogarth
Houdon
Jefferson
Locke
novel
Philosophes
Rousseau
salon
Swift
Voltaire
Wollstonecraft

Dates to Remember

1776, American Revolution

1789, French Revolution

Study Questions

1. How is the United States of America based upon Enlightenment concepts?

Images in chapters 24 and 25 are listed in the Study Guide for chapter 26.

STUDY GUIDE

Eighteenth-Century Art, Music, and Society

Fiero, Chapter 26

Rococo Style

Boffrand
Boucher
Chardin
Clodion
fête galante
Fischer
Fragonard
Greuze
Hogarth
Vigée Lebrun
Watteau

Neoclassical Style

Adam
~~Canova~~
Chalgrin
Copley
David
Gibbs
Houdin
Ingres
Jefferson
Kauffmann
Napoleon
Percier
Piranesi
Soufflot
Vignon
Wedgwood
West
Winckelmann

Music

Haydn
Mozart

orchestra
sonata form
(exposition, development, recapitulation)
string quartet
symphony

Study Questions

1. Discuss the concepts of form and structure in Neoclassical music and art. Discuss David's *Oath of the Horatii* and sonata form.
2. Distinguish several stylistic characteristics of the Rococo style. Note these characteristics in a painting, a work of architecture, and a work of music.
3. How did 18th-century Neoclassicism differ from the revival of ancient art that took place in the Renaissance? Why the difference?
4. Compare a painting by Chardin with one by Fragonard. How are they different and why?

Images from Fiero

24.2, 24.4, 25.3, 25.4, 25.5, 26.1, 26.4, 26.5, 26.6, 26.7, 26.8, 26.9, 26.10, 26.11, 26.12, 26.15, 26.16, 26.18, 26.19, 26.20, 26.21, 26.22, 26.24, 26.25, 26.26, 26.27, 26.31, 26.33

Additional Images on the Web

Copley, *Portrait of Paul Revere;* David, *Portrait of Napoleon* and *Intervention of the Sabine Women;* Hogarth, additional scenes from *Marriage à la Mode;* Kauffmann, *Cornelia;* Watteau, *Gersaint's Signboard;* West, *Agrippina With the Ashes of Germinicus*

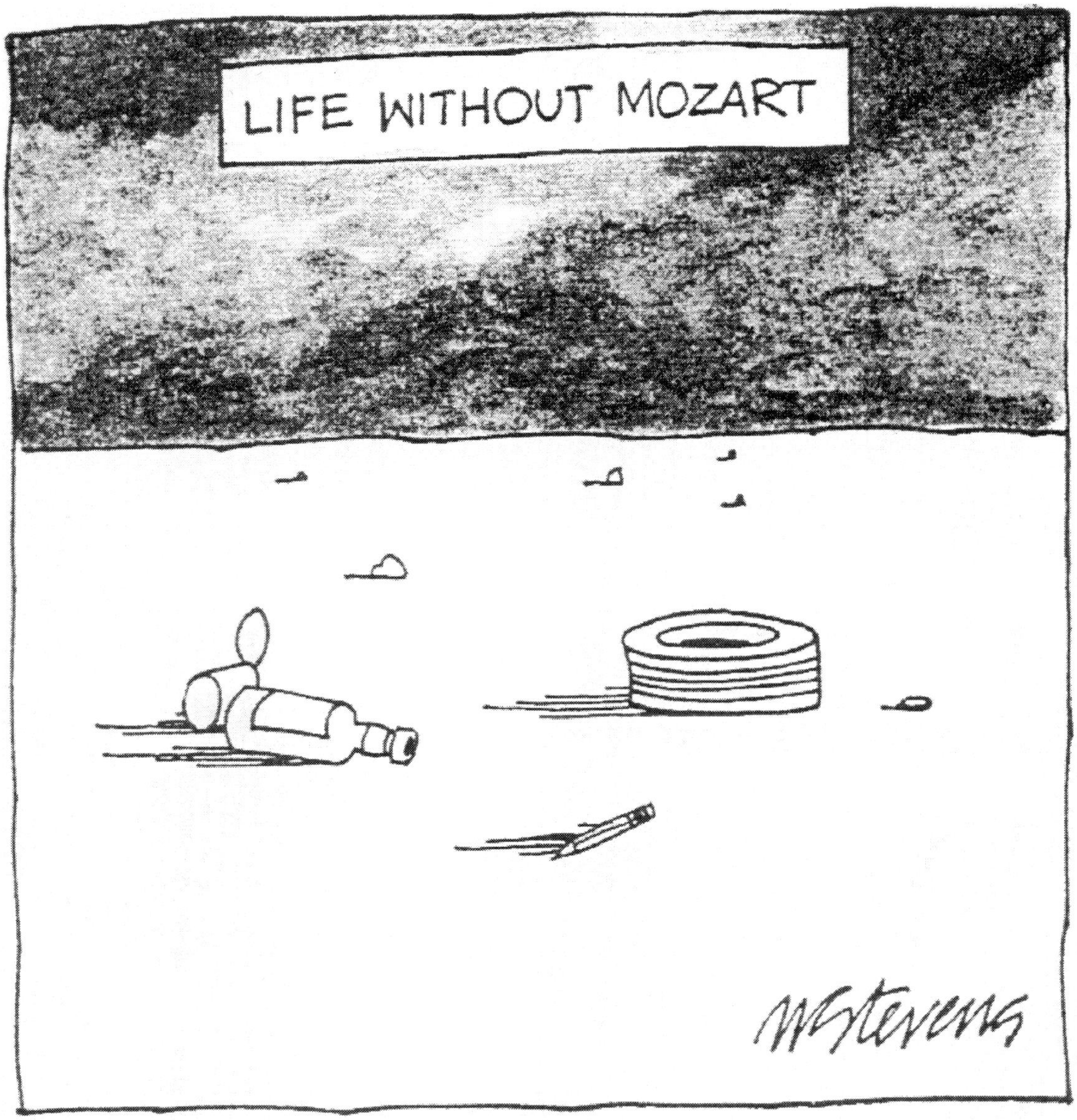
LIFE WITHOUT MOZART
MStevens

UNIT TWO

Romanticism, Realism, and the Nineteenth-Century World

STUDY GUIDE

The Romantic View of Nature, The Romantic Hero

Fiero, Chapters 27 and 28

Names

Bierstadt
Burke
Byron
Catlin
Church
Cole
Constable
Corot

Darwin
David
Douglas
Emerson
Faust
Fremiét
Friedrich
Goethe
Hicks

Keats
George Sand
Mary Shelley
Sojourner Truth
Thoreau
Turner
Whitman
Wordsworth

China

Tang Dynasty
Shen Zhou

Native America

Zuni

Roman
Realism
Symbolism
Impressionism

Study Questions

1. Describe the character and personality traits of a typical Romantic "anti-hero," a *femme fatale*? Name some contemporary people of note who fit these definitions.
2. Discuss an image of nature in a work of Romantic literature, art, and music. How do these images differ from earlier forms?
3. How is nature as described in Shen Fu's *Six Chapters from a Floating Life* similar to or different from European Romantic views?
4. Discuss the image of woman portrayed in the arts of Romanticism. Is this image still current? How or how not?

Images from Fiero

27.1, 27.3, 27.4, 27.5, 27.6, 27.7, 27.8, 27.9, 27.11, 27.12, 27.13, 27.14, 27.15, 27.18, 28.1, 28.3, 28.5

Additional Images on the Web

Cole, *Voyage of Life* (*Youth* and *Manhood*); Fremiét, *Woman Carried Off by a Gorilla*; Friedrich, *Wanderer*

STUDY GUIDE

The Romantic Style in Art and Music

Fiero, Chapter 29

Names

Bartholdi
Barry and Pugin
Chevreul
Cordier
Delacroix
Garnier
Géricault
Goya
Gros
Edmonia Lewis
Millais
Nash
Renwick
Rude

Music

ballet
Beethoven
Berlioz
Chopin
gesamtkunstwerk
idée fixe
leitmotif
lied
music drama
Paganini
piano forte
program symphony
Schubert
virtuoso
Wagner

Study Questions

1. Discuss the concept of "color" in romantic art, literature, and music.
2. Discuss the Wagnerian *gesamtkunstwerke*. How does it synthesize the romantic alliance of the arts?
3. Discuss romantic historicism. How does it differ from Neoclassical historical revivalism?
4. Compare the 19th-century concept of Romantic individualism in the works of an artist, composer, and writer/philosopher.

Images from Fiero

29.1, 29.2, 29.3, 29.4, 29.5, 29.6, 29.8, 29.9, 29.10, 29.11, 29.12, 29.13, 29.14, 29.17, 29.18

Additional Images on the Web

Delacroix, *Death of Sardanapolis* and *Paganini;* Géricault, *Mad Woman;* Millais, *Ophelia*

Program of Berlioz' Symphonie Fantastique

(from the Eulenburg Pocket Score E 422)

Introduction

A young musician of extraordinary sensibility and abundant imagination, in the depths of despair because of hopeless love, has poisoned himself with opium. The drug is too feeble to kill him but plunges him into a heavy sleep accompanied by weird visions. His sensations, emotion, and memories, as they pass through his affected mind, are transformed into musical images and ideas. The beloved one herself becomes to him a melody, a recurrent theme (the *idée fixe*) which haunts him continually.

First Movement: Reveries, Passions

First, he remembers that weariness of the soul, that indefinable longing, that somber melancholia and those object-less joys which he experienced before meeting his beloved. Then, the volcanic love with which she at once inspired him (the *idée fixe*), his delirious suffering, his return to tenderness, his religious consolations.

Second Movement: A Ball

At a ball, in the midst of a noisy, brilliant party, he finds his beloved again (*idée fixe*).

Third Movement: In the Country

On a summer evening in the country he hears two herders calling each other with their shepherd melodies. The pastoral duet in such surroundings, the gentle rustle of the trees softly swayed by the wind, some reasons for hope which had come to his knowledge recently—all unite to fill his heart with a rare tranquility and lend brighter colors to his fancies. But his beloved appears anew (the *idée fixe*), spasms contract his heart, and he is filled with dark premonitions. What if she proved faithless? Only one of the shepherds resumes his rustic tune. The sun sets. Far away there is rumbling thunder—solitude—silence.

Fourth Movement: March to the Scaffold

He dreams he has killed his loved one, that he is condemned to death and led to his execution. A march, now gloomy and ferocious, now solemn and brilliant, accompanies the procession. Noisy outbursts are followed without pause by the heavy sound of measured footsteps. Finally, like a last thought of love, the *idée fixe* appears for a moment, to be cut off by the fall of the axe.

Fifth Movement: Dream of a Witches' Sabbath

He sees himself at a witches' Sabbath surrounded by a fearful crowd of specters, sorcerers, and monsters of every kind, united for his burial. Unearthly sounds, groans, shrieks of laughter, distant cries, to which others seem to respond. The melody of his beloved is heard (the *idée fixe*), but it has lost its character of nobility and reserve. Instead, it is now an ignoble dance tune, trivial and grotesque. It is she who comes to the Sabbath! A shout of joy greets her arrival. She joins the diabolical orgy. The funeral knell, burlesque of the *Dies irae*. Dance of the witches. The dance and the *Dies irae* combined.

Franz Schubert's Erlkönig (Elf King)

(words by Johann Wolfgang von Goethe, from Deutsche Grammophon compact disc D105827)

This lied tells the exciting and frightening story of a desperate father riding on horseback through the forest with his sick child, pursued by the angel of death (the Elf King). The piano provides the momentum of the galloping horse while the singer changes his vocal timber each time a different character speaks.

Wer reitet so spät durch Nacht und Wind?
Es ist der Vater mit seinem Kind:
Er hat den Knaben wohl in dem Arm.
Er fasst ihnsicher, er hält ihn warm.

Who rides so late through night and wind?
It is the father with his child:
in his arms he has the boy,
he holds him safe, he keeps him warm.

"Mein Sohn, was birgst du so bang dein Gesicht?"
"Siehst, Vater, du den Erlkönig nicht?
Den Erlenkönig mit Kron und Schweif?"
"Mein Sohn, es ist ein Nebelstreif."

"My son, why do you hide your face in fear?"
"Father, don't you see the Elf-king,
the Elf-king with his crown and train?"
"My son, it's but a wisp of mist."

"Du liebes Kind, komm, geh mit mir!
Gar schöne Spiele spiel ich mit dir
Manch bunte Blumen sind an dem Strand,
Meine Mutter hat manch gülden Gewand."

"Dear child, come, go with me!
Wonderful games I'll play with you;
many gaily-colored flowers are on the shore,
my mother has many a garment of gold."

"Mein Vater, mein Vater, und hörest du nicht,
Was Erlenkönig mir leise verspricht?"
"Sei ruhig, bleibe ruhig, mein Kind:
In dürren Blättern säuselt der Wind."

"Father, father, don't you hear
what the Elf-king is softly promising me?"
"Be calm, keep calm, my child:
the wind is rustling in the dry leaves."

"Willst, feiner Knabe, du mit mir gehn?
Meine Töchter sollen dich warten schön;
Meine Töchter führen den nächtlichen Reihn
Und wiegen und tanzen und singen dich ein."

"Will you come with me, fine lad?
My daughters will care for you;
my daughters lead our nightly dance
and will rock and dance and sing you to sleep."

"Mein Vater, mein Vater, und siehst du
nicht dort
Erlkönigs Töchter am düstern Ort?"
"Mein Sohn, mein Sohn, ich seh es genau:
Es scheinen die alten Weiden so grau."

"Father, father, can't you see
the Elf-king's daughters there in the gloom?"
"My son, my son, I can see clearly:
it's the old willows gleaming so gray."

"Ich liebe dich, mich reizt deine schöne Gestalt;
Und bist du nicht willig, so brauch ich Gewalt."
"Mein Vater, mein Vater, jetzt fasst er mich an!
Erlkönig hat mir ein Leids getan!"

"I love you, your beauty allures me,
and if you're not willing, I shall use force."
"Father, father, he's seizing me now!
The Elf-king has hurt me!"

Dem Vater grausets, er reitet geschwind
Er hält in Armen das ächzende Kind,
Erreicht den Hof mit Müh' und Not:
In seinen Armen das Kind war tot.

The father shudders, swiftly he rides,
hugging the moaning child in his arms;
in fearful dread he reaches home.
In his arms the child is dead."

STUDY GUIDE

Industry, Empire, and the Realist Style

Fiero, Chapter 30

Names

Annan
Susan B. Anthony
Brady
Cameron
Courbet
Daguerre
Daumier
Dickens
Eakins
Eiffel
Flaubert
Harnett
Homer
Kollwitz
Manet
Marx and Engels
Millet
Nadar
Paxton
Puccini
Sullivan
Tanner
Twain

Terms

imperialism
industrial revolution
lithography
photography
socialism
verismo

Study Questions

1. What social and political factors provided the background for the realistic style in mid-19th-century France?
2. Discuss the impact of the invention of photography on 19th-century art.
3. Discuss the impact of the industrial revolution on the work of an artist, a writer, and a composer.
4. What aspects of realism run counter to the perceptions and beliefs of the romantics? Compare a realist painting with a romantic one.

Images from Fiero

30.3, 30.5, 30.6, 30.7, 30.8, 30.10, 30.12, 30.13, 30.14, 30.15, 30.18, 30.19, 30.22, 30.24, 30.25, 30.26, 30.27, 30.28

Additional Image on the Web

Eakins, *Gross Clinic,* Millet, *The Gleaners*

Declaration of Sentiments (Selected Excerpts)

This document launched the women's suffrage movement in 1848 in Seneca Falls, New York.

When, in the course of human events, it becomes necessary for one portion of the family of man to assume among the people of the earth a position different from that which they have hitherto occupied, but one to which the laws of nature and of nature's God entitle them, a decent respect to the opinions of mankind requires that they should declare the causes that impel them to such a course.

We hold these truths to be self-evident: that all men and women are created equal; that they are endowed by their Creator with certain inalienable rights; that among these are life, liberty, and the pursuit of happiness...

The history of mankind is a history of repeated injuries and usurpations on the part of man toward woman, having in direct object the establishment of an absolute tyranny over her. To prove this, let facts be submitted to a candid world.

He has never permitted her to exercise her inalienable right to the elective franchise.

He has compelled her to submit to laws, in the formation of which she had no voice.

He has withheld from her rights which are given to the most ignorant and degraded man—both natives and foreigners.

Having deprived her of this first right of a citizen, the elective franchise, thereby leaving her without representation in the halls of legislation, he has oppressed her on all sides.

He has made her, if married, in the eye of the law, civilly dead.

He has taken from her all right in property, even to the wages she earns.

He has made her, morally, an irresponsible being, as she can commit many crimes with impunity, provided they be done in the presence of her husband. In the covenant of marriage, she is compelled to promise obedience to her husband, he becoming to all intents and purposes, her master—the law giving him power to deprive her of her liberty, and to administer chastisement.

He has so framed the laws of divorce, as to what shall be the proper causes, and in case of separation, to whom the guardianship of the children shall be given, as to be wholly regardless of the happiness of women—the law, in all cases, going upon a false supposition of the supremacy of man, and giving all power into his hands.

After depriving her of all rights as a married woman, if single, and the owner of property, he has taxed her to support a government which recognizes her only when her property can be made profitable to it.

He has monopolized nearly all the profitable employments, and from those she is permitted to follow, she receives but a scanty remuneration. He closes against her all the avenues to wealth and distinction which he considers most honorable to himself. As a teacher of theology, medicine, or law, she is not known.

He has denied her the facilities for obtaining a thorough education, all colleges being closed against her.

He allows her in Church as well as State, but a subordinate position, claiming Apostolic authority for her exclusion from the ministry, and, with some exceptions, from any public participation in the affairs of the Church.

He has created a false public sentiment, by giving to the world a different code of morals for men and women, but which moral delinquencies which exclude women from society, are not only tolerated, but deemed of little account in man.

He has usurped the prerogative of Jehovah himself, claiming it as his right to assign for her a sphere of action, when that belongs to her conscience and to her God.

He has endeavored, in every way that he could, to destroy her confidence in her own powers, to lessen her self-respect, and to make her willing to lead a dependent and abject life.

Now, in view of this entire disfranchisement of one-half the people in this country, their social and religious degradation—in view of the unjust laws above mentioned, and because women do feel themselves aggrieved, oppressed, and fraudulently deprived of their most sacred rights, we insist that they have immediate admission to all the rights and privileges which belong to them as citizens of the United States...

STUDY GUIDE

The Move Toward Modernism

Fiero, Chapter 31

Names and Terms

art nouveau
Bergson
Cassatt
Cézanne
Debussy
Degas
Isadora Duncan
Gauguin
Grasset
Hodler
Horta
impressionism
japonisme
Mallarmé
Monet
Muybridge
Nietzsche
Pissaro
pointilism
poster
postimpressionism
Renoir
Rodin
Seurat
symbolism
Tiffany
Toulouse-Lautrec
Van Gogh

Japan

Hokusai
Kiyonobu
Kunisada
ukiyo
woodblock prints

Africa and Oceania

Yoruba

Study Questions

1. Discuss the impact of Japan on Western culture in the 19th century.
2. Discuss the music of Debussy, Mallarmé's poetry, and Monet's paintings. What do they have in common stylistically?
3. In what ways did Parisian urban life influence the art of the impressionists and postimpressionists?
4. Discuss the influence of Henri Bergson's theories on the arts of the late 19th century.

Images from Fiero

31.1, 31.2, 31.3, 31.4, 31.5, 31.6, 31.7, 31.8, 31.9, 31.10, 31.11, 31.12, 31.13, 31.14, 31.15, 31.16, 31.17, 31.18, 31.21, 31.22, 31.23, 31.24, 31.25, 31.26, 31.27, 31.28, 31.30, 31.31, 31.32

Additional Image on the Web

Degas, *Bather*

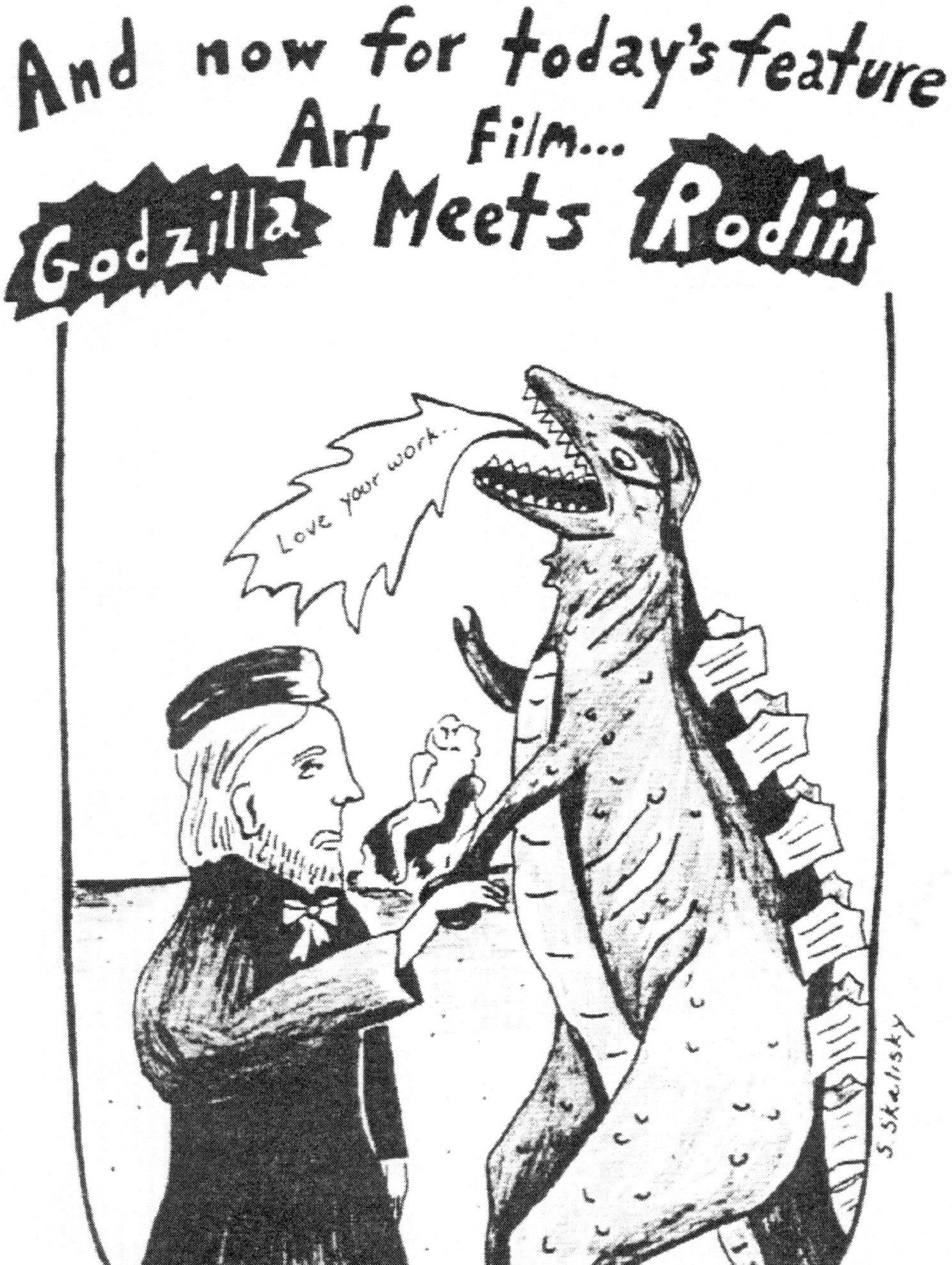
And now for today's feature
Art Film...
Godzilla Meets Rodin
Love your work...
S. Skalisky

UNIT THREE

Modernism, Globalism and the Information Age

STUDY GUIDE

The Modernist Assault

Fiero, Chapter 32

Names

Archipenko
Balla
Boccioni
Brancusi
Braque
Corbusier
Duchamp
Einstein
Robert Frost
Gropius
Kandinsky
Malevich
Matisse
Mondrian
Picasso
Popova
Rietveld
Severini
Weston
Wright

Terms

abstraction
Bauhaus-International Style
collage
cubism
De Stijl
fauvism
ferroconcrete
futurism
haiku
nonobjective art
Russian constructivism
suprematism
theosophy

Music

Nijinsky
Schoenberg
serial technique
Stravinsky
12-tone system

Film

Méliès
D.W. Griffith

Study Questions

1. What historical, scientific, and technological events set the stage for the cultural styles of the early 20th century?
2. Compare Picasso's *Demoiselles d'Avignon* with Stravinsky's *Rite of Spring*. What was the common inspiration for both?
3. How did the new medium of film respond to the modernist aesthetic?
4. Compare the architecture of Gropius with that of Frank Lloyd Wright? How and why are they different?

Images from Fiero

32.1, 32.2, 32.4, 32.5, 32.7, 32.8, 32.9, 32.10, 32.11, 32.12, 32.13, 32.14, 32.15, 32.16, 32.17, 32.19, 32.20, 32.21, 32.22, 32.23, 32.24, 32.25, 32.26, 32.28

Additional Image on the Web

Severini, *Armored Train*

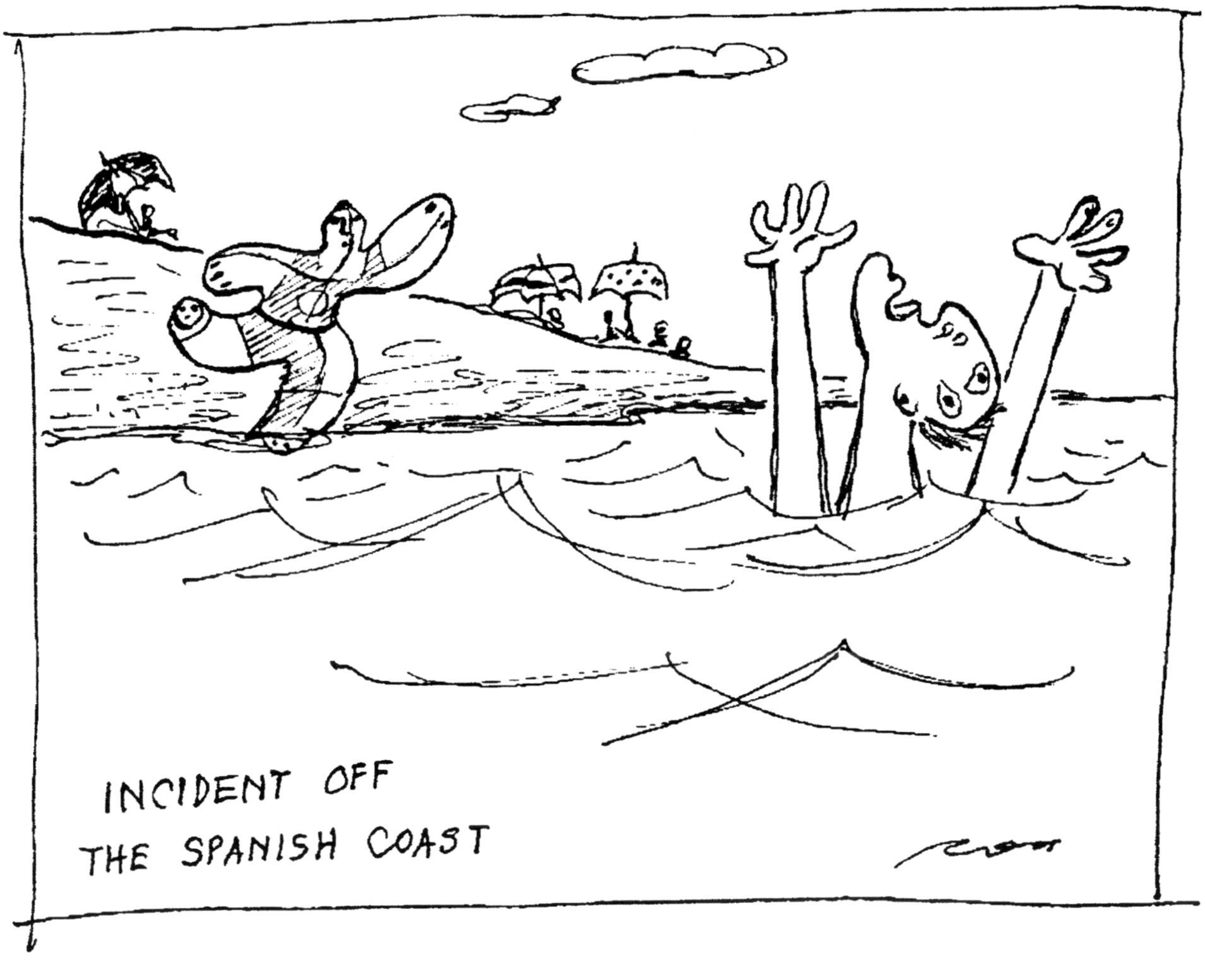
INCIDENT OFF
THE SPANISH COAST

STUDY GUIDE

The Freudian Revolution

Fiero, Chapter 33

Names and Terms

Chagall
de Chirico
Cummings
dada
Dali
Duchamp
expressionism
Freud
Höch
Kafka
Kahlo
Kirchner
Klee
Magritte
meta physical art
Miro
Munch
O'Keefe
Oppenheim
photomontage
surrealism, abstract and visionary

Study Questions

1. Discuss the impact of Freud's *Interpretation of Dreams* on art and literature.
2. To what specific event or events were the proponents of Dada responding? Why?

Images from Fiero

33.1, 33.2, 33.3, 33.4, 33.5, 33.6, 33.8, 33.9, 33.10, 33.11, 33.12, 33.13, 33.14, 33.15

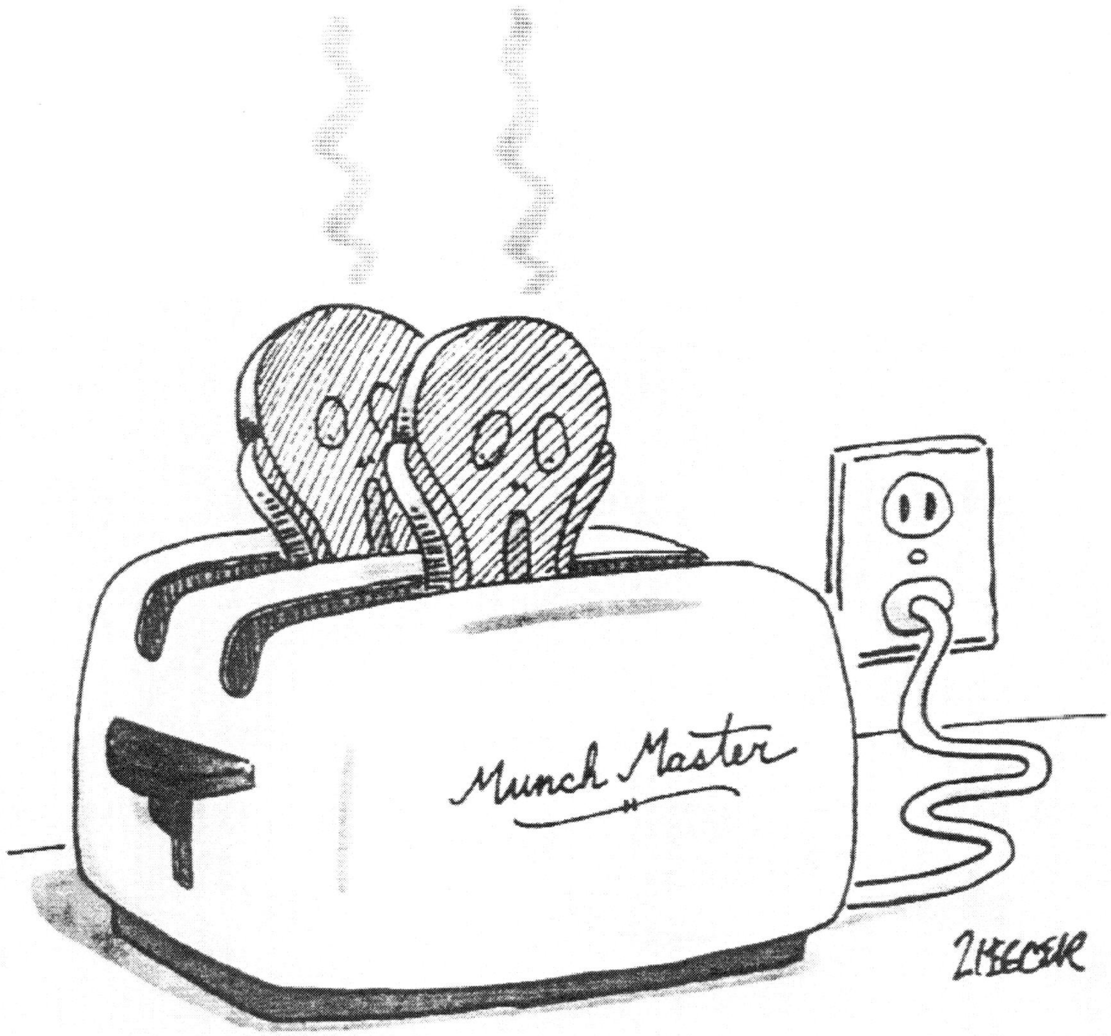
Munch Master
ZIEGLER

STUDY GUIDE

Total War, Totalitarianism, and the Arts

Fiero, Chapter 34

Names and Terms

art deco
Benton
Copland
communism
Eisenstein
Ernst
Grosz
Hitler
Lange
Léger
Lenin
Mao
Lee Miller
montage
Penderecki
Picasso
Riefenstahl
Rivera
Shahn
Steinbeck
Strakhov
Wiesel
Grant Wood

Important Dates

World War I, 1914–1918

The Great Depression, 1929

World War II, 1942–1945

Study Questions

1. What specific problems and concerns did social realist artists address in the early 20th century in the U.S.A., in Russia, in China?
2. Discuss a work of art, literature, and music that express a sense of despair in response to totalitarian conflict.
3. Compare the paintings of Ben Shahn with the music of Copland and the writing of Steinbeck. What elements do they share?
4. How did film and photojournalism serve in the war era? Discuss an example from a democratic context and one from a totalitarian regime.

Images from Fiero

34.1, 34.2, 34.3, 34.4, 34.5, 34.6, 34.7, 34.8, 34.9, 34.10, 34.11

Additional Images on the Web

Ben Shan, *Passion of Sacco and Vanzetti*, Grant Wood, *American Gothic*

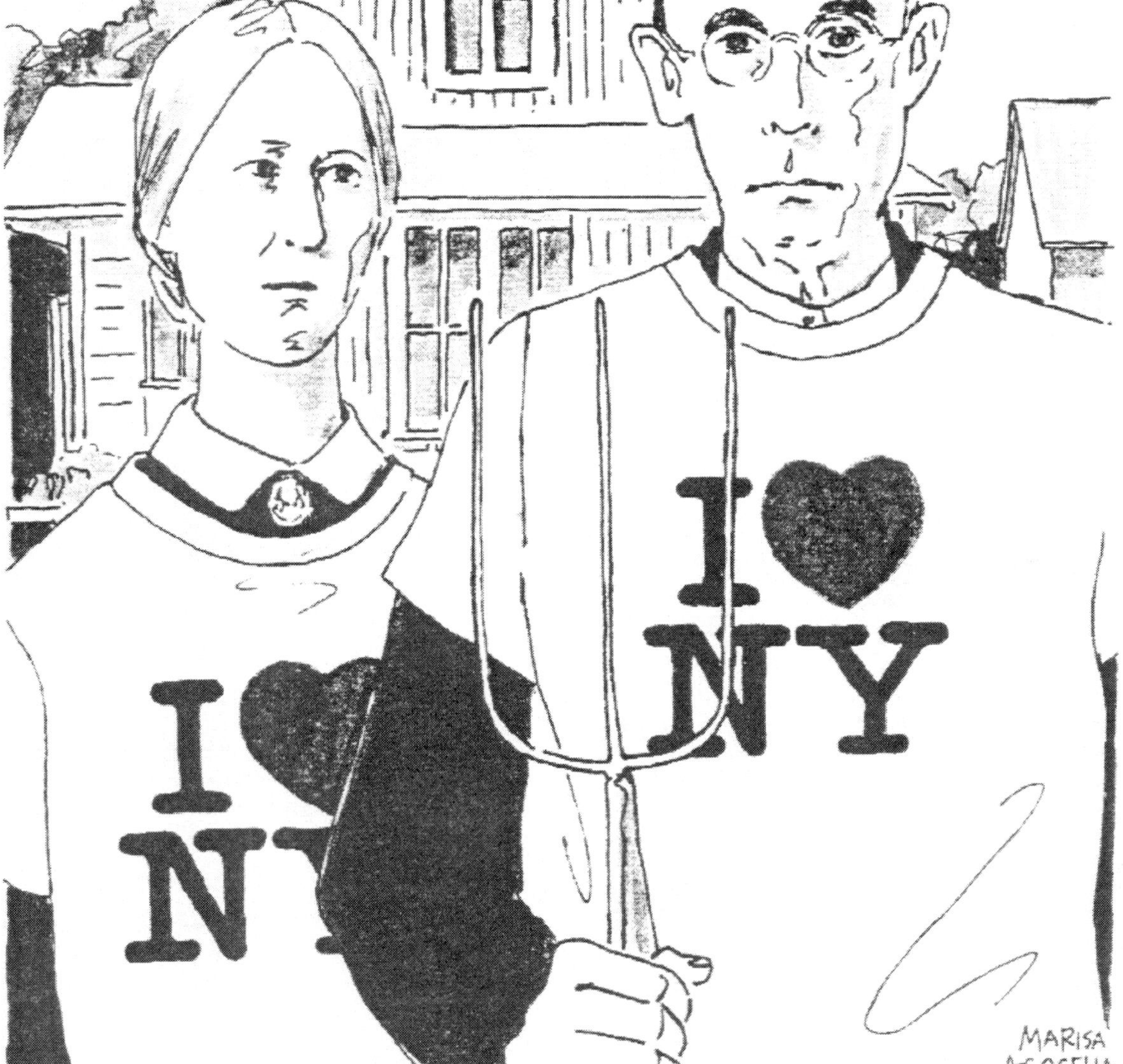
I ♥ NY
I ♥ NY
MARISA ACOCELLA

STUDY GUIDE

The Quest for Meaning

Fiero, Chapter 35

Names and Terms

action painting
Bacon
Bergman
Cage
Calder
color field
de Kooning
existentialism
film noir
Frankenthaler
Hitchcock
Hopper
Kline
Kurosawa
Mies van der Rohe
Pollock
Rothko
Saarinen
Sartre
Segal
David Smith
Welles
Wright

Study Questions

1. What factors combined to make New York the cultural center of the world after World War II?
2. Compare the concept of action painting with that of aleatory music.
3. Discuss the directions which film took internationally in the mid-20th century.
4. How did the concept of existentialism influence the attitudes of artists, composers, and writers in the years following World War II?

Images from Fiero

35.1, 35.2, 35.3, 35.5, 35.6, 35.7, 35.8, 35.9, 35.10, 35.11, 35.12, 35.13, 35.15, 35.16, 35.17, 35.18

Identity and Liberation

Fiero, Chapter 36

Names and Terms

Racial Identity and Ethnicity

apartheid
Basquiat
civil rights
Colescott
Ellington
Harlem Renaissance
Langston Hughes
improvisation
jazz
Luis Jiménez
Malcom X
Martin Luther King
Jacob Lawrence
Pépin Osorio
Betye Saar

Names and Terms

Gender and Women's Movement

Simon de Beauvoir
Judy Chicago
Marisol Escobar
feminism
Germaine Greer
Barbara Kruger
Robert Mapplethorpe
misogyny
Niki de St. Phalle
Cindy Sherman
Virginia Woolf

Study Questions

1. How did Malcom X's position on the status of blacks differ from that of Martin Luther King? Discuss in the context of two works of art that project these views.
2. What reason does Simone de Beauvoir give for woman's traditional subordination to men? Is there a work of art that suggests the same view?
3. Discuss the stereotypes of the black woman that are satirized and/or glorified in late 20th-century art. What traditional attitudes and/or expectations have contributed to these images?
4. Consider the ideas in this chapter in light of your own racial and gender identity. Discuss a work of art, music, or literature that speaks most closely to you.

Images from Fiero

36.1, 36.2, 36.3, 36.4, 36.6, 36.8, 36.9, 36.10, 36.11, 36.12, 36.13

The Information Age: Message and Meaning

Fiero, Chapter 37

Image and Sound

Fiero, Chapter 38

Names

Abacanowicz
Azaceta
Borofsky
Cai Guo-Qiang
Calatrava
Chamberlain
Christo & Jeanne-Claude
Chuck Close
Estes
Flavin
Galán
Gehry
Golub
Gursky
Hanson
Johns
Judd
Kiefer
Lichtenstein
Yolanda Lopez
Maya Ying Lin
Mariko Mori
Morimura
Neshat
Nevelson
Noguchi
Oldenburg
Ofili
Nam June Paik
Perez Associates
I. M. Pei
Rauschenberg
Riley
Serra
Smithson
Stella
Viola
Wang Guangyi
Warhol
Yvaral

Art Terms

assemblage
computer art
earth sculpture
environmental sculpture
geometric abstraction
globalism
kinetic art
magic realism
minimalism
neon
new expressionism
new realism
op art
pop art
postmodernism
public art
science fiction
silkscreen
social conscience art
total art
video art

Music

Philip Glass
Ligeti
microtonality
minimal music
synthesizer

Study Questions

1. How have computers become a new medium for artistic expressions? Discuss a work of art and music.
2. How have writers and artists worked to bring attention to the threat of ecological disaster? Cite specific examples.
3. Discuss humor in postmodern architecture and art, citing specific examples. Why is satire and humor important in this expressive style?
4. How is the concept of "science fiction" expressed in works of art, literature, and film? Cite an example of each medium and discuss why this idea become important in the last half of the 20th century.

Images from Fiero

37.1, 37.2, 37.3, 37.4, 37.5, 37.6, 38.1, 38.2, 38.3, 38.4, 38.5, 38.6, 38.7, 38.8, 38.9, 38.10, 38.11, 38.12, 38.13, 38.14, 38.15, 38.16, 38.17, 38.18, 38.19, 38.20, 38.22, 38.23, 38.24, 38.25, 38.26, 38.27, 38.28. 38.29, 39.30, 38.31, 38.32, 38.33, 38.34, 38.35, 38.36

Additional Image on the Web

Maya Ying Lin, Vietnam Memorial.

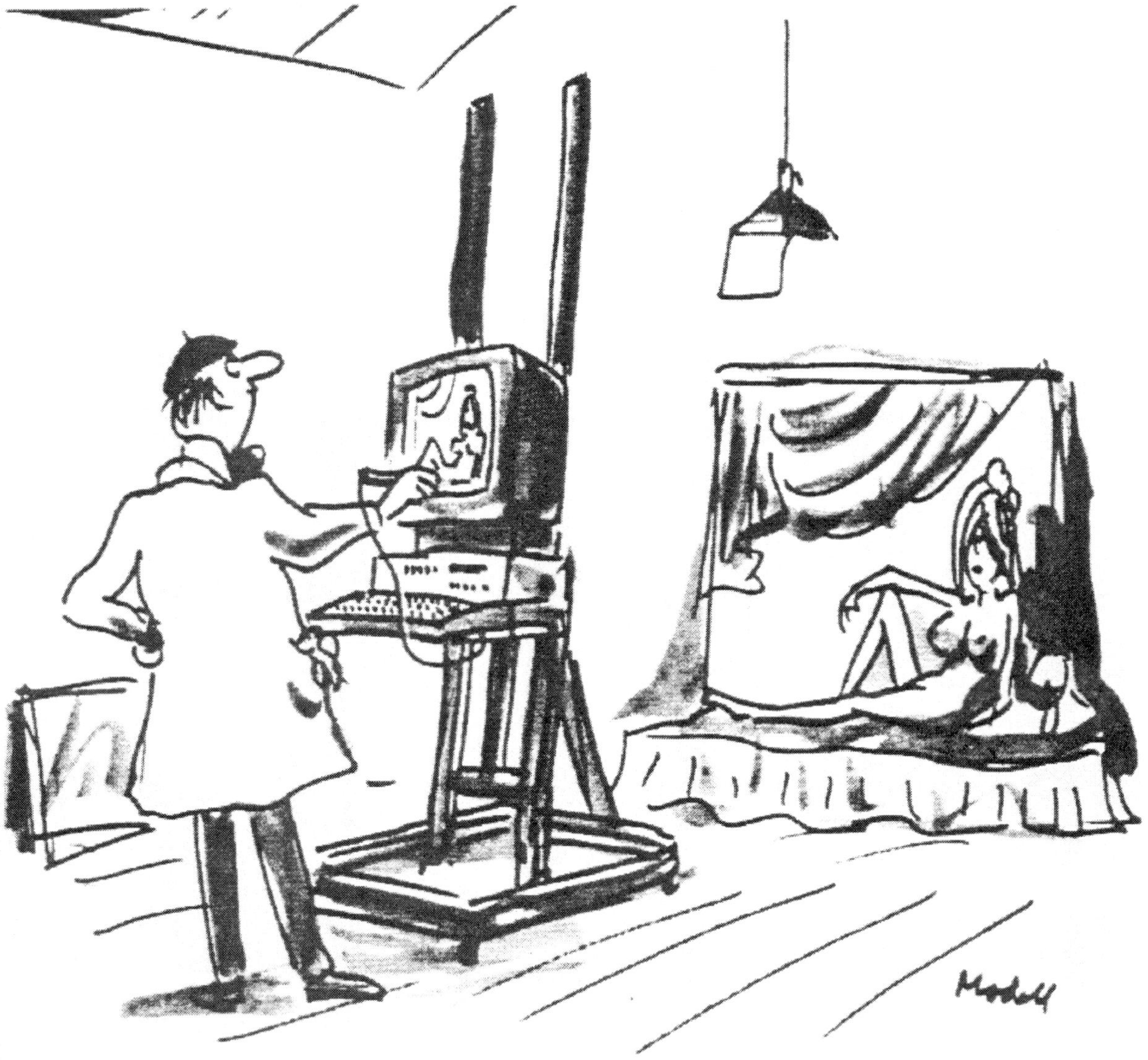
Modell

Visual Arts Vocabulary

Painting

The Illusion of Space Versus the Picture Plane

Painting is a two-dimensional art form, measured only by height and width. Depending upon the purpose of a painting, the artist could respect the *picture plane*—the actual flat surface of the wall, paper, or canvas—or the artist could create the illusion of three-dimensional objects occupying space, as though seen through a window. Throughout history, the illusion of space has been achieved in the following ways:

Overlap

An object or person is painted on top of and partially obscuring an image of something else to give the illusion that it is in front, and therefore closer to the viewer (example: Giotto, *Pieta* Arena Chapel).

Variation in Size

Objects or persons which the painter wishes to depict in the distance are made smaller than those perceived as nearer to the viewer (example: Bosch, *Garden of Earthly Delights*). This, of course, has not always been the case, particularly in Egyptian art (and in the works of children), where largeness is a function of importance, power or strength.

Position on the Picture Plane

Objects or things perceived as far away are placed closer to the top of the picture plane (example: Traini, *Triumph of Death*).

Aerial (or Atmospheric) Perspective

Shapes become lighter and less distinct the further away they are. Colors become less intense, more blurred or grayed as they recede (example: Masaccio, *Tribute Money*).

Linear Perspective

Space is organized so that all parallel lines and edges of surfaces ("orthogonals") receding at the same angle converge toward one or more "vanishing points." In "one point perspective," a single vanishing point is placed on the horizon at eye level (example: Leonardo, *Last Supper*).

Foreshortening

Foreshortening is a method of representing objects as if they were seen at an angle and receding into space instead of being seen in a strictly frontal or profile view. It is closely related to linear perspective (example: *Trinity*).

Realism and Abstraction

Before the invention of photography, early paintings were judged on their faithfulness to nature. The more realistic the image, the better the artist. Now, however, anyone can document the real world by simply aiming a camera and pressing a button. Painters are no longer obligated to record every detail of the objects they paint, and can even abandon the subject entirely, in which case the painting is "abstract." The more an artist leaves out of a representation, the more the viewer must supply, and the more abstract the work. Modern artists are not locked into the demands of realism, and are free to project thoughts and emotions into their work by developing and emphasizing elements of their craft, such as color, line, texture, shape, organization, and illusion of space.

Color

Warm and Cool Colors

Warm colors (red, orange, yellow) are exciting and advance toward us from the surface. Cool colors (blue, green, violet) calm us and tend to recede into the background (example: Constable, *Hay Wain*).

Primary Colors

Artists mix all their colors from three primary hues: red, yellow, and blue. (Example: Mondrian, *Composition*, is composed of primary colors.)

Hue, Value, and Saturation

Hue is the function of the wavelength of light reflected from the surface of the retina. Each identifiable wavelength is a hue: red, for example, has a wavelength of about 1/33,000 of an inch.

Value refers to the measure of lightness or darkness of a color achieved by adding white or black. Pastels have white added to the basic hue, and are therefore on the high end of the value scale (example: Fragonard, *The Swing*).

Saturation refers to the intensity of a color. Yellow, for example, can be both light and bright; but it can also be light and pale. Bright colors are highly saturated (example: Matisse, *The Dance*). Artists use color to affect the viewer's emotions, to suggest space, and to organize their works.

Line

Line is often contrasted with color in discussing styles of painting. In effect, color is perceived as taking up space and mass, while line often limits and defines areas of color. There are several types of line:

"Actual" Line

"Actual" line is the path of the pencil, pen, or other instruments of drawing and prints, or the unblended brushstroke in painting.

Contour Line

Contour line may be an actual line describing the outer limits of a figure or object, but in painting, contour line is often defined by the contrast between two color areas—that of the figure or object, and that of the background (note the continuous unbroken curvilinear contour in Miro's *Person Throwing a Stone*).

Implied Interior Line

Implied interior line. Figures and objects contain one or more directional lines which the viewer senses more than he or she actually sees. A figure such as Praxiteles' *Aphrodite*, for example, is basically vertical, but a closer analysis of its interior lines reveals the subtle "S" curve of its classical *contrapposto* posture.

Compositional Line

Compositional line leads the viewer's eye from one part of the work to another. It is also implied (that is, not actually seen) and directional. Compositions are made up of many such lines. Used properly, they can visually balance and unite a composition, create drama, and convey emotion or meaning (example: Michelangelo, *Creation of Adam*).

Vertical lines tend to be static, while horizontal lines are calm. Diagonal lines are dynamic and can suggest movement. Curved lines can also suggest movement as well as emotion.

Line is a two-dimensional phenomenon. However, some artists are able to suggest depth and shadow with line (example: Dürer, *Four Horsemen*, in which line suggests space and volume by hatching and shading). Architects and sculptors, whose media are three dimensional, sometimes inscribe lines on the surfaces of their works (example: *Kouros* from Attica), or define edges which are perceived as lines by the viewer (example: Wright, *Fallingwater*).

Sculpture

Sculpture is three-dimensional and is measured by height, width, and depth. Sometimes the adjective "sculptural," "sculpturesque," or "plastic" is applied to a painting, meaning that it is composed of strong, solid volumetric forms (example: Giotto, *Madonna Enthroned*). Sculpture can also be painted, in which case we refer to it as "polychromed" (example: Tuthmosis, *Queen Nefertiti*). Sculpture is often used in combination with architecture as decoration (example: west facade, Chartres Cathedral). On the other hand, a piece of sculpture can be "environmental" when, like architecture, it surrounds and involves the viewer (example: Chicago, *Dinner Party*). The formal elements defined above—line, light and dark, and sometimes even color—apply to sculpture as well as to painting.

Additive and Subtractive Means: Modeling and Carving

Until the 20th century, sculpture was made by two traditional means. The additive method is sometimes called "modeling" and often utilizes material that is soft and pliable to work with, such as clay, putty or wax. Often, soft clay or putty is applied to an interior support (an "armature") until the proper dimension is reached and modeling can take place (example: Maya Warrior). Another word for the subtractive method is "carving," which involves removing hard materials such as stone or wood to arrive at the surface (example: Michelangelo, *David*). These two techniques continue to be employed by modern sculptors, who have added several new techniques and media, such as construction and assemblage, "kinetic" or moving sculpture, earthworks or environmental art, performance art or "living sculpture," etc.

Positive and Negative Space: Closed and Open Forms

Sculptors work with both solid material and empty space. The way in which the sculptor manipulates matter ("positive" space) and void ("negative" space) causes the work to express "closed" and "open" forms. A sculpture composed primarily of closed forms and positive space gives the impression of a self-contained solid mass (example: *Venus of Willendorf*). Sculpture which is open in form utilizes negative space—i.e., hollows and voids, combined with projections into space (example: *Laocoon Group*).

Free-Standing and Relief Sculpture

"Free-standing" sculpture exists in space, displacing air, reflecting light and casting shadow (example: Pollaiuolo, *Hercules Strangling Antaeus*). A free-standing work of sculpture may or may not be intended to be viewed from all sides (Myron's *Discobolus*, is an example of a free-standing work meant to be seen from the front, but it stands alone, and a person can walk around it). "Relief" sculpture projects from a flat surface. It can be carved at "high" relief (example: *Zeus Hurling Thunderbolts* from the Altar of Zeus) or "low" relief (sometimes called "bas relief "—example: Parthenon frieze) depending upon the depth of cutting into the surface. Like painting, relief sculpture must be viewed from one vantage point.

Architecture

Architecture, like sculpture, is three-dimensional. However, unlike the other visual arts, architecture must be functional. The basic function of a building is, of course, to provide a protective enclosure for human beings and to house and shape their activities. In addition, architecture must be safe and structurally sound so that we need not worry about the ceiling falling or the floor buckling. In brief, architects must contend with three basic practical concerns:

Operational Function

Example: The Tower of London is a building whose function as a fortified castle is reflected in its appearance. The exterior of a cathedral such as Chartres indicates its function as a place of worship. The exterior of Gropius' Barhaus Building on the other hand, gives no indication of its function.

Relationship to the Environment

Example: The Seagram Building is a structure which exists independently of the natural environment. By contrast, Wright's "Fallingwater" is closely tied with its natural surroundings.

Expressive or Symbolic Connotations of Design

Example: Vignon, La Madeleine, patterned after a Roman temple, is symbolic of Napoleon's imperialistic ambitions. Saarinen's Trans World Airlines Terminal expresses in its design the smooth aerodynamic contours associated with flight.

More than a painter or a sculptor, an architect is at the mercy of factors other than aesthetic ones. He or she must consider the personal likes and dislikes of the person who is paying for the project (the "client" or "patron"), the other buildings surrounding the work and zoning laws, which can limit creativity.

Unlike painting and sculpture, architecture cannot be stored or put out of sight when the public tires of it. Groups of concerned citizens sometimes manage to save architectural monuments before it is too late. But all too often important structures are torn down with little or no thought for their artistic and historical value, only to be replaced in the name of "progress" by cheap and characterless substitutes. Incredible as it seems to us today, even such a venerable structure as the Cathedral of Notre Dame in Paris was once a candidate for the wrecker's ball.

Plans and Elevations

A *plan* is an architectural drawing that represents a view from above of the parts of a building or site that would lie on a horizontal plane if it were cut through at ground level. A plan shows, in two dimensions rather than three, the arrangement and distribution of interior spaces, walls, doors, windows, columns and ceiling support systems. Example: the plan of Chartres Cathedral, which shows the arrangement of the ceiling vaulting in the crosses along the nave and chapels.

An *elevation* is an architectural drawing of the side of a building without foreshortening or perspective distortion. The effect is somewhat like that achieved by sawing a building through from top to bottom and looking in from its gaping side. One example is the section view of the nave wall of Chartres Cathedral.

Like sculptors, architects compose with line, light and dark, solid and void.

Texture

Texture refers to the smoothness or roughness of a surface—its three-dimensional aspects. Painters can create the illusion of texture by expertly simulating the shiny surface of a mirror or the nub of an Oriental carpet even though the surface of their painting remains glossy and flat (example: Van Eyck, *Amolfini Marriage*). However, texture also refers to the actual thickness of paint as it projects from the surface of a painting. Paint which is thick and heavy on the surface is called impasto (example: Van Gogh, *Starry Night*).

Medium

In the visual arts, "medium" is the physical material with which the artist works. An artist may choose to work within the natural limitations of the medium, enhancing its natural characteristics, or he/she may defy the intrinsic nature of the medium, making it seem like another material altogether.

Painting

In general, medium implies the mode or means of painting, such as oil on canvas, watercolor, etc. In particular, "medium" refers to the fluid (the vehicle) in which the color (the pigment) is suspended to make paint. There are many painterly media. The most common are:

Tempera

The tempera medium uses egg as the vehicle for pigment, and was the favored medium of Italian Renaissance painters. The wooden support for the painting (the "panel") was painstakingly prepared by painting layers of chalky "gesso" over a thin linen cloth; then the preliminary design was drawn onto the panel, and the paint was applied in many layers according to the desired intensity of color. Tempera dries rapidly, hence the artist was unable to do much subtle blending of colors. As a result, figures in a tempera painting appear flat, and edges where colors meet are sharply defined (example: Botticelli, *Birth of Venus*).

Early panel painters used gold to enrich their designs, applying fragile gold leaf by means of a hair brush and static electricity to surfaces painted with a red gluelike substance called "bole." So much mundane labor was involved in painting a panel that an artist usually divided the less creative tasks, such as grinding pigments and preparing the gesso, among the apprentices in his shop. Often only the final painting or the most important figures were done by the master who signed his name to the work.

The most familiar medium to most students is oil on canvas, although these materials are relatively new to painting. The earliest use of the oil medium is thought to have been in 15th-century Flanders. Painters like Jan van Eyck applied thin transparent oil "glazes" onto wood panels prepared in much the same way as contemporary Italian tempera panels. Oil glaze does not dry as quickly as egg tempera. As a result, the artist had more time to blend and shade his colors and tones. The final effect is one of brilliant translucence and subtle blending that remains undiminished by time (example: van Eyck, *Amolfini Marriage*).

Later, in the 16th century, Venetian painters adapted oil painting to the wet lagoon climate of Venice by doing away with traditional wooden panels. They stretched prepared linen (called a "canvas") over a wood frame, thereby minimizing warping by moisture (example: Tintoretto, *Last Supper*). This method is still employed by modem artists (example: Lawrence, *Race Riots . . .*).

Fresco

In "fresco," pigments are applied to a wall. This medium was favored by Italian Renaissance artists as a means of covering vast areas with paintings (example: Brancacci Chapel). The pigments, once applied, become part of the wall's surface.

There were two ways of applying pigments to the wall surface. In "buon fresco," or true fresco, the colors were mixed with plaster and troweled directly onto the preliminary drawing, or "sinopia." In this type of fresco, the artist had to work rapidly, preparing only as much plaster as could be worked before it dried. Simple areas such as expanses of blue sky could be worked in less time and in larger areas than small detailed faces, for example. The other method, "fresco al secco," where watercolor paint was applied onto an already plastered wall, was a shortcut method which has not withstood the ravages of time as well as the "buon fresco" method. (Example: Giotto, *Lamentation*, Arena Chapel, shows the division of the plaster according to the daily work of the artist, as well as areas of "fresco al secco" which have flaked off with time.)

Watercolor

As the name suggests, the vehicle for watercolor is water. Soluble pigments are added, and the solution is thinly applied to paper. (Example: Dürer, *Wire Drawing Mill.*)

Acrylic Polymer

"Acrylic polymer" paints are watercolors formulated with acrylic polymer plastic latex emulsion as the vehicle. In the water base are suspended fine droplets of colorless synthetic resin which form a crystal clear film when the water evaporates. This film is tough, flexible and durable, and when dry it becomes water and oil resistant. There is very little change in the appearance of the colors from the wet to the dry stage, the colors remaining as intense and brilliant as when originally applied. The paint film is flexible so that both paper and canvas may be painted in either light or heavy applications of color. The paint is also adhesive, which makes it possible to add materials such as sand, cloth, wood, etc. to the surface without danger of their falling off. Acrylic is the choice of many modem painters (example: Stella, *Tahkt-i-Sulayman*).

The Graphic Arts

Drawing

A drawing often serves as a starting point for a painting, but a drawing can also be a finished work of art in its own right (example: Leonardo, *Wing Construction*). The traditional difference between drawing and painting is the use of color in the latter. There are, however, colored drawings, such as those using pastels," or colored chalks.

Prints

There are other two-dimensional media referred to collectively as prints. Included in this designation are woodcut, engraving (example: Dürer, *Four Horsemen*), etching (example: Rembrandt, *Christ Preaching*), lithography (example: Delacroix, *Mephistopheles*) and other forms of printing. Prints differ from painting and drawing in that they are reproduced mechanically A drawing or a painting is one of a kind, whereas a print exists in multiple of itself.

Note: Photography and computer-generated images can also be considered graphic media.

Study Tips

"How are we supposed to learn this stuff?"

Make the Most of Class Lectures and Discussions

It is essential to attend all lectures and discussion sections. The importance of attending all class meetings and keeping up with the reading in your textbook cannot be stressed enough. Besides having the benefit of a complete presentation, you will actually spend less time by coming to class than by trying to make up what you miss. Attending class is especially important since the slides shown in class are NOT available to students at any other time, and examinations include information presented in lectures that does not appear in your textbook.

Effective Note-Taking in Class

One of the most important things you can do to help yourself do well on art history exams is to take good notes in class and on the readings. There are some distinctive aspects to art history that can make note taking difficult. In class it can sometimes seem as if there are so many names, places, styles, and images that it is impossible to write everything down. Afterward, confronted by pages of cryptic scribbles, you may have difficulty sorting it all out or even remembering what the images were. Here are some ways to take effective notes.

Read the Relevant Chapter Before the Lecture

In lecture, it is most important that you are looking at the screen in front of you rather than trying to write down everything the professor says. If you have read the chapter before hand, you can limit your notes to those things not provided by the book: new facts, images or information that is not in the book, corrections to the book, emphasis on important objects or ideas. If the number of the image in the Fiero book is given in lecture, be sure to write it down. Bring your Student Manual with you to lecture, and consult it for terms, artists' names, and spellings.

Develop a Consistent Short Hand

Use abbreviations and symbols to help you write quickly and accurately in class. If your professor emphasizes a point (by saying something like "this is really important"), put stars or arrows next to it in the margin of your notes.

Taking Notes on Reading

When studying for an exam, it takes a long time to go through a chapter and find all the passages you've highlighted in your reading—often you end up having to reread the chapter to reconstruct the argument anyway. When you're highlighting or underlining, also make notes in the margins of the readings (as long as it's your book and not the library's) with cross-references to other images or observations that you find important. Also, integrate information in the text into your lecture notes so that you consolidate your studying in one place.

Your textbook and the class lectures will provide a conceptual framework upon which to base your study, as well as emphasizing important works and concepts likely to appear on exams. Make outlines for yourself, drawing upon lectures and text, relating works to the general character of a given place and time so that you may begin to identify things previously unknown to you on the basis of style.

For exams, you will be expected to identify works illustrated in your text and prints packet by style, artist, title, place (in the case of architecture) and medium. You are also expected to understand subject matter, meaning, and context for each work discussed in class. You will not have to know specific dates, but you will be responsible for remembering the general dates that define styles and historical eras.

Examinations will include material in the lectures that may not appear in your text. Make a friend, so that if you must miss a lecture, you may borrow the notes for that day. Then make an appointment with your discussion leader to discuss the missed lecture.

You will be encountering many new words, and are expected to know what they mean. Consult lists of terms in the Study Guide sections of your Student Manual, and pay particular attention to words that appear in *italics* in the Fiero text.

Studying for Exams

If you don't understand the goals and methods of examinations, and you don't study in the right way, a test can become a frustrating, unpleasant experience. Art history exams are typically designed to test your knowledge of works of art, artists, ideas, and time periods that you are studying and your ability to interpret this material. These goals are met through a variety of types of questions, including essays, slide identifications, and multiple-choice questions. There will often be a mix of questions addressing the visual images studied in the course, readings in your textbook, and lectures.

Here are a few study techniques that you may find helpful.

Slide Identifications and Multiple Choice Questions

A slide identification usually consists of a single slide, shown for one minute, which the student must identify according to artist, title, style, and/or medium. For example, a complete slide identification for Fiero Vol. 1, figure 5.10, would be:

Myron, *Discus Thrower*, Classical Greek Style, marble sculpture

A multiple-choice question will ask you to choose the best answer among several related to a specific slide.

If you are going to achieve even a beginner's level of mastery in an academic discipline, you must learn the material of that discipline. In art history, you need to be able to recall images visually, from memory, to help you understand works of art as you are exposed to them. For example if your professor discusses how an Archaic kouros looks like an Egyptian sculpture, you want to be able to remember what Egyptian sculpture looks like in order to fully appreciate the statement. A well-trained visual memory will enrich your life and enhance your appreciation of art in a variety of ways, even if you don't become an art history major.

How to Succeed at Slide Questions

There are two essential techniques in preparing for slide tests:

1. Don't leave your studying to the night before.
2. Make connections between images and group them in sets.

The first point may seem obvious—and I'm sure you've heard it before—but it can't be emphasized enough when it comes to art history Cramming for an art history exam is like trying to run a marathon without doing any training until the day before. The night before an exam you probably will need to refresh your memory, go over your weak points, and review major issues and images. But you must be "in training," working on images, all the time.

The second point is just as important. Rather than having unrelated bits of information floating around in your head, you want to understand them by making connections between images and ideas. You must create a context for the images, so that they make sense to you. You need to spend time studying images, and studying them in different ways. For example, if you're studying images from the first test unit in Arts & Ideas (Ancient Civilizations), you might create groups according to what I call the "five Ws:"

1. WHO (who is the artist, whom does the image depict, who ordered and paid for this work?). Group images around artists' names.
2. WHAT (what is the subject and title, what is the medium?). Group images according to subject matter and medium.
3. WHERE (where in the world does the object come from or, if architecture, where is it?). Group images by place.
4. WHEN (what style/chronological era produced it?). Group images by style, era, and chapter.
5. WHY (What ideas are reflected in the object? What does it communicate to viewers and why?). Group images by ideas.

In this way, you will connect each image to a variety of other images in different ways. They will start to form patterns, and these patterns are easier to remember than individual images or bits of information.

How to Remember Images

Here is an effective method for memorizing images, based on three simple steps.

Prioritize

If you feel overwhelmed by the number of images you need to know, prioritize them. Look for the works that were discussed at length in class and/or in your text. Look for works of art that reappear again and again in class as comparisons for other works. These are the images most likely to show up on an examination.

Familarize

Work with small groups of images at a time and study each one individually First, look at the image and see what you can recall about it. You may want to write down the information as you recall it, or just repeat it mentally. When you remember all that you can, look at the identification, note what you missed, and think about it in relation to the image. Try to explain to yourself why each element of the identification makes sense both historically and in the context of the lectures and book. As you get to know the images, take them out of the study groups and keep going over a smaller and smaller set of images until you've learned them all. Use the grouping technique described above to extract subsets of images for review. A good reverse way to test yourself is to look at the written identification, and see if you can mentally recall the image.

Contextualize

You need to have as firm a grasp of historical context for slide questions as you do for essays. The historical context generates the groupings you use for review, and ties together the images so that they make meaningful patterns. The Fiero book does a good job of providing the ideas and historical information you need to know One of the worst mistakes students make in reading their texts is skipping over this information as "filler" and reading only the parts that directly pertain to the images. Learning the ideas and history will enrich your understanding of the works of art and give you necessary information for interpreting art in essays and in class discussion. It will also save you from making unnecessary mistakes on slide questions.

Flash Cards

If you are having trouble connecting artists, images, styles, and ideas, it may be worthwhile to make a set of flashcards. On one side of an index card, paste or tape a photocopy of a required image (don't cut up your textbook!). On the other side of the card, write the "five Ws" for that image. Include the figure number from the textbook for easy reference. Flash cards take time, but they are worth it, because the learning process occurs while you are making the cards, as well as in using the finished cards. Plus, if you make them up each week, they won't seem like such a burden. I have had students whose exams improved by several letter grades after they studied with flashcards.

In the exam, if you see a slide that you don't recognize, it sometimes helps to eliminate those artists or styles you know it can't possibly be, for whatever reasons. Try to narrow it down to two or three possibilities, then reconstruct your list of distinctive "Ws" for each and see which one fits best. You can then make an "educated guess" and perhaps get partial credit.

Essay Questions

Art history exams often include essay questions because they provide a more in-depth way to test your interpretive ability and knowledge of the larger themes and issues addressed in lectures.

The best way to prepare for essay questions is obviously to attend class consistently and complete all the readings. Pay attention to images that reappear often, themes or issues that are discussed repeatedly, and readings that are a frequent point of reference. Put yourself in the position of the professor. If you were teaching this course, what would you think are the most important issues to know? Your Student Manual lists several study questions for each chapter in Fiero, emphasizing art historical context. Two of these will appear in some form on each exam. If you can answer all of them, you are home free.

Essay questions often ask you to identify the slides upon which the question is based as a starting point, just as you would in a slide identification, so the slide memorization that you do will help you here, too. Also, the groups that you create as you memorize slides may give you some ideas for your essays.

Text Taking Strategies for Essays

Think Before You Write

During exams, I see many students just plunge into writing as soon as a slide flashes on the screen. This is usually a bad idea. Although students are understandably anxious about having a limited amount of time to write, in actuality it is usually enough. Give yourself time to think and be sure of your answer. If you're nervous, it is easy to make a mistake at first glance.

Outline Before You Write

As a follow-up to the previous suggestion, it is very important to outline your essay before you begin to write. For a fifteen-minute essay, I recommend spending a full five minutes outlining your answer. This will help you organize your thoughts and answer the question as completely as possible. It is always better to write a cogent and focused answer to the question rather than a large number of disorganized words. Remember to keep consulting your outline as you write to make sure that you don't forget important points. Content is more important than number of words written.

Be Specific

Discuss key visual elements of the images in detail to support your interpretation. Be specific in your references to ideas. Demonstrate that you understand the ideas and information offered by lectures and text and can use them to build an insightful interpretation.

Be Clear and Concise

Focus on answering the question and don't provide a lot of extra background material that doesn't directly pertain to the subject at hand. State your basic idea in your opening sentence. Have a clear topic sentence for each paragraph in the body of your essay (easy to do if you've outlined your answer first). If you have time, use the conclusion to summarize or extend your arguments. Don't worry too much about your writing style, but do try to write clear, straightforward sentences. It can help to underline a few key terms or sentences in your answer, to help the person who reads your essay find your main points.

Do What You Can to Get Partial Credit

Many students don't put anything down because they didn't know one part of it, even though they may know all the other parts. Be sure to write as much as you can, even if you don't know everything. If you can't answer the whole question, do the parts that you can as thoroughly as possible.

Stay Calm!

Many students get so tense about the process of memorizing slides and taking slide tests that they freeze during the exam. There are several different strategies for staying calm during a test—including deep breathing, stretching, etc. Stay in the moment: focus on the question you're answering, not the one you just finished or the one that's coming up next.

In closing, if you are serious about getting a good grade in *Arts and Ideas*, and follow all these suggestions, you will succeed. Good luck!

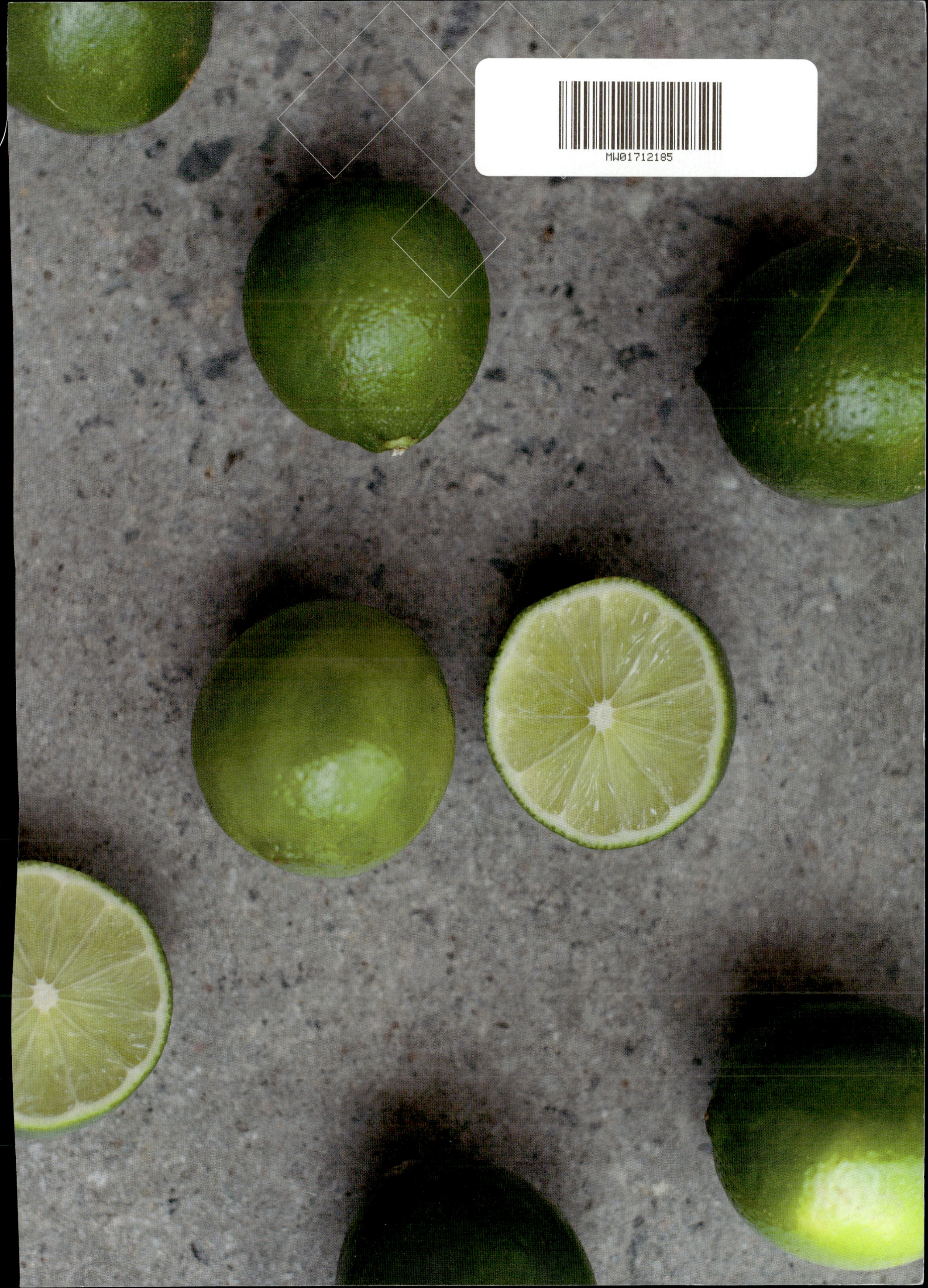

La cuisine de Jean-Philippe
Ses 100 meilleures recettes véganes
Jean-Philippe Cyr

Textes : Jean-Philippe Cyr
Photographies et retouches : Samuel Joubert
Photographies de la couverture et de la page 212 : Emilie Villeneuve
Conception graphique et mise en page : Nathalie Caron
Stylisme culinaire : Noémie Graugnard
Édition : Emilie Villeneuve et Marie Guarnera
Révision : Louise Faucher
Correction d'épreuves : Chantale Landry et Vincent Fortier
Coordination : Mathilde Bessière

Un ouvrage sous la direction d'Antoine Ross Trempe

Publié par :
Les Éditions Cardinal inc.
7240, rue Saint-Hubert
Montréal (Québec) H2R 2N1
editions-cardinal.ca

Dépôt légal : 3e trimestre 2017
Bibliothèque et Archives nationales du Québec
Bibliothèque et Archives Canada
ISBN : 978-2-924646-17-5

Financé par le gouvernement du Canada
Funded by the Government of Canada
Canada

Nous reconnaissons avoir reçu l'aide financière du gouvernement du Québec – Crédit d'impôt remboursable pour l'édition de livres et Programme d'aide à l'édition et à la promotion – SODEC.

ISBN : 978-2-924646-17-5

Imprimé au Canada

LA CUISINE DE
JEAN-PHILIPPE

Ses 100 meilleures recettes véganes

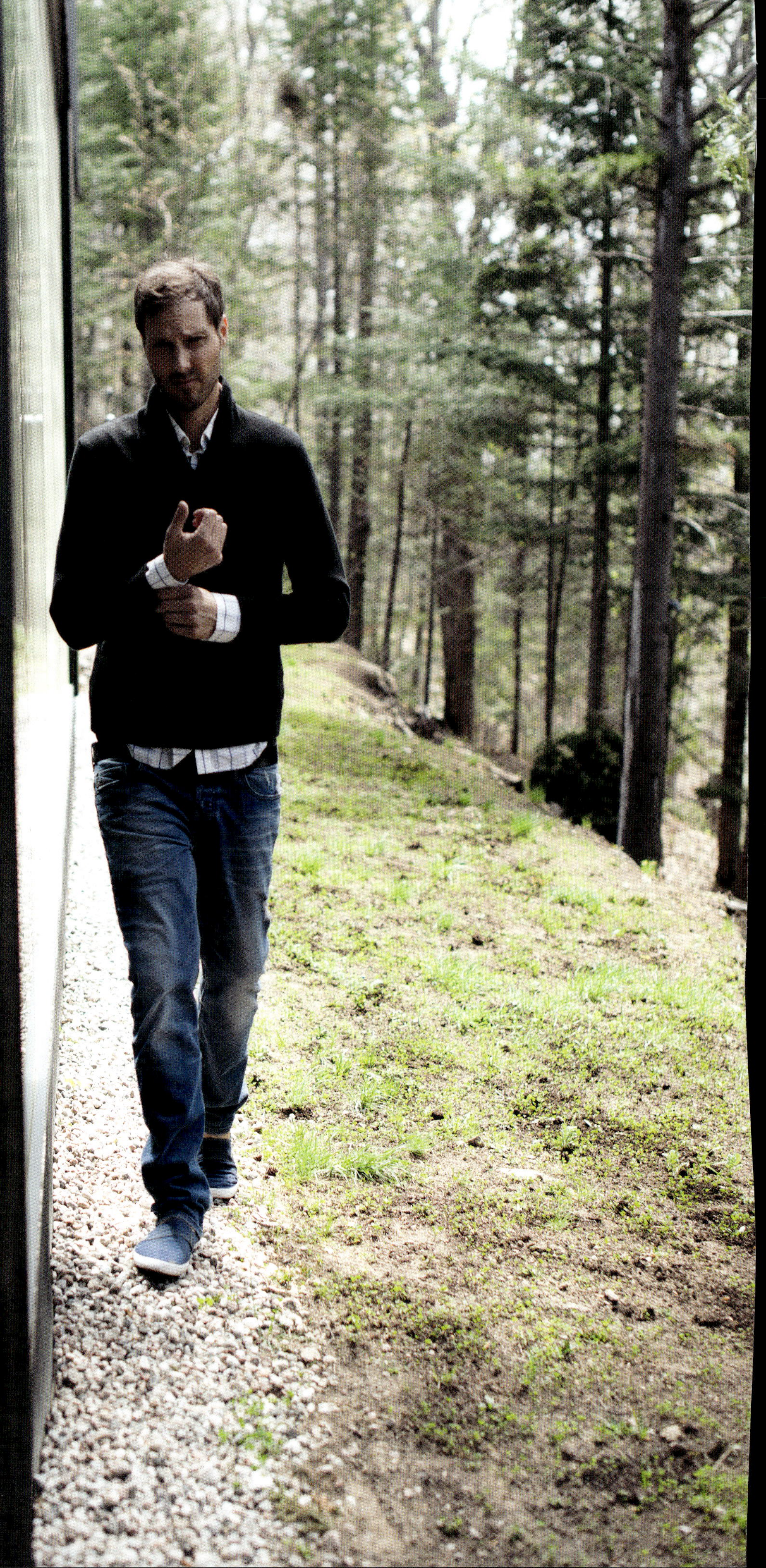

LA CUISINE DE JEAN-PHILIPPE

Ses 100 meilleures recettes véganes

cardinal

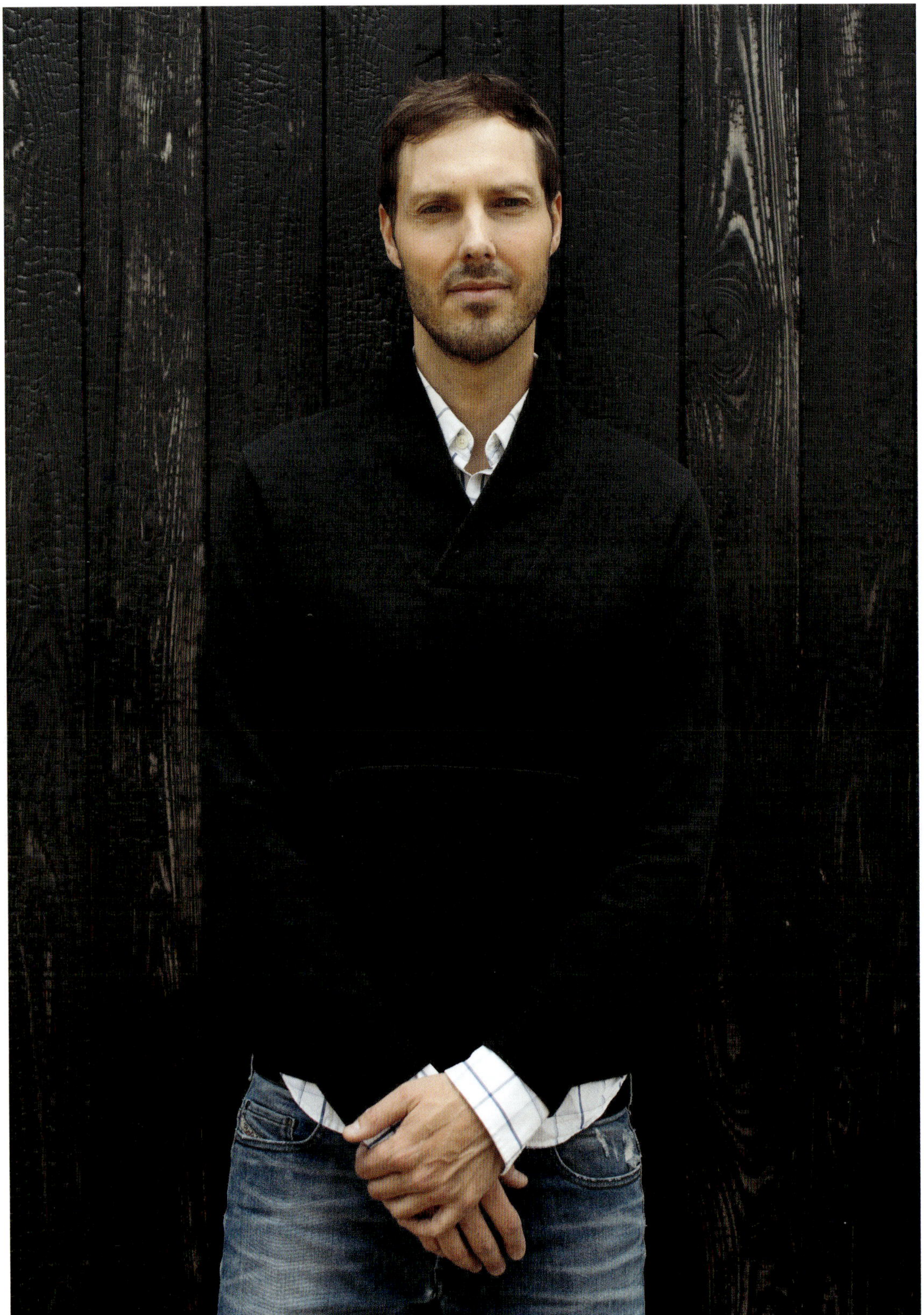

Introduction

Les goûts, les textures et les odeurs de la bouffe me fascinent depuis que je suis tout petit. Pour pouvoir jouer avec ces éléments et me retrouver le plus souvent possible en cuisine, j'ai fait des études dans ce domaine, puis j'ai exploré pendant de nombreuses années l'univers de la restauration. Cent fois sur le métier et dans des établissements en tout genre, j'ai appris à peaufiner mes techniques avant de partir à la découverte de l'Asie. Là, j'ai goûté des mariages de saveurs sublimes, qui m'ont subjugué. Cette recherche d'équilibre entre le sucré, le salé, l'acidulé et le piquant m'a grandement inspiré. Je me suis dès lors mis à appliquer ces nouveaux concepts aux plats que j'élaborais. J'ai fait évoluer ma cuisine, tout en me concentrant exclusivement sur des ingrédients à base de plantes. Ma transition vers une alimentation végane s'est faite en parallèle à mon parcours en restauration, tout en douceur.

Ces dernières années ont vu naître un engouement pour la cuisine végane, et c'est tant mieux pour la santé, pour l'environnement et pour les droits des animaux. Le mouvement vers une alimentation privilégiant les végétaux et les grains attire de plus en plus de monde à qui j'ai le plaisir de proposer des recettes simples à réaliser, et surtout, gourmandes! Depuis les débuts de mon blogue *La cuisine de Jean-Philippe* et de mon arrivée sur les réseaux sociaux, j'ai le plaisir de proposer le fruit de ma réflexion et de mon expérience au monde entier. J'essaie, avec mes capsules vidéo et à travers mes recettes, de démocratiser le véganisme, de montrer à quel point il est facile de réaliser un repas savoureux, avec des ingrédients végétaux que l'on peut trouver facilement à l'épicerie.

Dans ce premier livre, j'ai réuni mes recettes «classiques», celles qui sont les plus appréciées des membres de ma communauté virtuelle. Il contient aussi beaucoup de nouveaux plats conviviaux qui feront l'unanimité autour de votre table.

Cet ouvrage est l'occasion pour moi de vous aider à cuisiner simple, végé et délicieux. Que vous soyez véganes, végétariens ou simplement attirés par l'idée de consommer moins de viande, ce livre a été fait avec beaucoup de plaisir, pour vous.

Table des matières

LÉGENDE

Temps de préparation / **NOMBRE DE PORTIONS**

Temps de cuisson

Temps de repos

Note spécifique

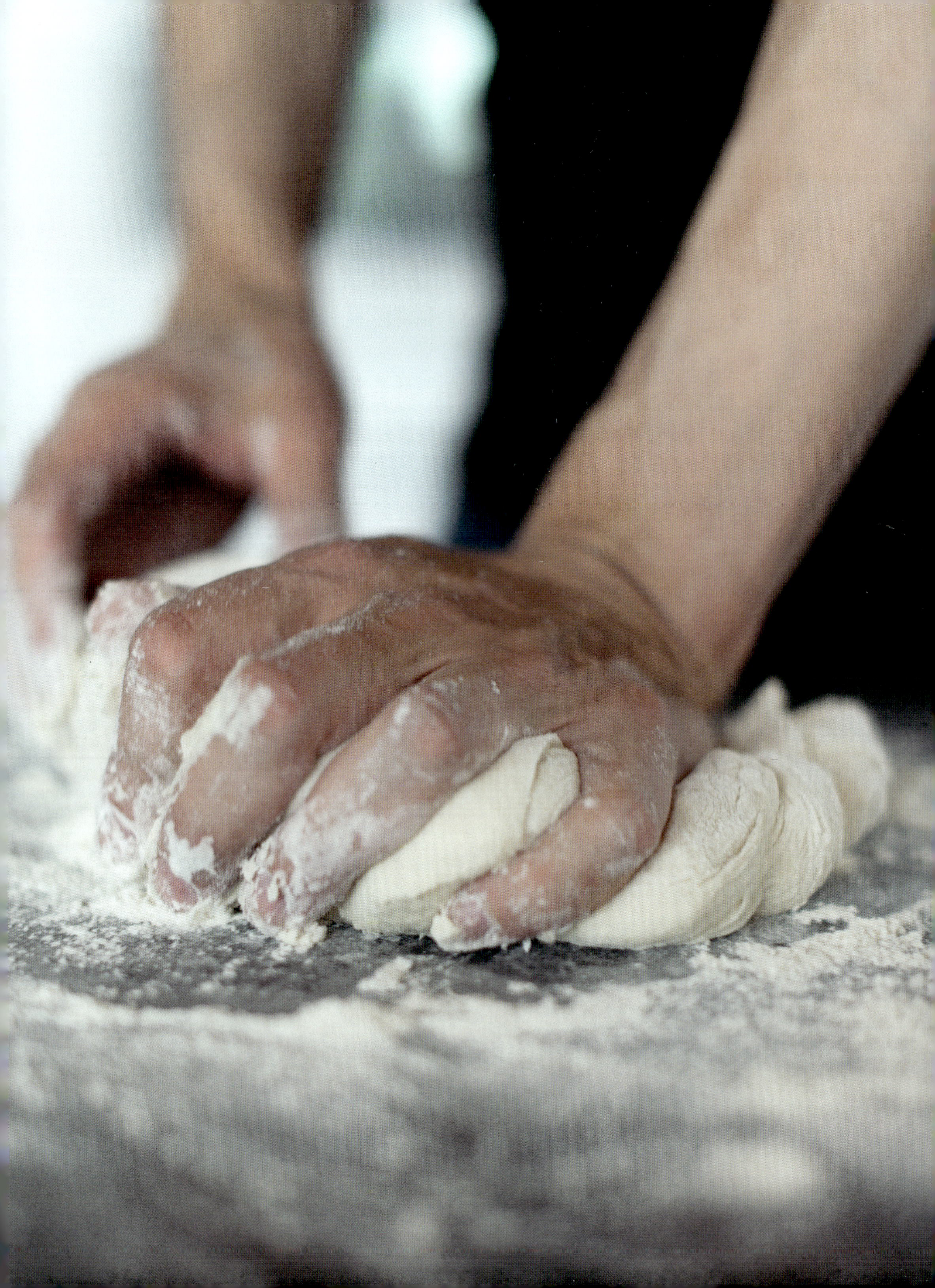

Les produits et les équipements de base

L'agar agar est un produit gélifiant extrait d'une algue qu'on utilise en très petite quantité pour changer la texture d'une préparation. C'est un ingrédient végétal parfait pour remplacer la gélatine animale. Pour activer l'agar agar, il faut le dissoudre dans un liquide, porter la préparation à ébullition, puis c'est lors du refroidissement que la magie s'opère. On retrouve deux types d'agar agar sur le marché, en poudre et en flocons. Je suggère l'agar agar en poudre, mais si vous utilisez la variété en flocons, il est important de doubler la quantité recommandée pour un résultat similaire.

La levure alimentaire, aussi appelée levure nutritionnelle, est une levure inactive qu'on utilise comme condiment dans la cuisine végétalienne. En plus d'être riche en vitamines du complexe B, elle apporte une saveur fromagée aux préparations auxquelles elle est ajoutée. On la retrouve en grande surface sous forme de flocons. À ne pas confondre avec la levure à pain ou la levure de bière.

La farine de gluten est une farine à haute teneur en protéines qui est extraite de la farine de blé. C'est le gluten qui procure son élasticité au pain. La farine de gluten est utilisée pour préparer le seitan, un substitut végétal à la viande.

La fumée liquide est un condiment qu'on utilise en très petite quantité et qui apporte, comme son nom l'indique, un arôme de fumée aux préparations auxquelles elle est ajoutée. Vous la retrouverez en épicerie (habituellement près des sauces barbecue).

La protéine végétale texturée (PVT) est une protéine alimentaire fabriquée à partir de farine de soya. On l'utilise comme substitut de viande hachée dans les plats végétaliens, après l'avoir réhydratée.

Le millet est une céréale très nutritive qu'on cuit comme le riz et qu'on peut utiliser pour remplacer la viande dans les burgers ou les pâtés, par exemple. Il est sans gluten.

Le riz brun à grain court est un riz à grain entier très riche en fibres et qui contient encore le son et le germe. Il est très nutritif, car seule l'écorce a été enlevée. Il est délicieux en accompagnement, et je l'utilise aussi comme liant dans les végéburgers. Comme il requiert plus de temps de cuisson que le riz blanc, on peut le faire tremper au préalable, si désiré.

Le quinoa est un grain entier très protéiné ayant une teneur élevée en fer. Il est excellent, entre autres, en accompagnement et en salade. On le cuit comme le riz dans 1 ½ à 2 fois son volume d'eau. Il est à noter que les grains de quinoa sont recouverts d'une résine légèrement amère (appelée « saponine ») qu'il faut retirer en rinçant abondamment le quinoa à l'eau avant de le faire cuire.

Le tempeh, originaire d'Indonésie, est fait à base de soya fermenté. Très protéiné, riche en fibres et en fer, il est un excellent substitut à la viande. Son goût unique rappelle celui d'un fromage très fort.

Le tofu est fabriqué à partir de fèves de soya. C'est un aliment riche en protéines et faible en gras. Très polyvalent, et ayant un goût assez neutre, le tofu absorbe la saveur des assaisonnements qu'on lui ajoute. Pour les plats salés, je suggère d'acheter le tofu le plus ferme que vous pourrez trouver. L'étiquetage laissant parfois perplexe, il faut vérifier la texture du tofu au toucher. Le tofu ferme ou extra-ferme devrait avoir la texture d'un fromage cheddar, par exemple.

Un mélangeur (de type *blender*) ou un mélangeur à main (aussi appelé « pied mélangeur ») vous sera très utile afin de réduire des aliments en purée, pour un potage, par exemple. À ne pas confondre avec un robot culinaire.

Un robot culinaire est un outil indispensable en cuisine végétalienne. Il permet de broyer des ingrédients à sec, comparativement au mélangeur qui requiert un liquide afin de bien fonctionner. Le robot culinaire dispose aussi de lames interchangeables qui permettent d'obtenir différentes coupes de légumes. Il est important d'acheter un robot qui convient à votre situation : un étudiant pourra se contenter d'un robot d'une capacité de 7 tasses (1,75 L), alors qu'une famille de quatre aura besoin d'un robot d'une plus grande capacité. Le prix d'un robot culinaire peut varier en fonction de sa puissance.

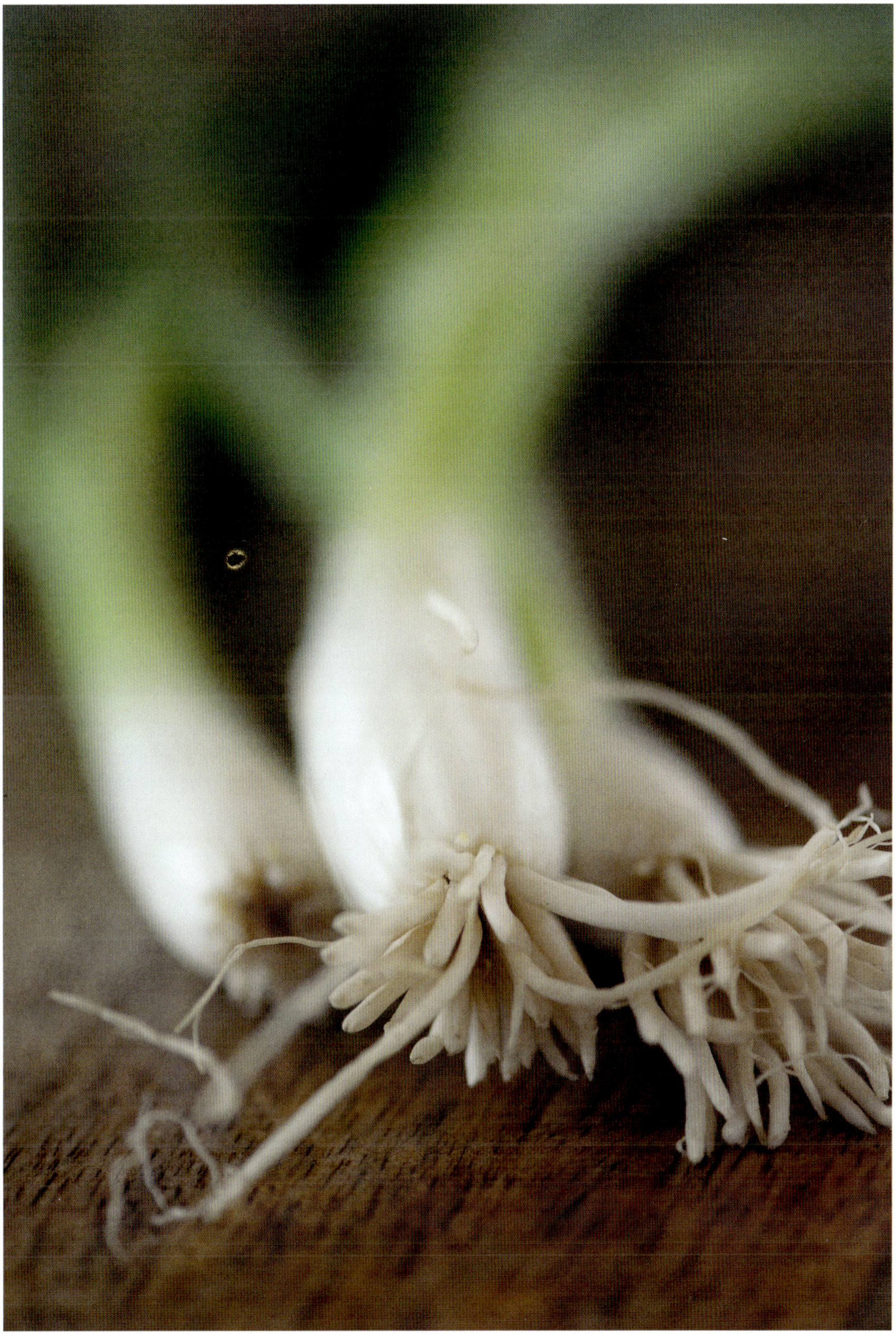

DÉJEUNERS ET BRUNCHS

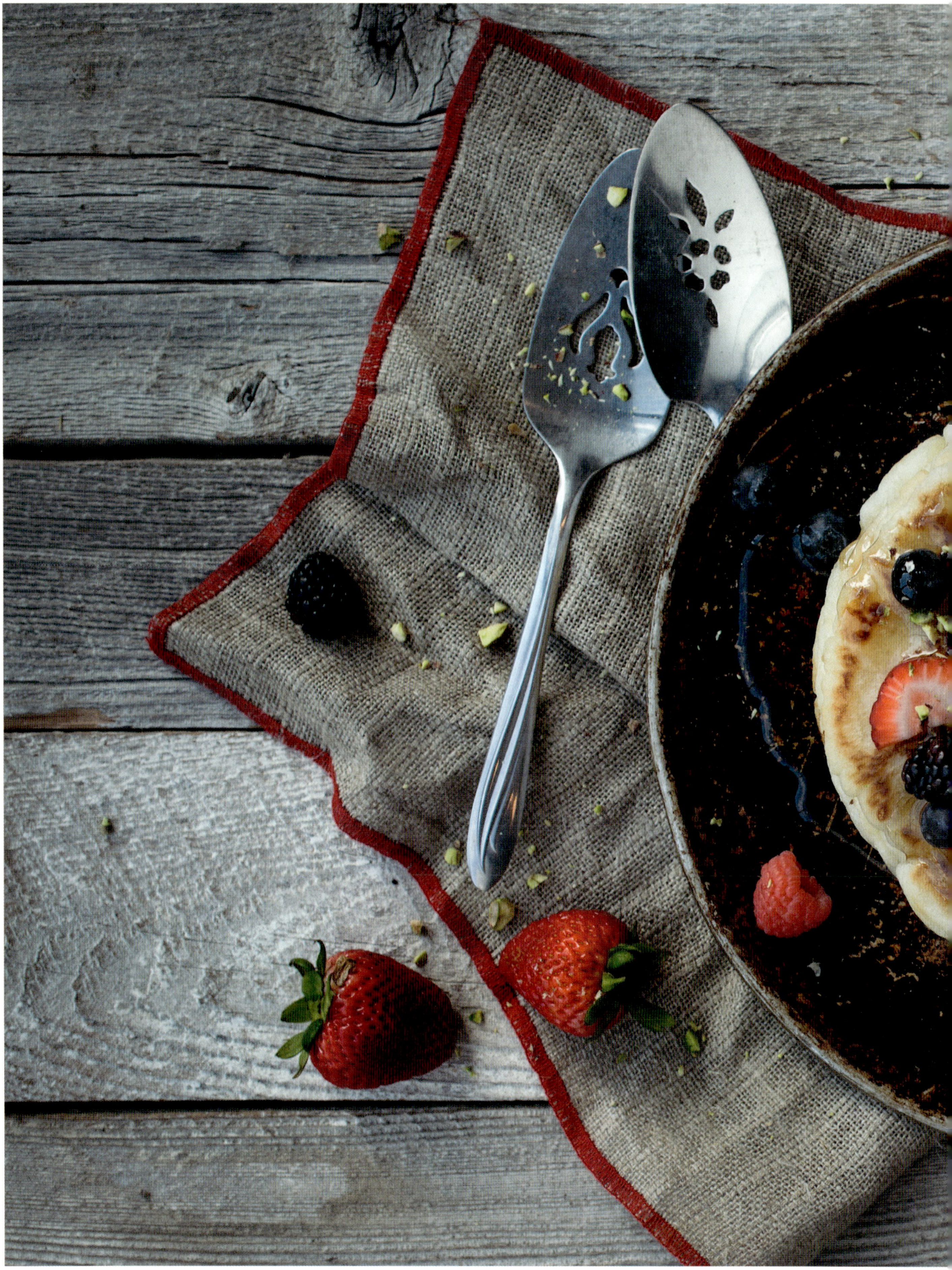

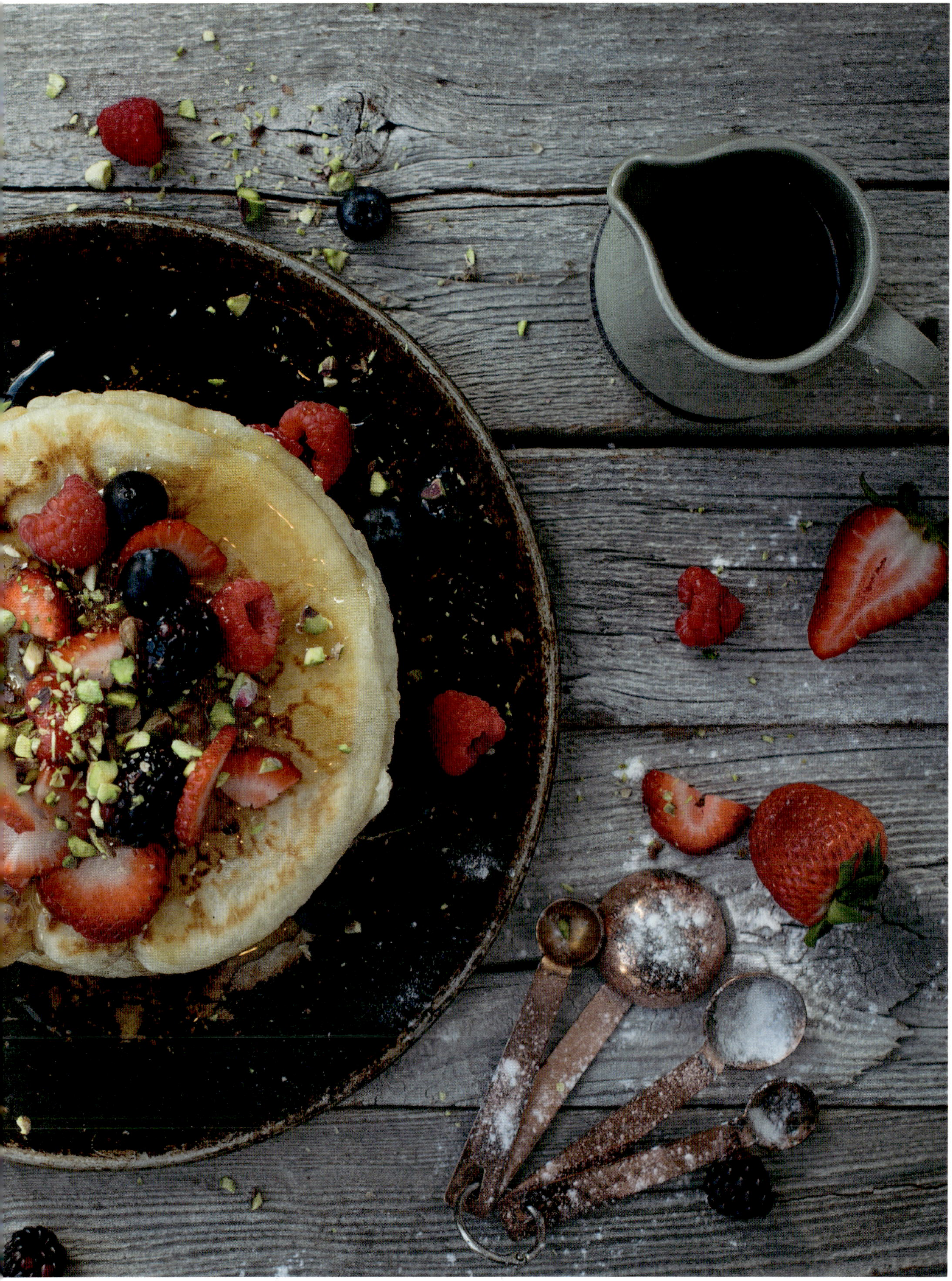

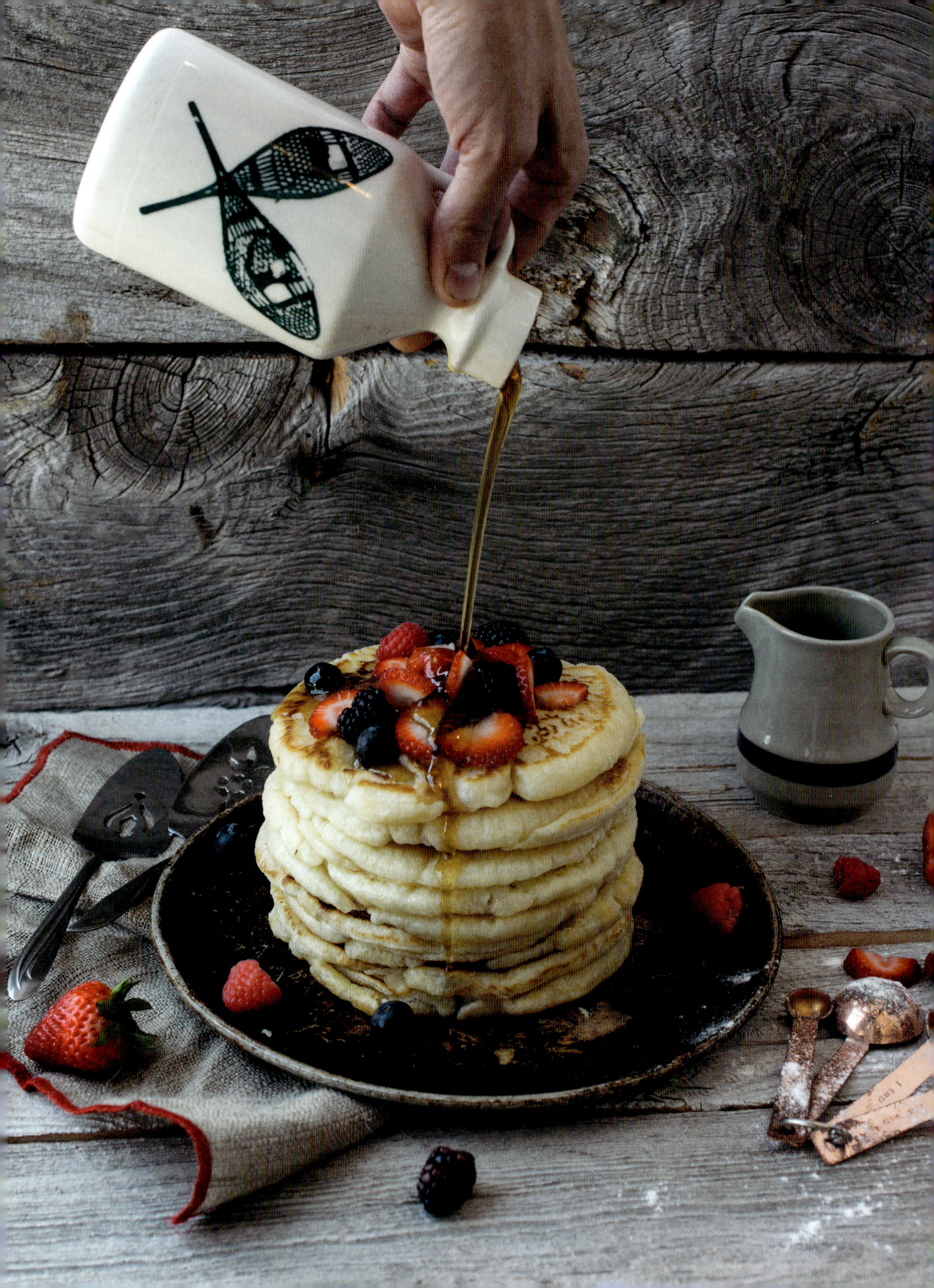

Crêpes

Ce ne sont pas les meilleures crêpes véganes, ce sont les meilleures crêpes, point !

10 min / **10 CRÊPES**
40 min

INGRÉDIENTS

3 tasses (450 g) farine

2 c. à soupe (30 ml) sucre

1 c. à thé (5 ml) poudre à pâte

1 c. à thé (5 ml) sel

¼ tasse (60 ml) huile végétale (+ pour la cuisson)

½ c. à thé (2,5 ml) vanille

3 tasses (750 ml) lait végétal

Sirop d'érable, pour garnir

Quelques fruits de saison, pour garnir

PRÉPARATION

1. Dans un bol, mélanger la farine, le sucre, la poudre à pâte et le sel. Ajouter le reste des ingrédients, puis mélanger à l'aide d'un fouet jusqu'à ce que le mélange soit homogène.
2. Dans une poêle, faire chauffer de l'huile, puis verser environ ¼ tasse (60 ml) de la pâte et incliner le poêlon pour l'étendre uniformément.
3. Faire cuire chaque crêpe pendant environ 2 minutes de chaque côté, en ajoutant de l'huile, au besoin.
4. Garnir les crêpes de sirop d'érable et/ou de fruits de saison. Déguster.

Pain aux bananes

20 min / **8 À 10 PORTIONS**

45 min

INGRÉDIENTS

2 bananes bien mûres

1 c. à soupe (15 ml) jus de citron

½ tasse (125 ml) huile végétale (+ 1 c. à soupe/15 ml, pour huiler le moule)

½ tasse (125 ml) lait végétal

1 tasse (210 g) cassonade tassée

2 tasses (300 g) farine tout usage

1 c. à thé (5 ml) sel

1 c. à thé (5 ml) poudre à pâte

1 c. à thé (5 ml) bicarbonate de sodium

3 c. à soupe (45 ml) farine de lin

⅓ tasse (40 g) noix de Grenoble, hachées

PRÉPARATION

1. Préchauffer le four à 350 °F (180 °C).
2. Huiler un moule à pain de 9 po x 5 po (23 cm x 13 cm). Réserver.
3. Dans un bol, réduire les bananes en purée. Ajouter le jus de citron, l'huile, le lait végétal et la cassonade, puis battre le tout à l'aide d'un batteur électrique, jusqu'à ce que le mélange soit homogène. Réserver.
4. Dans un autre bol, mélanger la farine, le sel, la poudre à pâte, le bicarbonate de sodium, la farine de lin et les noix.
5. Ajouter le mélange liquide aux ingrédients secs et mélanger à l'aide d'une cuillère en bois.
6. Étaler la pâte dans le moule. Cuire au four pendant environ 45 minutes, ou jusqu'à ce qu'un cure-dent inséré au centre du pain en ressorte propre.
7. Laisser refroidir le pain pendant 15 minutes. Démouler le pain et le laisser refroidir complètement sur une grille, puis le trancher. Déguster.

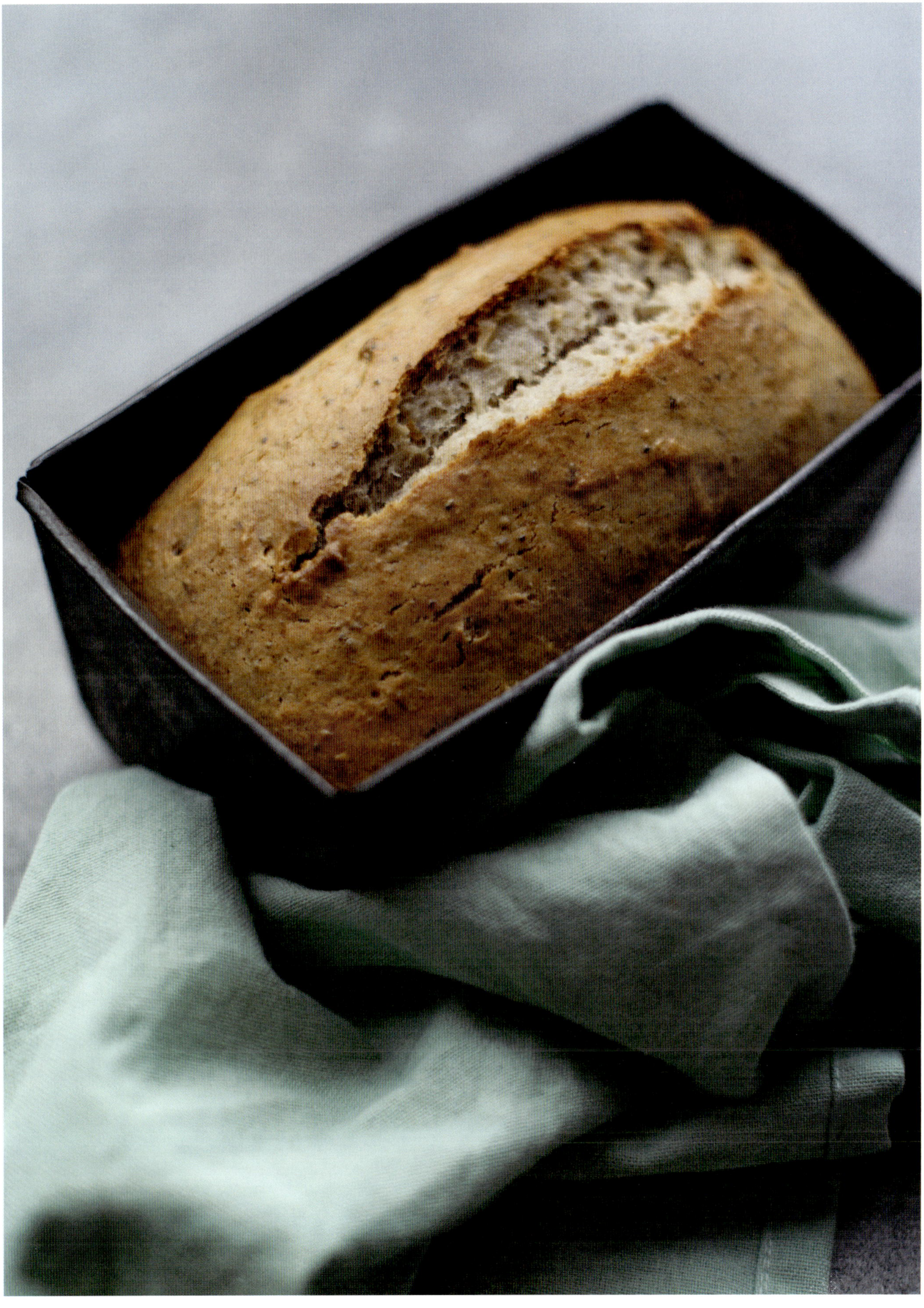

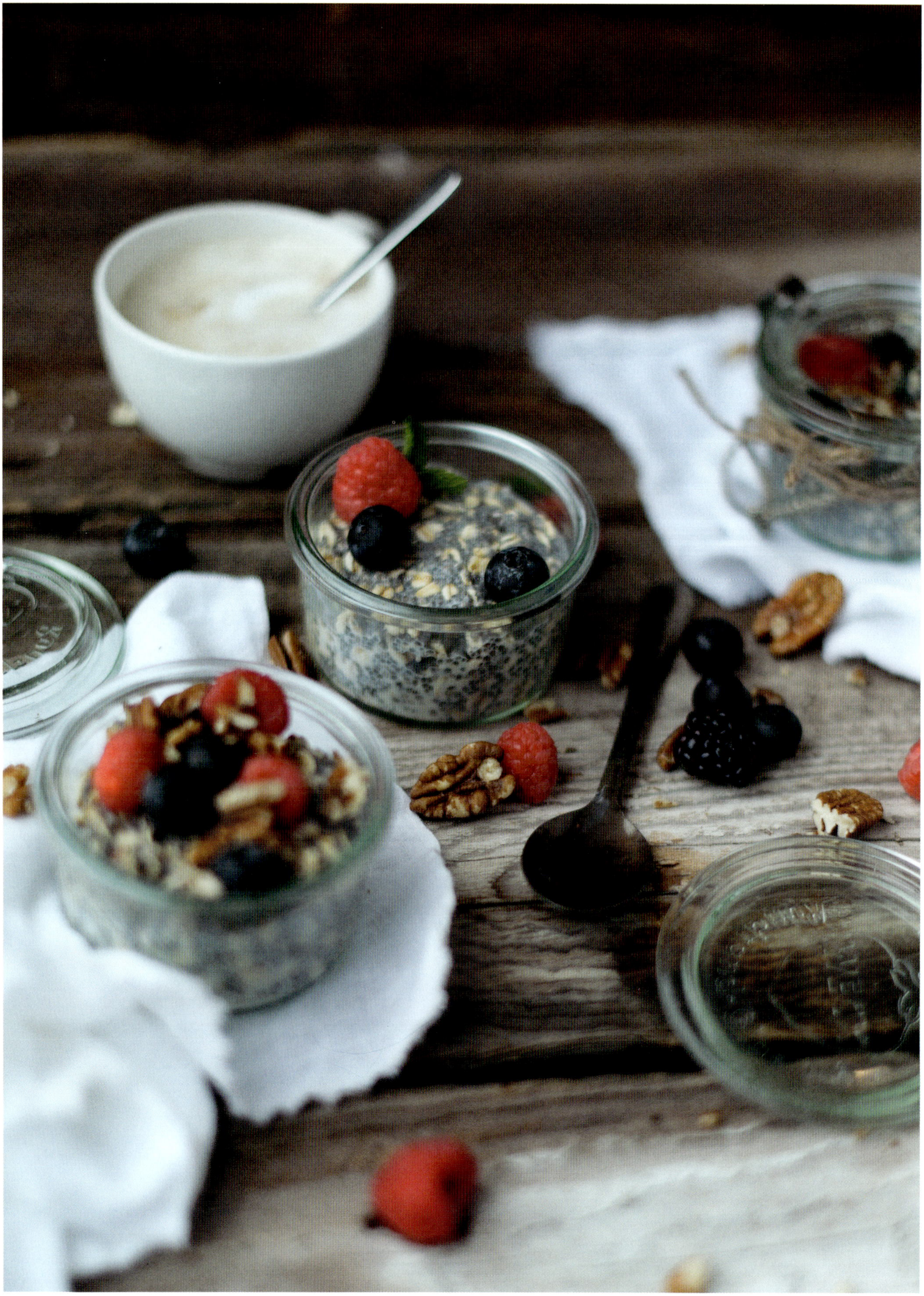

Flocons d'avoine et chia sans cuisson

Pour les matins pressés, vous pouvez même les apporter pour les manger sur le pouce.

5 min / **1 PORTION**

40 min

Temps de réfrigération 2 à 12 h

INGRÉDIENTS

1 tasse (250 ml) lait végétal non sucré

½ tasse (50 g) flocons d'avoine

2 c. à soupe (30 ml) graines de chia entières

1 c. à soupe (15 ml) sirop d'érable

Quelques fruits, pour garnir

PRÉPARATION

1. Dans un pot en verre muni d'un couvercle ou dans un petit bol, mélanger le lait végétal, l'avoine et les graines de chia.
2. Fermer le pot ou couvrir le bol d'une pellicule plastique, puis réfrigérer pendant au moins 2 heures, ou jusqu'au lendemain.
3. Ajouter le sirop d'érable et garnir de vos fruits préférés avant de déguster.

NOTE: Se conservent jusqu'à 2 jours au réfrigérateur.

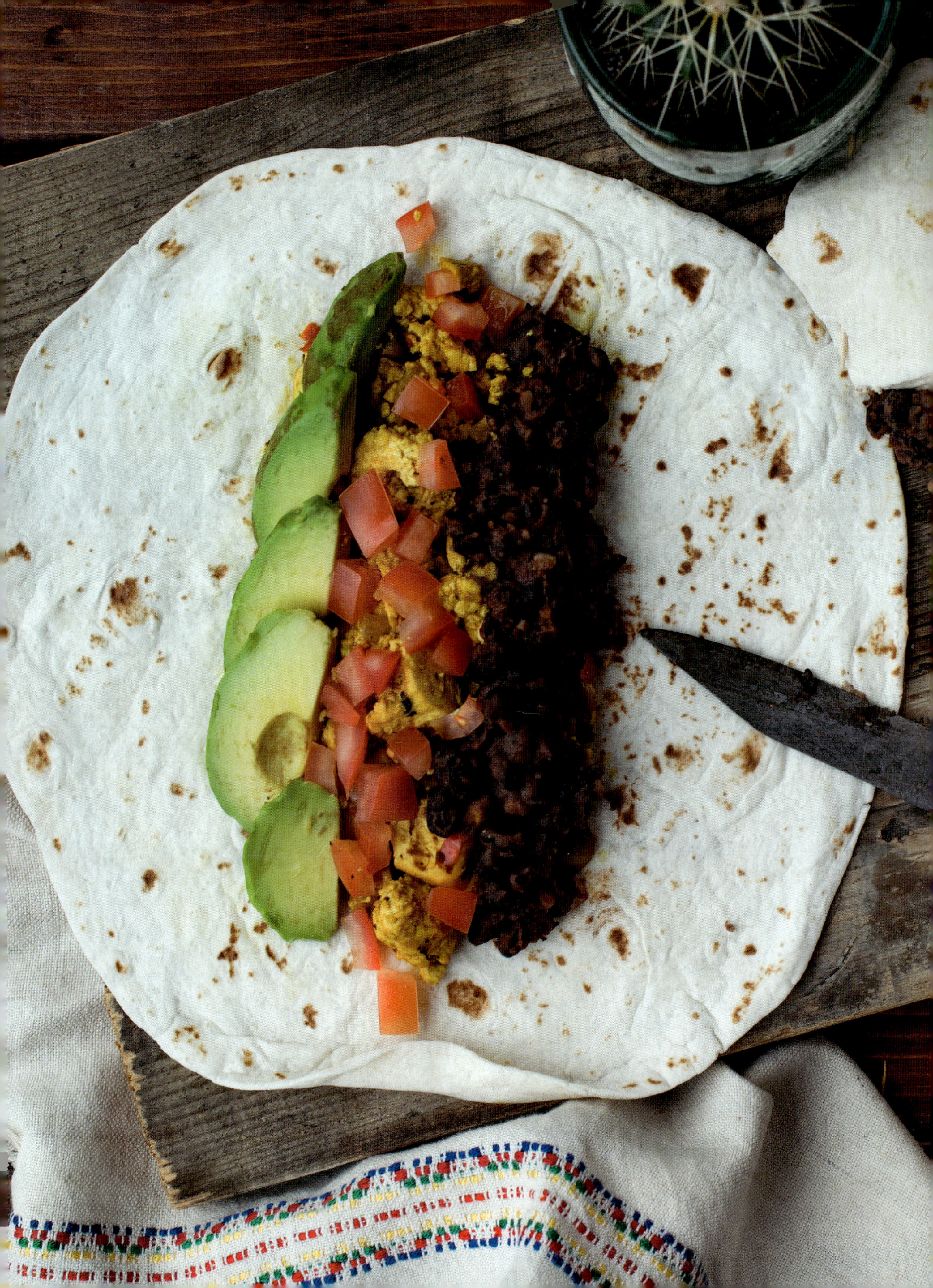

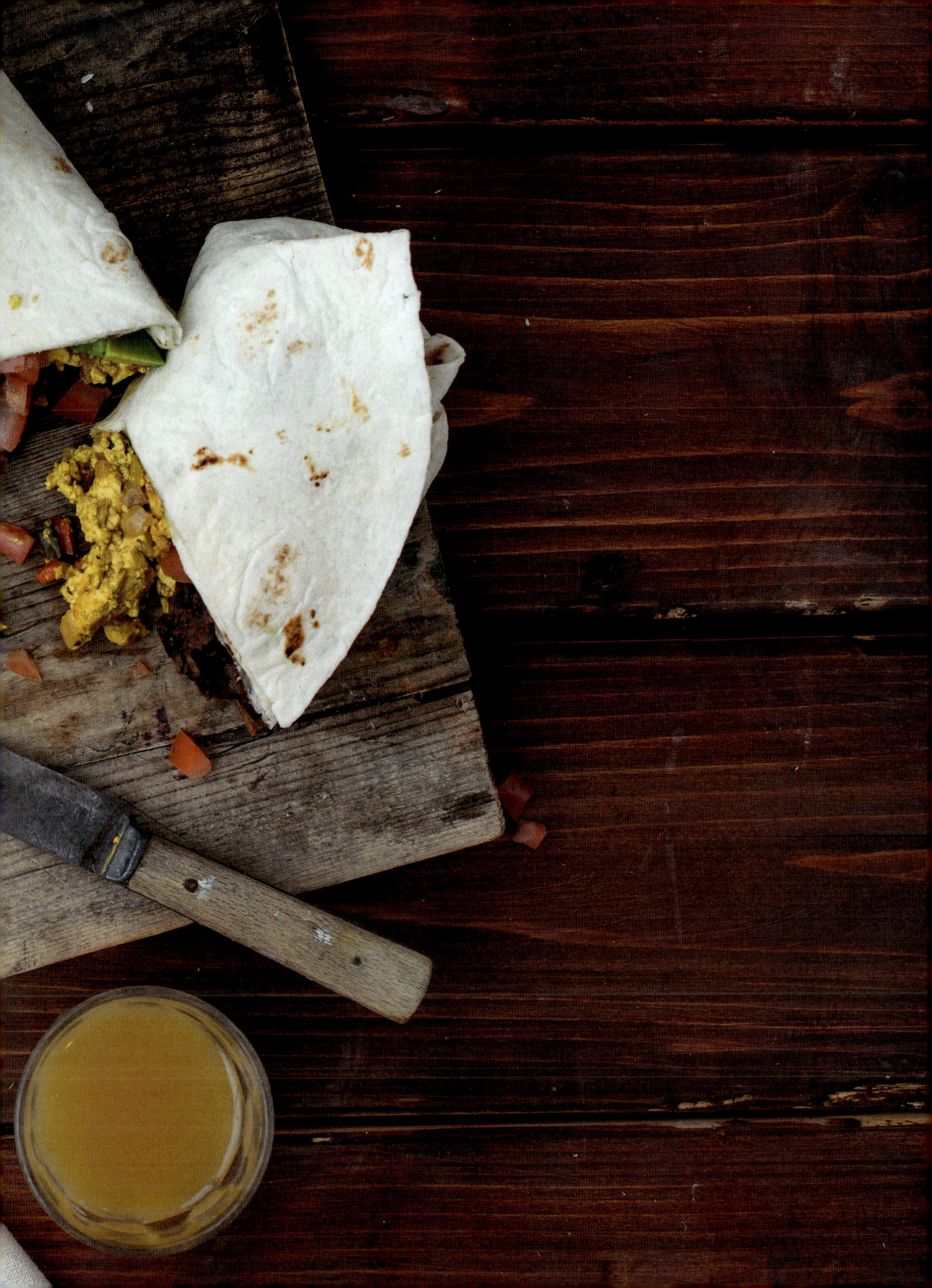

Burritos déjeuner

25 min / **4 PORTIONS**
15 min

FRIJOLES NEGROS

1 boîte (540 ml) haricots noirs, rincés et égouttés

2 c. à soupe (30 ml) huile végétale

2 gousses d'ail, hachées

1 c. à thé (5 ml) origan séché

1 c. à thé (5 ml) cumin moulu

1 c. à thé (5 ml) pâte de tomate

1 c. à thé (5 ml) sirop d'érable

⅛ c. à thé (0,5 ml) piment de Cayenne

½ c. à thé (2,5 ml) sel

½ tasse (125 ml) eau

PRÉPARER LES FRIJOLES NEGROS

1. Dans une poêle à frire, faire revenir les haricots à feu vif dans l'huile, pendant 2 minutes.
2. Ajouter l'ail, l'origan, le cumin, la pâte de tomate, le sirop d'érable, le piment de Cayenne et le sel, puis poursuivre la cuisson à feu vif de 2 à 3 minutes, ou jusqu'à ce que les haricots commencent à coller au fond de la poêle.
3. Ajouter l'eau. (Si votre poêle est suffisamment chaude, le mélange devrait frémir.)
4. Poursuivre la cuisson à feu vif pendant environ 2 minutes, ou jusqu'à ce que tout le liquide soit absorbé. Réserver.

TOFU BROUILLÉ

1 petit oignon, haché

½ poivron rouge, coupé en dés

4 gros champignons de Paris, émincés

2 c. à soupe (30 ml) huile de canola

1 bloc (454 g) tofu ferme, émietté

¼ c. à thé (1 ml) curcuma

¼ c. à thé (1 ml) paprika

1 c. à thé (5 ml) poudre d'oignon

½ c. à thé (2,5 ml) basilic séché

3 c. à soupe (45 ml) levure alimentaire

1 c. à thé (5 ml) sirop d'érable

¾ tasse (180 ml) lait végétal

1 c. à thé (5 ml) sel

Poivre, au goût

4 tortillas, au choix

Quelques tranches d'avocat, pour garnir

Quelques tomates coupées en dés, pour garnir

PRÉPARER LE TOFU BROUILLÉ

1. Dans une poêle, faire revenir à feu moyen l'oignon, le poivron rouge et les champignons dans l'huile pendant 2 minutes.
2. Incorporer le tofu émietté, le curcuma, le paprika, la poudre d'oignon, le basilic, la levure alimentaire, le sirop d'érable, le lait végétal, le sel et le poivre.
3. Poursuivre la cuisson pendant quelques minutes.

ASSEMBLER LES BURRITOS

1. Garnir les tortillas des frijoles negros, du tofu brouillé, de tomates et d'avocat. Replier la base et le haut des tortillas sur la garniture et rouler. Déguster.

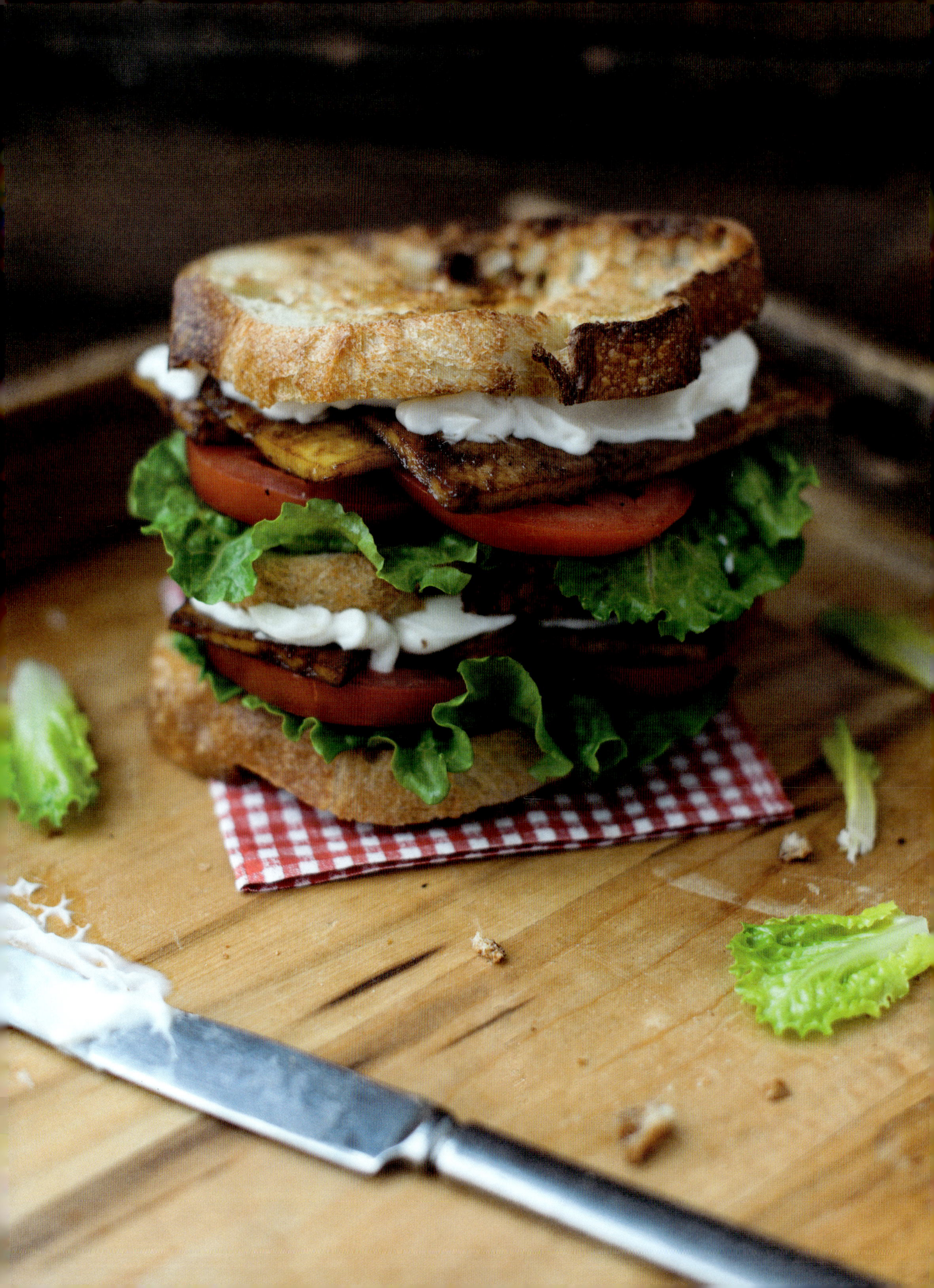

BLT

20 à 25 min / **2 À 3 SANDWICHS**

15 min

BACON DE TOFU

1 c. à thé (5 ml) poudre d'oignon

1 c. à soupe (15 ml) levure alimentaire

2 c. à soupe (30 ml) sauce soya

1 ½ c. à soupe (23 ml) sirop d'érable

1 c. à soupe (15 ml) huile végétale (+ 2 c. à soupe pour huiler la plaque)

1 ½ c. à thé (8 ml) fumée liquide

1 bloc de tofu ferme, tranché finement (350 g)

Pain grillé

Mayonnaise végétale (voir recette p. 209), pour garnir

Quelques tranches de tomates, pour garnir

Quelques feuilles de laitue, pour garnir

PRÉPARER LE BACON DE TOFU

1. Préchauffer le four à 375 °F (190 °C).
2. Dans un bol, mélanger la poudre d'oignon, la levure alimentaire, la sauce soya, le sirop d'érable, l'huile et la fumée liquide.
3. Verser sur les tranches de tofu et laisser mariner de 10 à 15 minutes.
4. Huiler une plaque à pâtisserie et y déposer les tranches de tofu.
5. Cuire au four pendant 15 minutes, ou jusqu'à ce que le tofu soit bien croustillant.

DRESSER LES SANDWICHS

1. Garnir le pain grillé du bacon de tofu, de la mayonnaise, des tranches de tomates et de la laitue. Déguster.

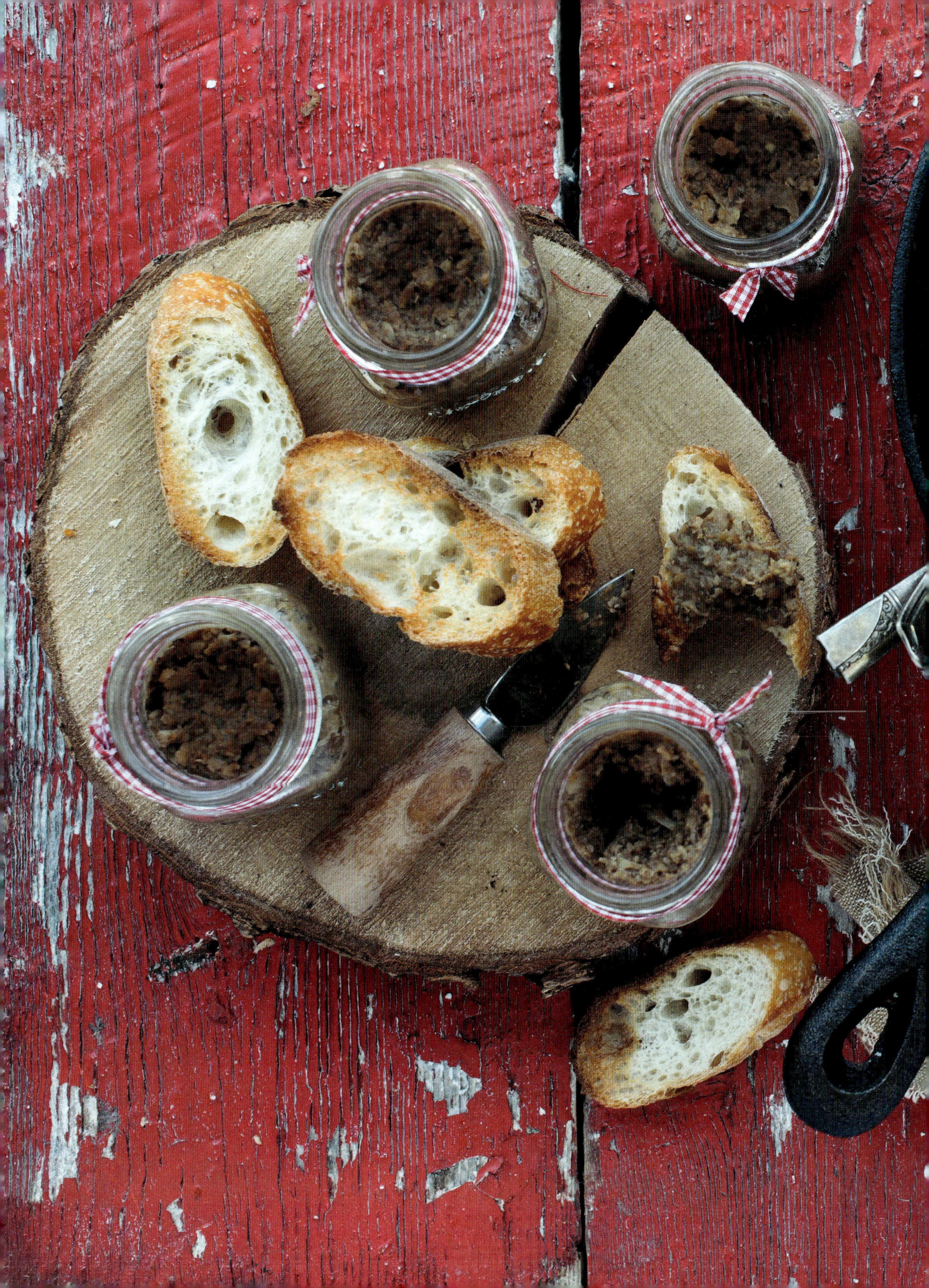

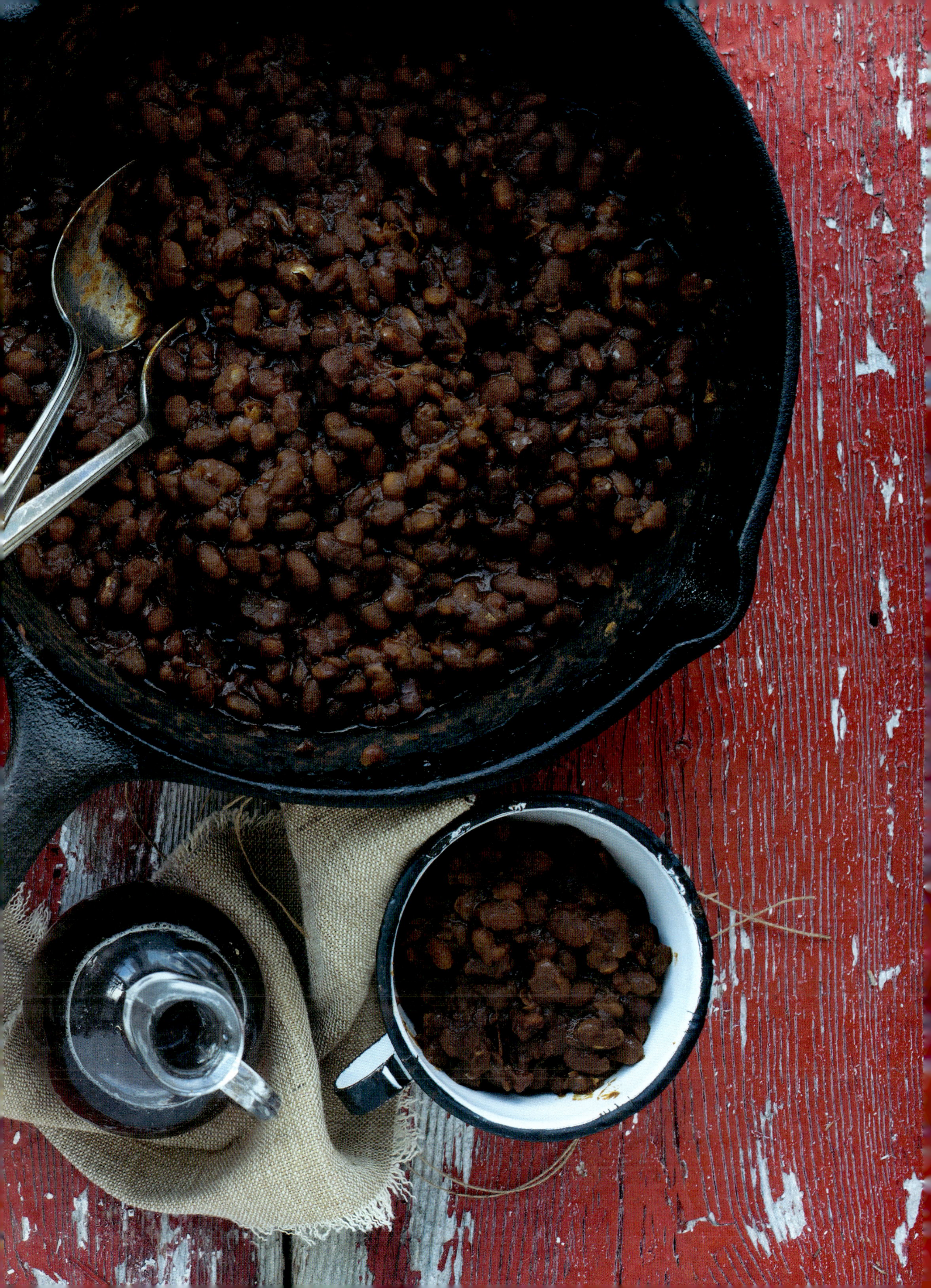

Cretons

15 min / **ENVIRON 4 TASSES (600 G)**

20 min

INGRÉDIENTS

1 tasse (80 g) protéines végétales texturées (PVT)

2 tasses (500 ml) eau bouillante

1 oignon, haché

4 tasses (227 g) champignons de Paris, émincés

3 c. à soupe (45 ml) huile végétale

1 gousse d'ail, hachée

1 boîte (540 ml) lentilles, rincées et égouttées

2 tasses (500 ml) bouillon de légumes

1 c. à soupe (15 ml) tamari ou sauce soya

1 c. à soupe (15 ml) sirop d'érable

2 c. à soupe (30 ml) levure alimentaire

1 c. à thé (5 ml) basilic séché

1 c. à thé (5 ml) origan séché

½ c. à thé (2,5 ml) clou de girofle moulu

Sel et poivre

PRÉPARATION

1. Dans un bol, plonger les PVT dans l'eau bouillante et laisser reposer pendant 5 minutes afin de les réhydrater. Égoutter et réserver.
2. Dans une poêle à fond épais, faire revenir l'oignon et les champignons dans l'huile pendant 4 minutes.
3. Ajouter l'ail et les PVT, puis poursuivre la cuisson pendant 4 minutes.
4. Ajouter le reste des ingrédients et poursuivre la cuisson pendant 15 minutes, ou jusqu'à ce que le liquide soit presque complètement absorbé.
5. Verser le mélange dans un récipient, puis le broyer à l'aide d'un mélangeur à main jusqu'à l'obtention d'une texture légèrement grumeleuse.
6. Laisser refroidir, couvrir et réfrigérer avant de servir.

Fèves au sirop d'érable

30 min / **6 PORTIONS**

3 h

12 à 24 h

INGRÉDIENTS

2 tasses (400 g) haricots blancs secs

2 c. à soupe (30 ml) huile végétale

1 oignon, émincé

½ tasse (125 ml) mélasse

¼ tasse (60 ml) sirop d'érable

1 c. à thé (5 ml) moutarde en poudre

2 c. à soupe (30 ml) pâte de tomate

2 c. à soupe (30 ml) miso

1 c. à thé (5 ml) sel

Poivre, au goût

5 tasses (1,25 L) eau

PRÉPARATION

1. Faire tremper les haricots dans de l'eau de 12 à 24 heures (facultatif). Bien rincer et égoutter.
2. Préchauffer le four à 325°F (160°C).
3. Déposer les haricots dans une casserole. Couvrir d'eau et porter à ébullition. Réduire le feu et laisser mijoter pendant 15 minutes. Bien égoutter. Réserver.
4. Dans une marmite allant au four ou une cocotte en fonte émaillée, faire chauffer l'huile, ajouter l'oignon et faire suer pendant 5 minutes.
5. Ajouter la mélasse, le sirop d'érable, la moutarde en poudre, la pâte de tomate, le miso, le sel et le poivre. Bien mélanger.
6. Ajouter les haricots et l'eau. Porter à ébullition, puis couvrir la marmite de papier d'aluminium. Cuire au four pendant 3 heures, ou jusqu'à ce que les haricots soient tendres. Ajouter de l'eau chaude et poursuivre la cuisson, au besoin. Servir bien chaud.

Miniquiches

À manger avec les doigts, s'il vous plaît !

20 min / **24 MINIQUICHES**

25 min

INGRÉDIENTS

2 c. à soupe (30 ml) huile végétale (+ 2 c. à soupe/30 ml pour huiler les moules)

4 tasses (227 g) champignons de Paris, émincés

1 ½ tasse (120 g) poireau, émincé

1 gousse d'ail, hachée

½ c. à thé (2,5 ml) basilic séché

½ c. à thé (2,5 ml) origan séché

1 tasse (120 g) farine de pois chiches

¼ tasse (20 g) levure alimentaire

1 tasse (250 ml) bouillon de légumes

Sel et poivre, au goût

PRÉPARATION

1. Préchauffer le four à 375 °F (190 °C).
2. Huiler une plaque de 24 minimuffins.
3. Dans une poêle à fond épais, faire chauffer l'huile à feu moyen.
4. Ajouter les champignons et le poireau, puis faire suer pendant 10 minutes.
5. Ajouter l'ail, le basilic et l'origan, puis poursuivre la cuisson pendant 2 minutes.
6. Dans un bol, mélanger la farine de pois chiches, la levure alimentaire et le bouillon de légumes.
7. Retirer la poêle du feu et incorporer le mélange à base de farine aux légumes.
8. Bien mélanger, puis saler et poivrer.
9. Répartir le mélange dans le moule à minimuffins. Cuire au four de 10 à 12 minutes.
10. Laisser légèrement refroidir sur une grille avant de démouler et de déguster.

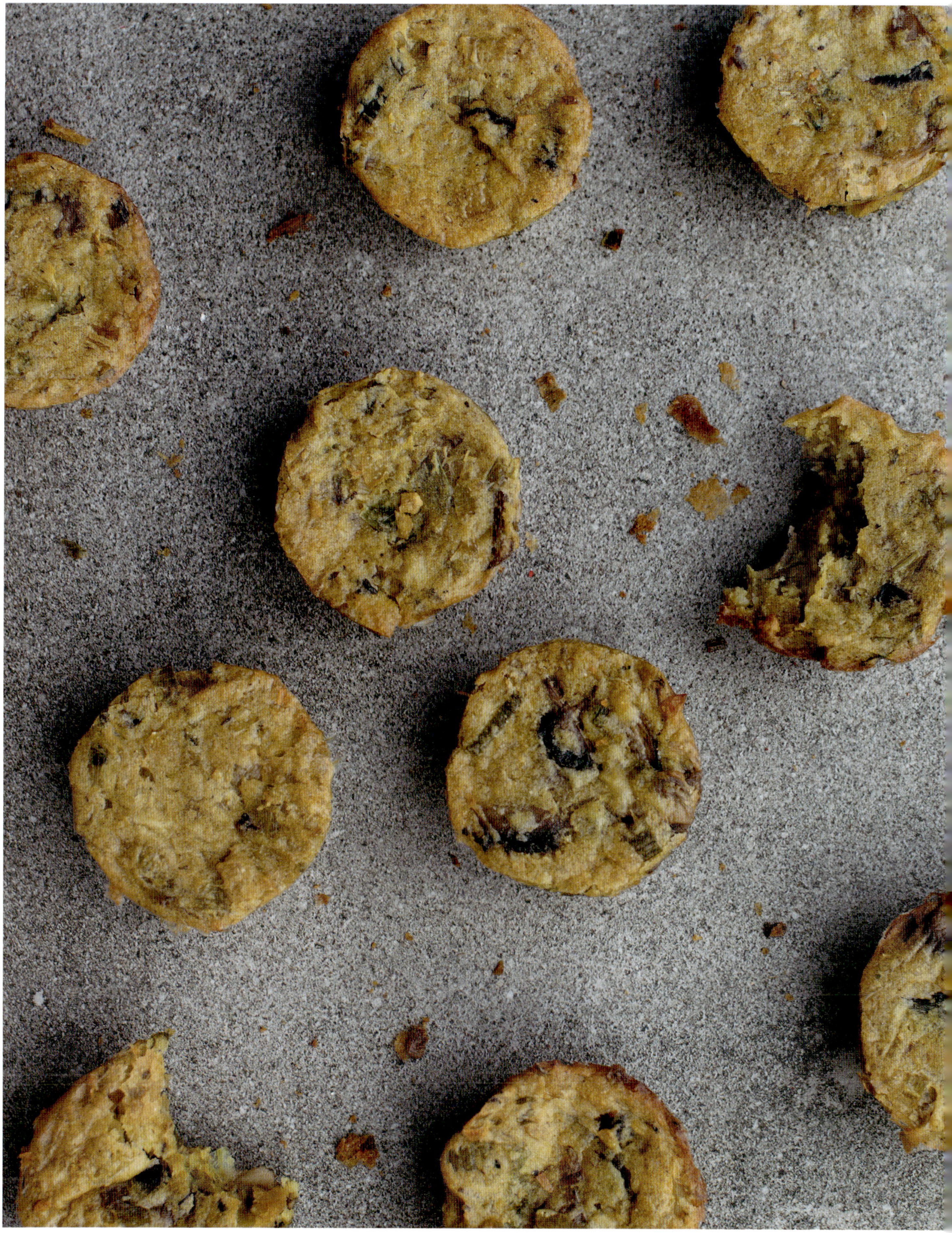

Sandwichs à la tartinade de tofu

10 min / **4 SANDWICHS**

INGRÉDIENTS

1 bloc (350 g) tofu ferme

1 c. à thé (5 ml) jus de citron

¼ tasse (20 g) levure alimentaire

1 c. à thé (5 ml) poudre d'ail

¼ tasse (60 ml) mayonnaise végétale (voir recette p. 209)

1 c. à thé (5 ml) sirop d'érable

Sel et poivre, au goût

2 branches de céleri, hachées

8 tranches de pain

Laitue, pour garnir

PRÉPARATION

1. Dans le bol d'un robot culinaire, mettre tous les ingrédients, sauf le céleri et le pain. Mélanger quelques secondes à la fois, jusqu'à ce que la garniture soit homogène.
2. Transvider la garniture dans un bol, ajouter le céleri et mélanger.
3. Couvrir les tranches de pain de la tartinade de tofu et garnir de laitue, puis déguster.

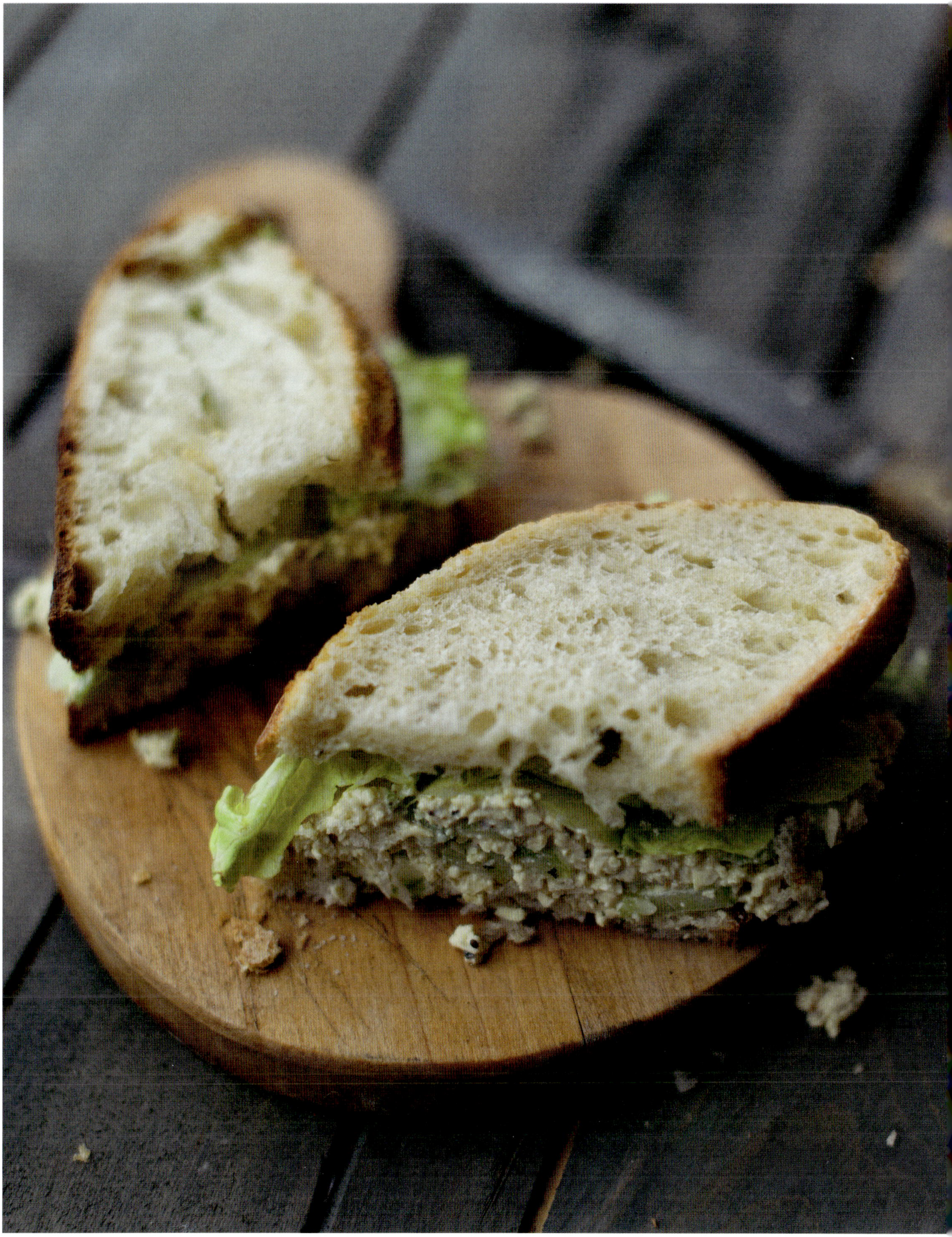

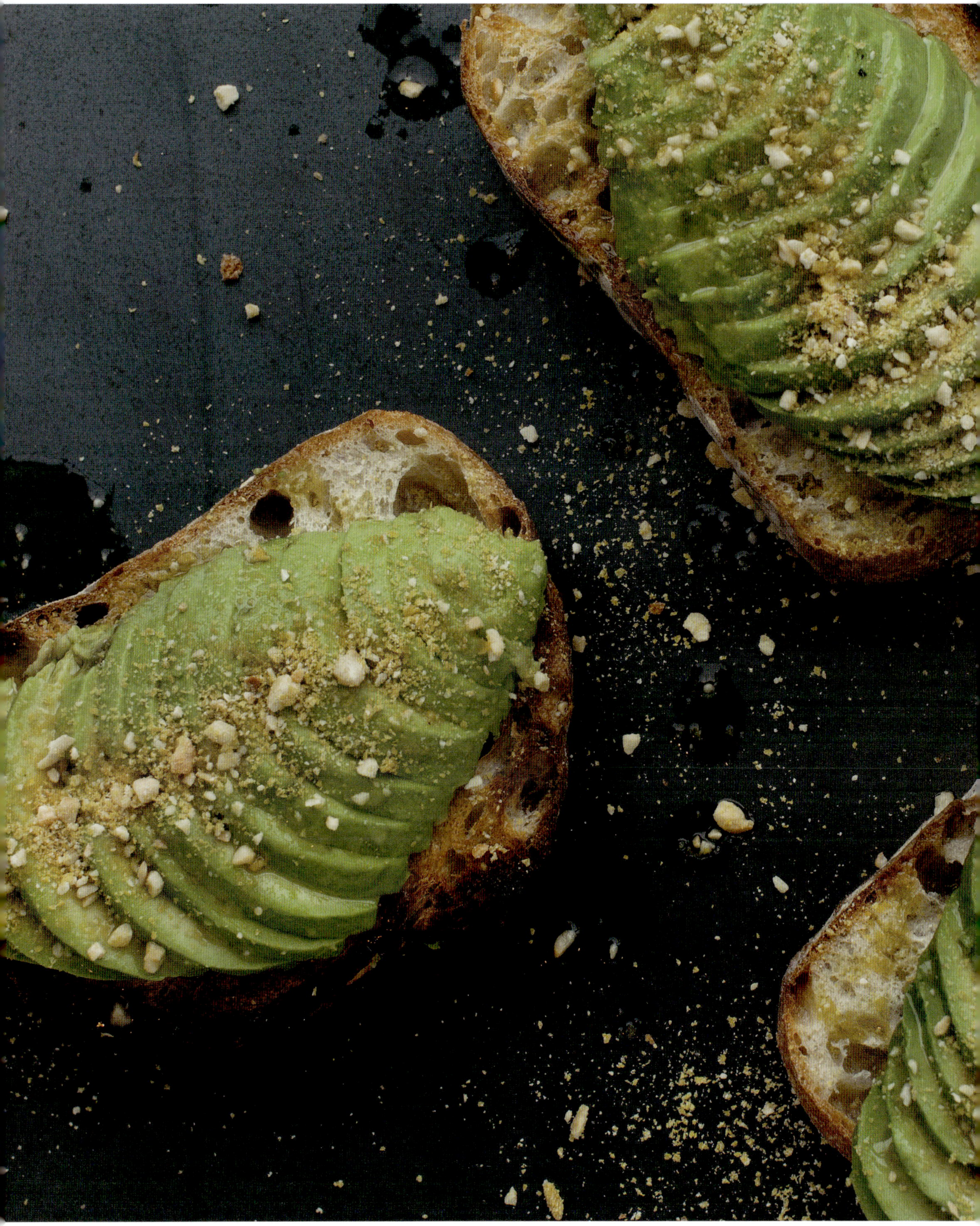

Toasts à l'avocat

5 min / **2 TOASTS**

INGRÉDIENTS

2 tranches de pain grillé

1 avocat bien mûr

2 c. à soupe (30 ml) parmesan de cajou (voir recette p. 208)

Huile d'olive

PRÉPARATION

1. Peler et dénoyauter l'avocat, puis le trancher finement.
2. Déposer les tranches d'avocat en éventail sur le pain grillé.
3. Saupoudrer du parmesan de cajou et arroser d'un trait d'huile d'olive. Déguster.

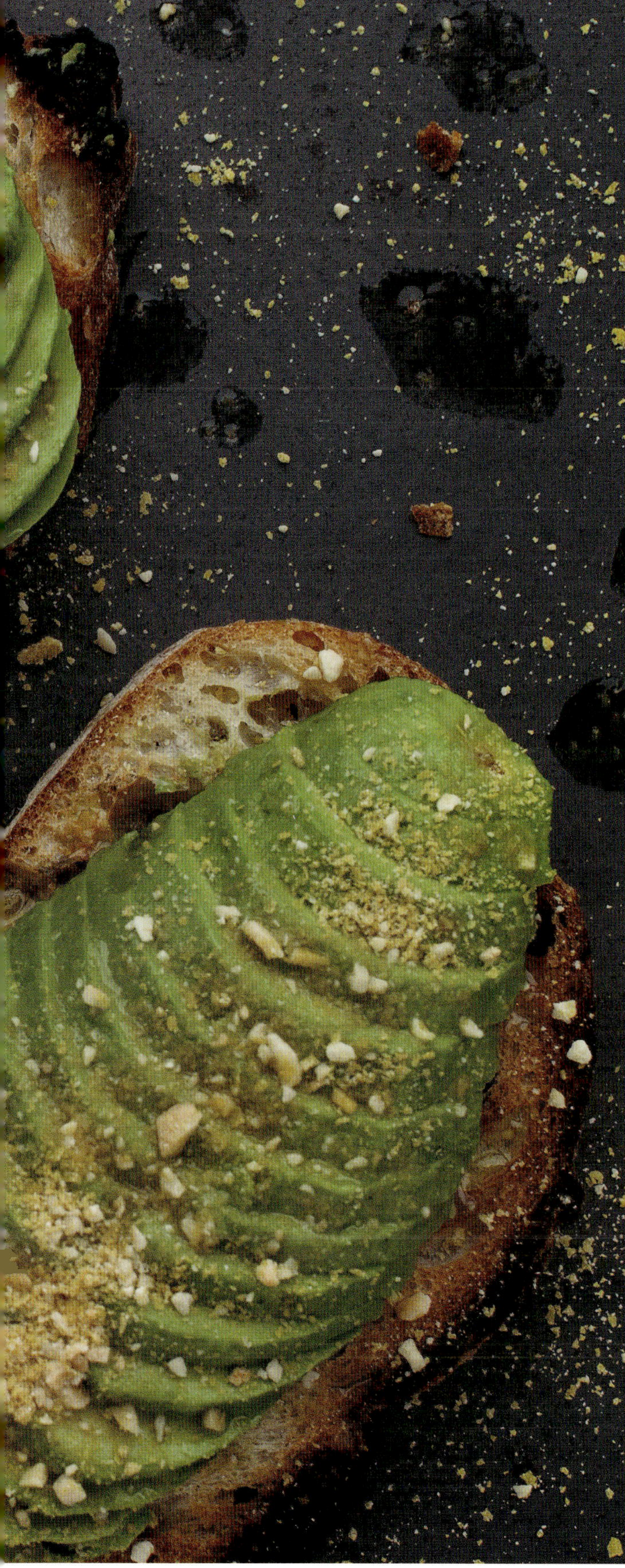

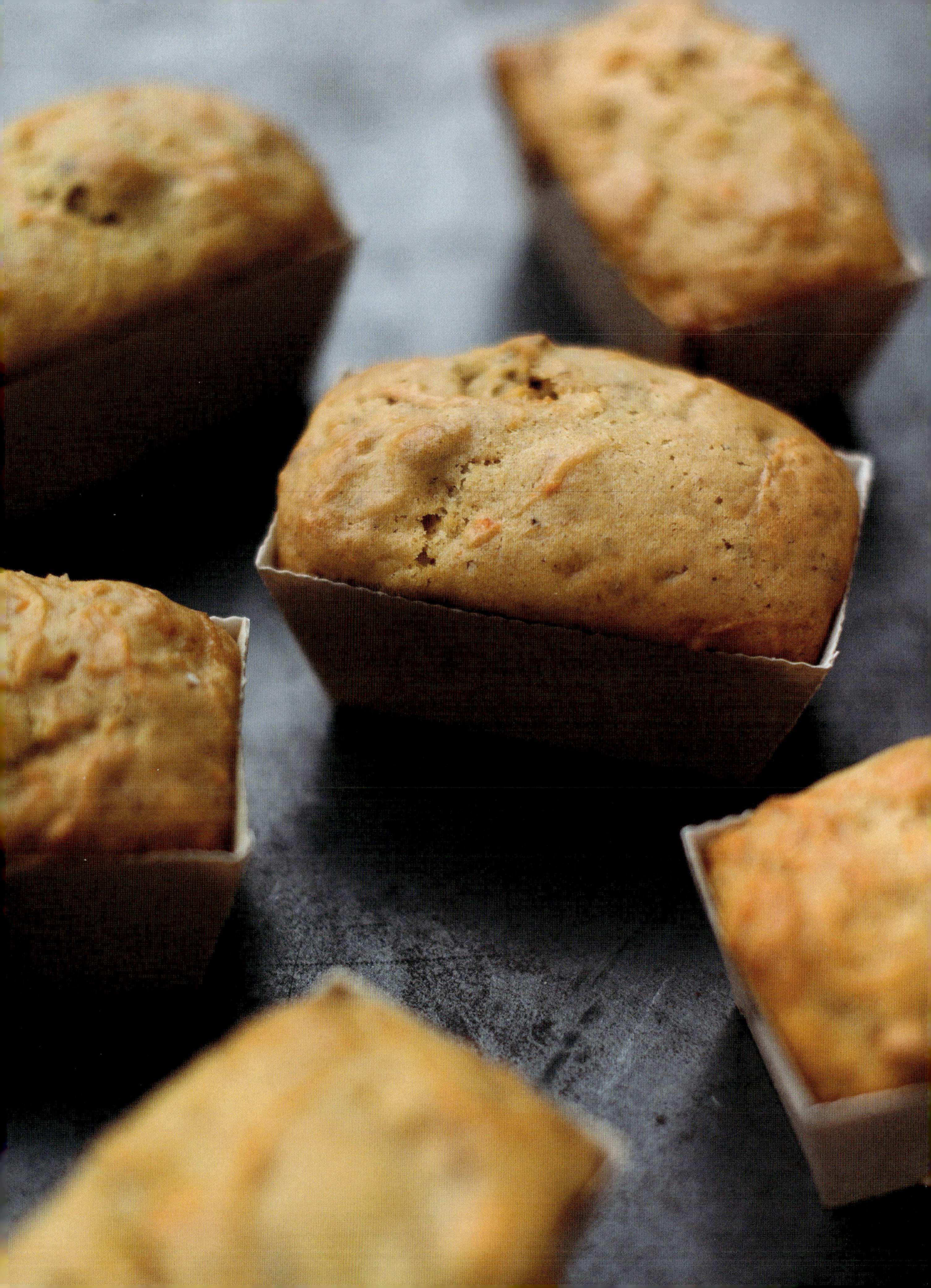

Petits gâteaux à la patate douce

20 min / **12 GÂTEAUX**

30 min

INGRÉDIENTS

1 tasse (210 g) cassonade tassée

¾ tasse (180 ml) huile végétale

½ tasse (125 ml) compote de pommes

1 c. à thé (5 ml) jus de citron

2 tasses (200 g) patate douce, râpée

½ tasse (125 ml) lait végétal

2 tasses (300 g) farine

1 c. à thé (5 ml) sel

1 c. à thé (5 ml) poudre à pâte

1 c. à thé (5 ml) bicarbonate de sodium

½ c. à thé (2,5 ml) cannelle moulue

½ tasse (60 g) noix de Grenoble, hachées

PRÉPARATION

1. Préchauffer le four à 375 °F (190 °C).
2. Chemiser 12 moules à muffins de caissettes en papier ou les huiler.
3. Dans un grand bol, battre la cassonade, l'huile végétale et la compote de pommes pendant 2 minutes.
4. Ajouter le jus de citron, la patate douce et le lait végétal. Bien mélanger.
5. Dans un autre bol, mélanger la farine, le sel, la poudre à pâte, le bicarbonate de sodium, la cannelle et les noix.
6. Ajouter les ingrédients secs aux ingrédients humides en mélangeant à la cuillère.
7. Répartir la pâte dans les moules.
8. Cuire au four pendant environ 30 minutes, ou jusqu'à ce qu'un cure-dent inséré au centre des muffins en ressorte propre.
9. Démouler et laisser refroidir sur une grille avant de déguster.

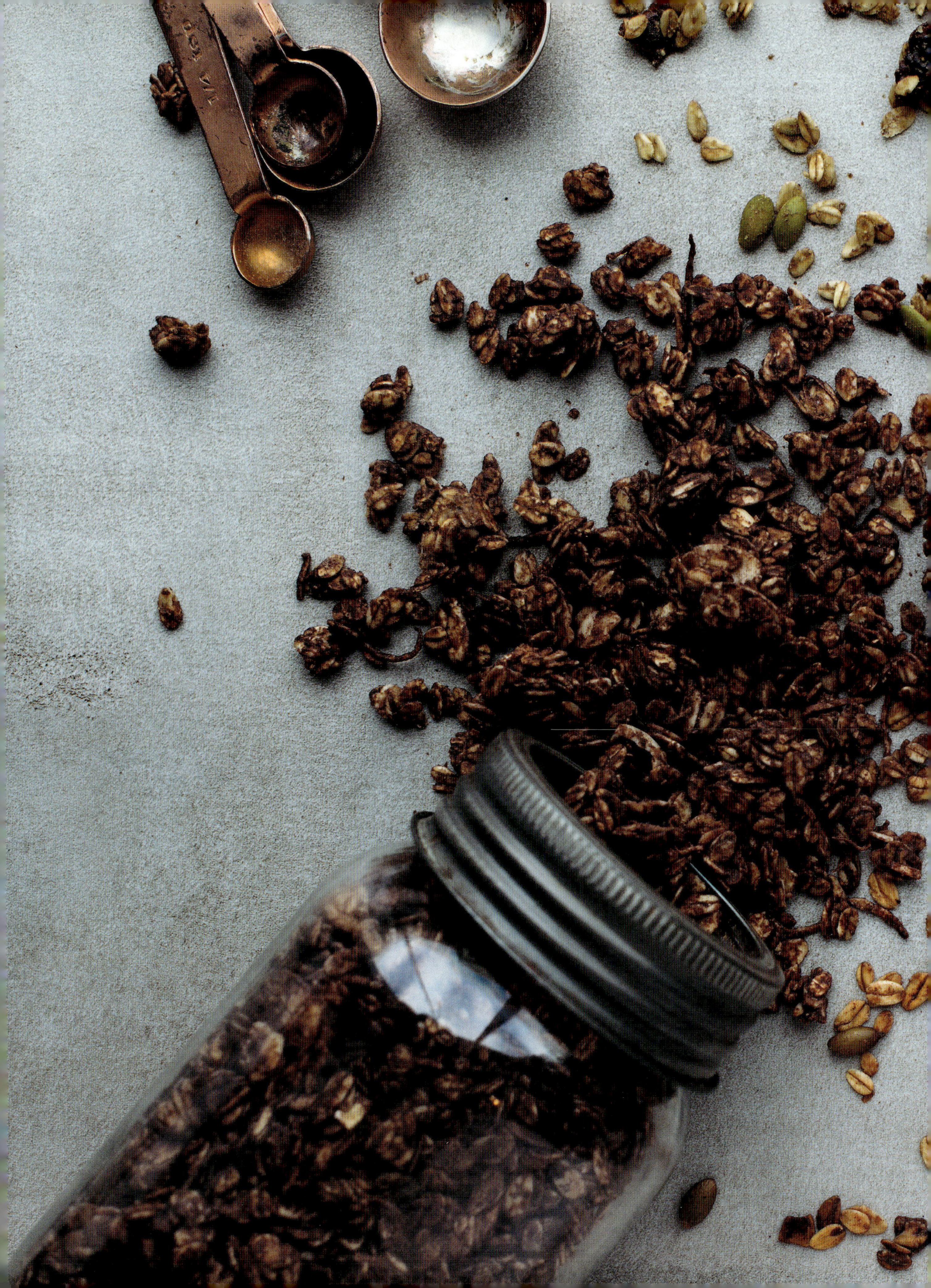

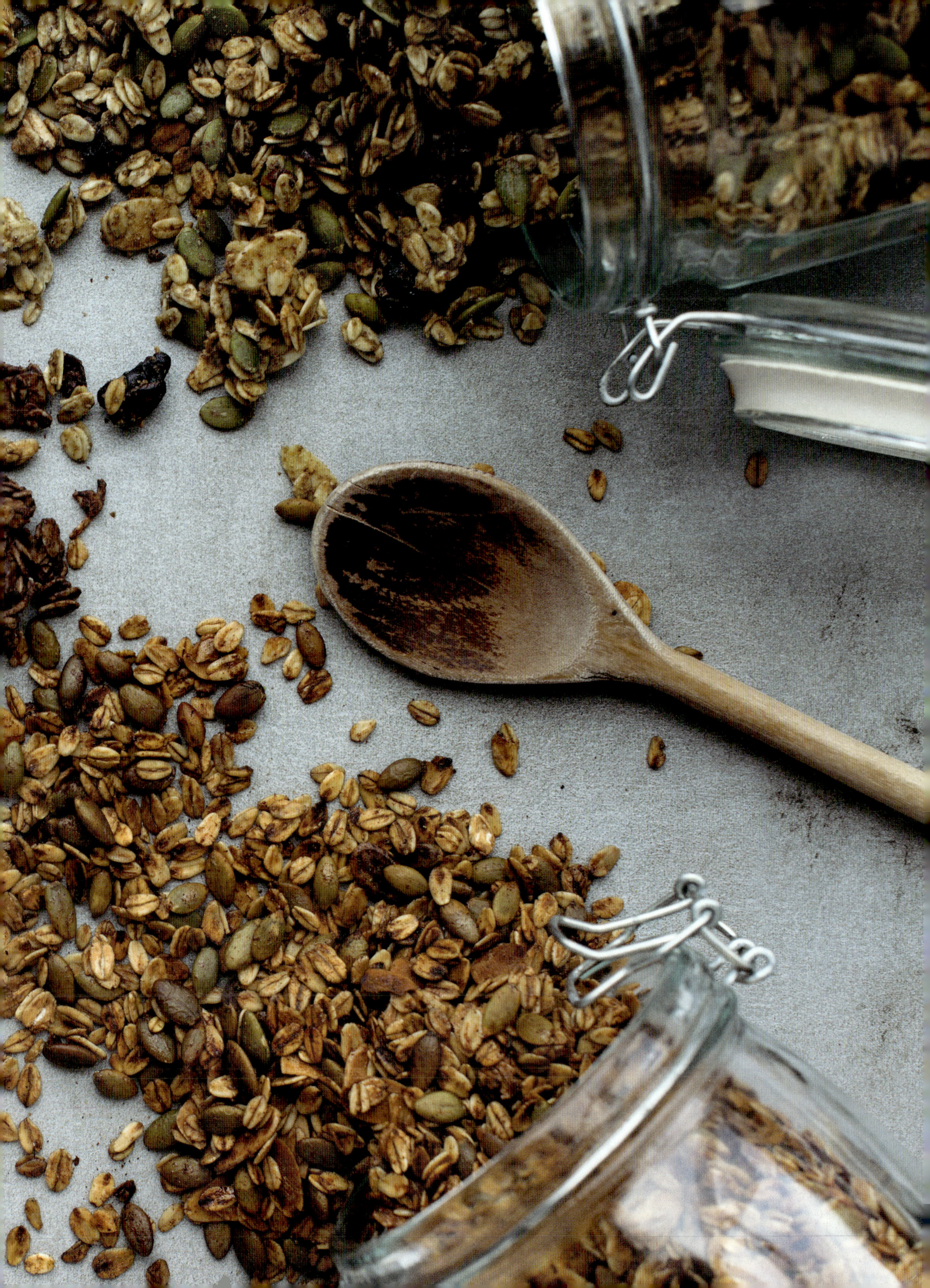

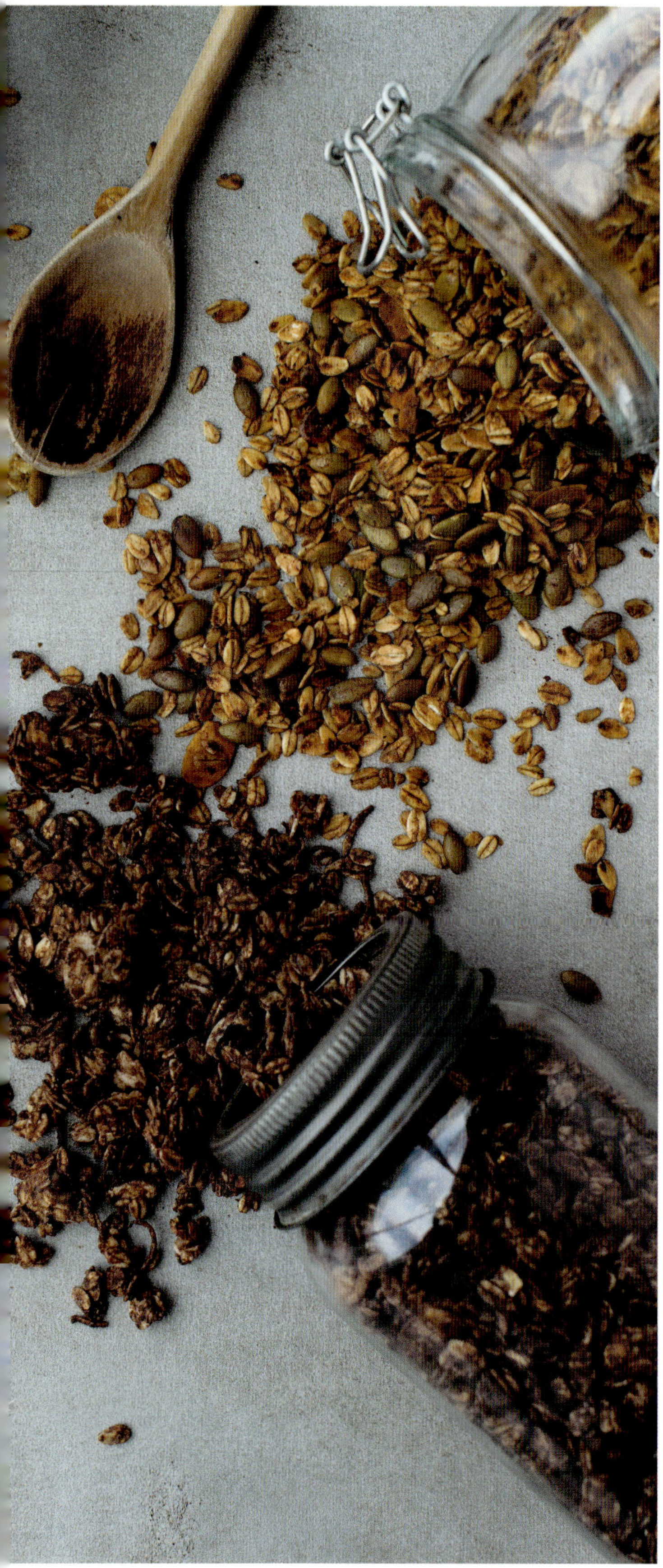

Granola aux arachides et au chocolat

Pour vos collations, vos toppings et vos grignotines santé!

15 min / **4 TASSES (500 G)**

15 à 20 min

INGRÉDIENTS

3 c. à soupe (45 ml) huile de coco fondue

¼ tasse (70 g) beurre d'arachide naturel

¼ tasse (60 ml) sirop d'érable

1 c. à thé (5 ml) vanille

¼ tasse (20 g) noix de coco râpée non sucrée

¼ tasse (20 g) cacao en poudre

½ tasse (50 g) amandes effilées

2 ½ tasses (250 g) flocons d'avoine

½ c. à thé (2,5 ml) fleur de sel

PRÉPARATION

1. Préchauffer le four à 350 °F (180 °C).
2. Dans un bol, mélanger l'huile de coco fondue, le beurre d'arachide et le sirop d'érable.
3. Incorporer le reste des ingrédients.
4. Étendre uniformément le mélange sur une plaque à pâtisserie.
5. Cuire au four de 15 à 20 minutes, en remuant à mi-cuisson.

NOTE : Se conservent jusqu'à 4 semaines à température ambiante.

Granola aux épices d'automne

15 min / **4 TASSES (500 G)**

15 à 20 min

INGRÉDIENTS

3 c. à soupe (45 ml) huile de coco fondue

¼ tasse (60 ml) sirop d'érable

2 ½ tasses (250 g) flocons d'avoine

¾ tasse (100 g) graines de citrouille

½ tasse (50 g) amandes effilées

2 c. à thé (10 ml) cannelle

¼ c. à thé (1 ml) muscade

¼ c. à thé (1 ml) clou de girofle moulu

½ c. à thé (2,5 ml) fleur de sel

PRÉPARATION

1. Préchauffer le four à 350°F (180°C).
2. Dans un bol, mélanger l'huile de coco fondue et le sirop d'érable.
3. Incorporer le reste des ingrédients.
4. Étendre uniformément le mélange sur une plaque à pâtisserie.
5. Cuire au four de 15 à 20 minutes, en remuant à mi-cuisson.

Granola au matcha et aux canneberges

15 min / **4 TASSES (500 G)**

15 à 20 min

INGRÉDIENTS

3 c. à soupe (45 ml) huile de coco fondue

¼ tasse (60 ml) tahini

¼ tasse (60 ml) sirop d'érable

2 ½ tasses (250 g) flocons d'avoine

¾ tasse (100 g) graines de citrouille

¼ tasse (25 g) amandes effilées

¼ tasse (30 g) farine de lin

1 c. à soupe (15 ml) thé matcha en poudre

½ c. à thé (2,5 ml) fleur de sel

½ tasse (75 g) canneberges séchées

PRÉPARATION

1. Préchauffer le four à 350°F (180°C).
2. Dans un bol, mélanger l'huile de coco fondue, le tahini et le sirop d'érable.
3. Incorporer le reste des ingrédients.
4. Étendre uniformément le mélange sur une plaque à pâtisserie.
5. Cuire au four de 15 à 20 minutes, en remuant à mi-cuisson.

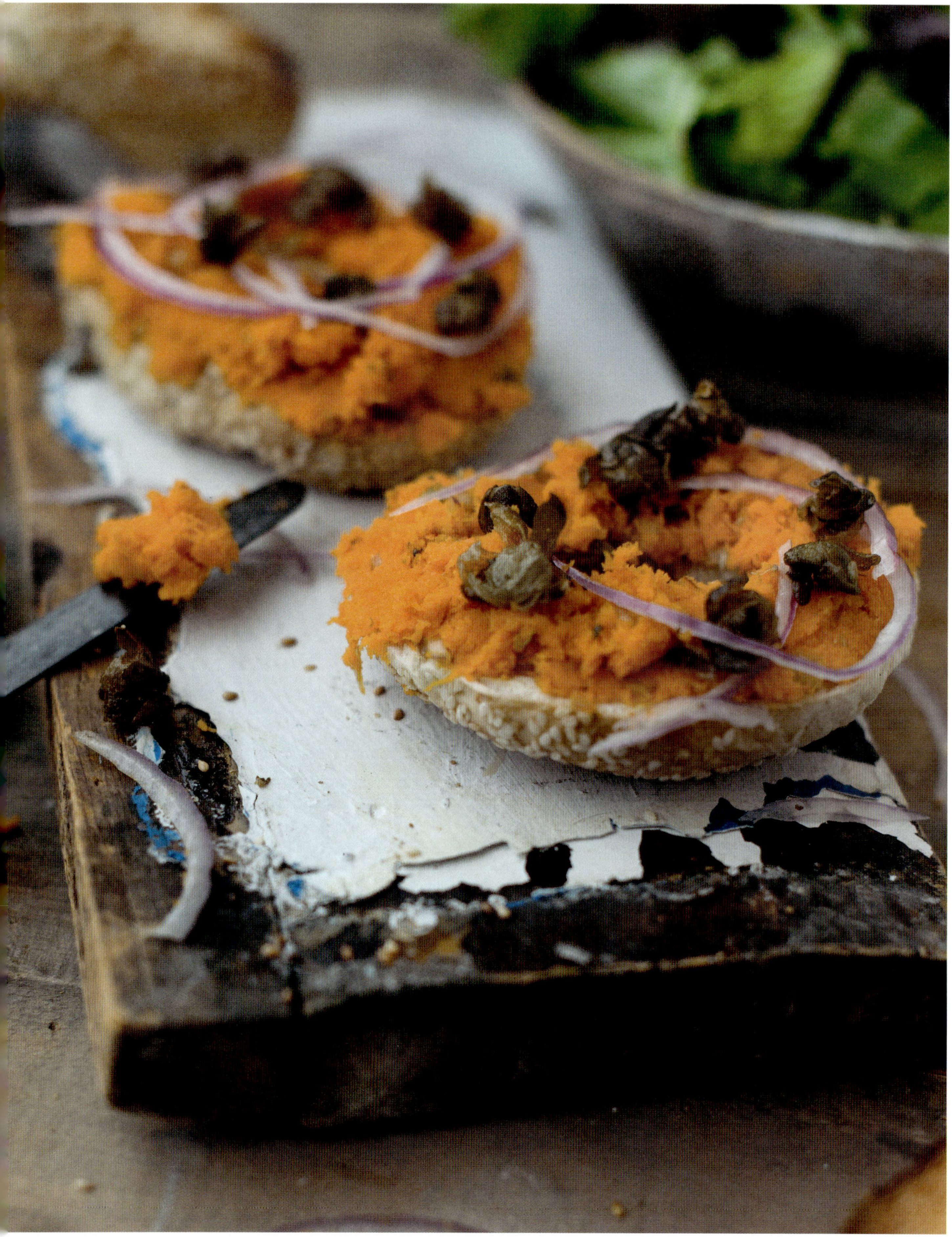

Bagels au fauxmon et aux câpres frites

15 min / **4 À 6 PORTIONS**

2 min

60 min

FAUXMON

4 tasses (440 g) pulpe de carottes ou carottes râpées finement

½ oignon rouge, haché

3 c. à soupe (45 ml) câpres, hachées

2 c. à soupe (30 ml) huile d'olive

1 c. à soupe (15 ml) fumée liquide

1 c. à soupe (15 ml) sirop d'érable

2 c. à soupe (30 ml) jus de citron

Sel, au goût

CÂPRES FRITES

3 c. à soupe (45 ml) câpres

¼ tasse (60 ml) huile végétale

4 à 6 bagels

Oignon rouge, facultatif

PRÉPARER LE FAUXMON

1. Mélanger tous les ingrédients et laisser reposer pendant 1 heure à température ambiante afin de permettre aux saveurs de se développer.

FAIRE FRIRE LES CÂPRES

1. Bien rincer et assécher les câpres à l'aide d'un essuie-tout.
2. Dans une petite casserole, faire chauffer l'huile.
3. Ajouter les câpres et faire frire pendant 2 minutes.
4. Transférer sur un essuie-tout.

GARNIR LES BAGELS

1. Tartiner les bagels de fauxmon, ajouter les câpres frites et garnir de quelques rondelles d'oignon rouge, si désiré. Déguster.

SALADES ET ACCOMPAGNEMENTS

Carpaccio de betteraves

30 min / **2 À 4 PORTIONS**

55 min

INGRÉDIENTS

2 c. à soupe (30 ml) amandes effilées, pour garnir

2 betteraves rouges

2 betteraves jaunes

2 c. à soupe (30 ml) huile d'olive

2 c. à soupe (30 ml) vinaigre de cidre

1 piment chipotle, haché

Sel, au goût

Quelques micropousses, pour garnir

PRÉPARATION

1. Préchauffer le four à 375 °F (190 °C).
2. Déposer les amandes effilées dans un plat allant au four et les faire griller de 3 à 5 minutes. Réserver.
3. Déposer les betteraves dans deux grandes casseroles et couvrir d'eau fraîche. (Il est important de faire cuire les betteraves rouges et jaunes séparément.) Porter à ébullition, réduire le feu, couvrir et laisser mijoter pendant 50 minutes.
4. Égoutter les betteraves et les laisser tiédir. Retirer la pelure avec les mains ou avec une cuillère sous l'eau froide.
5. Dans un bol, mélanger l'huile d'olive, le vinaigre de cidre, le piment haché et le sel.
6. Trancher finement les betteraves et les ajouter à la vinaigrette.
7. Réserver au froid.
8. Au moment de servir, disposer les betteraves dans une assiette, puis garnir de micropousses et d'amandes grillées.

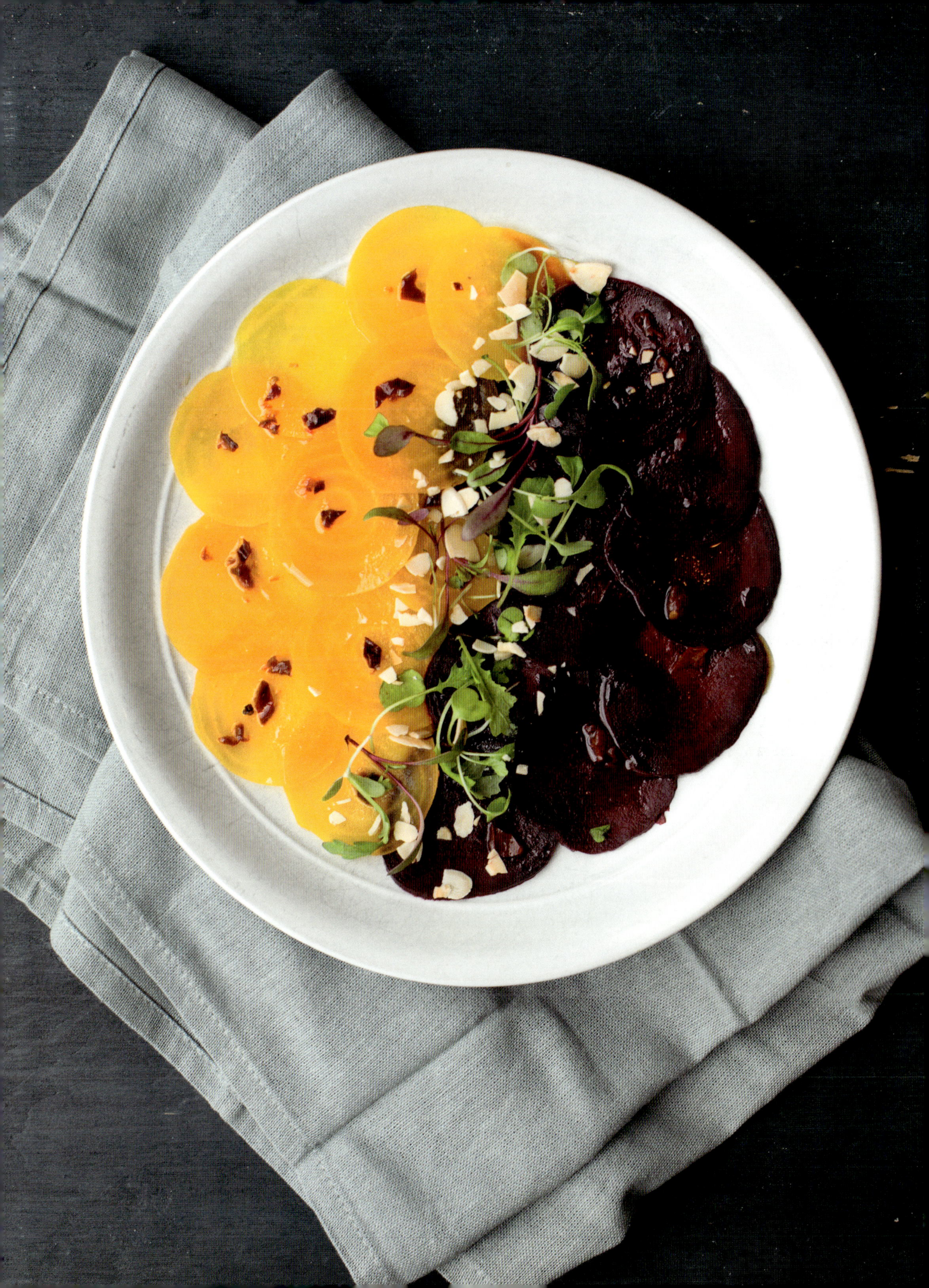

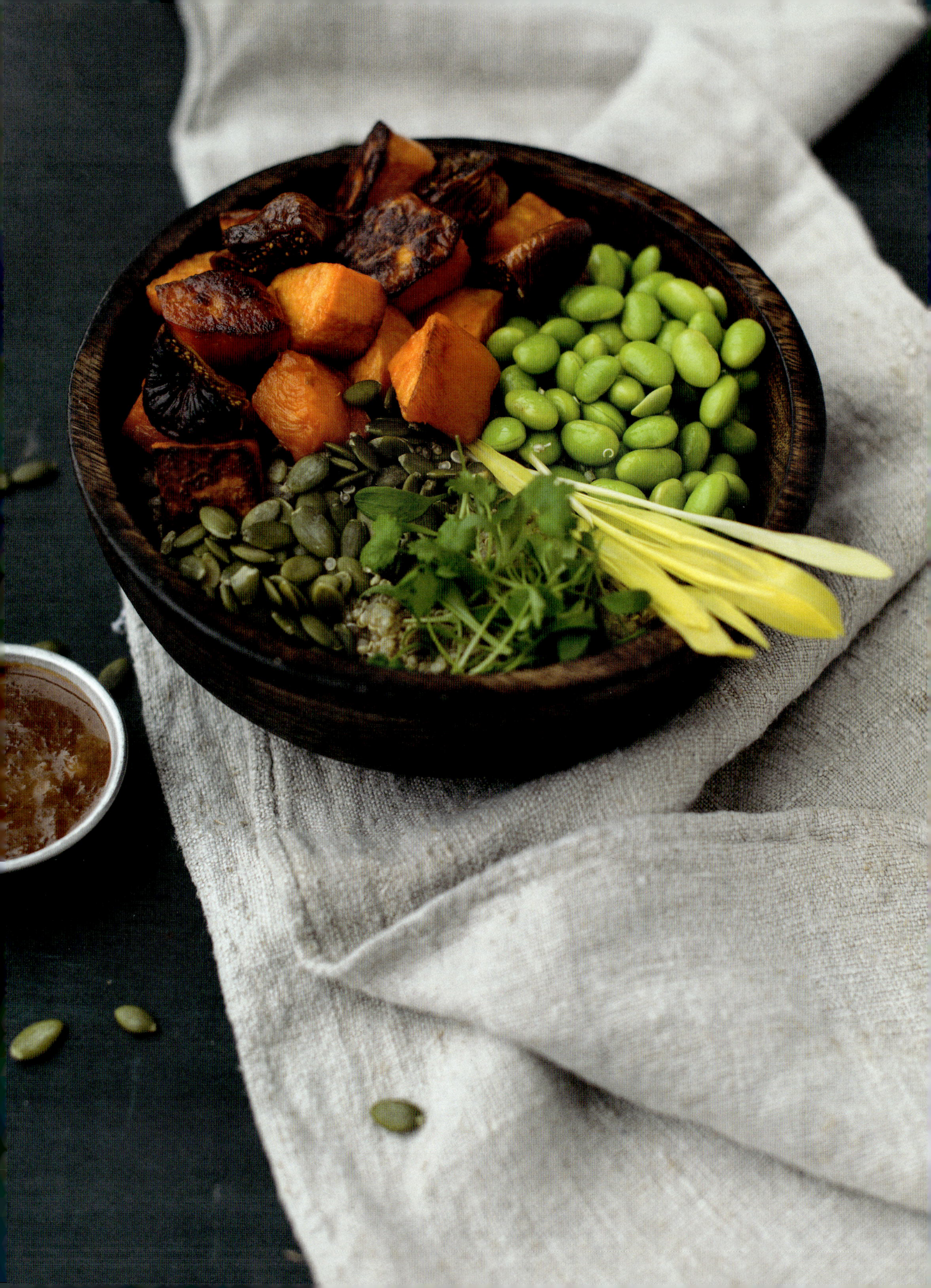

Bol du bouddha

20 min / **1 BOL**

30 min

BOL

1 patate douce, coupée en dés

2 figues séchées, tranchées

2 c. à soupe (30 ml) huile végétale

Sel, au goût

1 ½ tasse (375 ml) quinoa cuit

¼ tasse (35 g) edamames écossés surgelés, réchauffés

Quelques graines de citrouille, pour garnir

Quelques micropousses, au choix

VINAIGRETTE

1 gousse d'ail, hachée*

1 morceau de ¾ po (2 cm) de gingembre frais, haché

1 pincée de sel

1 c. à soupe (15 ml) sauce soya

1 c. à soupe (15 ml) jus de citron

1 c. à soupe (15 ml) huile végétale

1 c. à soupe (15 ml) sirop d'érable

2 c. à soupe (30 ml) tahini

PRÉPARER LE BOL

1. Préchauffer le four à 350 °F (180 °C).
2. Dans un plat allant au four, déposer la patate douce et les figues séchées. Huiler, saler, mélanger et enfourner pendant 30 minutes.
3. Dans un bol, mettre la patate douce, le quinoa, les figues et les edamames, puis verser la vinaigrette. Garnir de graines de citrouille et de micropousses. Servir.

PRÉPARER LA VINAIGRETTE

1. Dans un mortier**, déposer l'ail, le gingembre et le sel, puis broyer les ingrédients ensemble. Ajouter la sauce soya, le jus de citron, l'huile, le sirop d'érable et le tahini. Mélanger.

* Si vous ne digérez pas l'ail cru, n'en mettez pas ou faites-le cuire préalablement.

** Si vous n'avez pas de mortier, broyez tous les ingrédients de la vinaigrette à l'aide d'un mélangeur.

Choux de Bruxelles grillés

20 min / **4 PORTIONS**

20 min

CHOUX DE BRUXELLES

4 tasses (500 g) choux de Bruxelles, coupés en deux

2 c. à soupe (30 ml) huile végétale

SAUCE

2 c. à soupe (30 ml) huile végétale

4 oignons verts, émincés

¼ tasse (60 ml) sauce soya

¼ tasse (60 ml) sirop d'érable

1 gousse d'ail, hachée

¼ c. à thé (1 ml) piment rouge broyé

FAIRE CUIRE LES CHOUX DE BRUXELLES

1. Dans une casserole, porter 8 tasses (2 L) d'eau à ébullition et y plonger les choux de Bruxelles. Faire bouillir pendant 3 minutes.
2. Transférer dans un bol et ajouter l'huile végétale. Bien mélanger.
3. Étendre les choux de Bruxelles sur une plaque à pâtisserie, puis passer sous le gril préchauffé du four de 3 à 4 minutes.
4. Retourner les choux de Bruxelles, puis les passer de nouveau sous le gril jusqu'à ce qu'ils soient bien grillés.

ENTRE-TEMPS, PRÉPARER LA SAUCE

1. Dans une casserole, faire chauffer l'huile. Ajouter les oignons verts et faire frire pendant 2 minutes.
2. Ajouter la sauce soya, le sirop d'érable, l'ail et le piment. Laisser réduire pendant 5 minutes.
3. Retirer les choux de Bruxelles du four et les arroser de la sauce, puis servir.

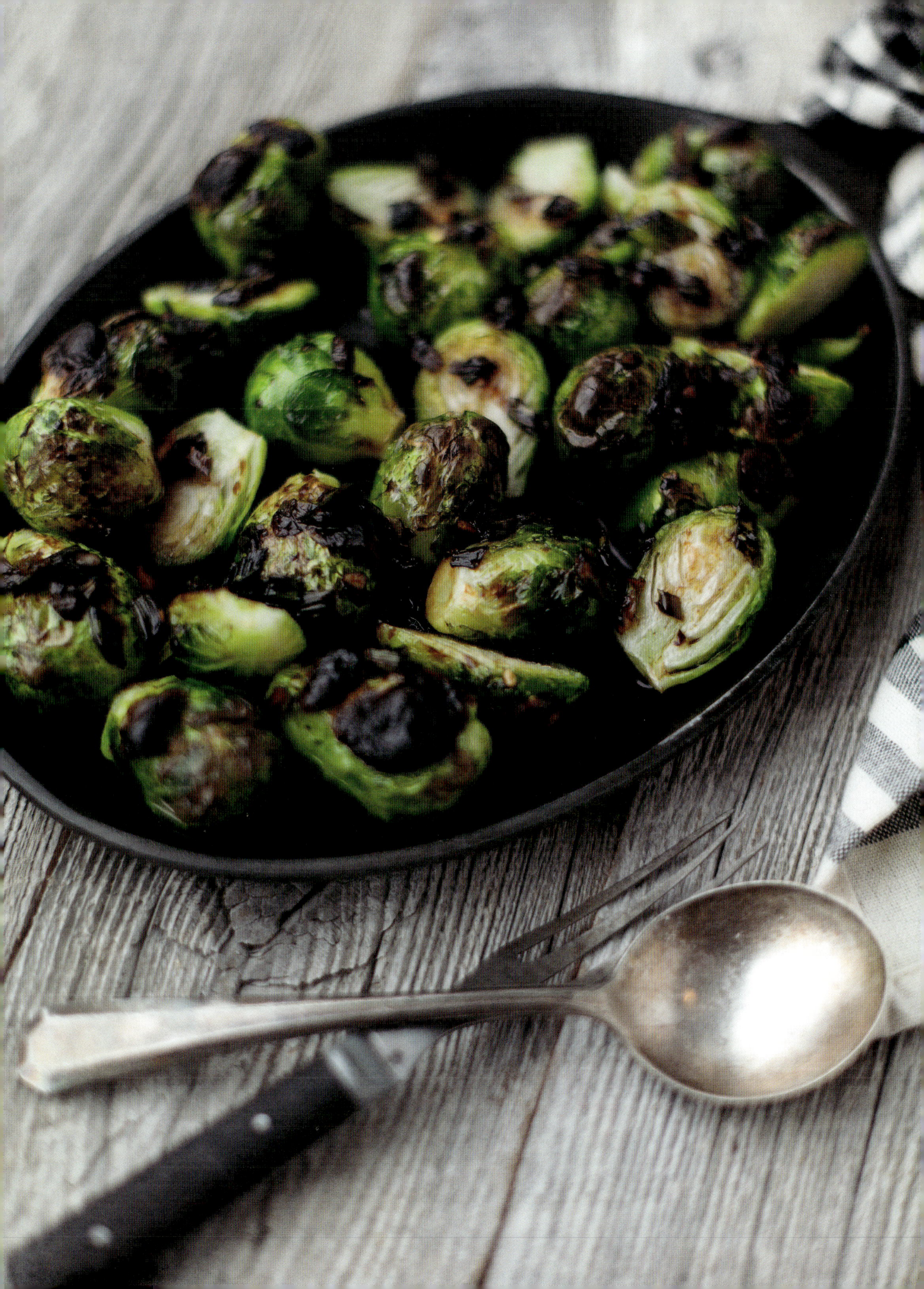

Salade de pommes de terre

15 min / **6 PORTIONS**

30 min

INGRÉDIENTS

1 lb (454 g) pommes de terre à chair jaune

1 lb (454 g) pommes de terre bleues

2 branches de céleri, hachées

⅔ tasse (160 ml) mayonnaise végétale (voir recette p. 209)

1 c. à soupe (15 ml) raifort

1 c. à thé (5 ml) poudre d'oignon

1 c. à thé (5 ml) sel ou kala namak* (sel noir de l'Himalaya)

PRÉPARATION

1. Dans une grande casserole, déposer les pommes de terre entières. Ajouter de l'eau pour les recouvrir complètement.
2. Porter à ébullition et laisser mijoter pendant environ 30 minutes, ou jusqu'à ce que les pommes de terre soient tendres. (Ne pas trop cuire.)
3. Égoutter et laisser refroidir.
4. Lorsque les pommes de terre ont refroidi, les peler et les couper en dés.
5. Dans un grand bol, mélanger le céleri hâché, la mayonnaise végétale, le raifort, la poudre d'oignon et le sel. Bien mélanger et ajouter les pommes de terre. Remuer délicatement pour bien les enrober. Servir.

* Le kala namak, aussi appelé sel noir de l'Himalaya, contient des composés soufrés qui lui confèrent une saveur d'œuf dur très particulière.

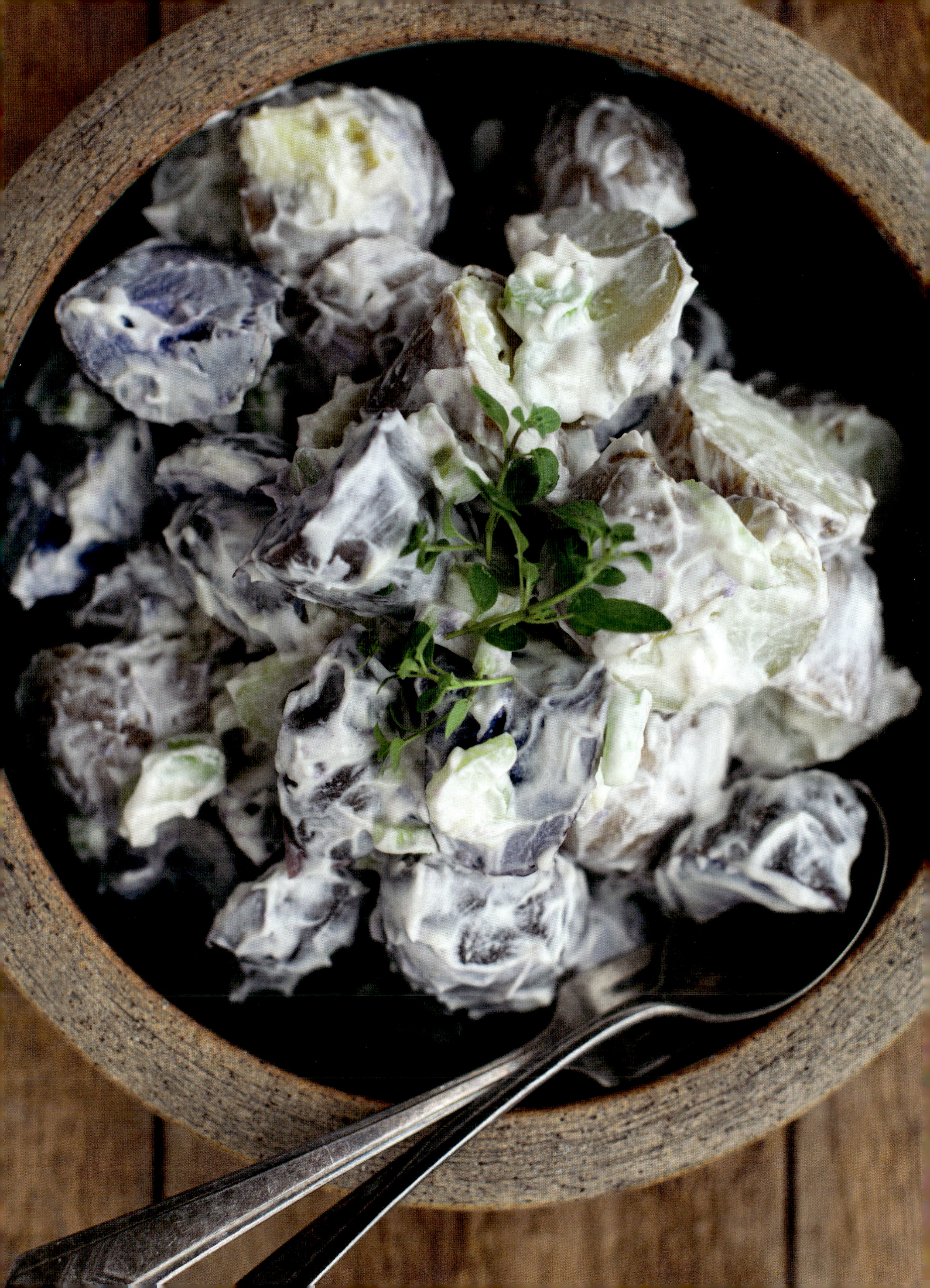

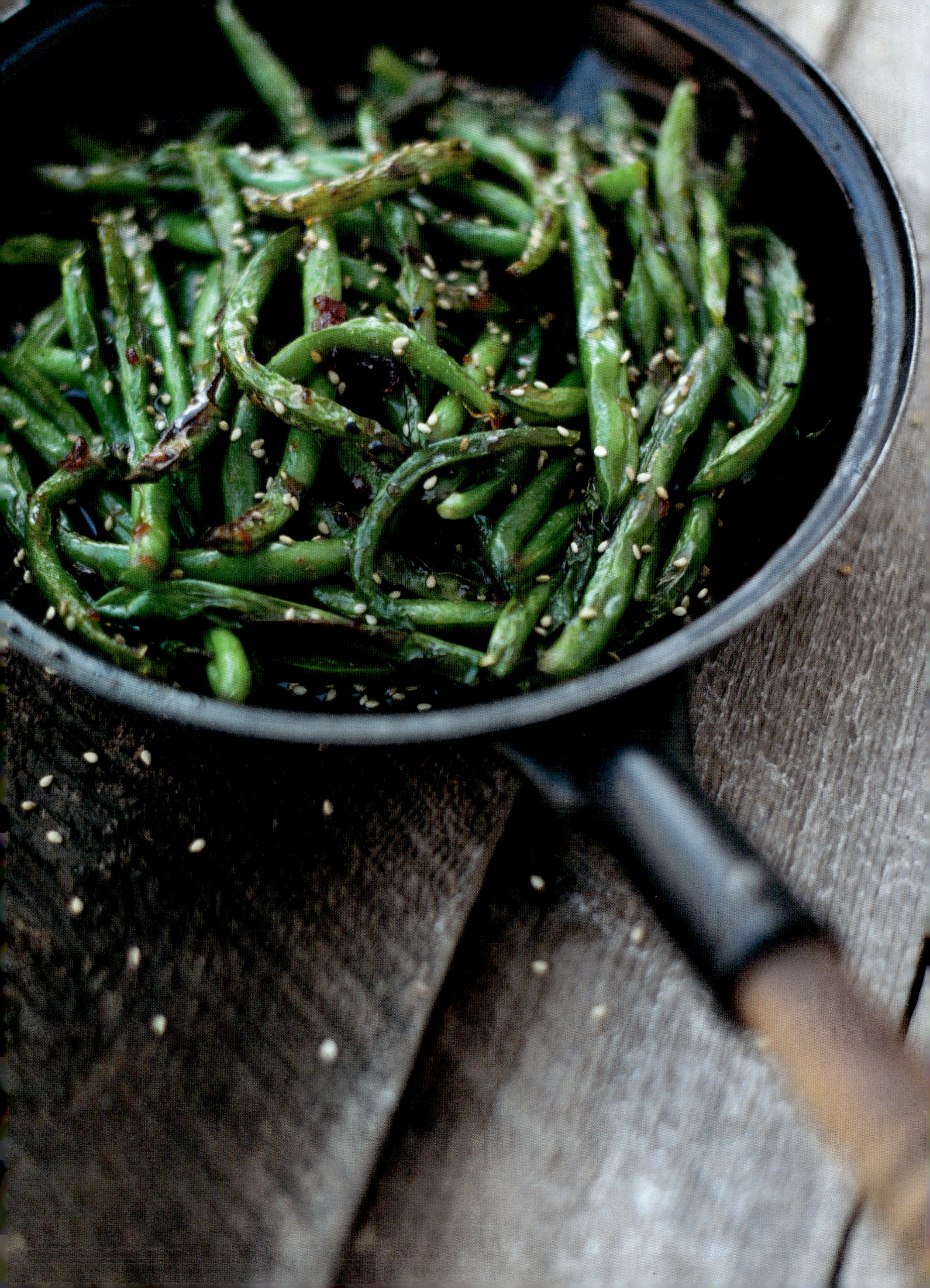

Haricots verts grillés à la sichuanaise

20 min / **4 PORTIONS**

10 min

INGRÉDIENTS

10 tasses (1 kg) haricots verts parés

2 c. à soupe (30 ml) huile de sésame grillé

¼ tasse (60 ml) sirop d'érable

2 c. à soupe (30 ml) vinaigre de cidre

1 c. à thé (5 ml) sambal oelek

2 c. à soupe (30 ml) graines de sésame

Sel

PRÉPARATION

1. Dans une grande casserole, porter de l'eau à ébullition.
2. Ajouter les haricots verts, puis cuire pendant 1 minute à partir du moment où l'eau recommence à bouillir.
3. Égoutter les haricots, bien les éponger, puis les déposer dans un grand bol.
4. Ajouter l'huile de sésame grillé, saler généreusement et mélanger.
5. Disposer les haricots sur une plaque de cuisson et cuire quelques minutes sous le gril préchauffé du four, jusqu'à ce que les haricots commencent à dorer. Remuer et poursuivre la cuisson sous le gril pendant quelques minutes.
6. Entre-temps, verser le sirop d'érable, le vinaigre de cidre et le sambal oelek dans une petite casserole. Porter à ébullition et laisser réduire jusqu'à l'obtention d'une consistance sirupeuse.
7. Retirer les haricots du four, puis les placer dans un grand bol. Ajouter la vinaigrette chaude.
8. Bien mélanger et garnir de graines de sésame avant de servir.

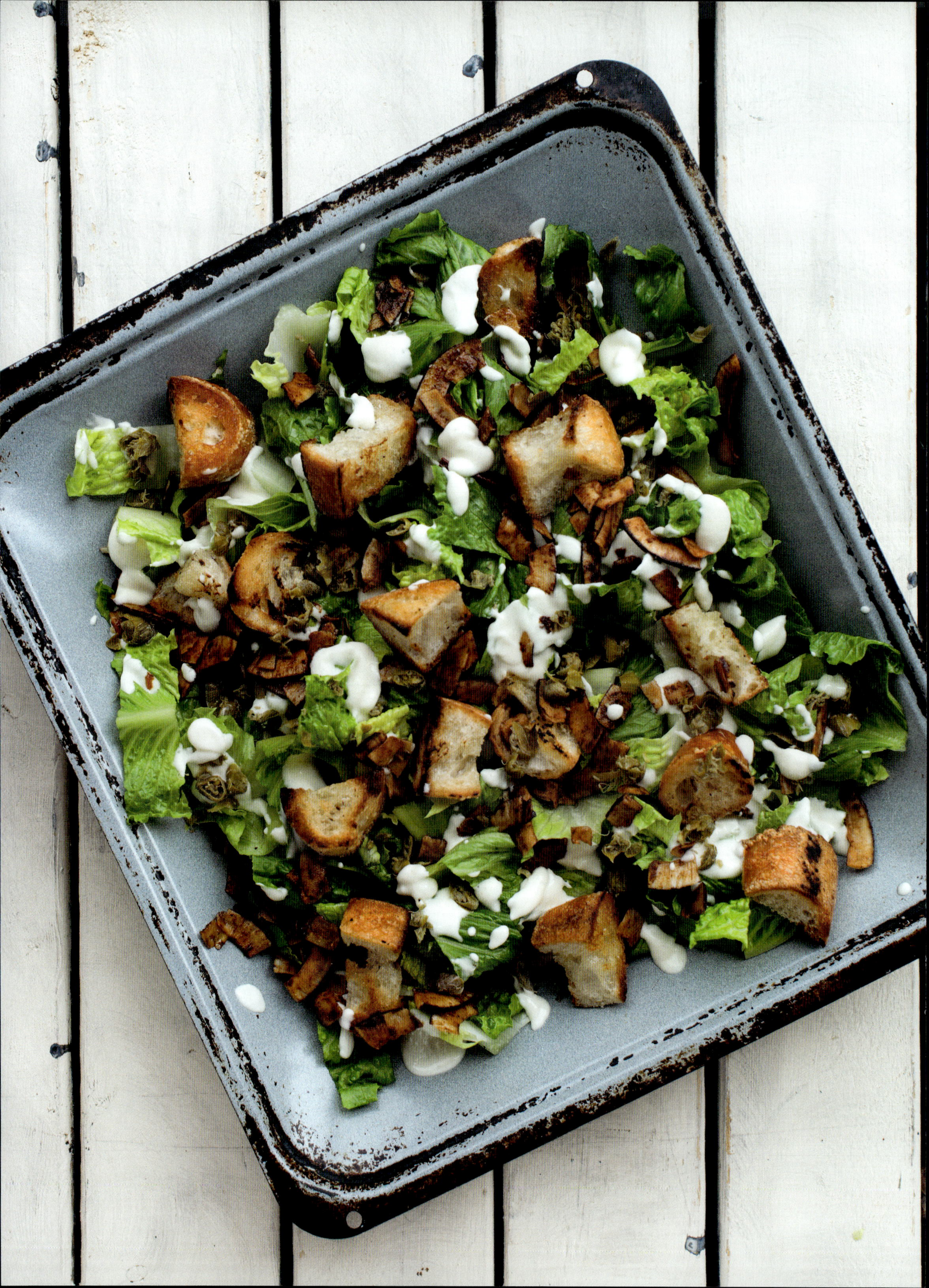

Salade César

15 min / **2 PORTIONS**

10 à 15 min

BACON DE NOIX DE COCO

2 c. à soupe (30 ml) sauce soya

1 ½ c. à soupe (23 ml) fumée liquide

2 c. à soupe (30 ml) levure alimentaire

1 ½ c. à soupe (23 ml) sirop d'érable

1 c. à soupe (15 ml) huile végétale

1 tasse (70 g) copeaux de noix de coco

CROÛTONS

⅓ de baguette, coupée en dés de 1 po (2 cm) de largeur

3 c. à soupe (45 ml) huile d'olive

SAUCE

¼ tasse (60 ml) lait végétal non sucré

1 c. à thé (5 ml) moutarde de Dijon

1 c. à thé (5 ml) raifort préparé

1 c. à thé (5 ml) sirop d'érable

1 c. à soupe (15 ml) câpres égouttées

¼ tasse (60 ml) huile végétale

Sel, au goût

1 laitue romaine, déchiquetée

Quelques croûtons de pain

PRÉPARER LE BACON DE NOIX DE COCO

1. Préchauffer le four à 375 °F (190 °C).
2. Dans un bol, mélanger la sauce soya, la fumée liquide, la levure alimentaire, le sirop d'érable et l'huile végétale.
3. Ajouter les copeaux de noix de coco et bien mélanger.
4. Étendre la préparation sur une plaque à pâtisserie et cuire de 10 à 15 minutes en remuant de temps à autre. Réserver.

PRÉPARER LES CROÛTONS

1. Dans une poêle, faire revenir les morceaux de pain dans l'huile d'olive en remuant jusqu'à l'obtention d'une belle coloration. Réserver.

PRÉPARER LA SAUCE

1. Dans un récipient, mettre le lait végétal, la moutarde de Dijon, le raifort, le sirop d'érable et les câpres. Mélanger avec un pied mélangeur, en versant très lentement l'huile en filet, jusqu'à ce que la mayonnaise prenne. Aussitôt que la mayonnaise a épaissi, cesser de mélanger.
2. Au moment de servir, déposer la sauce au fond d'un grand bol, ajouter la laitue, puis mélanger délicatement. Parsemer du bacon de noix de coco et des croûtons de pain.

Bol du dragon

20 min / **2 BOLS**

15 min

TEMPEH

1 c. à soupe (15 ml) huile de sésame grillé

½ c. à soupe (8 ml) sauce soya

1 c. à soupe (15 ml) nectar d'agave ou sirop d'érable

½ tasse (125 ml) bouillon de légumes

½ paquet (120 g) tempeh

SAUCE

½ c. à soupe (8 ml) sirop d'érable

1 ½ c. à soupe (23 ml) huile végétale

½ c. à thé (2,5 ml) ail en poudre

1 c. à soupe (15 ml) sauce soya

2 c. à soupe (30 ml) levure alimentaire

Un peu d'eau, pour détendre la sauce

BOLS

1 tasse (160 g) riz brun cuit

Un peu de chou rouge, râpé

Un peu de poivron rouge, émincé

Un peu de patate douce, râpée

Quelques micropousses, au choix

PRÉPARER LE TEMPEH

1. Dans un bol, mélanger l'huile de sésame grillé, la sauce soya, le nectar d'agave et le bouillon de légumes.
2. Couper le tempeh en triangles et le disposer dans une casserole. Verser le mélange liquide sur le tempeh. Faire mijoter pendant environ 15 minutes, ou jusqu'à ce que le bouillon soit absorbé. Réserver.

PRÉPARER LA SAUCE

1. Mélanger le sirop d'érable, l'huile, l'ail en poudre, la sauce soya et la levure alimentaire. Incorporer un peu d'eau, au besoin.

ASSEMBLER LES BOLS

1. Dans deux bols, mettre le riz brun, du chou rouge, du poivron rouge et de la patate douce, puis ajouter le tempeh et verser la sauce. Garnir de micropousses, puis servir.

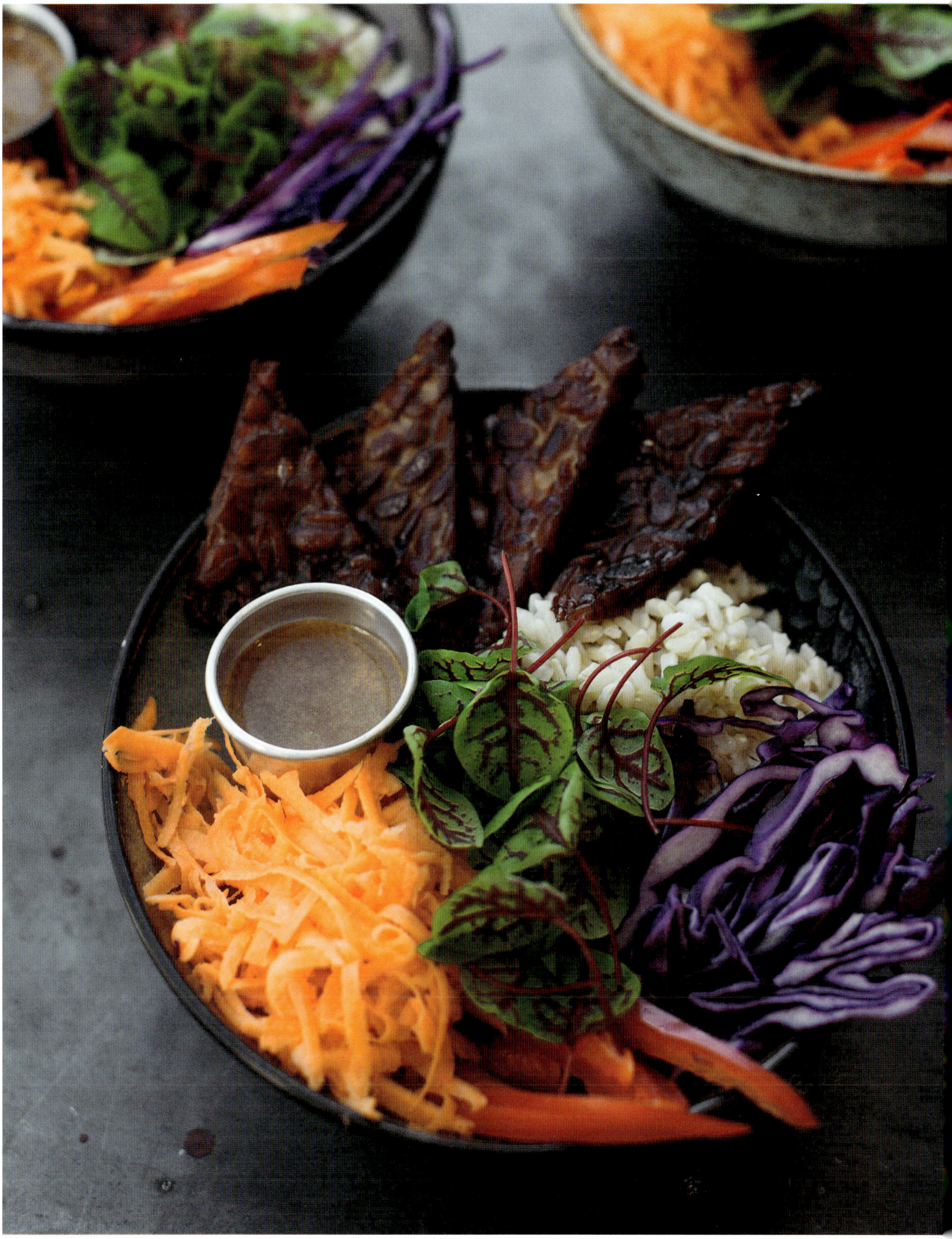

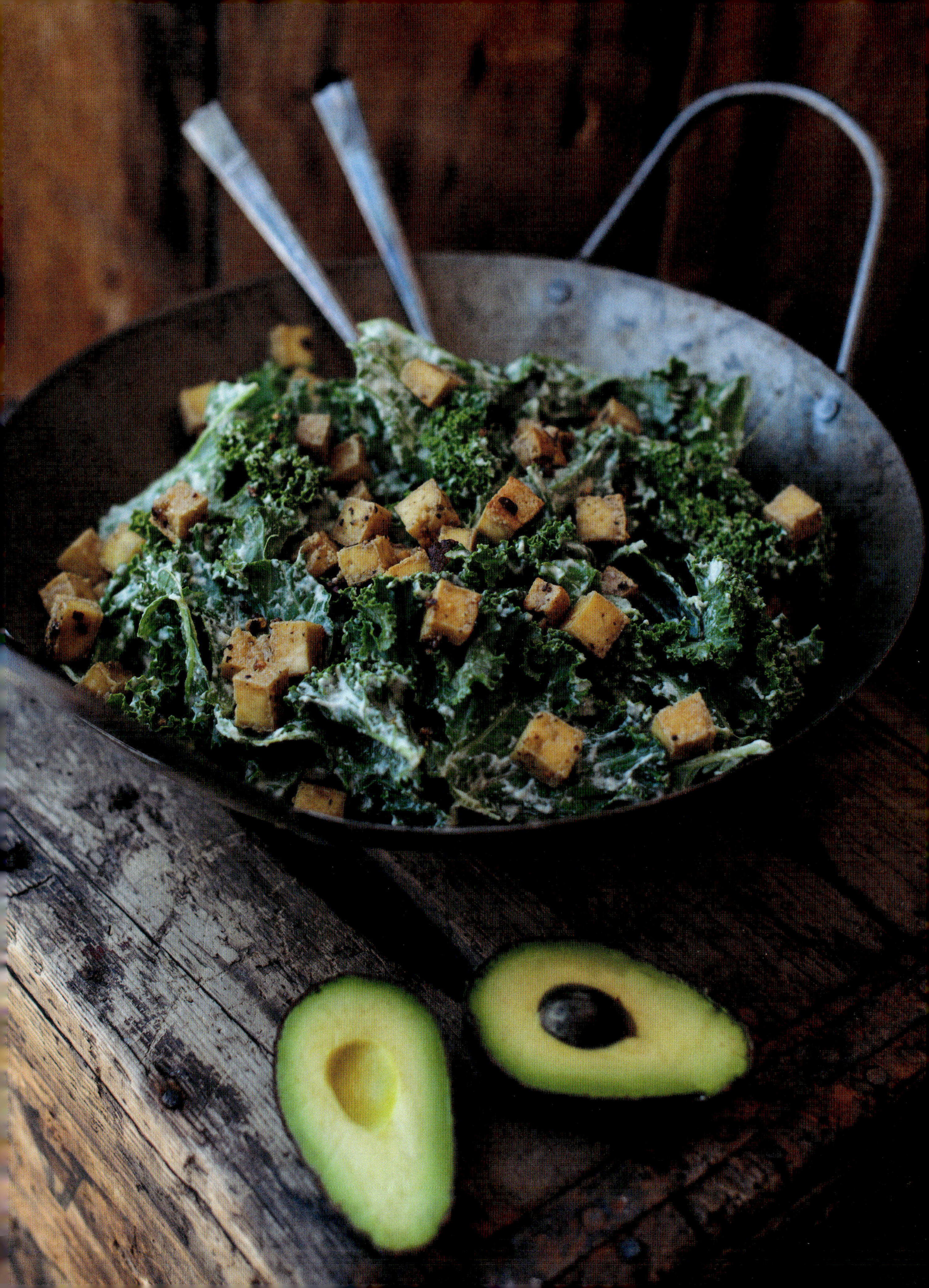

Salade de kale et vinaigrette ranch

Quoi? Faire manger du kale à ma famille? Oui, c'est possible, et tout le monde en redemandera.

15 min / **2 PORTIONS**

5 min

15 min

VINAIGRETTE RANCH

½ tasse (65 g) noix de cajou

1 c. à thé (5 ml) poudre d'oignon

1 c. à thé (5 ml) poudre d'ail

1 c. à soupe (15 ml) jus de citron

1 c. à soupe (15 ml) vinaigre de cidre

2 oignons verts, hachés

¾ tasse (180 ml) lait végétal

½ c. à thé (2,5 ml) sel

CROÛTONS

2 c. à soupe (30 ml) huile d'olive

1 tasse (180 g) tofu ferme, coupé en dés

¼ c. à thé (1 ml) piment rouge broyé

1 c. à thé (5 ml) poivre en grains grossièrement moulu

½ c. à thé (2,5 ml) graines de moutarde

1 c. à thé (5 ml) sirop d'érable

Sel, au goût

1 botte (environ 150 g) chou frisé (kale)

PRÉPARER LA VINAIGRETTE RANCH

1. Faire tremper les noix de cajou dans l'eau bouillante pendant 15 minutes.
2. Égoutter les noix de cajou et les déposer dans le récipient d'un mélangeur.
3. Ajouter le reste des ingrédients et broyer jusqu'à l'obtention d'une texture homogène. Réserver.

PRÉPARER LES CROÛTONS

1. Dans une poêle, faire revenir les dés de tofu dans l'huile à feu vif de 3 à 5 minutes.
2. Ajouter le reste des ingrédients et poursuivre la cuisson pendant 2 minutes, en remuant de temps à autre. Réserver.

PRÉPARER LA SALADE

1. Débarrasser les feuilles de chou frisé de leur tige centrale en faisant glisser la lame d'un couteau de part et d'autre de la tige.
2. Déchirer les feuilles grossièrement.
3. Nettoyer les feuilles à l'eau et bien les essorer (idéalement, avec une essoreuse à salade).
4. Déposer les feuilles dans un grand bol. Ajouter la vinaigrette et bien mélanger. Parsemer des croûtons de tofu. Servir.

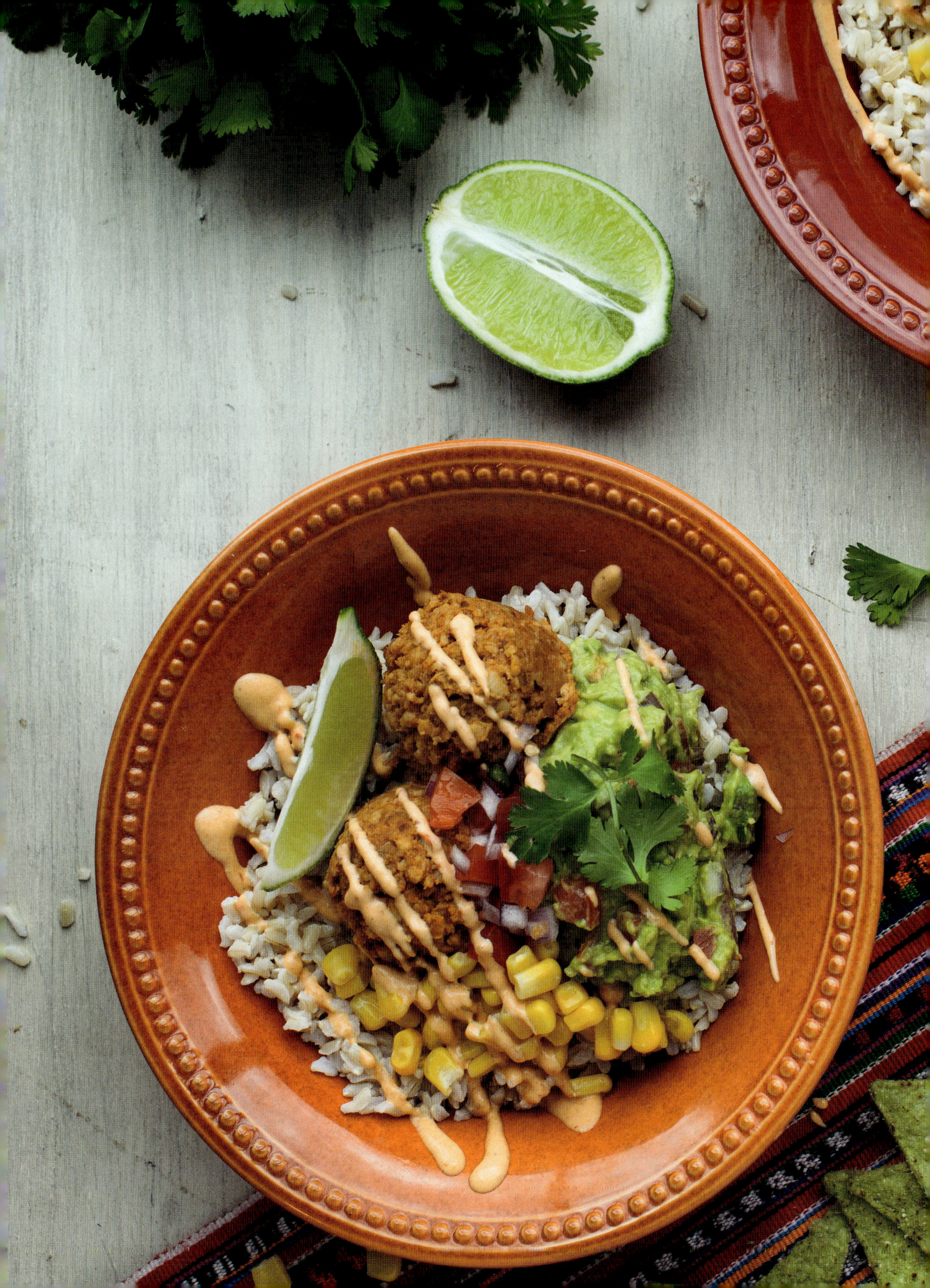

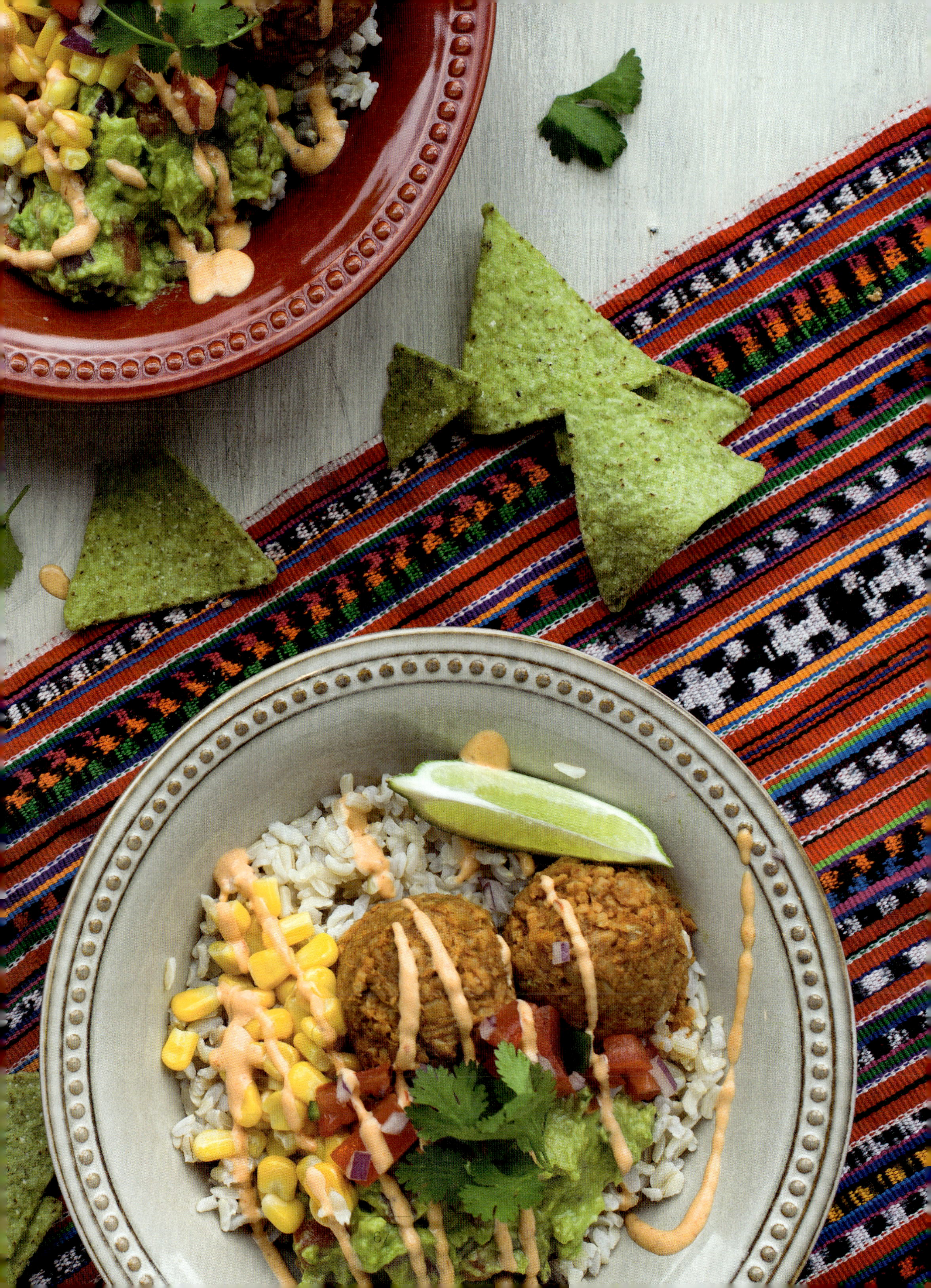

Bol mexicain

35 min / **2 BOLS**

30 min

20 min

RIZ BRUN

1 tasse (200 g) riz brun à grain court

2 tasses (500 ml) bouillon de légumes ou eau

CHORIZO DE TEMPEH

1 paquet de tempeh (240 g)

2 gousses d'ail, hachées

¼ tasse (60 ml) huile végétale

1 c. à thé (5 ml) assaisonnement au chili

2 c. à soupe (30 ml) ketchup

2 c. à thé (10 ml) sirop d'érable

½ tasse (125 ml) bouillon de légumes

Sel, au goût

BRUSCHETTA

1 tomate, coupée en dés

½ piment jalapeño, haché finement

½ oignon rouge, haché finement

1 c. à soupe (15 ml) huile d'olive

1 avocat, coupé en dés

Fleur de sel, au goût

Le jus de ½ citron ou de 1 lime

PRÉPARER LE RIZ BRUN

1. Déposer le riz dans une casserole à fond épais.
2. Ajouter le bouillon de légumes. Porter à ébullition, réduire le feu, couvrir et laisser mijoter de 20 à 30 minutes, ou jusqu'à ce que le liquide soit absorbé.
3. Retirer du feu et laisser reposer à couvert pendant 20 minutes.

PRÉPARER LE CHORIZO DE TEMPEH

1. Broyer le tempeh au robot culinaire, jusqu'à l'obtention d'une texture de grains de riz. (Ne pas trop broyer.)
2. Dans une poêle à frire, faire revenir l'ail dans l'huile pendant 1 minute. Ajouter le reste des ingrédients et poursuivre la cuisson à feu moyen, jusqu'à ce que tout le liquide soit absorbé.
3. Poursuivre la cuisson quelques minutes pour faire griller le tempeh. Réserver.

PRÉPARER LA BRUSCHETTA

1. Dans un grand bol, mélanger tous les ingrédients et laisser reposer pendant 15 minutes avant de servir.

GUACAMOLE

2 à 3 avocats bien mûrs

½ oignon rouge, haché finement

1 tomate, coupée en dés

1 petit piment jalapeño, haché finement

½ tasse (20 g) coriandre fraîche, hachée

Le jus de 1 lime

Sel, au goût

SAUCE CHIPOTLE

¼ tasse (60 ml) mayonnaise végétale (voir recette p. 209)

1 piment chipotle en conserve, haché

½ c. à thé (2,5 ml) sirop d'érable

½ c. à thé (2,5 ml) jus de citron

1 pincée de sel

Maïs, pour garnir

Tranches de lime, pour garnir

Coriandre, pour garnir

PRÉPARER LE GUACAMOLE

1. Peler et dénoyauter les avocats.
2. Dans un bol, piler grossièrement les avocats à l'aide d'une fourchette.
3. Ajouter le reste des ingrédients et bien mélanger. Réserver.

PRÉPARER LA SAUCE CHIPOTLE

1. Dans un bol, mélanger tous les ingrédients. Réserver.

ASSEMBLER LES BOLS

1. Dans chaque bol, déposer une portion de riz brun, ajouter le chorizo de tempeh, le guacamole, la bruschetta, le maïs, la lime, la coriandre et garnir de sauce chipotle. Servir.

Coleslaw

20 min / **4 À 6 PORTIONS**

1 à 24 h

INGRÉDIENTS

1 petit chou vert (environ 1 ¼ lb/625 g)

½ tasse (125 ml) mayonnaise végétale (voir recette p. 209)

2 c. à soupe (30 ml) vinaigre de cidre

1 c. à soupe (15 ml) sirop d'érable

1 c. à thé (5 ml) sel

1 c. à thé (5 ml) poudre d'oignon

2 carottes, râpées

PRÉPARATION

1. Couper le chou en quatre, puis retirer le cœur.
2. Au robot culinaire ou à la mandoline, émincer le chou finement. Réserver.
3. Dans un grand bol, mélanger la mayonnaise, le vinaigre, le sirop d'érable, le sel et la poudre d'oignon.
4. Ajouter le chou et les carottes et bien mélanger.
5. Laisser mariner pendant 1 heure, ou jusqu'au lendemain. Servir en accompagnement de burgers de millet (voir recette p. 100), par exemple.

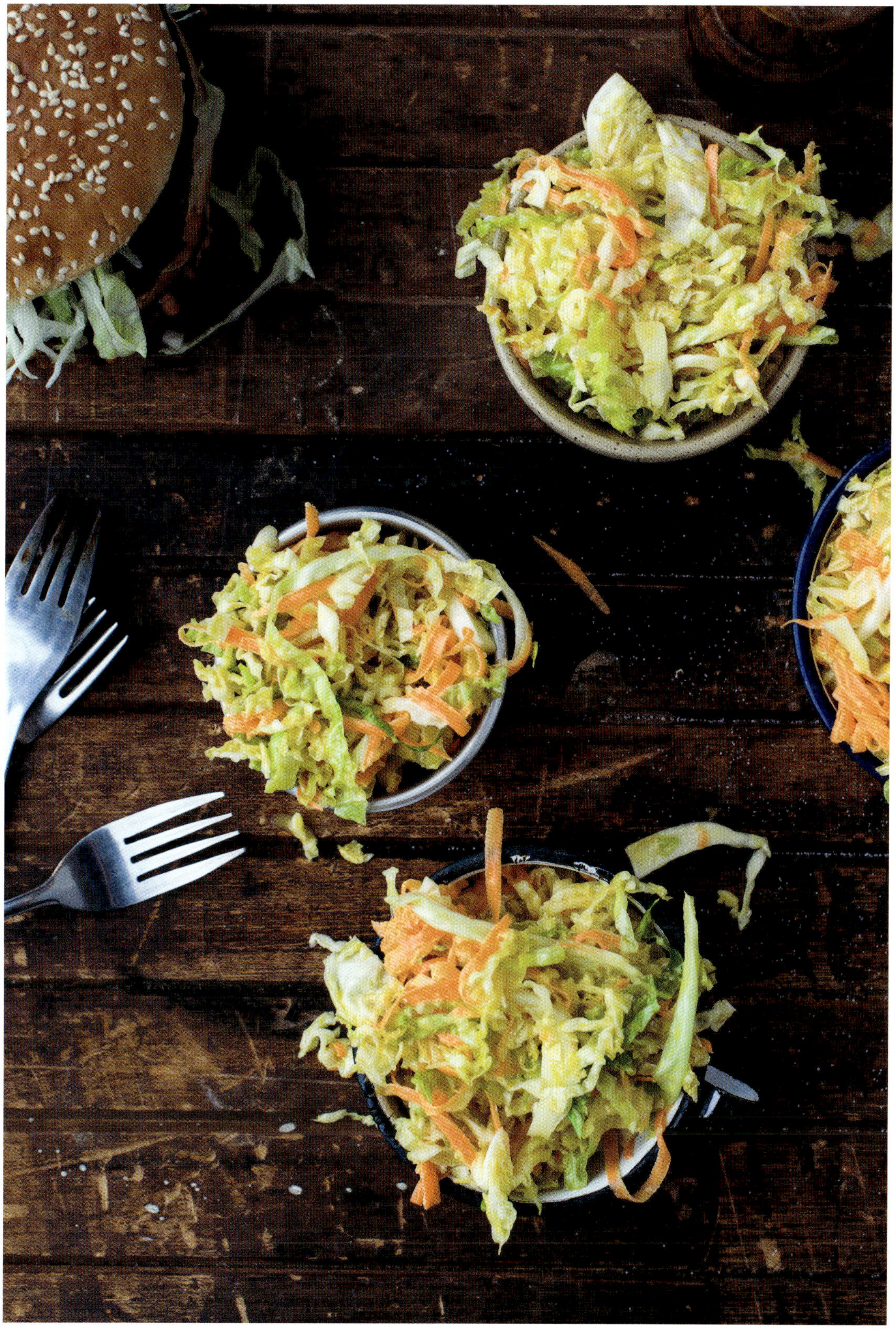

Salade de pommes épicée à la thaïe

Inspirée de la populaire recette de salade de papaye verte que j'ai découverte en Asie du sud-est, cette salade épicée-sucrée-amère est encore meilleure préparée avec un fruit local comme la pomme. Un coup de cœur assuré lors de vos pique-niques.

10 min / **2 PORTIONS**

30 min

INGRÉDIENTS

2 grosses pommes, émincées

Le jus de 1 lime

2 c. à soupe (30 ml) sirop d'érable

1 piment thaï, épépiné et émincé finement

2 oignons verts, émincés

1 bouquet de coriandre fraîche, hachée

Sel, au goût

PRÉPARATION

1. Dans un bol, mélanger tous les ingrédients et laisser mariner 30 minutes avant de servir.

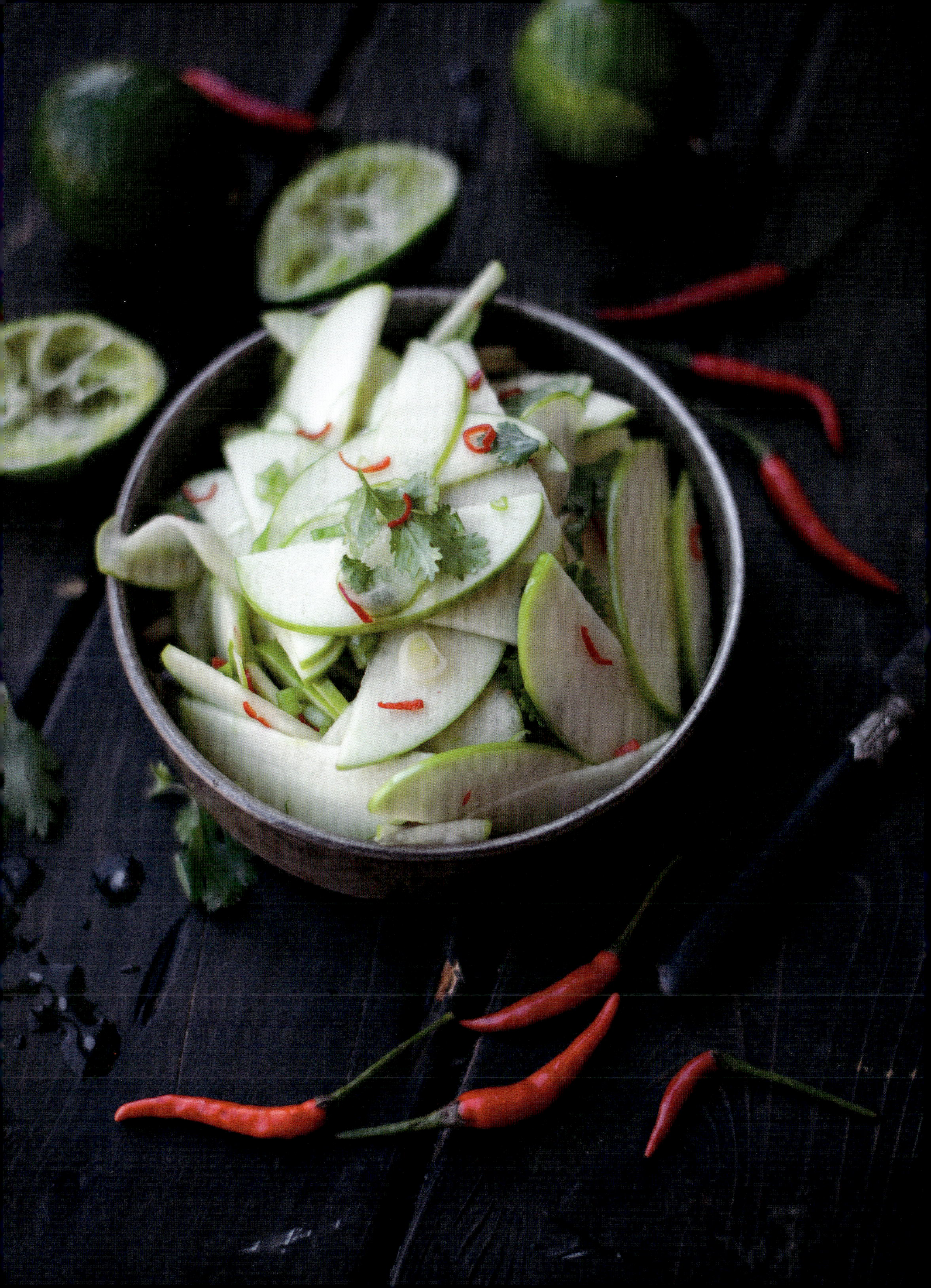

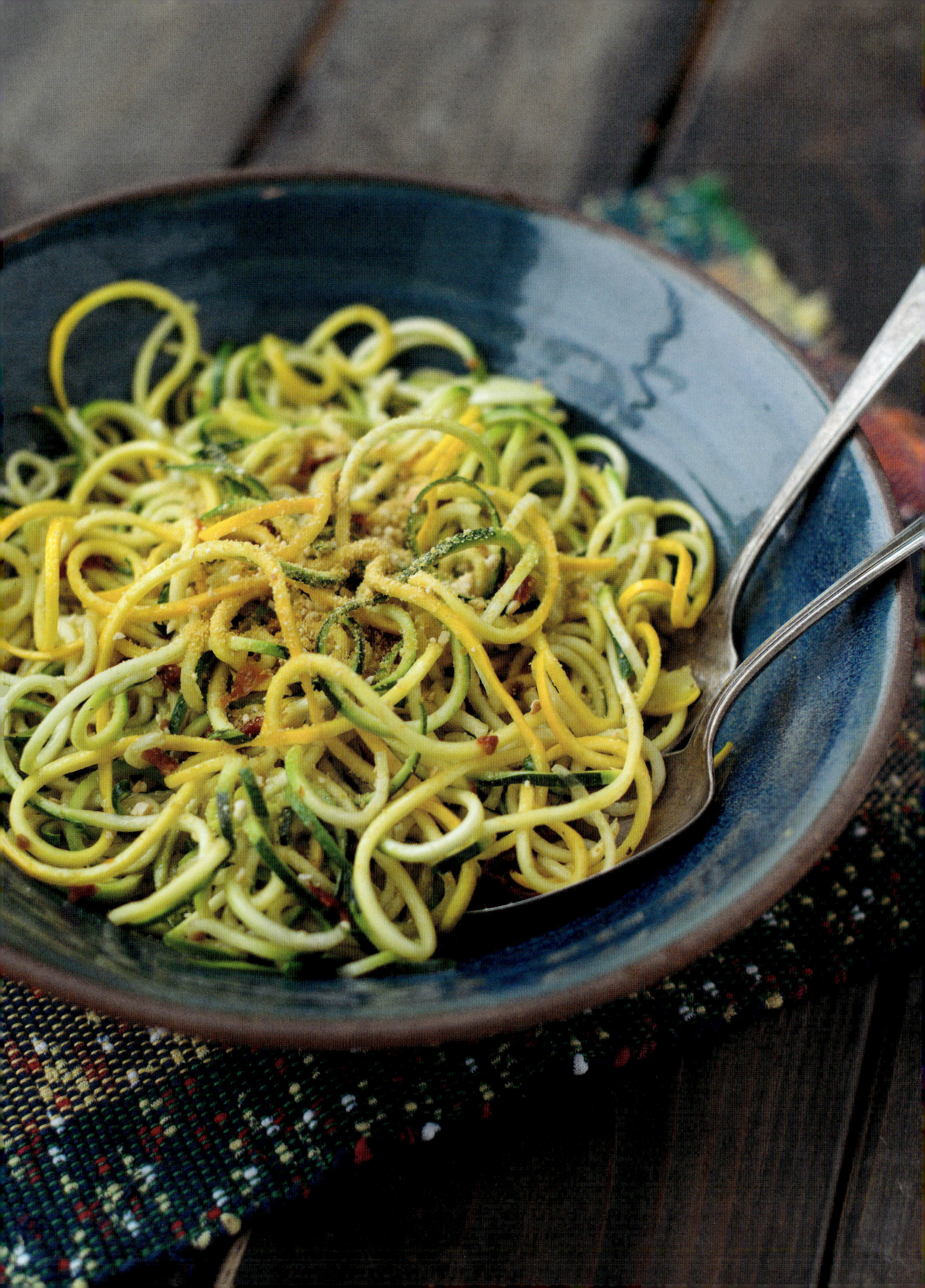

Spirales de courgettes

15 min / **2 PORTIONS**

10 min

INGRÉDIENTS

2 courgettes vertes

2 courgettes jaunes

3 c. à soupe (45 ml) huile d'olive

2 gousses d'ail, hachées

3 c. à soupe (45 ml) tomates séchées, hachées finement

¼ c. à thé (1 ml) piment rouge broyé

Sel et poivre, au goût

4 c. à soupe (60 ml) parmesan de cajou (voir recette p. 208)

PRÉPARATION

1. Couper les courgettes en spaghettis à l'aide d'un coupe-spirales.
2. Dans une poêle moyenne, faire chauffer l'huile à feu moyen-vif.
3. Ajouter l'ail, les tomates séchées et le piment rouge broyé. Cuire de 1 à 2 minutes, en brassant fréquemment, jusqu'à ce que l'ail soit légèrement rôti.
4. Ajouter les courgettes. Saler, poivrer et faire cuire à feu moyen-vif, en brassant fréquemment, de 2 à 4 minutes, ou jusqu'à ce que le mélange soit chaud.
5. Répartir les spirales de courgettes dans deux assiettes et saupoudrer du parmesan de cajou avant de servir.

Steaks de chou-fleur

20 min / **2 PORTIONS**

20 min

INGRÉDIENTS

¼ tasse (25 g) amandes effilées

1 tête de chou-fleur (2 lb/1 kg)*

Sel, au goût

3 c. à soupe (45 ml) huile végétale

1 petit bouquet de persil plat, haché (25 g)

1 c. à soupe (15 ml) vinaigre de cidre

1 c. à soupe (15 ml) sirop d'érable

¼ c. à thé (1 ml) piment rouge broyé

⅓ tasse (80 ml) vin blanc

Fleur de sel, au goût

PRÉPARATION

1. Préchauffer le four à 375°F (190°C).
2. Étendre les amandes sur une assiette allant au four. Faire griller de 2 à 3 minutes. Réserver.
3. Couper le chou-fleur en tranches d'environ 1 ½ po (4 cm) d'épaisseur, puis saler généreusement les tranches de chaque côté.
4. Dans une poêle à fond épais, faire chauffer l'huile à feu très vif. Attendre que l'huile soit très chaude et y déposer les tranches de chou-fleur. Couvrir pour éviter les éclaboussures et poursuivre la cuisson pendant 5 minutes en évitant de déplacer les tranches dans la poêle.
5. Lorsque les tranches de chou-fleur sont bien grillées en dessous, les retourner et poursuivre la cuisson pendant 5 minutes.
6. Entre-temps, dans un bol, mélanger le persil haché, le vinaigre de cidre, le sirop d'érable et le piment rouge broyé.
7. Déglacer avec le vin blanc et laisser réduire presque à sec.
8. Verser la vinaigrette dans la poêle et poursuivre la cuisson à feu vif pendant quelques minutes.
9. Répartir les steaks de chou-fleur dans deux assiettes. Arroser de la vinaigrette chaude, puis parsemer des amandes effilées et de fleur de sel avant de servir.

* Il est important de choisir une tête de chou-fleur bien ferme pour cette recette.

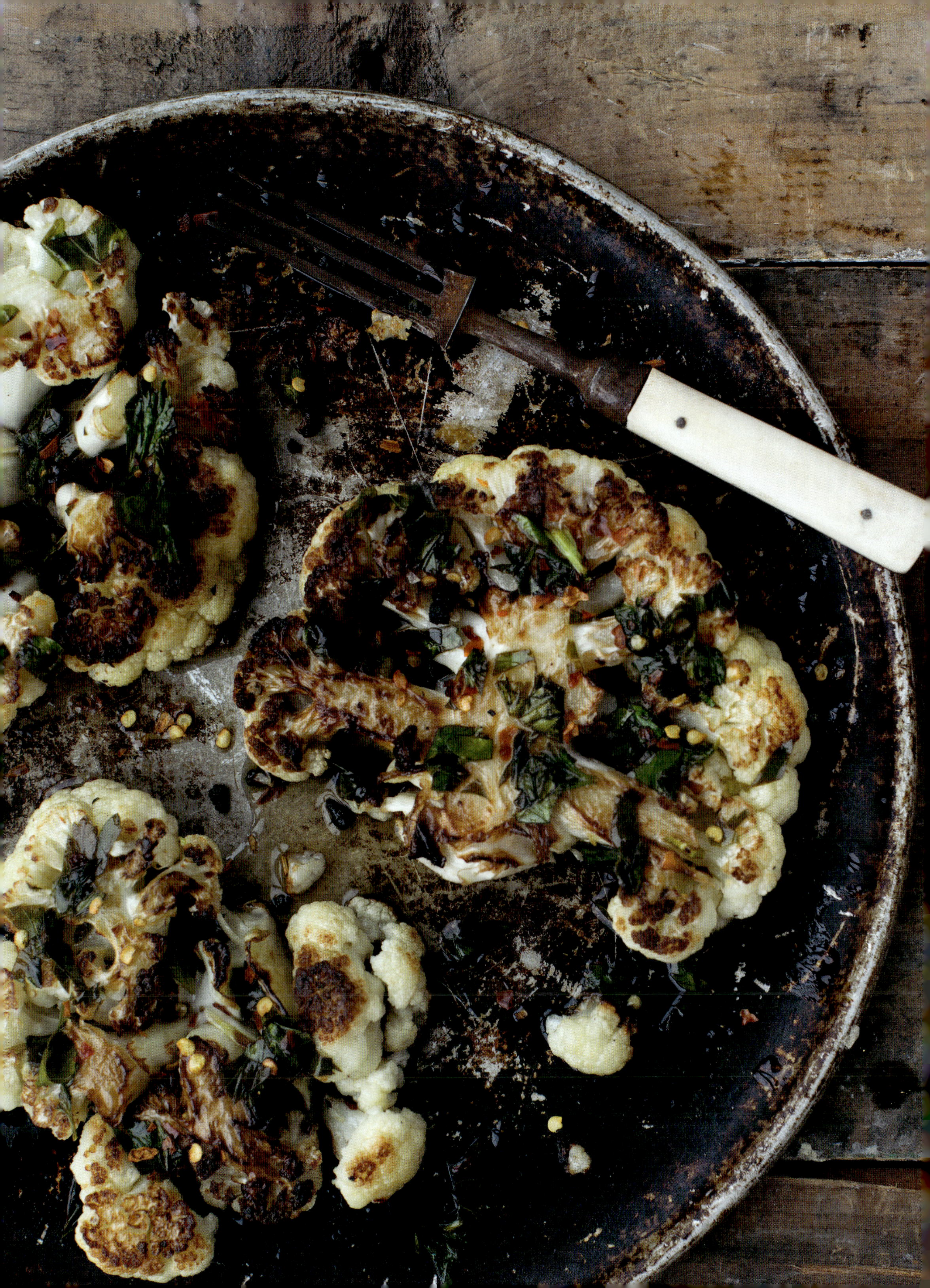

Tartare d'avocat

15 min / **1 PORTION**

5 min

INGRÉDIENTS

1 avocat, coupé en dés

1 c. à soupe (15 ml) mayonnaise végétale (voir recette p. 209)

Quelques gouttes de tabasco

Fleur de sel, au goût

1 petite tortilla de maïs

Huile d'olive

¼ c. à thé (1 ml) origan séché

1 petite tomate, coupée en dés

Coulis de vinaigre balsamique, pour garnir

1 boîte de conserve vide de 796 ml, dont on a enlevé les extrémités (à utiliser comme emporte-pièce)

PRÉPARATION

1. Préchauffer le four à 375 °F (190 °C).
2. Dans un bol, mélanger délicatement l'avocat, la mayonnaise, le tabasco et une pincée de fleur de sel. Réserver.
3. Découper une rondelle dans la tortilla avec l'emporte-pièce.
4. Déposer la rondelle de tortilla sur une plaque à pâtisserie.
5. Huiler légèrement la tortilla et parsemer d'une pincée de fleur de sel et d'origan.
6. Faire griller au four pendant 5 minutes.
7. Déposer la boîte de conserve sur une assiette, puis y mettre la préparation d'avocat, en la tassant légèrement avec une cuillère.
8. Couvrir de la rondelle de tortilla grillée.
9. Ajouter la tomate en dés et presser légèrement.
10. Retirer délicatement la boîte de conserve et arroser de coulis de vinaigre balsamique avant de servir.

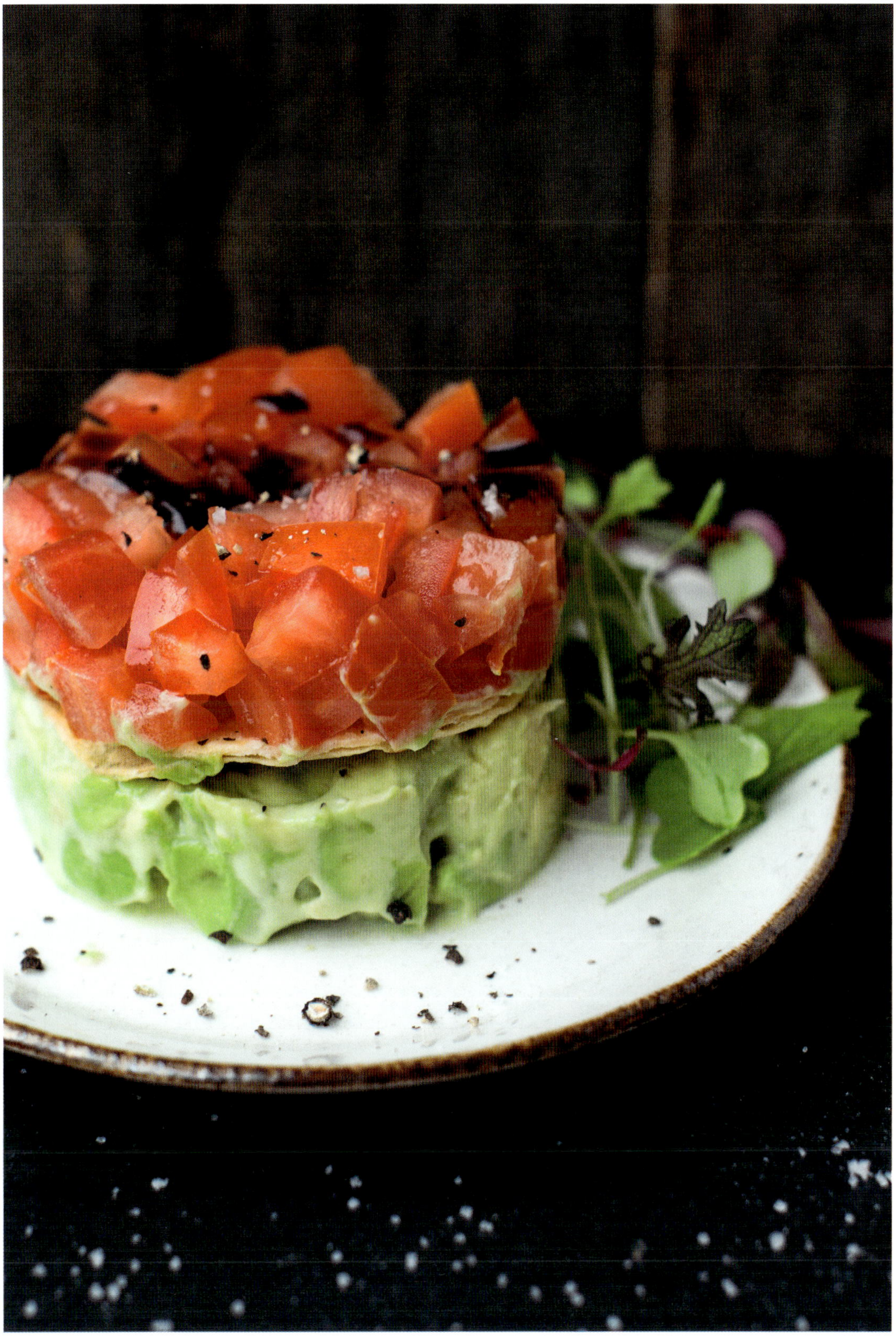

SOUPES
ET POTAGES

Potage de chou-fleur au curcuma

15 min / **6 PORTIONS**

35 min

INGRÉDIENTS

1 oignon, émincé

2 c. à soupe (30 ml) huile végétale

1 tête de chou-fleur (environ 600 g)

2 pommes de terre à chair jaune, pelées et coupées en dés (environ 300 g)

8 tasses (2 L) bouillon de légumes

1 c. à thé (5 ml) curcuma

Sel, au goût

PRÉPARATION

1. Dans une casserole, faire revenir l'oignon dans l'huile à feu doux pendant 3 minutes.
2. Ajouter le reste des ingrédients et porter à ébullition. Réduire le feu, couvrir et laisser mijoter pendant 30 minutes, ou jusqu'à ce que les légumes soient tendres.
3. Passer la soupe au bras mélangeur ou au mélangeur, jusqu'à ce qu'elle soit lisse. Servir bien chaud.

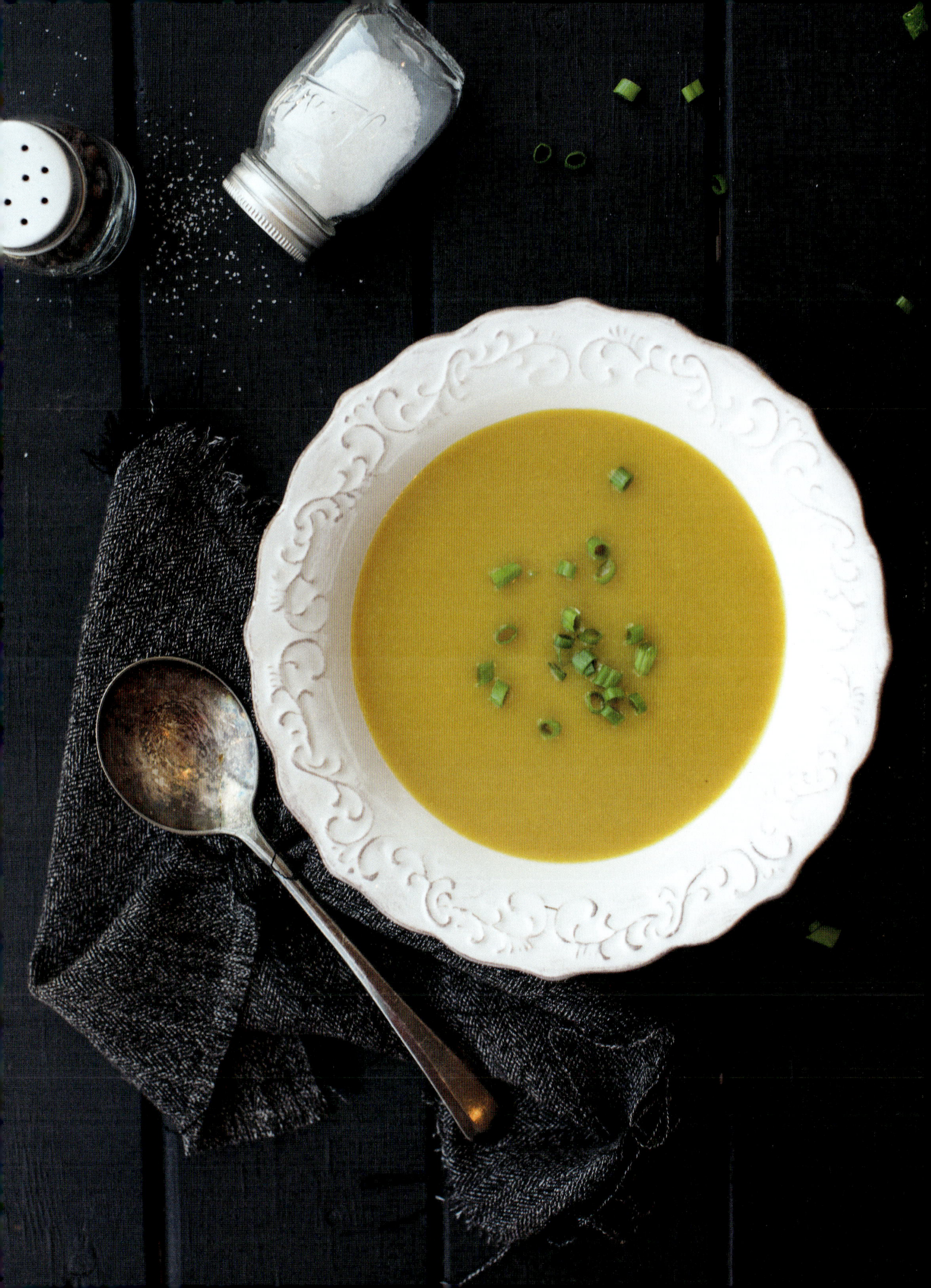

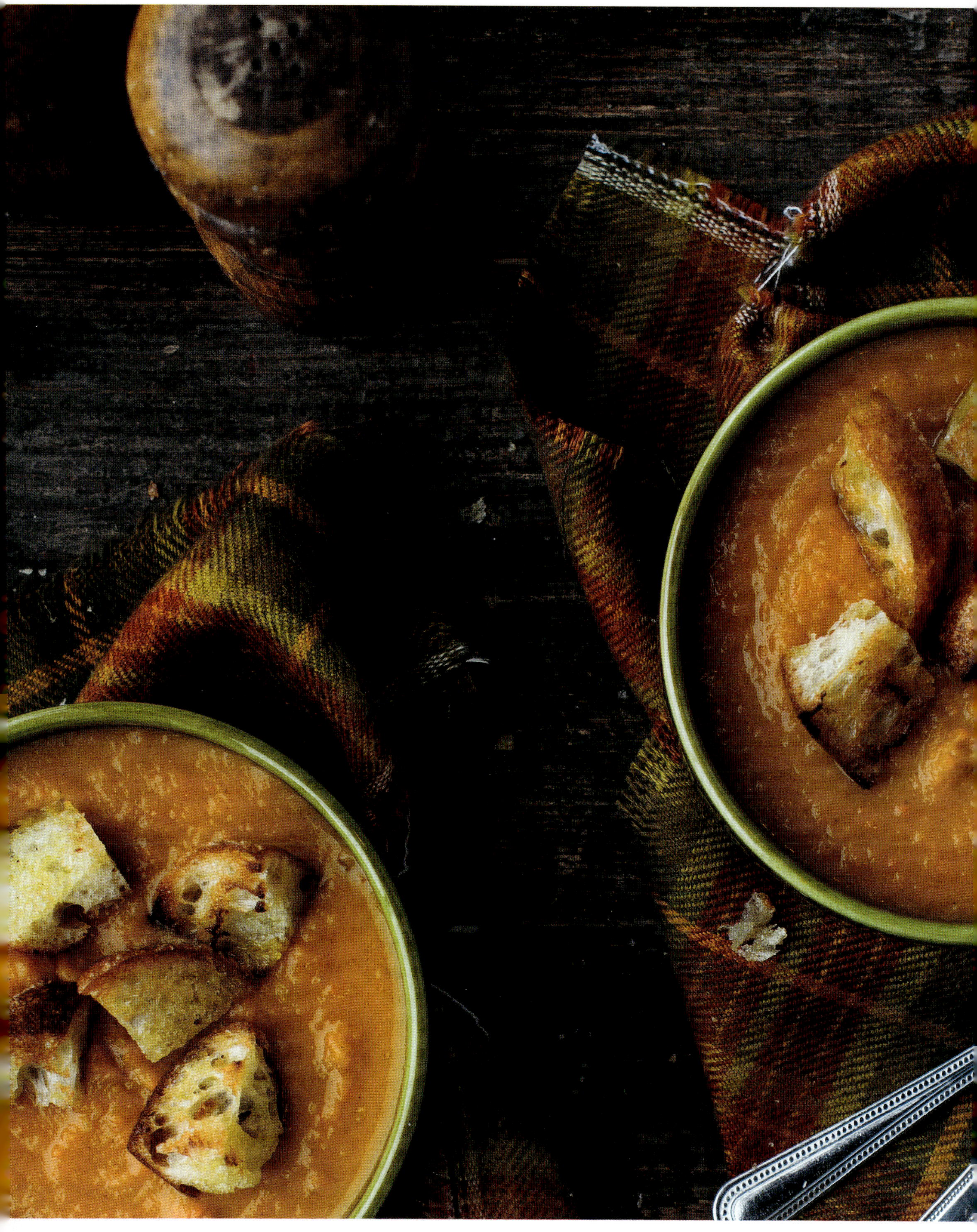

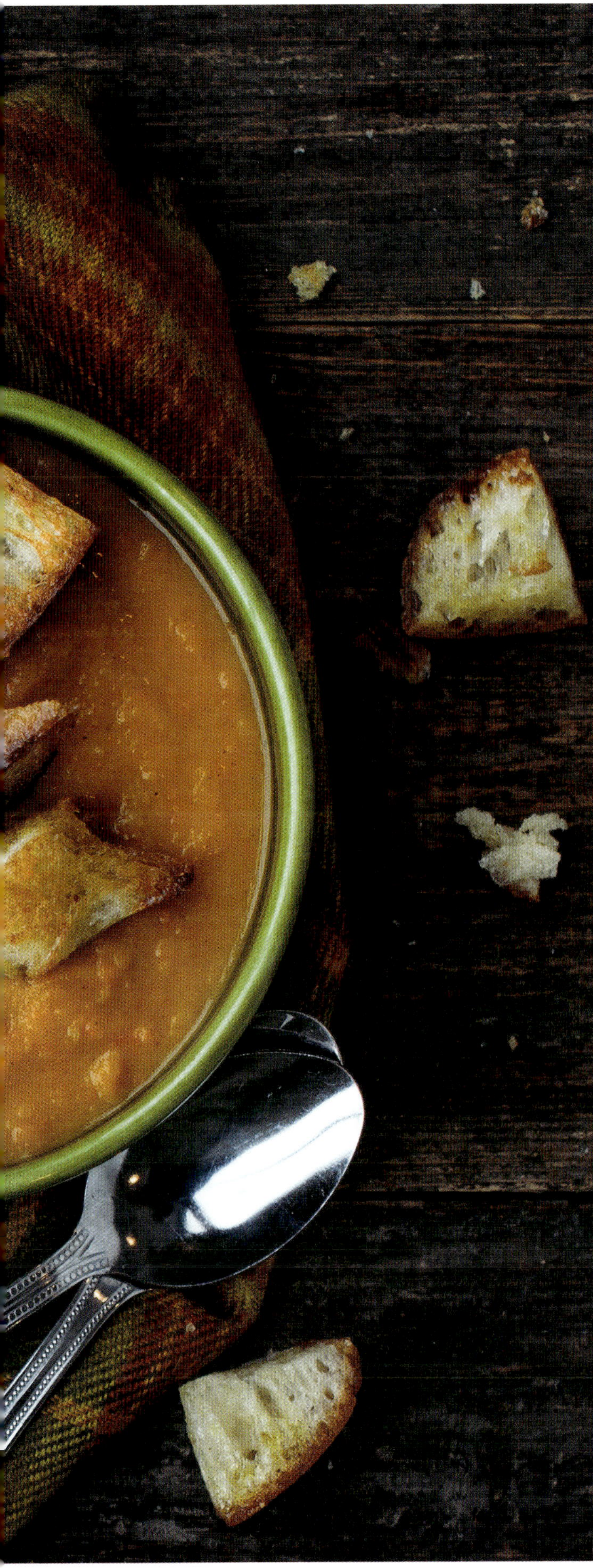

Potage de légumes d'automne grillés

Faire griller les légumes au four confère à ce potage un petit goût de légumes caramélisés. Mais c'est un secret!

20 min / **4 PORTIONS**

45 min

INGRÉDIENTS

1 patate douce
1 oignon
3 carottes
2 c. à soupe (30 ml) huile d'olive
⅛ c. à thé (0,5 ml) muscade moulue
¼ c. à thé (1 ml) cannelle moulue
¼ c. à thé (1 ml) cumin moulu
¼ c. à thé (1 ml) curcuma
Sel et poivre, au goût
4 tasses (1 L) bouillon de légumes
Croûtons (voir recette p. 61), pour garnir

PRÉPARATION

1. Préchauffer le four à 350˚F (180˚C).
2. Couper grossièrement les légumes, puis les déposer dans un grand bol.
3. Ajouter l'huile, la muscade, la cannelle, le cumin, le curcuma, le sel et le poivre, puis bien mélanger.
4. Étaler les légumes sur une plaque à pâtisserie ou dans un grand plat allant au four. Faire griller 30 minutes.
5. Retirer les légumes du four et les mettre dans une marmite. Ajouter le bouillon de légumes et porter à ébullition. Couvrir et laisser mijoter pendant 15 minutes, ou jusqu'a ce que les légumes soient tendres.
6. Passer la soupe au pied mélangeur ou au mélangeur, jusqu'à ce qu'elle soit lisse. Garnir des croûtons et servir bien chaud.

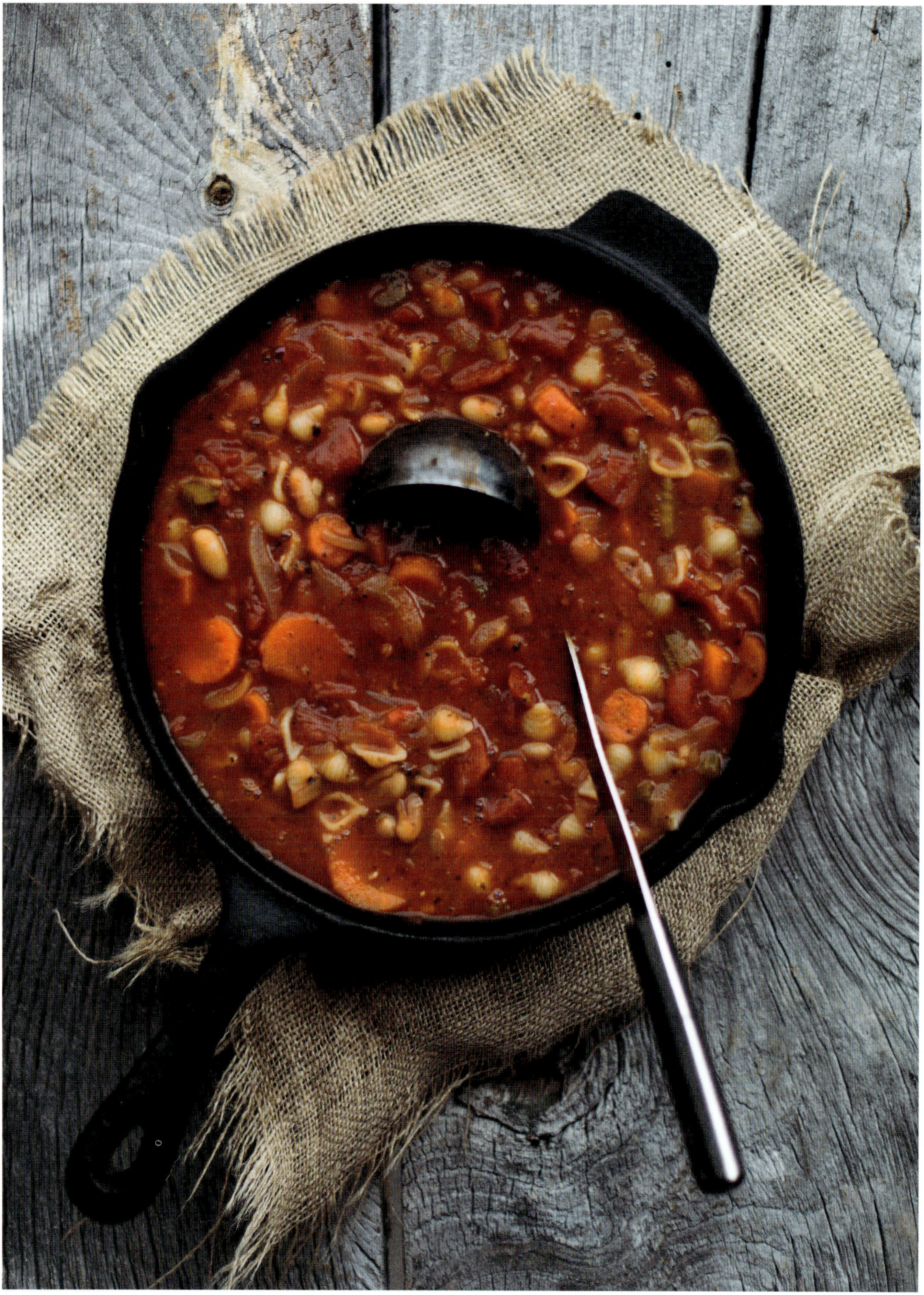

Soupe minestrone

30 min / **8 À 10 PORTIONS**

75 min

INGRÉDIENTS

2 c. à soupe (30 ml) huile d'olive

2 oignons, émincés

4 carottes, tranchées en rondelles

2 branches de céleri, émincées

2 gousses d'ail, hachées

1 c. à soupe (15 ml) basilic séché

1 c. à soupe (15 ml) origan séché

1 c. à thé (5 ml) sel

1 boîte (796 ml) tomates en dés

6 tasses (1,5 L) bouillon de légumes

1 boîte (540 ml) jus de tomate

1 boîte (540 ml) haricots blancs, rincés et égouttés

1 tasse (90 g) petites pâtes en forme de coquilles

PRÉPARATION

1. Dans une casserole à fond épais, faire chauffer l'huile à feu moyen pendant 1 minute.
2. Ajouter les oignons et faire suer de 2 à 3 minutes.
3. Ajouter les carottes et le céleri. Poursuivre la cuisson, en remuant fréquemment, pendant 5 minutes, ou jusqu'à ce que les légumes aient ramolli.
4. Ajouter le reste des ingrédients et porter à ébullition.
5. Réduire le feu, couvrir et laisser mijoter pendant 1 heure, en remuant de temps à autre. Servir bien chaud.

Potage Saint-Germain

On dit que ce sont les recettes les plus simples qui sont les meilleures. Cet adage prend tout son sens ici. Grâce à ce classique de la cuisine française revisité, vous serez épatés de redécouvrir, sous un nouveau jour, les petits pois que nos mères nous servaient.

15 min / **6 PORTIONS**
50 min

INGRÉDIENTS

1 oignon, émincé
2 c. à soupe (30 ml) huile végétale
1 grosse pomme de terre
5 tasses (750 g) petits pois surgelés
6 tasses (1,5 L) bouillon de légumes
Sel, au goût

PRÉPARATION

1. Dans une casserole, faire revenir l'oignon dans l'huile à feu moyen pendant 5 minutes.
2. Ajouter le reste des ingrédients, porter à ébullition, réduire le feu, couvrir et laisser mijoter pendant 45 minutes.
3. Passer la soupe au pied mélangeur ou au mélangeur, jusqu'à ce qu'elle soit lisse. Servir bien chaud.

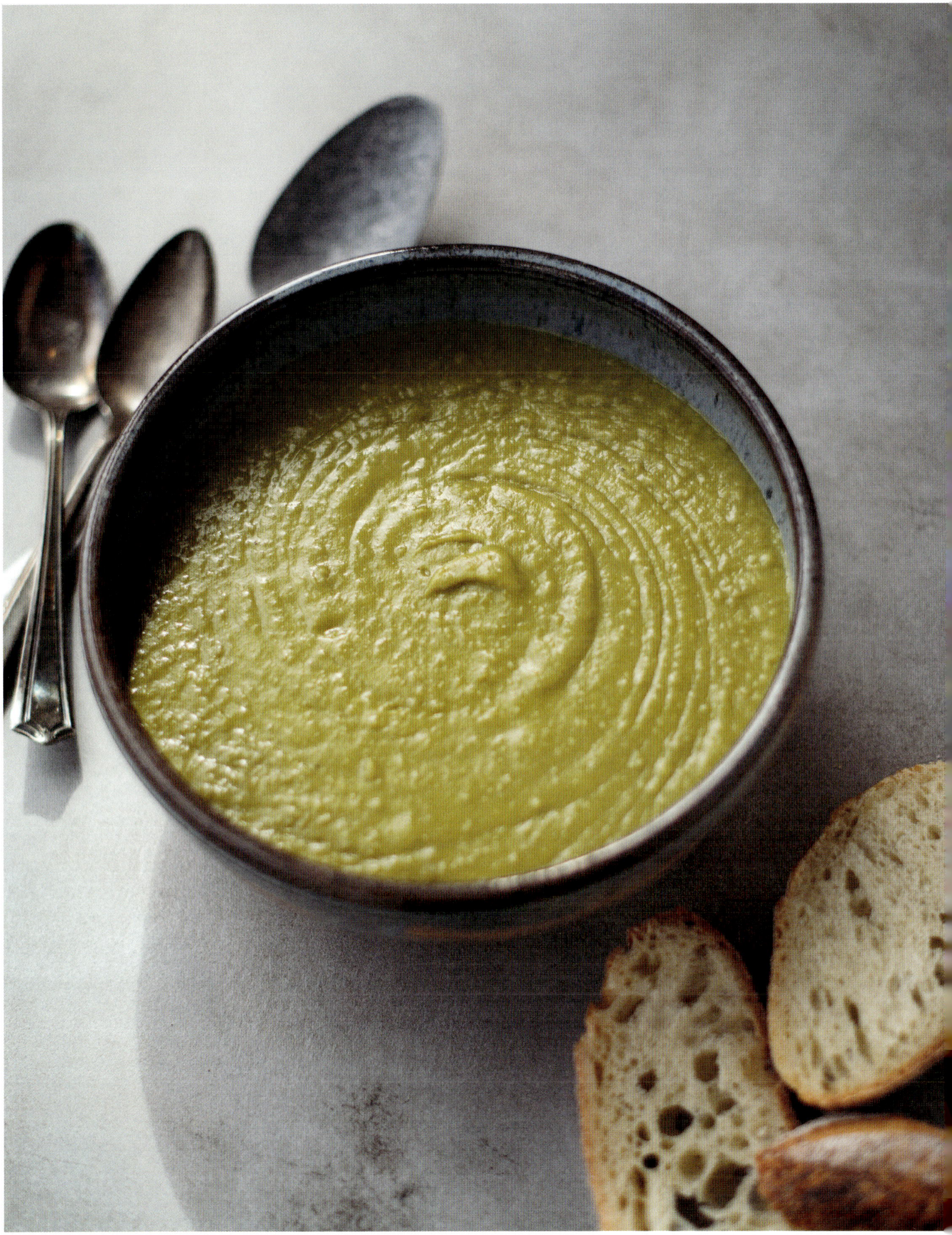

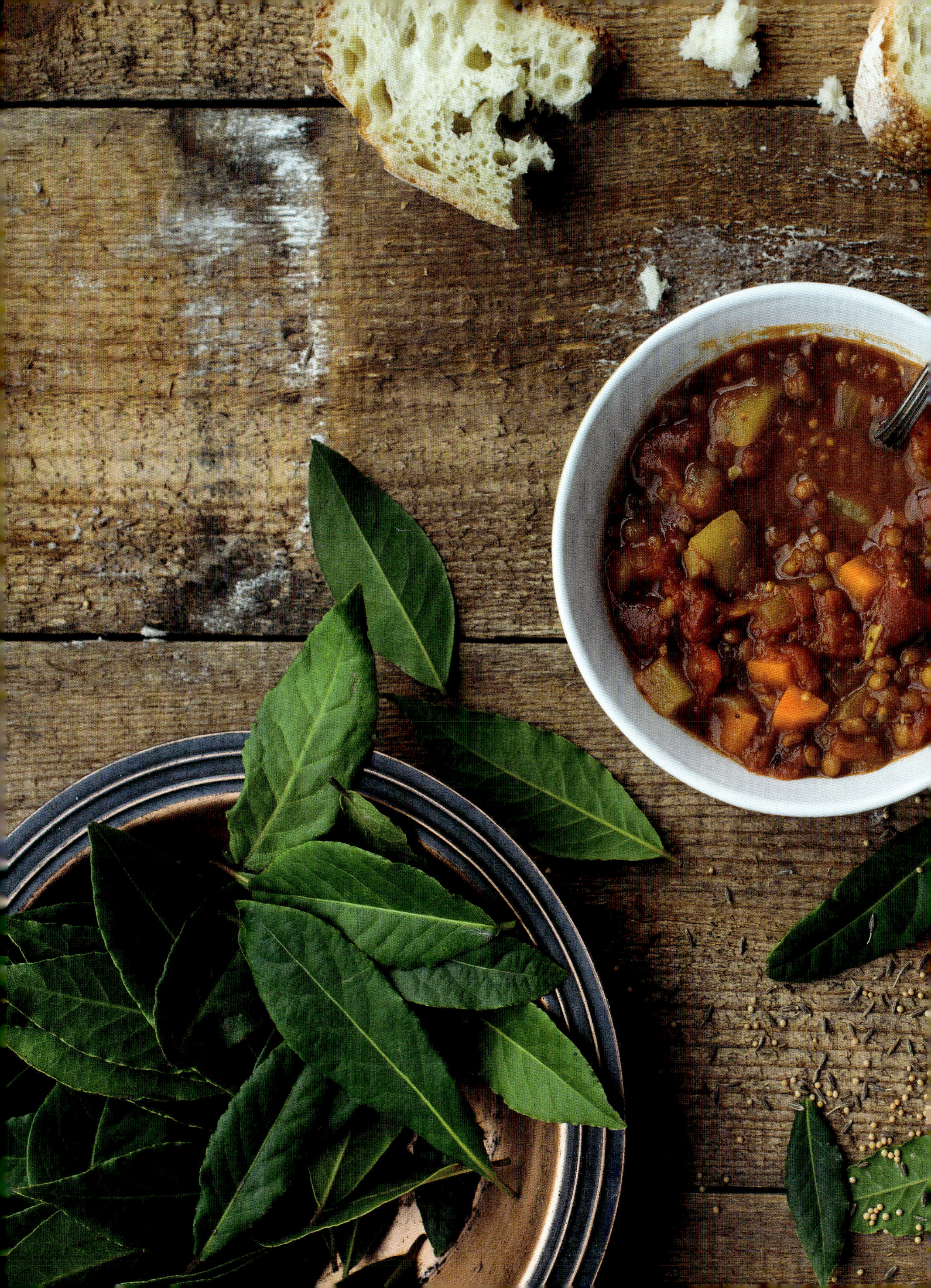

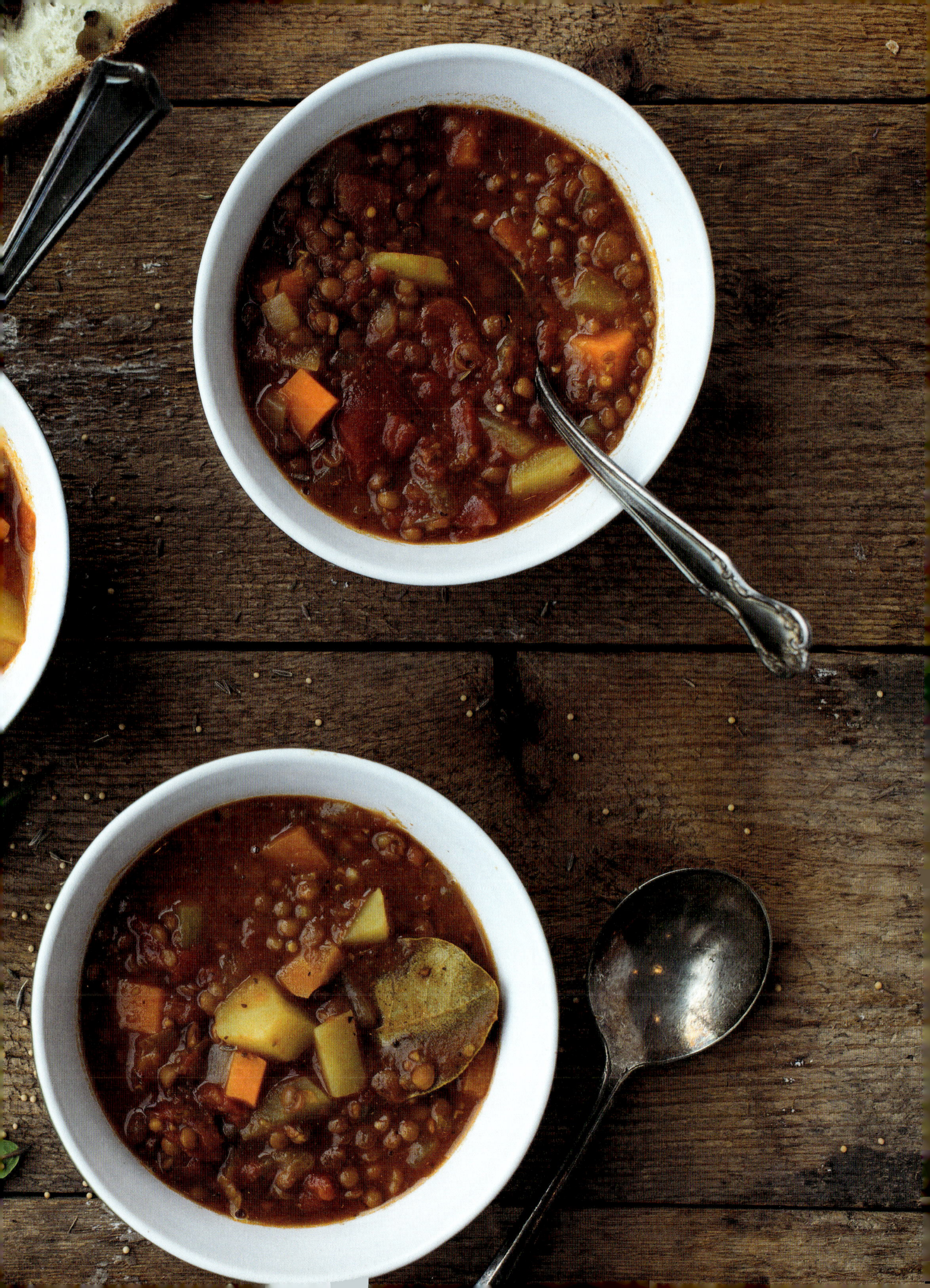

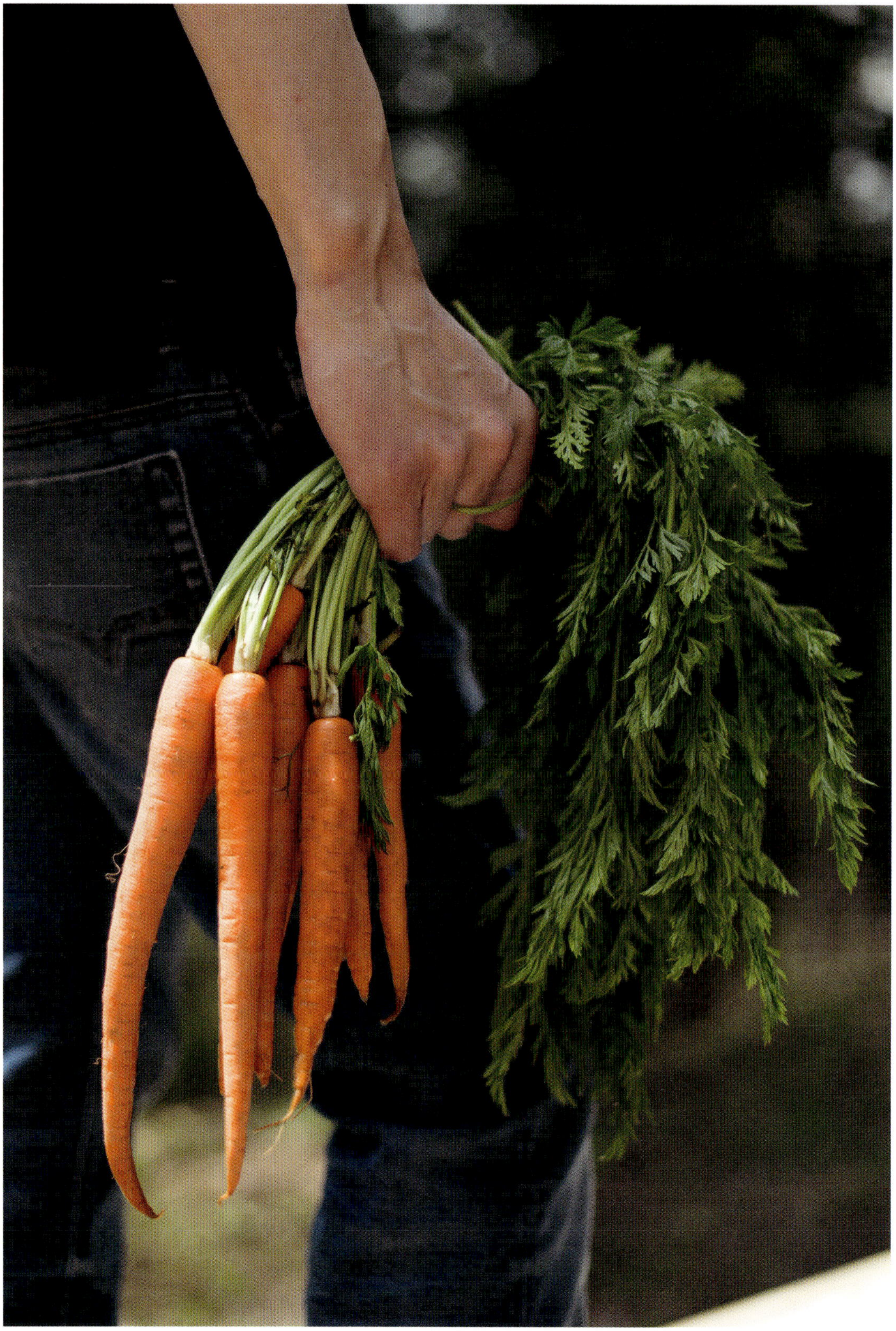

Soupe-repas marocaine

30 min / **8 À 10 PORTIONS**

70 min

INGRÉDIENTS

1 oignon, coupé en dés

3 c. à soupe (45 ml) huile végétale

1 c. à thé (5 ml) graines de moutarde

1 c. à thé (5 ml) graines de céleri

1 c. à thé (5 ml) cumin moulu

1 c. à thé (5 ml) coriandre moulue

1 c. à thé (5 ml) origan séché

½ c. à thé (2,5 ml) curcuma

1 gousse d'ail, hachée

1 c. à soupe (15 ml) sauce harissa

3 feuilles de laurier

2 carottes, coupées en dés

1 boîte (540 ml) lentilles vertes, rincées et égouttées

2 pommes de terre à chair jaune, pelées et coupées en dés

8 tasses (2 L) bouillon de légumes

1 boîte (796 ml) tomates en dés

Sel et poivre, au goût

PRÉPARATION

1. Dans une grande casserole, faire revenir l'oignon dans l'huile à feu moyen pendant 4 minutes.
2. Ajouter les graines de moutarde, les graines de céleri, le cumin, la coriandre, l'origan, le curcuma et l'ail, puis poursuivre la cuisson pendant 2 minutes.
3. Ajouter le reste des ingrédients et porter à ébullition. Réduire le feu, couvrir et laisser mijoter pendant 1 heure, en remuant de temps à autre. Servir bien chaud.

PLATS PRINCIPAUX

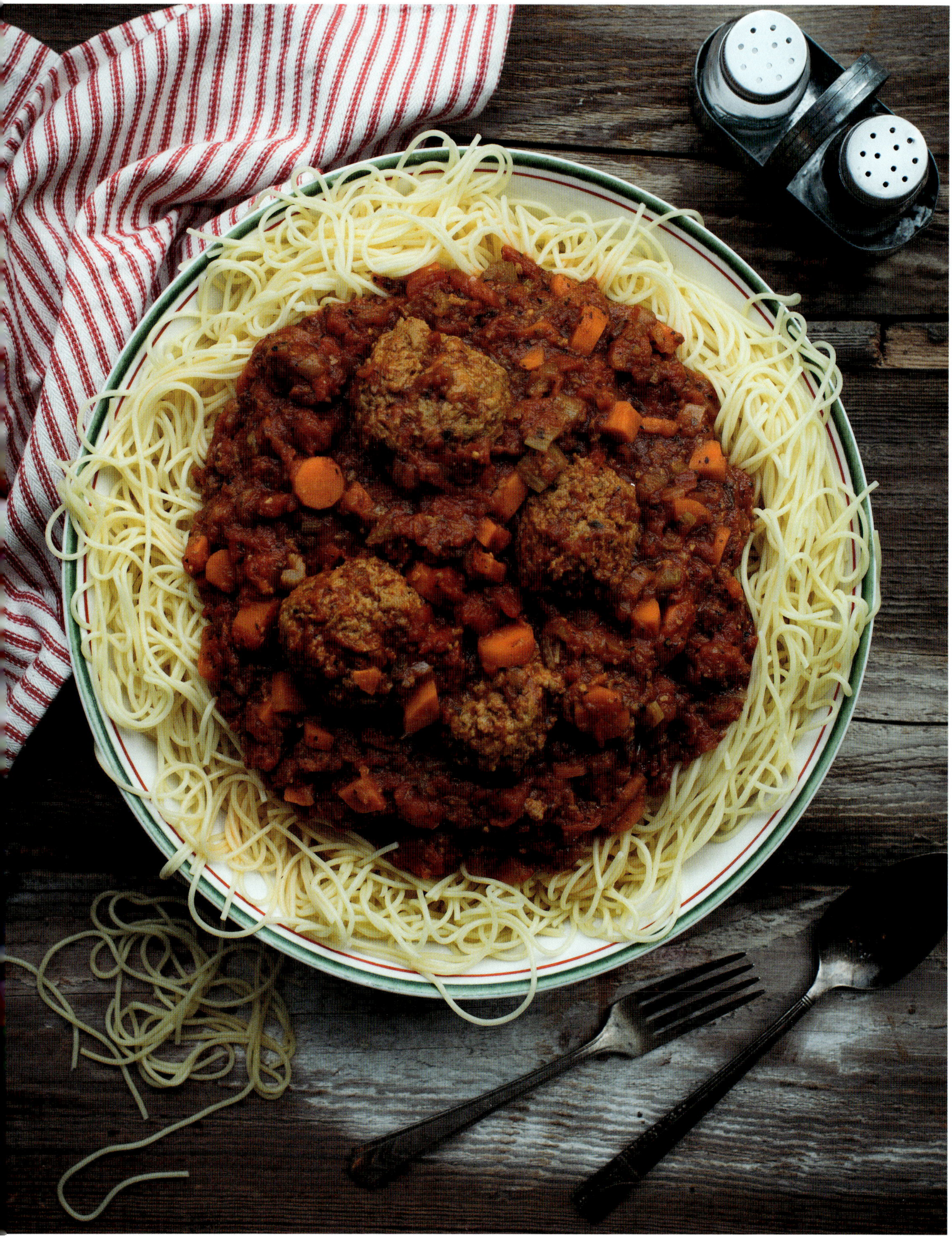

Sauce aux boulettes

30 min / **4 PORTIONS**

45 à 55 min

INGRÉDIENTS

1 tasse (80 g) protéines végétales texturées (PVT)

2 tasses (500 ml) eau bouillante

1 oignon, haché

4 tasses (227 g) champignons de Paris, grossièrement hachés

2 c. à soupe (30 ml) huile d'olive

2 gousses d'ail, hachées

3 c. à soupe (45 ml) sauce soya

½ c. à thé (2,5 ml) sel

½ tasse (40 g) levure alimentaire

¼ tasse (10 g) persil, haché

2 tasses (260 g) farine de gluten

6 tasses (1,5 L) sauce tomate (voir recette p. 103 et la doubler)

PRÉPARATION

1. Dans un bol, plonger les PVT dans l'eau bouillante et laisser reposer pendant 5 minutes afin de les réhydrater. Égoutter et réserver.
2. Dans une poêle, faire revenir l'oignon et les champignons dans l'huile pendant 10 minutes. Ajouter l'ail et poursuivre la cuisson pendant 2 minutes.
3. Transvider les oignons et les champignons dans le bol d'un robot culinaire.
4. Égoutter les PVT et les ajouter dans le bol du robot.
5. Ajouter la sauce soya, le sel, la levure et le persil. Broyer pendant 1 minute.
6. Transférer la préparation dans un bol et ajouter la farine.
7. Pétrir pendant 2 minutes, jusqu'à ce que la farine soit bien absorbée.
8. Former de petites boulettes, chauffer la sauce tomate et y faire pocher les boulettes de 30 à 45 minutes en les retournant à mi-cuisson si elles ne sont pas complètement plongées dans la sauce. (Les boulettes prendront de l'expansion à la cuisson.) Servir sur des pâtes.

Bourguignon de portobellos

30 min / **2 PORTIONS**

50 min

INGRÉDIENTS

3 champignons portobellos, coupés en quartiers

2 carottes, coupées en rondelles

1 oignon, émincé

1 c. à thé (5 ml) cumin

¼ c. à thé (1 ml) piment de la Jamaïque

1 c. à thé (5 ml) sel

3 c. à soupe (45 ml) huile végétale

Poivre en grains, au goût

1 ½ tasse (375 ml) vin rouge

4 c. à soupe (60 ml) sauce soya

2 c. à soupe (30 ml) sirop d'érable

3 c. à soupe (45 ml) pâte de tomate

2 tasses (500 ml) bouillon de légumes

3 feuilles de laurier

1 c. à soupe (15 ml) fécule de maïs

3 c. à soupe (45 ml) eau

Quelques feuilles de persil, pour garnir

PRÉPARATION

1. Préchauffer le four à 400°F (200°C).
2. Dans une grande casserole allant au four, bien mélanger les champignons, les carottes, l'oignon, le cumin, le piment, le sel, l'huile végétale et le poivre.
3. Faire rôtir au four pendant 30 minutes.
4. À la sortie du four, déposer sur la cuisinière et déglacer avec le vin. Laisser mijoter pendant environ 5 minutes à feu moyen-vif.
5. Ajouter la sauce soya, le sirop d'érable, la pâte de tomate, le bouillon de légumes et les feuilles de laurier. Porter à ébullition et laisser mijoter pendant 15 minutes.
6. Dans un petit bol, mélanger la fécule de maïs et l'eau.
7. Ajouter le mélange de fécule au bourguignon, en remuant constamment. Porter à ébullition et retirer du feu aussitôt que la sauce a épaissi (après environ 1 minute).
8. Garnir de persil et servir.

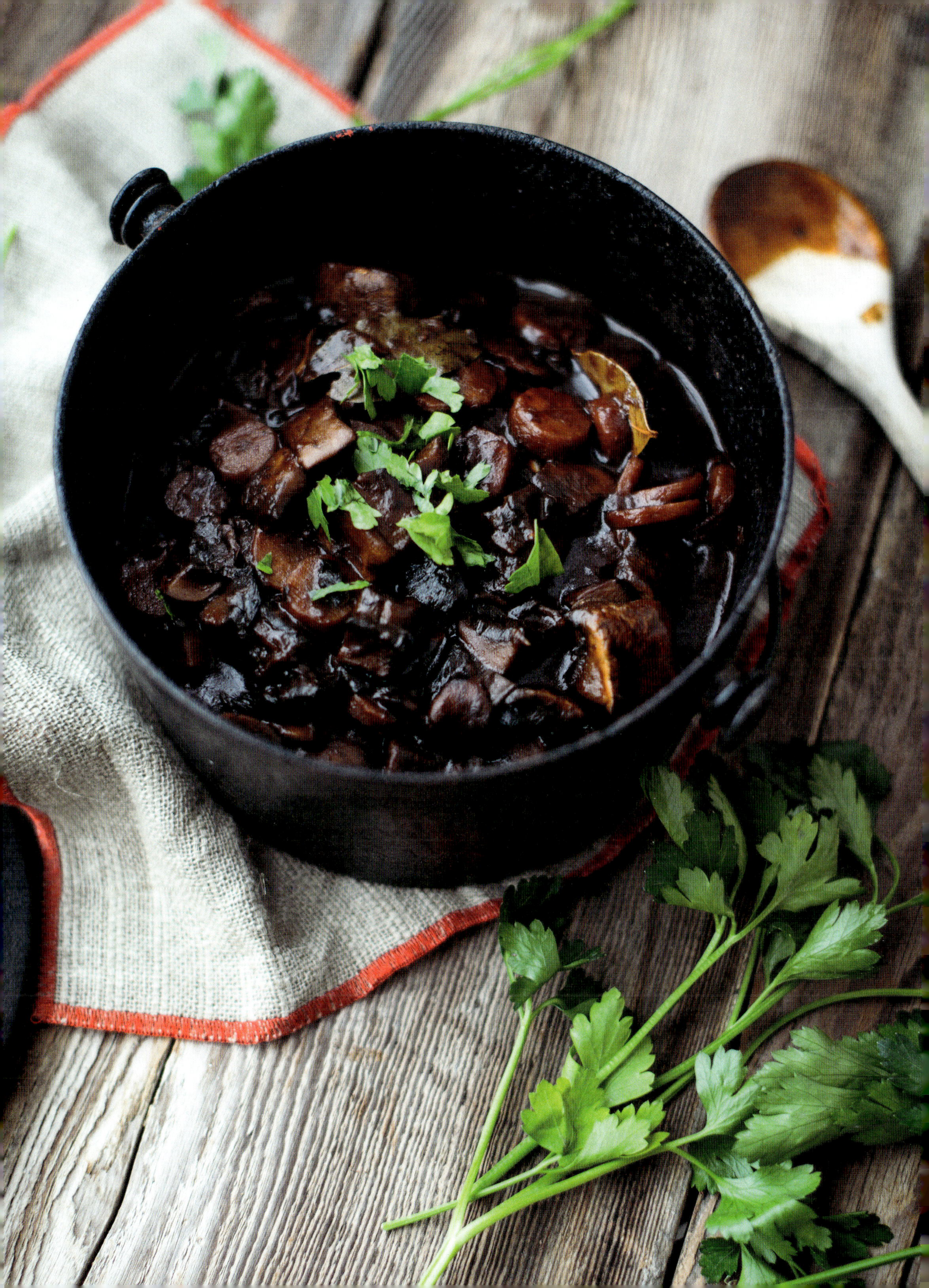

Burgers de millet

45 min / **6 PORTIONS**

10 min

20 min

MILLET

1 tasse (190 g) millet cru

2 c. à soupe (30 ml) huile d'olive

2 tasses (500 ml) bouillon de légumes (ou eau)

SAUCE

1 c. à soupe (15 ml) cornichons, hachés

½ tasse (125 ml) mayonnaise végétale (voir recette p. 209)

1 c. à soupe (15 ml) moutarde

½ c. à thé (2,5 ml) sel de céleri

1 c. à thé (5 ml) paprika

1 c. à thé (5 ml) poudre d'oignon

1 c. à thé (5 ml) sirop d'érable

1 c. à thé (5 ml) ketchup

1 c. à thé (5 ml) vinaigre (facultatif)

BOULETTES DE MILLET

1 oignon, haché

1 ½ tasse (120 g) champignons de Paris, émincés

2 c. à soupe (30 ml) huile d'olive

2 ½ tasses (250 g) millet cuit (voir « Cuire le millet »)

1 tasse (160 g) riz brun cuit (voir recette p. 68)

1 tasse (125 g) chapelure

¼ tasse (60 ml) ketchup

1 c. à thé (5 ml) sel

1 c. à thé (5 ml) poudre d'ail

6 pains à hamburger

Un peu de laitue, pour garnir

Quelques tranches de tomate, pour garnir

Un peu d'oignon émincé, pour garnir

CUIRE LE MILLET

1. Bien rincer le millet, puis l'égoutter.
2. Dans une casserole, faire revenir le millet dans l'huile de 3 à 4 minutes en le faisant griller légèrement.
3. Ajouter le bouillon de légumes. Porter à ébullition, puis réduire le feu et couvrir. Laisser mijoter pendant 20 minutes, ou jusqu'à ce que le liquide soit absorbé. Retirer du feu et laisser reposer à couvert pendant 20 minutes.

PRÉPARER LA SAUCE

1. Dans un petit bol, mélanger tous les ingrédients. Réserver.

PRÉPARER LES BOULETTES DE MILLET

1. Préchauffer le four à 375 °F (190 °C).
2. Dans une casserole, faire revenir l'oignon et les champignons dans l'huile de 3 à 4 minutes.
3. Transvider le mélange et le reste des ingrédients dans le bol d'un robot culinaire. Mélanger quelques secondes à la fois pendant environ 1 minute, ou jusqu'à l'obtention d'une texture granulaire.
4. Former des boulettes à l'aide d'une cuillère à crème glacée.
5. Dans une poêle huilée, faire cuire les boulettes pendant 2 minutes de chaque côté et transférer sur une plaque allant au four.
6. Poursuivre la cuisson au four pendant 10 minutes. Servir sur des pains à hamburger garnis de laitue, de tomates et d'oignon, et accompagner de coleslaw (voir recette p. 70), par exemple.

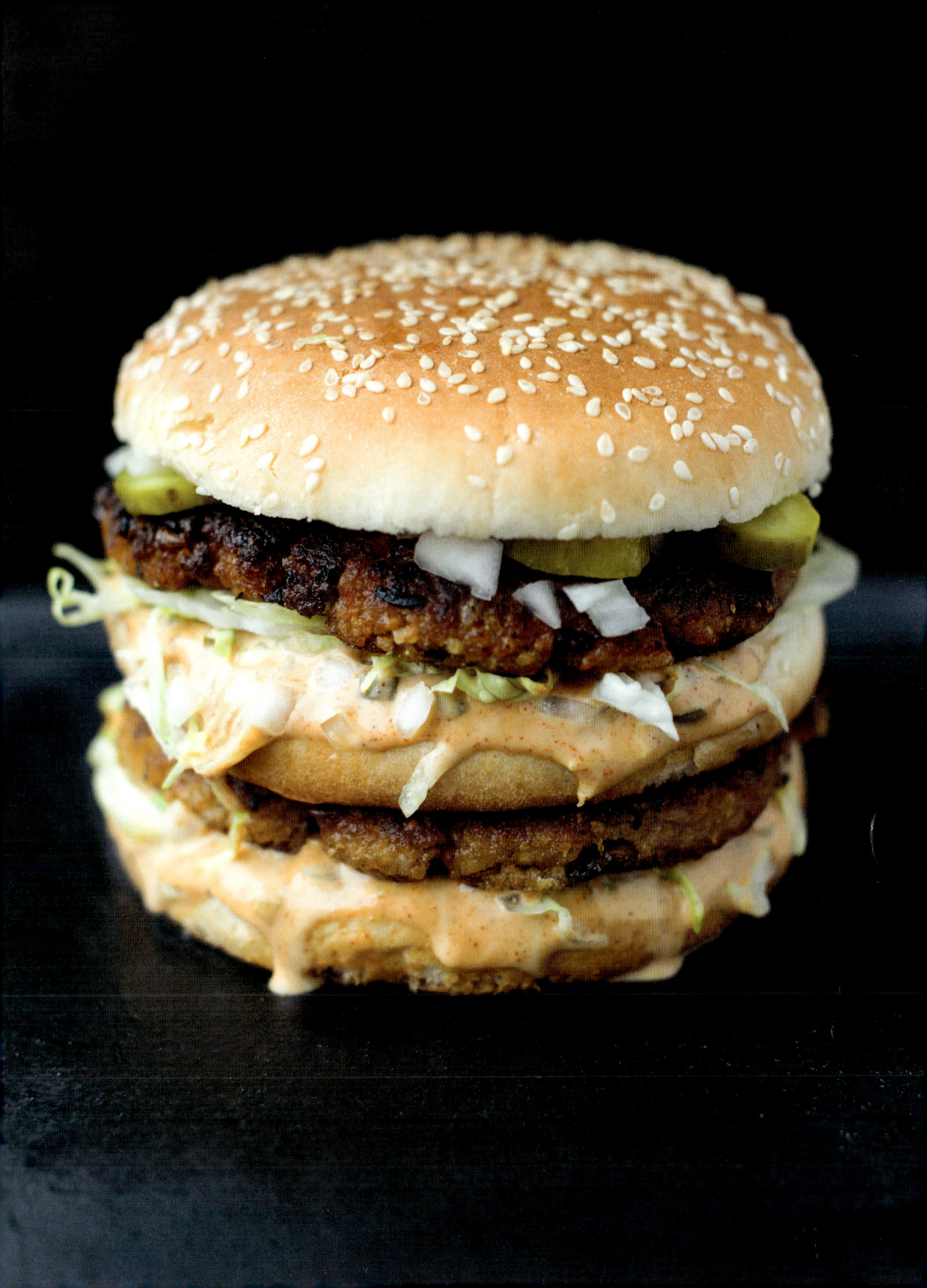

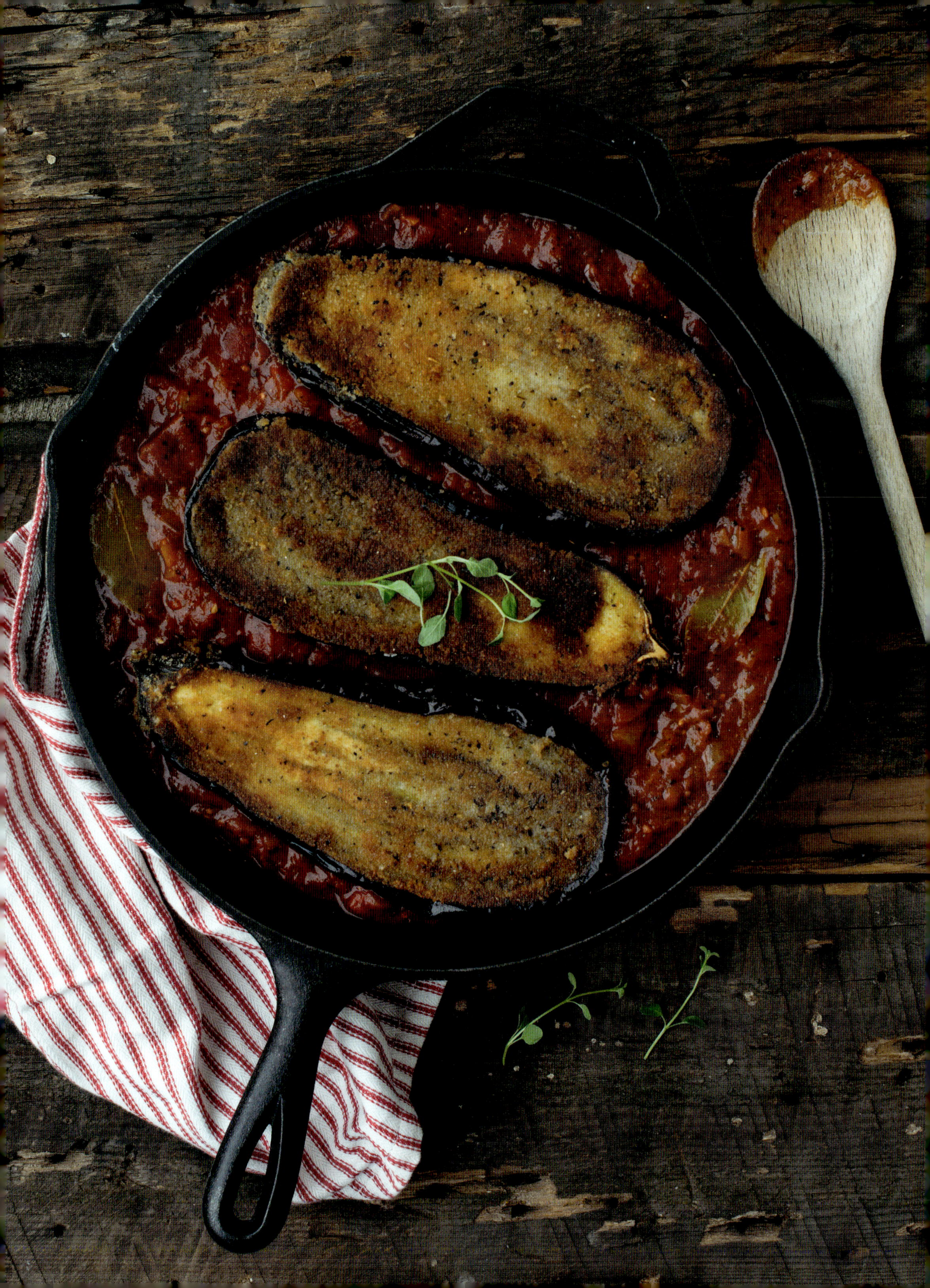

Aubergines à la parmigiana

25 min / **2 À 4 PORTIONS**

40 à 60 min

SAUCE TOMATE

3 c. à soupe (45 ml) huile d'olive

1 oignon, haché

1 carotte, hachée

2 gousses d'ail, hachées

1 c. à soupe (15 ml) basilic séché

1 c. à soupe (15 ml) origan séché

¼ c. à thé (1 ml) piment rouge broyé

3 feuilles de laurier

2 boîtes (2 x 796 ml) tomates en dés

2 c. à soupe (30 ml) pâte de tomate

2 c. à soupe (30 ml) sucre de canne

1 c. à thé (5 ml) sel

AUBERGINES

¼ tasse (60 ml) huile végétale

1 grosse aubergine

Sel

½ tasse (70 g) fécule de maïs

Eau

1 tasse (125 g) chapelure

1 c. à thé (5 ml) origan séché

PRÉPARER LA SAUCE TOMATE

1. Dans une grande casserole, faire chauffer l'huile à feu moyen-vif. Ajouter l'oignon et la carotte. Faire cuire à feu moyen de 10 à 15 minutes, ou jusqu'à ce que les légumes soient tendres (ne pas les faire dorer).
2. Ajouter l'ail et poursuivre la cuisson pendant 1 minute.
3. Ajouter le basilic, l'origan, le piment rouge broyé, les feuilles de laurier, les tomates, la pâte de tomate, le sucre de canne et le sel. Porter à ébullition, réduire le feu et laisser mijoter de 30 à 45 minutes.

ENTRE-TEMPS, PRÉPARER LES AUBERGINES

1. Préchauffer le four à 375 °F (190 °C).
2. Huiler généreusement une plaque à pâtisserie.
3. Trancher l'aubergine dans le sens de la longueur (les tranches devraient avoir environ ¾ po/2 cm d'épaisseur).
4. Saler les aubergines sur les deux côtés et les laisser reposer pendant 5 minutes.
5. Entre-temps, préparer trois récipients. Verser la fécule de maïs dans le premier bol, un peu d'eau dans le deuxième, et la chapelure et l'origan dans le troisième.
6. Prendre une première tranche d'aubergine et l'enrober de fécule de maïs (secouer un peu pour en enlever l'excédent). Ensuite, immerger rapidement l'aubergine dans l'eau, puis l'enrober généreusement de chapelure. Répéter l'opération avec chaque tranche d'aubergine.
7. Disposer les tranches sur la plaque à pâtisserie, en prenant soin de les retourner afin de répartir l'huile sur les deux côtés.
8. Faire griller au four pendant environ 20 minutes, en retournant les aubergines à mi-cuisson.
9. Servir sur la sauce tomate.

Cari de courge

30 min / **4 PORTIONS**

55 à 75 min

INGRÉDIENTS

1 courge Butternut

1 oignon, haché

2 c. à soupe (30 ml) huile végétale

½ c. à thé (2,5 ml) graines de moutarde

2 c. à thé (10 ml) poudre de cari

½ c. à thé (2,5 ml) cannelle moulue

½ c. à thé (2,5 ml) curcuma

½ c. à thé (2,5 ml) cumin moulu

1 c. à thé (5 ml) sambal oelek
ou ¼ c. à thé (1 ml) piment rouge broyé

1 c. à thé (5 ml) sirop d'érable

1 tasse (250 ml) lait de coco

1 tomate, coupée en dés

1 c. à thé (5 ml) sel

Poivre, au goût

PRÉPARATION

1. Préchauffer le four à 375°F (190°C).
2. Éplucher la courge, l'épépiner et la couper en cubes, puis la déposer dans un plat allant au four. Réserver.
3. Dans une casserole, faire attendrir l'oignon dans l'huile. (Ajouter un peu d'eau, au besoin.)
4. Ajouter les graines de moutarde, la poudre de cari, la cannelle, le curcuma, le cumin, le sambal oelek et le sirop d'érable, puis poursuivre la cuisson pendant 2 minutes.
5. Incorporer le lait de coco, la tomate, le sel et le poivre, puis laisser mijoter pendant 5 minutes.
6. Verser le mélange sur la courge.
7. Cuire au four de 45 à 60 minutes, ou jusqu'à ce que la courge soit tendre et dorée sur le dessus. Déguster.

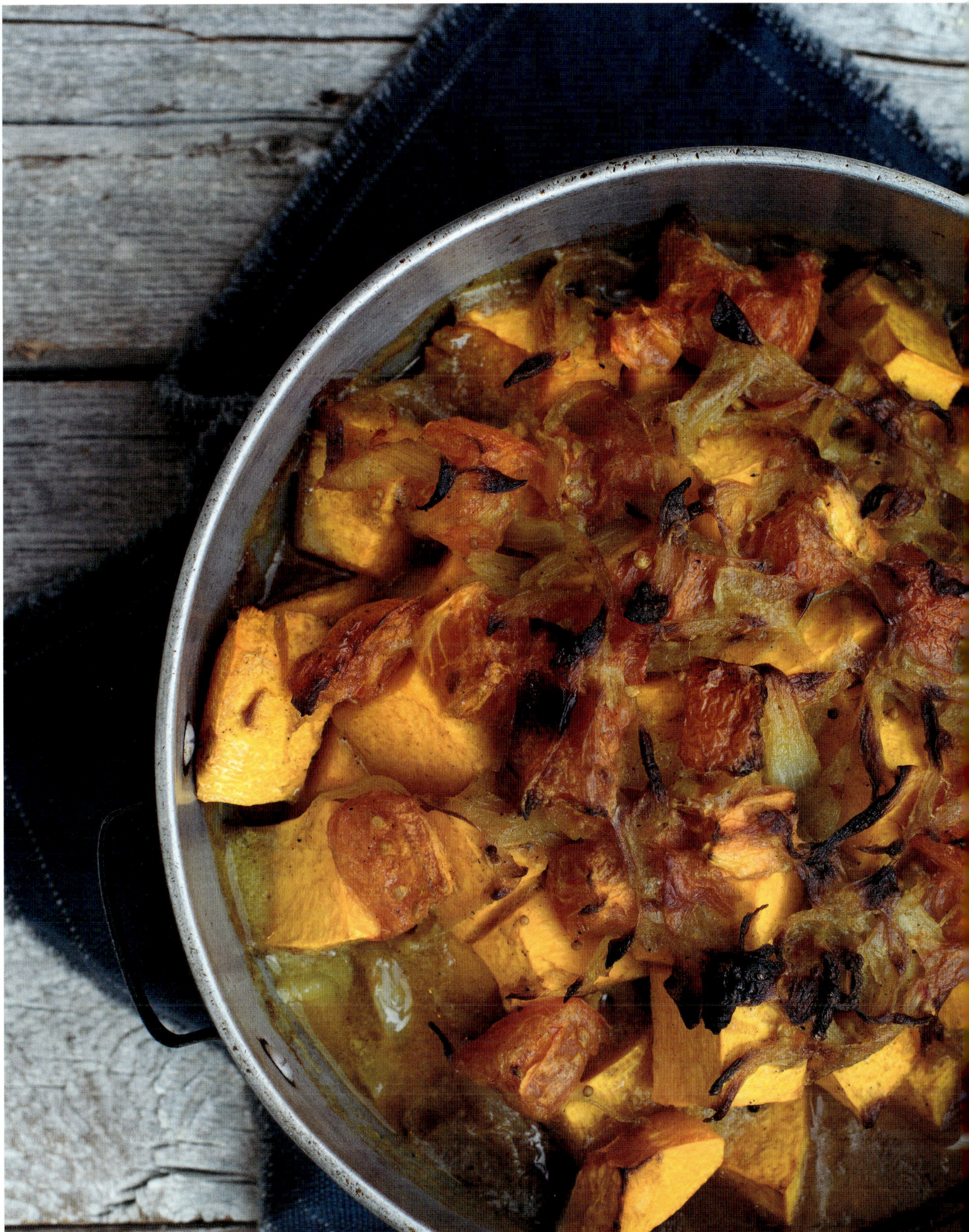

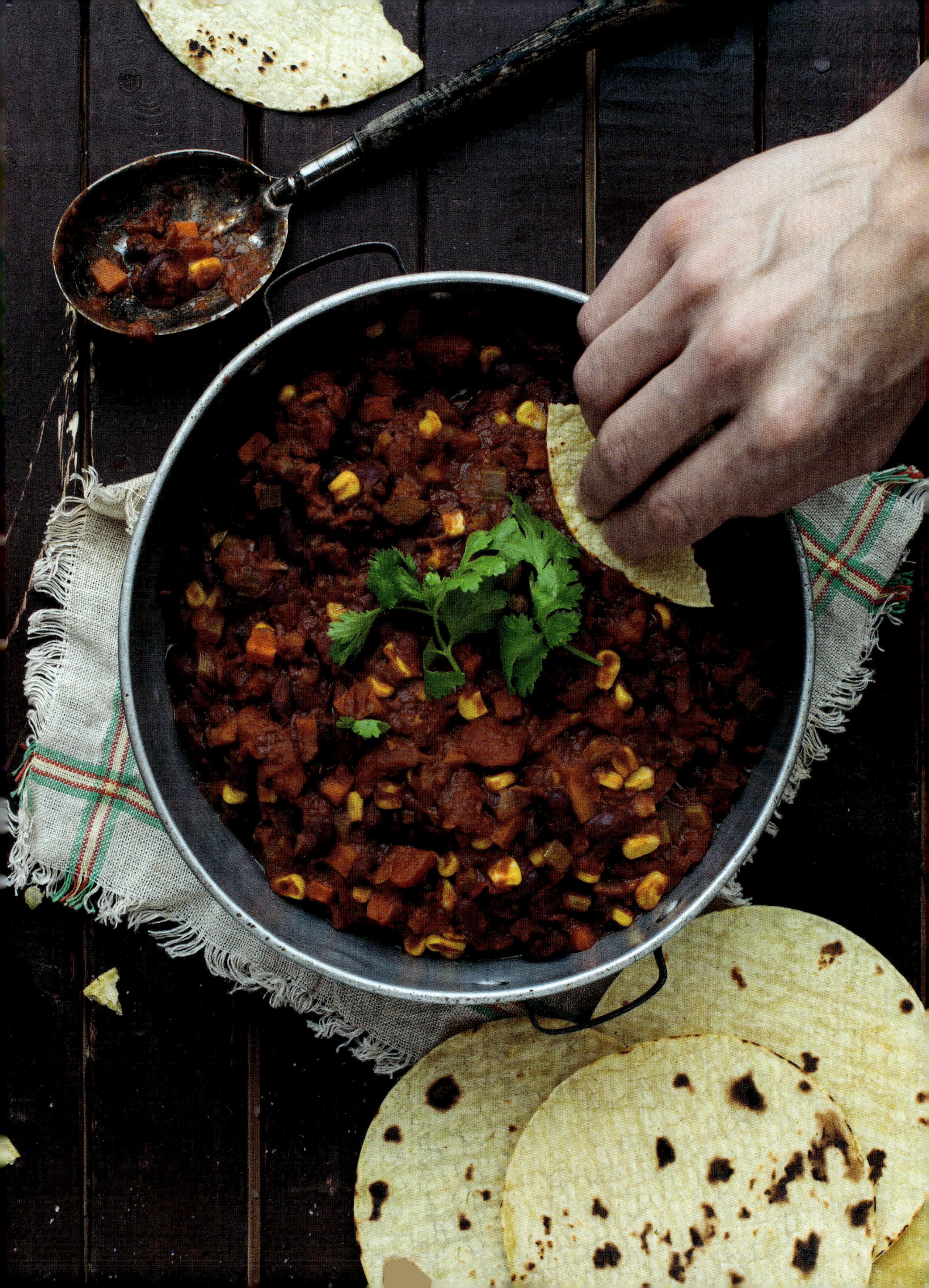

Chili sin carne

30 min / **4 À 6 PORTIONS**

70 min

INGRÉDIENTS

1 oignon, émincé

2 c. à soupe (30 ml) huile végétale

2 branches de céleri, hachées

2 carottes, émincées

1 c. à soupe (15 ml) assaisonnement au chili

1 c. à thé (5 ml) cumin moulu

1 c. à thé (5 ml) coriandre moulue

½ c. à thé (2,5 ml) piment rouge broyé

1 c. à soupe (15 ml) cacao en poudre

2 c. à thé (10 ml) ail, haché

¼ tasse (50 g) cassonade

Sel et poivre, au goût

1 boîte (540 ml) haricots rouges, rincés et égouttés

1 tasse (150 g) maïs en grains surgelé

2 boîtes (2 x 796 ml) tomates en dés

PRÉPARATION

1. Dans une casserole, faire revenir l'oignon dans l'huile pendant 2 minutes. Ajouter le céleri et les carottes. Saler et poursuivre la cuisson pendant 5 minutes.
2. Ajouter l'assaisonnement au chili, le cumin, la coriandre, le piment, le cacao, l'ail, la cassonade, le sel et le poivre. Bien mélanger et faire revenir pendant 2 minutes.
3. Incorporer les haricots rouges, le maïs et les tomates.
4. Laisser mijoter pendant 1 heure, puis servir bien chaud avec du riz ou comme garniture à tacos.

Dhal

15 min / **4 PORTIONS**

20 min

INGRÉDIENTS

1 tasse (190 g) lentilles corail, rincées

2 ½ tasses (625 ml) eau

2 oignons moyens, hachés

¼ tasse (60 ml) huile d'olive ou de sésame

½ c. à thé (2,5 ml) graines de cumin

1 ½ c. à thé (8 ml) poudre de cari

½ c. à thé (2,5 ml) curcuma

½ c. à thé (2,5 ml) coriandre moulue

1 c. à soupe (15 ml) ail, haché

1 c. à soupe (15 ml) gingembre frais, haché

2 c. à soupe (30 ml) pâte de tomate

1 tomate, coupée en morceaux

Sel et poivre, au goût

Coriandre, pour garnir

PRÉPARATION

1. Déposer les lentilles dans une marmite. Ajouter l'eau et porter à ébullition. Réduire le feu et laisser mijoter pendant 12 minutes. Réserver.
2. Dans une casserole, faire revenir les oignons dans l'huile à feu moyen-vif pendant environ 10 minutes, ou jusqu'à ce qu'ils soient tendres. Ajouter un peu d'eau, au besoin.
3. Ajouter les graines de cumin, la poudre de cari, le curcuma, la coriandre, l'ail, le gingembre, la pâte de tomate et la tomate.
4. Saler et poivrer, puis poursuivre la cuisson pendant quelques minutes.
5. Ajouter les lentilles cuites et mélanger. Garnir de coriandre et servir.

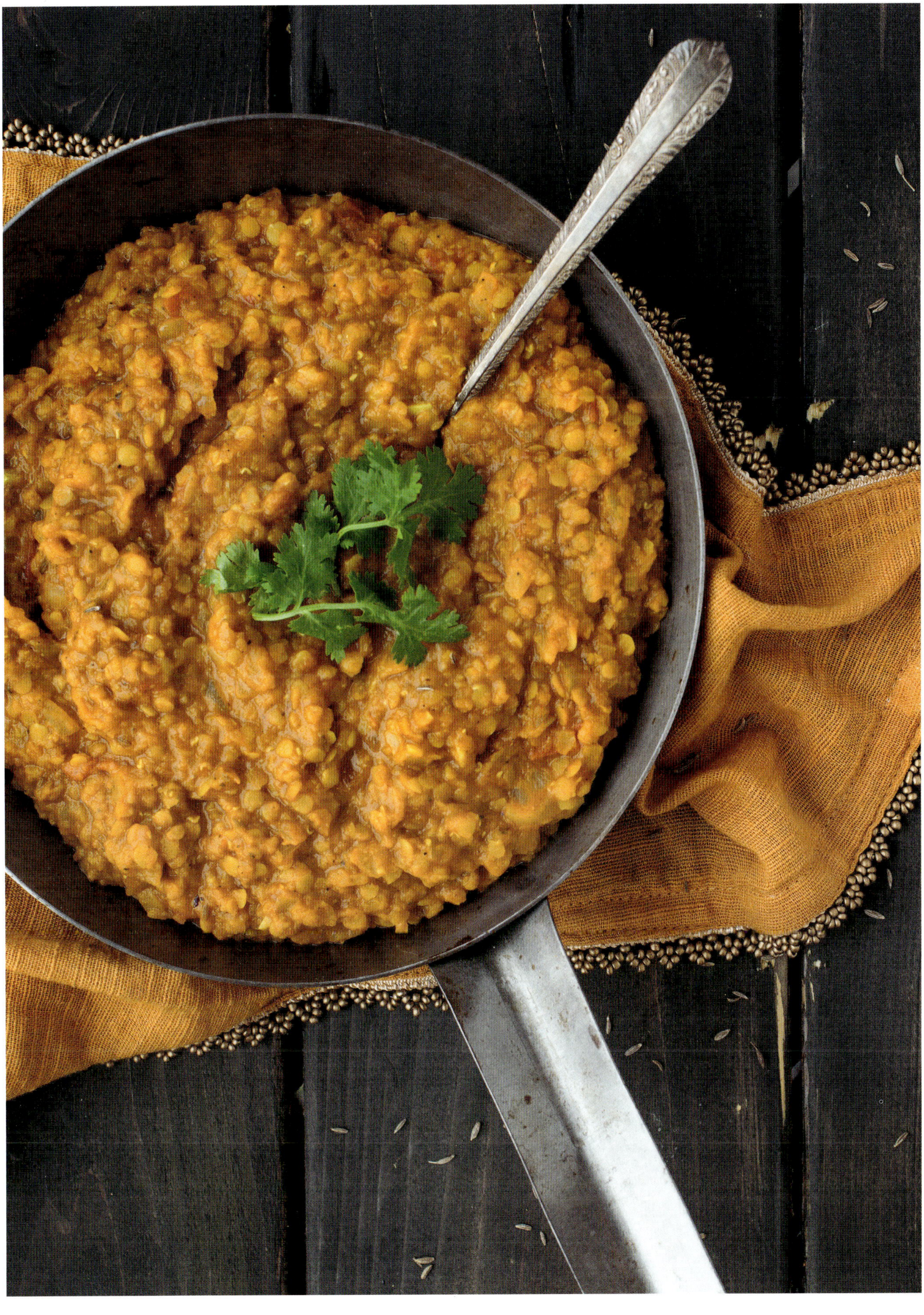

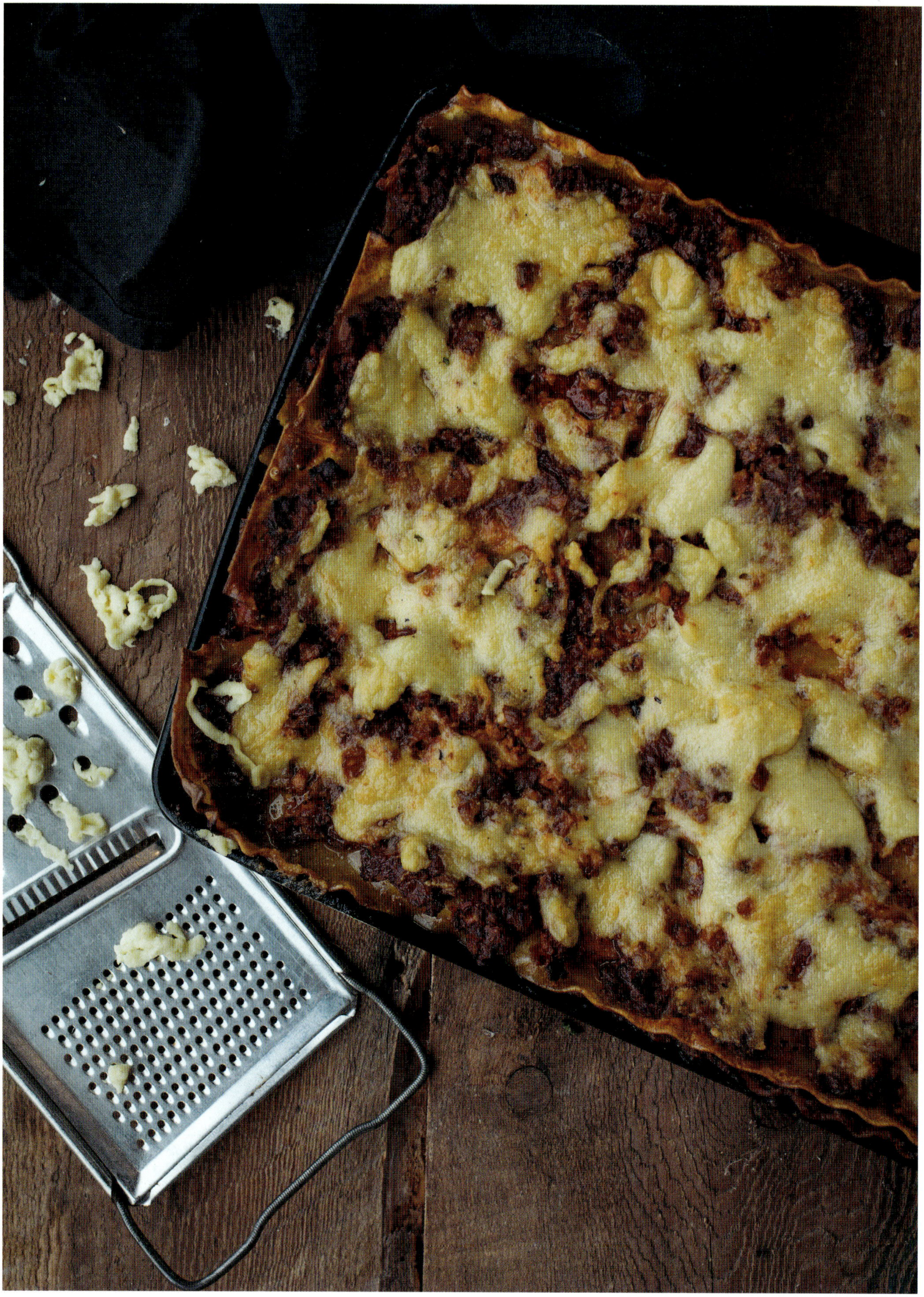

Lasagne à l'aubergine et à la sauce bolognaise au tofu

40 min / **6 PORTIONS**

145 min
90 min (sauce) + 55 min (lasagne)

SAUCE BOLOGNAISE AU TOFU

1 bloc (454 g) tofu ferme, coupé en gros dés

3 c. à soupe (45 ml) huile végétale

1 oignon, haché

3 branches de céleri, émincées

2 carottes, hachées

1 c. à thé (5 ml) sel

¼ tasse (60 ml) sauce soya

¼ tasse (50 g) cassonade, sucre de canne ou sirop d'érable

3 gousses d'ail, hachées

2 c. à soupe (30 ml) basilic séché

2 c. à soupe (30 ml) origan séché

½ c. à thé (2,5 ml) piment rouge broyé

3 boîtes (3 x 796 ml) tomates en dés

Sel et poivre, au goût

LASAGNE

12 pâtes à lasagne

1 aubergine, tranchée

10 tasses (2,5 L) sauce bolognaise au tofu

Mozzarella végane (voir recette p. 132), au goût

PRÉPARER LA SAUCE BOLOGNAISE AU TOFU

1. Broyer le tofu au robot culinaire ou à la fourchette. Réserver.
2. Dans une grande casserole, faire chauffer l'huile. Ajouter l'oignon, le céleri, les carottes et le sel. Faire cuire pendant environ 15 minutes à feu moyen-vif, afin d'attendrir les légumes.
3. Ajouter le tofu broyé, la sauce soya, la cassonade, l'ail, le basilic, l'origan, le piment, les tomates, le sel et le poivre. Couvrir et laisser mijoter pendant 45 minutes.
4. Retirer le couvercle de la casserole et poursuivre la cuisson pendant 30 minutes, ou jusqu'à ce que la sauce ait la consistance désirée.

MONTER LA LASAGNE

1. Préchauffer le four à 375 °F (190 °C).
2. Dans une casserole d'eau bouillante salée, cuire les pâtes jusqu'à ce qu'elles soient *al dente*. Rincer les pâtes sous l'eau froide, les égoutter, puis les huiler légèrement. Réserver.
3. Dans un plat de cuisson de 13 po x 9 po (33 cm x 23 cm), répartir le quart de la sauce. Couvrir d'un rang de lasagnes.
4. Ajouter un autre quart de la sauce, puis couvrir d'un autre rang de lasagnes.
5. Ajouter un autre quart de la sauce, puis un rang de tranches d'aubergine. Couvrir d'un rang de pâtes. Ajouter le reste de la sauce et parsemer de la mozzarella végane.
6. Cuire au four pendant environ 45 minutes, ou jusqu'à ce que la lasagne soit bouillonnante. Servir bien chaud.

Koftas de courgettes et de carottes

30 min / **4 PORTIONS**

20 à 30 min

KOFTAS

1 boîte (540 ml) pois chiches, rincés et égouttés

1 oignon, haché

2 c. à soupe (30 ml) huile d'olive (+ 2 c. à soupe/30 ml pour huiler la plaque)

2 courgettes, râpées

3 carottes, râpées

1 c. à thé (5 ml) sel

1 c. à thé (5 ml) cumin moulu

1 c. à soupe (15 ml) poudre de cari

¼ tasse (20 g) levure alimentaire

1 tasse (120 g) farine de pois chiches

½ tasse (125 ml) eau

SAUCE

1 boîte (400 ml) lait de coco

1 c. à soupe (15 ml) poudre de cari

¼ c. à thé (1 ml) piment rouge broyé

1 c. à soupe (15 ml) sucre de canne

¼ tasse (20 g) levure alimentaire

½ c. à thé (2,5 ml) sel

PRÉPARER LES KOFTAS

1. Préchauffer le four à 375 °F (190 °C).
2. À l'aide d'un pilon à pommes de terre, piler les pois chiches grossièrement. Réserver.
3. Dans une casserole à fond épais, faire revenir l'oignon dans l'huile pendant 4 minutes, ou jusqu'à ce qu'il ait ramolli.
4. Ajouter les courgettes et les carottes râpées, puis poursuivre la cuisson de 3 à 4 minutes.
5. Ajouter les pois chiches, le sel, le cumin, la poudre de cari, la levure alimentaire, la farine de pois chiches et l'eau.
6. Bien mélanger et retirer du feu.
7. Huiler une plaque à pâtisserie de 17 po x 12 po (43 cm x 30 cm).
8. Façonner des boules avec la préparation de pois chiches et les disposer sur la plaque à pâtisserie.
9. Cuire au four de 20 à 30 minutes.

PRÉPARER LA SAUCE

1. Dans une casserole, mélanger tous les ingrédients de la sauce et porter à ébullition. Laisser réduire à feu moyen pendant 5 minutes.
2. Servir les koftas nappés de la sauce.

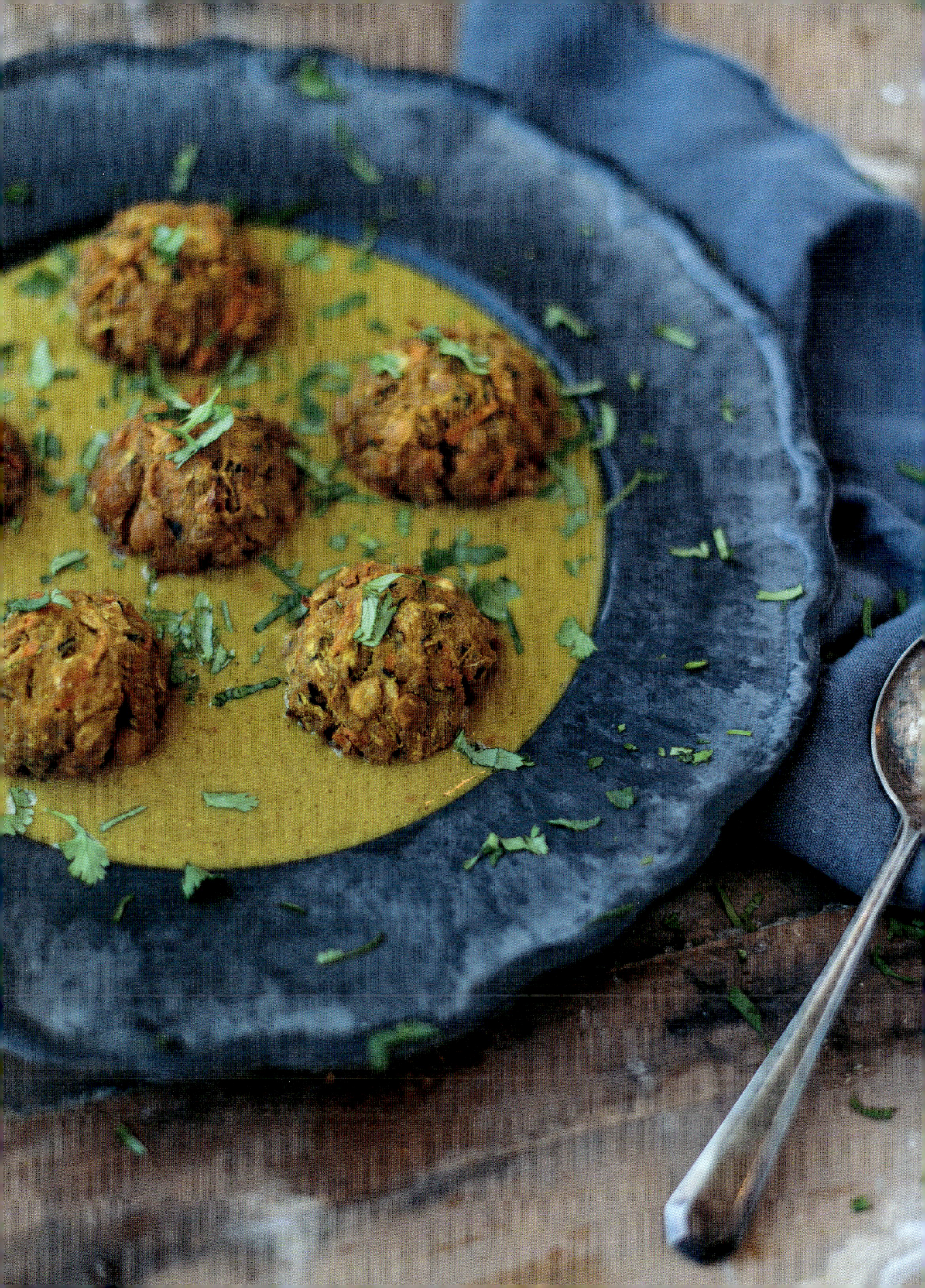

Tacos

20 min / **16 TACOS**

50 min

JACQUIER GRILLÉ

2 c. soupe (30 ml) huile végétale

1 oignon, émincé

2 boîtes (2 x 20 oz) jacquier (*jackfruit*) en saumure (pas dans le sirop)

1 tasse (250 ml) bouillon de légumes

¼ tasse (60 ml) ketchup

1 c. à soupe (15 ml) poudre de chili

1 c. à thé (5 ml) poudre d'oignon

3 c. à soupe (45 ml) mélasse

1 c. à thé (5 ml) cacao en poudre

1 c. à thé (5 ml) vinaigre de cidre

1 c. à thé (5 ml) sel

16 petits tortillas

Bruschetta mexicaine (voir recette p. 68)

Avocat, coupé en dés

Oignon rouge, émincé

Oignons rouges marinés (voir recette p. 208)

Fines herbes fraîches

Quartiers de lime

PRÉPARER LE JACQUIER

1. Préchauffer le four à 350°F (180°C).
2. Dans une casserole, faire revenir l'oignon dans l'huile pendant 2 minutes. Égoutter le jacquier, en retirer les pépins et l'ajouter à l'oignon. Poursuivre la cuisson pendant 2 minutes.
3. Ajouter le reste des ingrédients, puis porter à ébullition. Réduire le feu, couvrir et laisser mijoter pendant 10 minutes.
4. Transférer dans un plat allant au four. Cuire au four pendant 45 minutes.
5. Retirer le jacquier du four, puis l'effilocher avec une fourchette.

ASSEMBLER LES TACOS

1. Garnir les tortillas du jacquier effiloché, de bruschetta, d'avocat, d'oignon et de fines herbes. Servir avec des quartiers de lime.

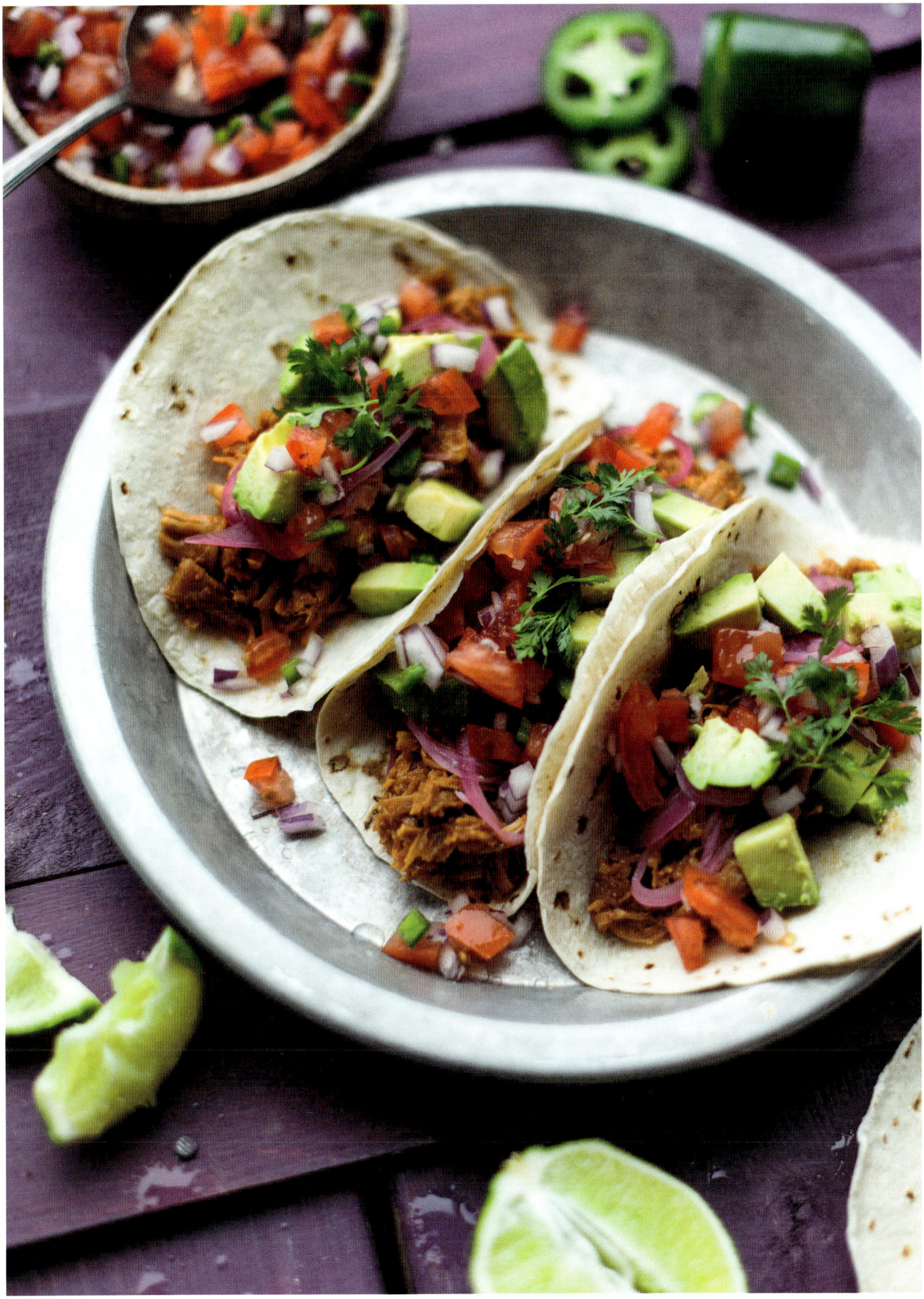

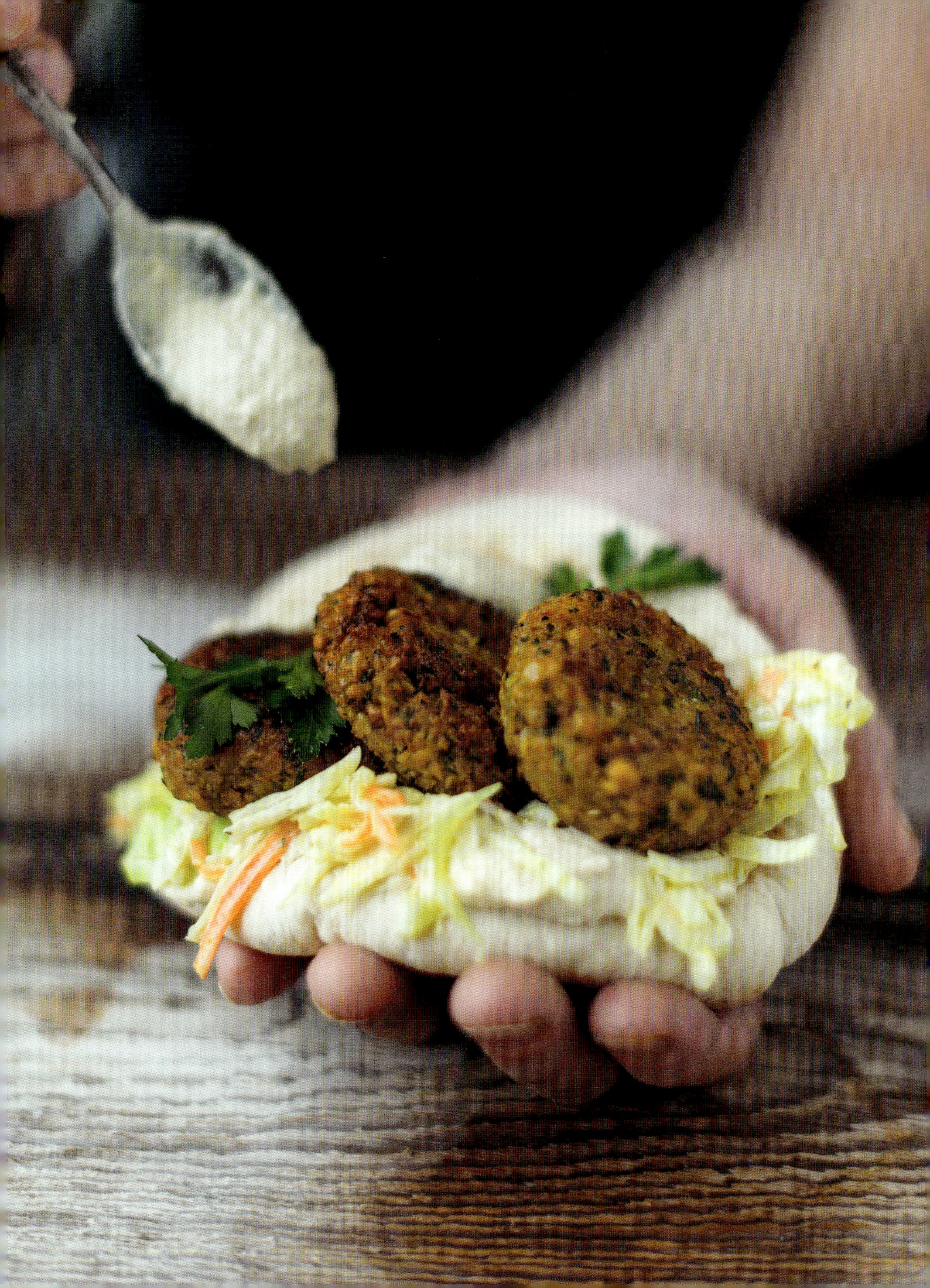

Falafels

30 min / **12 FALAFELS**

25 à 30 min

12 à 24 h

INGRÉDIENTS

1 tasse (255 g) pois chiches secs*

1 oignon, coupé en quartiers

3/4 tasse (30 g) persil plat, haché

2 gousses d'ail, hachées

1/3 tasse (40 g) amandes en bâtonnets

1 c. à thé (5 ml) cumin

1 c. à thé (5 ml) sel

Le jus de 1 citron

1 c. à thé (5 ml) sauce harissa (ou 1 c. à soupe/15 ml, si vous préférez la version épicée)

1 c. à soupe (15 ml) sirop d'érable

1/2 c. à thé (2,5 ml) bicarbonate de sodium

1/2 tasse (75 g) farine

Huile végétale

* Ne pas utiliser de pois chiches en boîte pour cette recette.

PRÉPARATION

1. Faire tremper les pois chiches dans l'eau de 12 à 24 heures. Bien rincer et égoutter. (Ils auront doublé de volume, ce qui vous fournira les 2 tasses/500 ml nécessaires à la préparation.)
2. Préchauffer le four à 375 °F (190 °C).
3. Au robot culinaire, broyer les pois chiches jusqu'à l'obtention d'une texture semblable à celle du couscous. (Ne pas trop broyer.)
4. Retirer les pois chiches du bol du robot culinaire, puis y mettre le reste des ingrédients, sauf la farine et l'huile. Broyer, puis verser dans un bol.
5. Ajouter les pois chiches et la farine. Bien mélanger.
6. Façonner le mélange de pois chiches en 12 petites galettes.
7. Mettre un peu d'huile dans une poêle, puis faire dorer les galettes, quelques-unes à la fois, de 2 à 3 minutes de chaque côté.
8. Déposer les galettes sur une plaque de cuisson et poursuivre la cuisson au four de 5 à 10 minutes.
9. Servir avec du coleslaw (voir recette p. 70) et du houmous (voir recette p. 194) sur du pain naan, par exemple.

Mac n' cheese

20 min / **4 PORTIONS**
15 min

PÂTES

1 boîte (375 g) macaronis

SAUCE

1 ½ tasse (375 ml) bouillon de légumes

¼ tasse (30 g) fécule de tapioca

½ tasse (65 g) noix de cajou

¼ tasse (60 ml) huile de coco désodorisée ou beurre végétalien

¼ tasse (20 g) levure alimentaire

1 c. à thé (5 ml) vinaigre de cidre

1 c. à thé (5 ml) poudre d'oignon

1 c. à thé (5 ml) poudre d'ail

1 c. à thé (5 ml) sirop d'érable

1 c. à thé (5 ml) sel

FAIRE CUIRE LES PÂTES

1. Faire cuire les pâtes selon les indications sur l'emballage. Égoutter et réserver.

PRÉPARER LA SAUCE

1. Au mélangeur, broyer tous les ingrédients.
2. Verser le mélange dans une casserole à fond épais, puis porter à ébullition en remuant constamment.
3. Laisser mijoter pendant 1 minute.
4. Ajouter les pâtes égouttées et poursuivre la cuisson quelques minutes pour réchauffer les pâtes. Déguster.

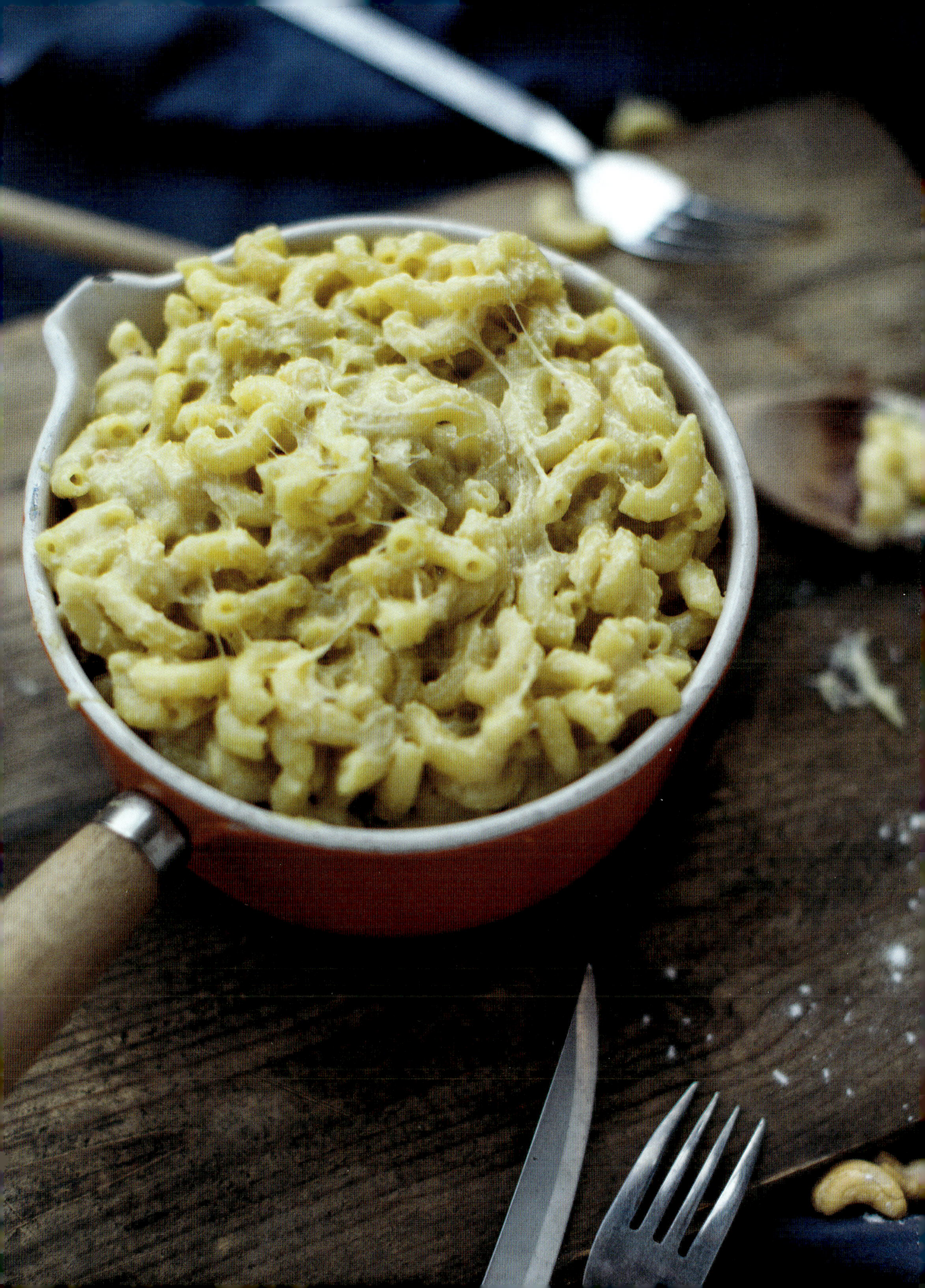

Mac foulet

45 min / **4 PORTIONS**

70 min

ESCALOPES

1 tasse (130 g) farine de gluten

¼ tasse (30 g) farine de riz

¼ tasse (20 g) levure alimentaire

1 c. à thé (5 ml) poudre d'oignon

1 c. à thé (5 ml) poudre d'ail

1 c. à thé (5 ml) basilic séché

1 c. à thé (5 ml) origan séché

¾ c. à thé (4 ml) sel

½ c. à thé (2,5 ml) épices à volaille

¾ tasse (180 ml) bouillon de légumes (+ 4 tasses/1 L)

PÂTE À FRIRE

½ tasse (75 g) farine tout usage

1 c. à thé (5 ml) poudre d'ail

1 c. à thé (5 ml) poudre d'oignon

½ c. à thé (2,5 ml) sel

Poivre, au goût

½ tasse (125 ml) lait végétal

1 c. à thé (5 ml) sirop d'érable

1 tasse (125 g) chapelure

Huile végétale, pour la friture

4 pains à hamburger

Mayonnaise végétale (voir recette p. 209)

Laitue, pour garnir

Quelques tranches de tomate, pour garnir

PRÉPARER LES ESCALOPES

1. Dans un grand bol, mélanger la farine de gluten, la farine de riz, la levure alimentaire, la poudre d'oignon, la poudre d'ail, le basilic, l'origan, le sel et les épices à volaille.
2. Ajouter le bouillon de légumes chaud et bien mélanger.
3. Pétrir la pâte de 2 à 3 minutes.
4. Façonner la pâte en boule, puis la trancher de manière à obtenir 4 escalopes.
5. Dans une casserole, porter à ébullition le reste du bouillon de légumes.
6. Plonger les escalopes dans le bouillon de légumes, puis réduire le feu au minimum. Couvrir et laisser mijoter à feu très doux pendant 1 heure.
7. Retirer du feu et laisser les escalopes refroidir dans le bouillon.

PRÉPARER LA PÂTE À FRIRE

1. Dans un bol, mélanger la farine, la poudre d'ail, la poudre d'oignon, le sel et le poivre.
2. Ajouter le lait végétal et le sirop d'érable et mélanger.
3. Dans une friteuse (ou sur la cuisinière, si on utilise une plaque à induction), faire chauffer à 325 °F (160 °C) une quantité suffisante d'huile pour recouvrir entièrement les escalopes.
4. Bien enrober chaque escalope de pâte à frire, puis la passer dans la chapelure.
5. Plonger les escalopes dans l'huile chaude et les faire frire de 4 à 5 minutes, ou jusqu'à ce qu'elles soient bien dorées.
6. Retirer les escalopes de l'huile, puis les égoutter sur un essuie-tout afin de retirer l'excédent d'huile.
7. Servir des pains à hamburger tartinés de mayonnaise végétale et garnis de laitue et de tomate.

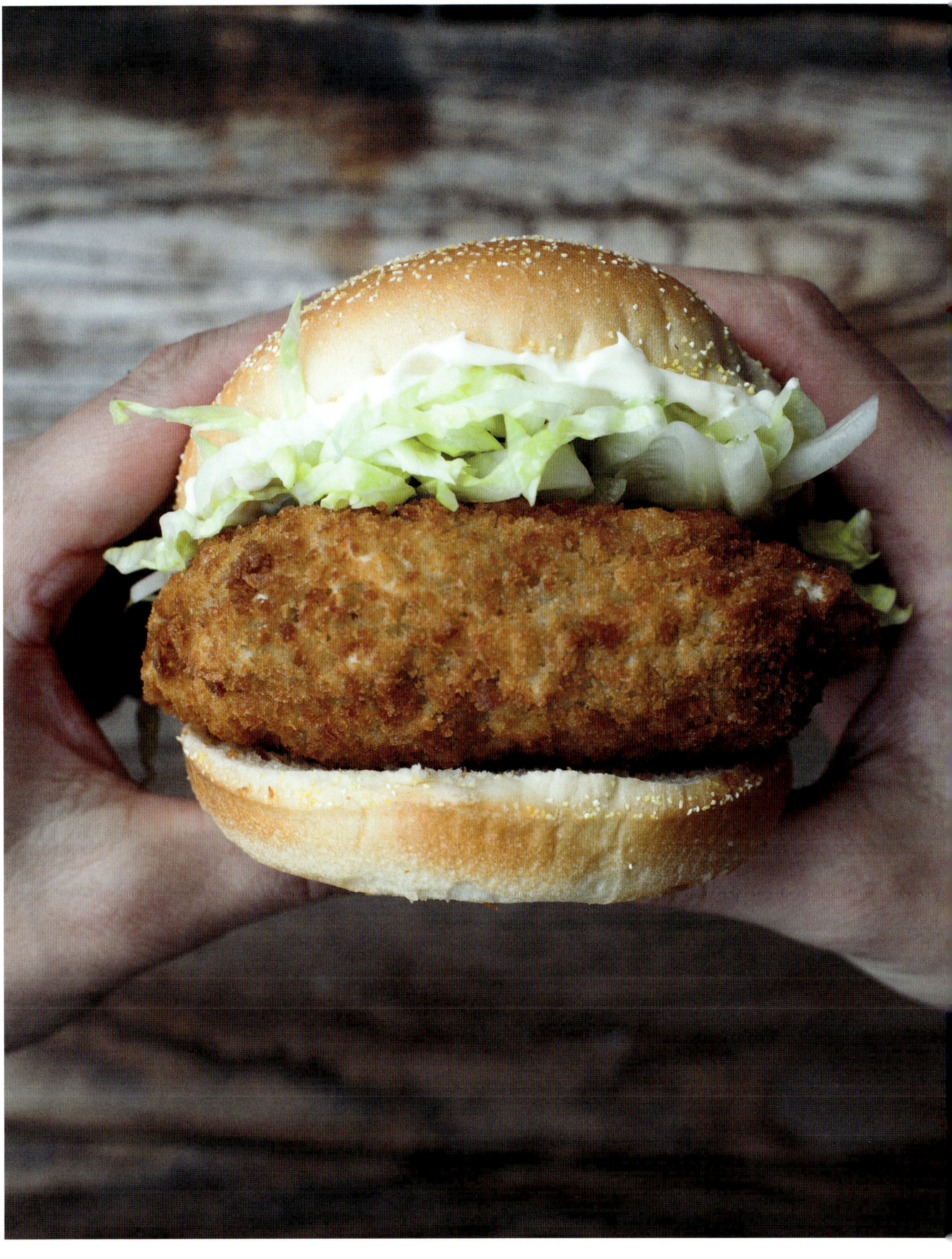

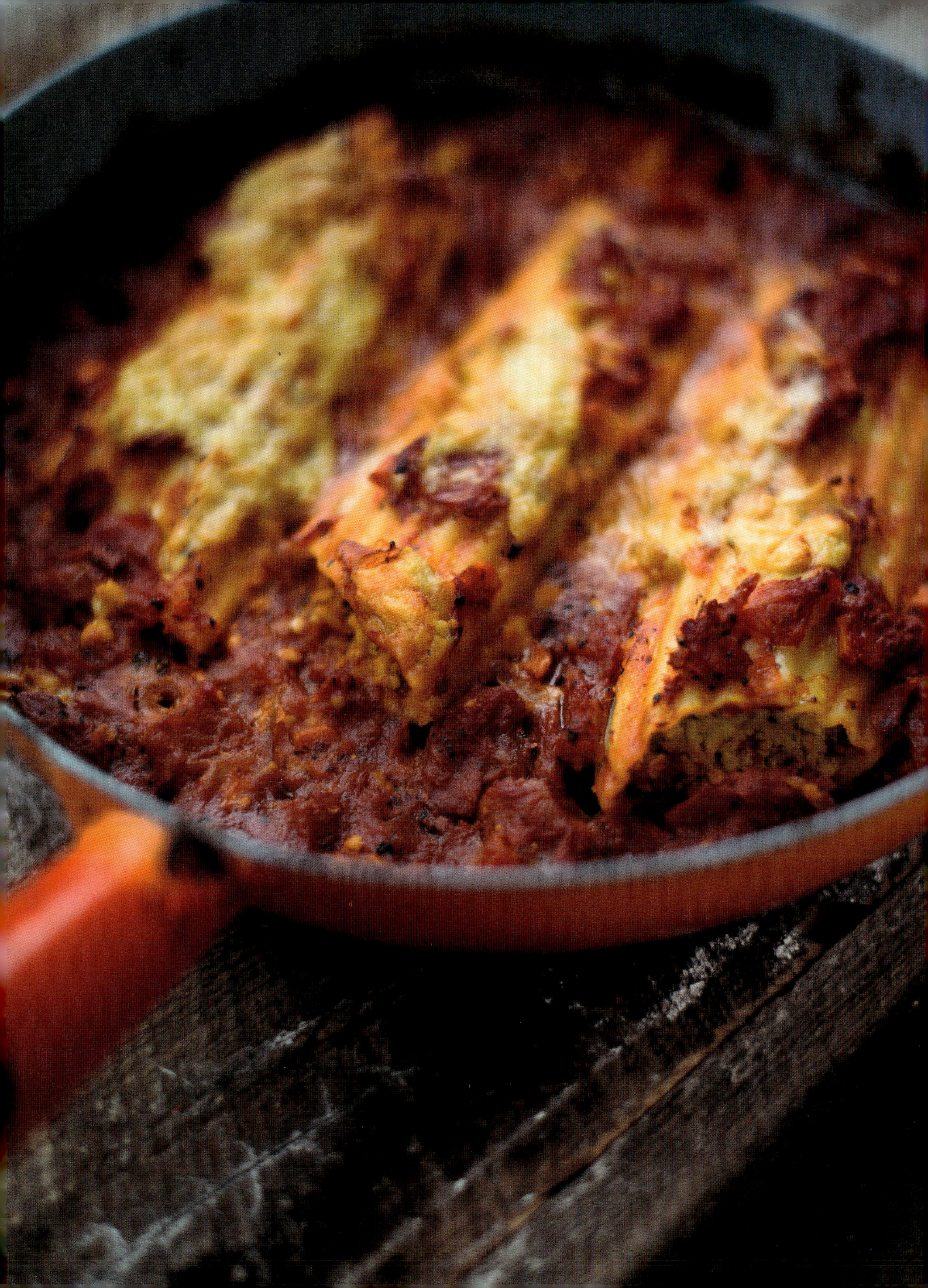

Manicottis

30 min / **4 PORTIONS**

60 min

RICOTTA DE TOFU

1 bloc (350 g) tofu ferme

1 c. à thé (5 ml) jus de citron

1 c. à thé (5 ml) basilic séché

1 c. à thé (5 ml) origan séché

¼ tasse (20 g) levure alimentaire

1 gousse d'ail, hachée

2 c. à soupe (30 ml) huile d'olive

1 c. à thé (5 ml) sirop d'érable

1 c. à thé (5 ml) sel

Poivre

MANICOTTIS

1 oignon, haché

2 c. à soupe (30 ml) huile d'olive

1 paquet (142 g) bébés épinards

1 aubergine

Sel

8 manicottis

6 tasses (1,5 L) sauce tomate (voir recette p. 103 et la doubler)

PRÉPARER LA RICOTTA DE TOFU

1. Mettre tous les ingrédients dans le bol d'un robot culinaire. Mélanger quelques secondes à la fois afin de broyer légèrement les ingrédients.

PRÉPARER LES MANICOTTIS

1. Préchauffer le four à 375 °F (190 °C).
2. Faire revenir l'oignon dans la moitié de l'huile pendant 4 minutes.
3. Ajouter les bébés épinards et poursuivre la cuisson pendant 2 minutes.
4. Ajouter à la ricotta de tofu et mélanger. Réserver.
5. Couper l'aubergine en tranches de ¾ po (2 cm) d'épaisseur. Saler généreusement et les faire revenir dans le reste de l'huile d'olive.
6. Déposer les tranches d'aubergines au fond d'un plat allant au four.
7. À l'aide d'une poche à douille, farcir les manicottis du mélange de tofu.
8. Déposer les manicottis farcis sur les aubergines et y verser la sauce.
9. Cuire au four pendant 45 minutes. Déguster.

Palak tofu

Faire pocher le tofu pendant 2 minutes dans l'eau avant de l'utiliser pour cette recette fait toute la différence. Ça lui confère une texture se rapprochant du fromage indien paneer, traditionnellement utilisé dans cette recette.

15 min / **4 PORTIONS**

20 min

INGRÉDIENTS

1 bloc (350 g) tofu ferme, coupé en dés

1 paquet (142 g) bébés épinards

1 boîte (400 ml) lait de coco

1 c. à soupe (15 ml) gingembre, haché

1 c. à soupe (15 ml) pâte de tomate (ou 2 c. à soupe/30 ml de ketchup)

2 gousses d'ail, hachées

1 c. à thé (5 ml) garam masala

1 c. à thé (5 ml) sirop d'érable

Sel, au goût

PRÉPARATION

1. Dans une casserole, porter de l'eau à ébullition, y plonger le tofu et faire bouillir pendant 2 minutes. Égoutter et réserver.
2. Dans la même casserole, mélanger le reste des ingrédients.
3. Porter à ébullition, réduire le feu et laisser mijoter pendant 15 minutes, ou jusqu'à ce que la sauce épaississe.
4. Passer la sauce au pied mélangeur ou au mélangeur, jusqu'à ce qu'elle soit lisse.
5. Remettre la sauce dans la casserole et y ajouter le tofu.
6. Réchauffer pendant 2 minutes et servir avec du riz, par exemple.

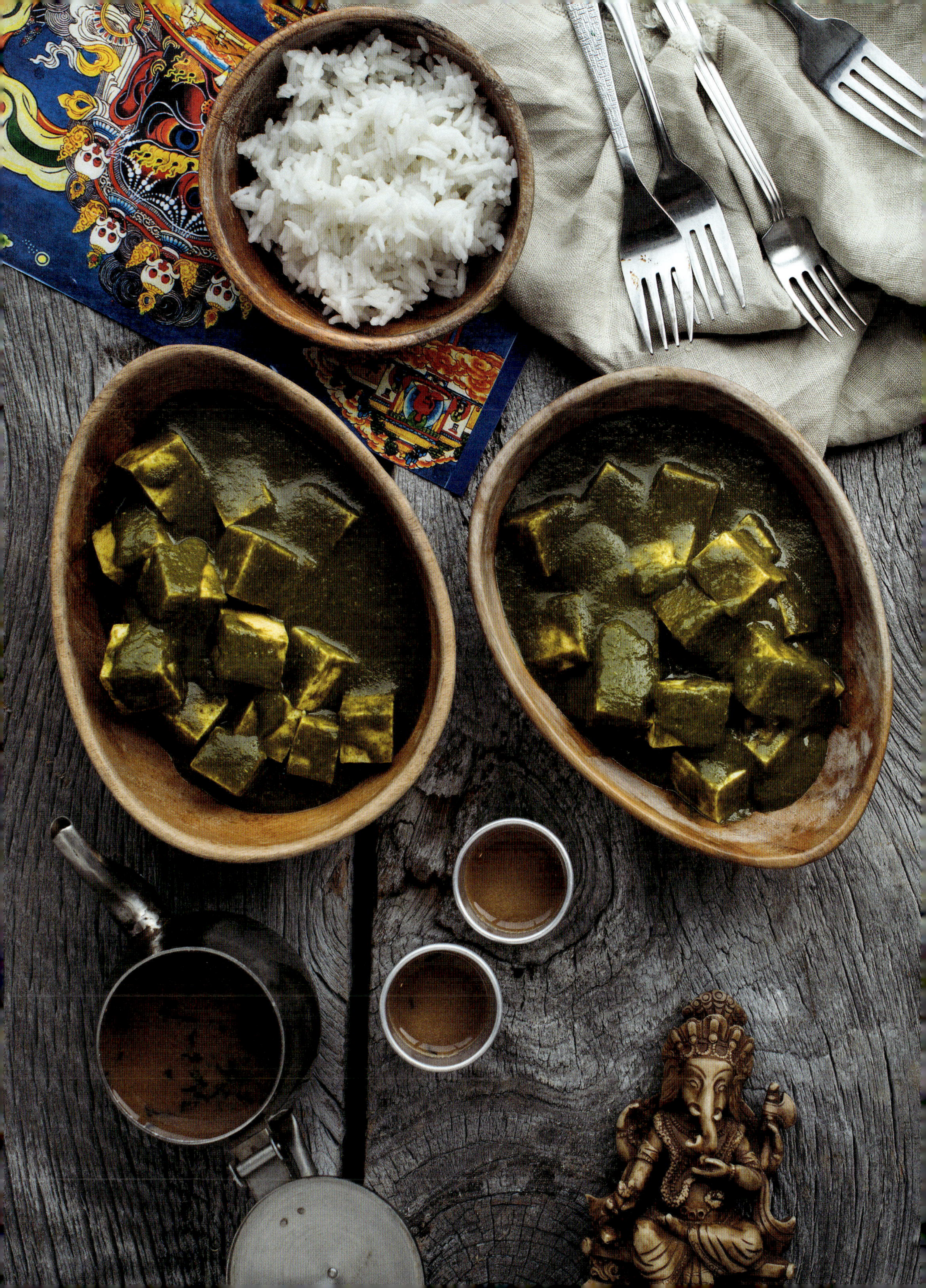

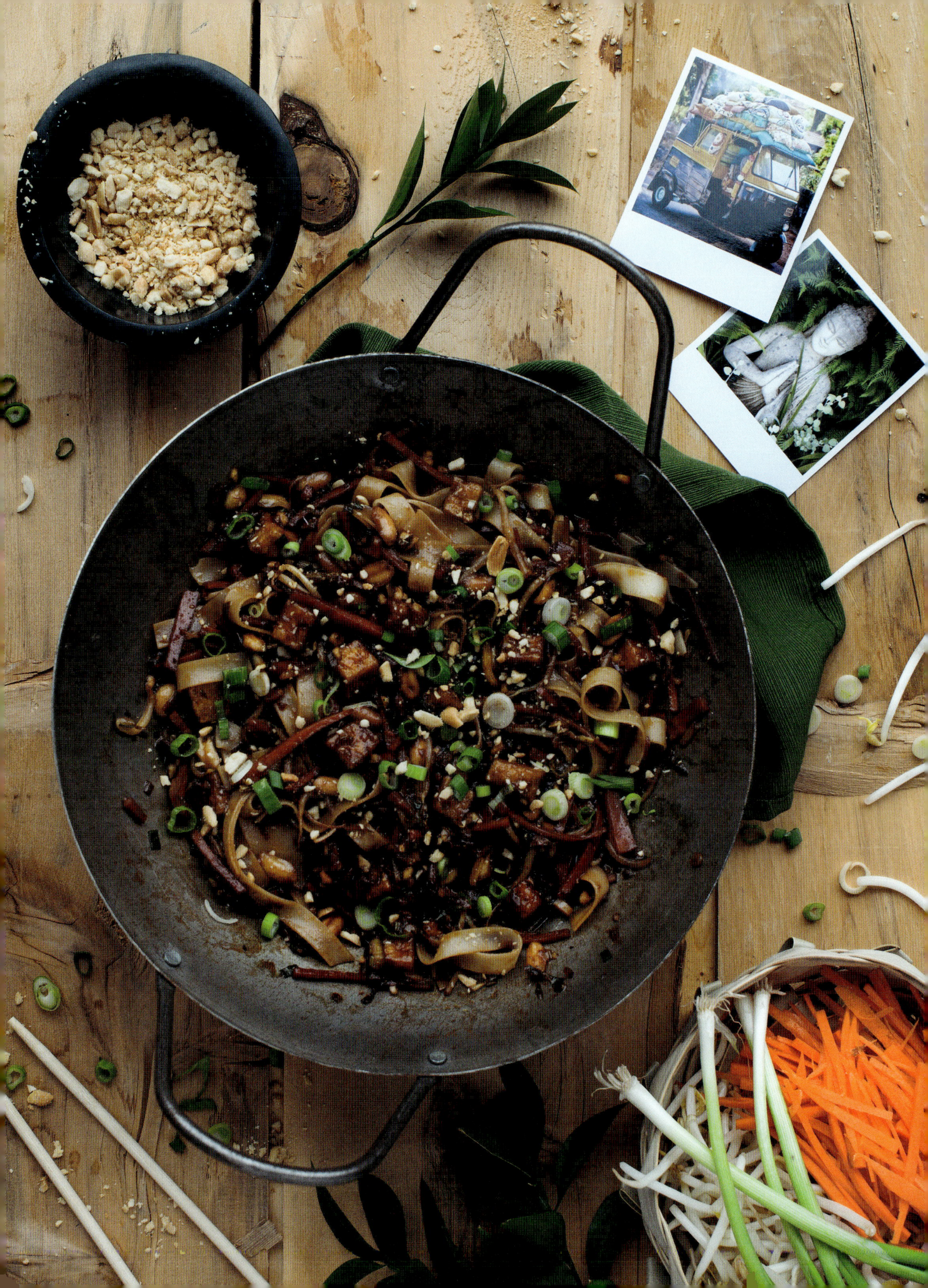

Pad thaï

La cuisine thaïe est probablement l'une des plus excitantes du monde et certainement l'une de mes favorites. Tout repose sur l'interaction entre ces quatre saveurs : salé, sucré, piquant et aigre. Lorsque l'équilibre est atteint, le résultat est spectaculaire !

30 min / **2 PORTIONS**
15 min

INGRÉDIENTS

5 oz (150 g) nouilles de riz

½ bloc (la moitié de 1 bloc de 454 g) tofu ferme, coupé en dés

¼ tasse (35 g) fécule de maïs

¼ tasse (60 ml) huile végétale

2 échalotes françaises, hachées

2 oignons verts, émincés

2 c. à thé (10 ml) ail, haché

2 carottes, coupées en julienne ou râpées

1 tomate, coupée en dés

¼ tasse (60 ml) sauce soya

¼ tasse (50 g) sucre de canne ou autre sucre

1 c. à thé (5 ml) purée de piment ou piment séché, au goût

2 tasses (150 g) fèves germées

½ tasse (75 g) arachides, hachées

2 c. à thé (10 ml) vinaigre de riz

Sel et poivre, au goût

PRÉPARATION

1. Dans un grand bol d'eau bouillante, plonger les nouilles de riz et les laisser se réhydrater pendant quelques minutes. Égoutter et réserver.
2. Enrober le tofu de la fécule de maïs. Dans un wok, faire frire le tofu dans un peu d'huile, jusqu'à ce qu'il soit doré. Retirer du wok et réserver.
3. Dans le wok, faire sauter les échalotes françaises, les oignons verts, l'ail, les carottes et la tomate dans le reste de l'huile à feu moyen-vif pendant 5 minutes.
4. Ajouter la sauce soya, le sucre et la purée de piment. Mélanger.
5. Ajouter les nouilles de riz égouttées, les fèves germées, le tofu frit, les arachides broyées et le vinaigre de riz. Poursuivre la cuisson pendant 3 minutes en remuant constamment. Déguster.

Parmentier de lentilles

Pour changer du traditionnel pâté chinois ! Lorsque vous aurez essayé la levure alimentaire dans la purée de pommes de terre, vous ne pourrez plus vous en passer.

30 min / **6 PORTIONS**

90 min

PURÉE

2 lb (1 kg) pommes de terre, pelées

⅓ tasse (25 g) levure alimentaire

1 ½ c. à thé (8 ml) sel

1 c. à thé (5 ml) poudre d'oignon

2 c. à soupe (30 ml) huile d'olive

LENTILLES

2 c. à soupe (30 ml) huile végétale

1 oignon, haché

2 carottes, hachées

10 champignons de Paris, tranchés

3 branches de céleri, émincées

2 gousses d'ail, hachées

1 c. à soupe (15 ml) pâte de tomate

3 c. à soupe (45 ml) sauce soya

1 c. à soupe (15 ml) basilic séché

1 c. à soupe (15 ml) origan séché

3 feuilles de laurier

2 c. à soupe (30 ml) sirop d'érable

1 boîte (540 ml) lentilles vertes, égouttées et rincées

½ tasse (125 ml) eau

Sel et poivre, au goût

PRÉPARER LA PURÉE

1. Dans une grande casserole, déposer les pommes de terre et les couvrir d'eau fraîche.
2. Porter à ébullition, réduire le feu, couvrir et laisser mijoter de 30 à 45 minutes.
3. Égoutter les pommes de terre et ajouter le reste des ingrédients*. Piler et réserver.

PRÉPARER LES LENTILLES

1. Préchauffer le four à 350 °F (180 °C).
2. Dans une grande casserole, chauffer l'huile à feu moyen. Ajouter les légumes et cuire de 10 à 15 minutes, ou jusqu'à ce qu'ils aient ramolli.
3. Ajouter le reste des ingrédients et cuire de 5 à 10 minutes.
4. Étendre la préparation dans un moule allant au four, puis couvrir de la purée de pommes de terre.
5. Cuire de 30 à 45 minutes. Laisser reposer pendant 10 minutes avant de servir avec une salade.

* Ajouter du bouillon de légumes ou du lait végétal pour détendre la purée, au besoin.

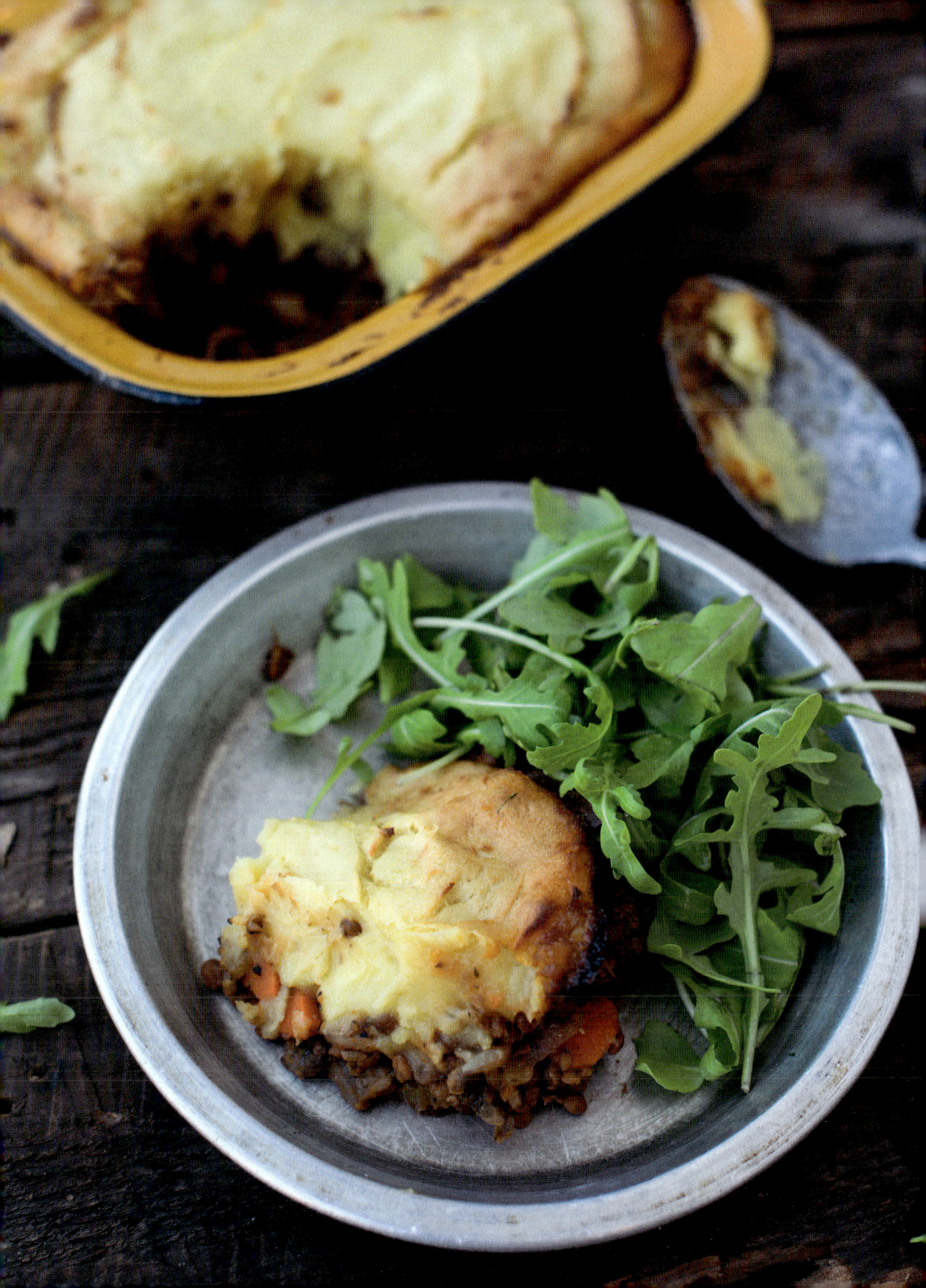

Pâtes à la puttanesca

20 min / **4 PORTIONS**

20 min

INGRÉDIENTS

6 tasses (450 g) rigatonis

4 c. à soupe (60 ml) huile d'olive

1 oignon, haché grossièrement

1 tasse (140 g) olives Kalamata, dénoyautées

1 pot (105 ml) câpres, égouttées

6 tasses (1,5 L) sauce tomate (voir recette p. 103 et la doubler)

Sel et poivre, au goût

Un peu de basilic frais

Parmesan de cajou (voir recette p. 208)

PRÉPARATION

1. Dans une grande casserole d'eau bouillante salée, cuire les pâtes jusqu'à ce qu'elles soient *al dente*. Égoutter, huiler légèrement et réserver.
2. Dans la même casserole, faire revenir l'oignon et les olives dans l'huile pendant environ 5 minutes. Ajouter les câpres, la sauce tomate et les pâtes. Poursuivre la cuisson pendant 5 minutes. Rectifier l'assaisonnement. Servir garni de basilic et de parmesan de cajou, puis arroser d'un filet d'huile d'olive.

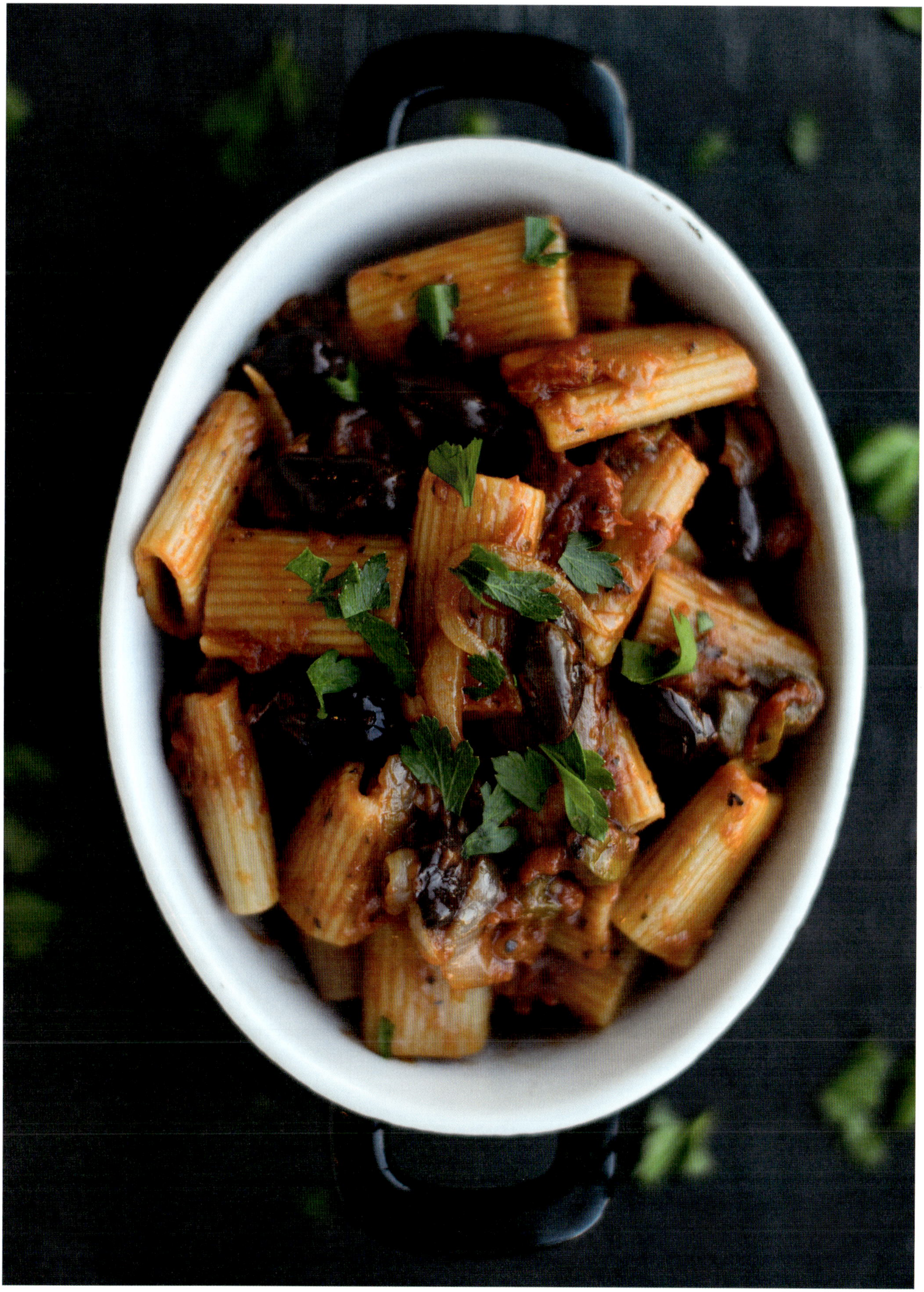

Pizzas trois façons

1 h / **3 PIZZAS**
12 à 15 min
45 min
Temps de réfrigération 2 h (mozzarella)

MOZZARELLA VÉGANE

¼ tasse (35 g) noix de cajou
1 c. à thé (5 ml) jus de citron
1 c. à thé (5 ml) sirop d'érable
2 c. à soupe (30 ml) levure alimentaire
4 c. à thé (10 g) agar agar en poudre
2 c. à soupe (30 ml) fécule de tapioca
1 c. à thé (5 ml) sel
⅓ tasse (80 ml) huile de coco désodorisée
1 ½ tasse (375 ml) eau

PÂTE À PIZZA

2 tasses (500 ml) eau tiède
1 sachet (8 g) levure
1 c. à soupe (15 ml) sucre
4 tasses (600 g) farine
1 c. à thé (5 ml) sel

3 tasses (750 ml) sauce tomate (voir recette p. 103)
Champignons coupés en tranches
Poivrons verts émincés
Pepperoni de tofu (voir recette p. 209)
Roquette
Tomates cerises

PRÉPARER LA MOZZARELLA VÉGANE

1. Faire tremper les noix de cajou dans de l'eau chaude pendant 15 minutes.
2. Égoutter et déposer les noix de cajou dans le récipient d'un mélangeur. Ajouter le reste des ingrédients et broyer jusqu'à l'obtention d'une texture crémeuse.
3. Verser le mélange dans une casserole et porter à ébullition en remuant sans arrêt. Lorsque des bulles commencent à se former à la surface du mélange, poursuivre la cuisson en remuant de 1 à 2 minutes. (La préparation aura épaissi à ce stade.)
4. Verser la préparation dans deux ramequins. Réfrigérer pendant au moins 2 heures, ou jusqu'à 5 jours.
5. Démouler la mozzarella en retournant délicatement les ramequins sur une assiette. Râper et réserver.

PRÉPARER LA PÂTE À PIZZA

1. Dans un bol, mélanger l'eau, la levure et le sucre. Laisser reposer pendant environ 5 minutes, ou jusqu'à ce que la préparation soit mousseuse.
2. Dans un grand bol, mélanger 3 tasses (450 g) de la farine et le sel. Ajouter la préparation de levure à la farine et bien mélanger. Couvrir d'un linge propre et humide. Laisser gonfler la pâte pendant environ 30 minutes dans un endroit chaud et à l'abri des courants d'air.
3. Déposer la pâte sur un plan de travail fariné ou dans le bol d'un batteur sur socle.
4. Pétrir la pâte, en ajoutant 1 tasse (150 g) de la farine, pendant environ 5 minutes, ou jusqu'à ce qu'elle soit lisse.

PRÉPARER LES PIZZAS

1. Préchauffer le four à 450 °F (230 °C).
2. Séparer la pâte en trois portions. Sur un plan de travail fariné, abaisser chaque portion de pâte en un disque de 10 po (27 cm) de diamètre, en formant une bordure épaisse.
3. Déposer chaque abaisse sur une plaque à pizza.
4. Étaler uniformément 1 tasse (250 ml) de sauce tomate sur chaque abaisse.
5. Garnir la première pizza de champignons, de poivrons et de mozzarella, la deuxième de pepperoni de tofu et de mozzarella, et la troisième de mozzarella.
6. Cuire au four de 12 à 15 minutes, ou jusqu'à ce que le fromage soit bien doré.
7. Au moment de servir, garnir la pizza à la mozzarella de roquette et de tomates cerises.

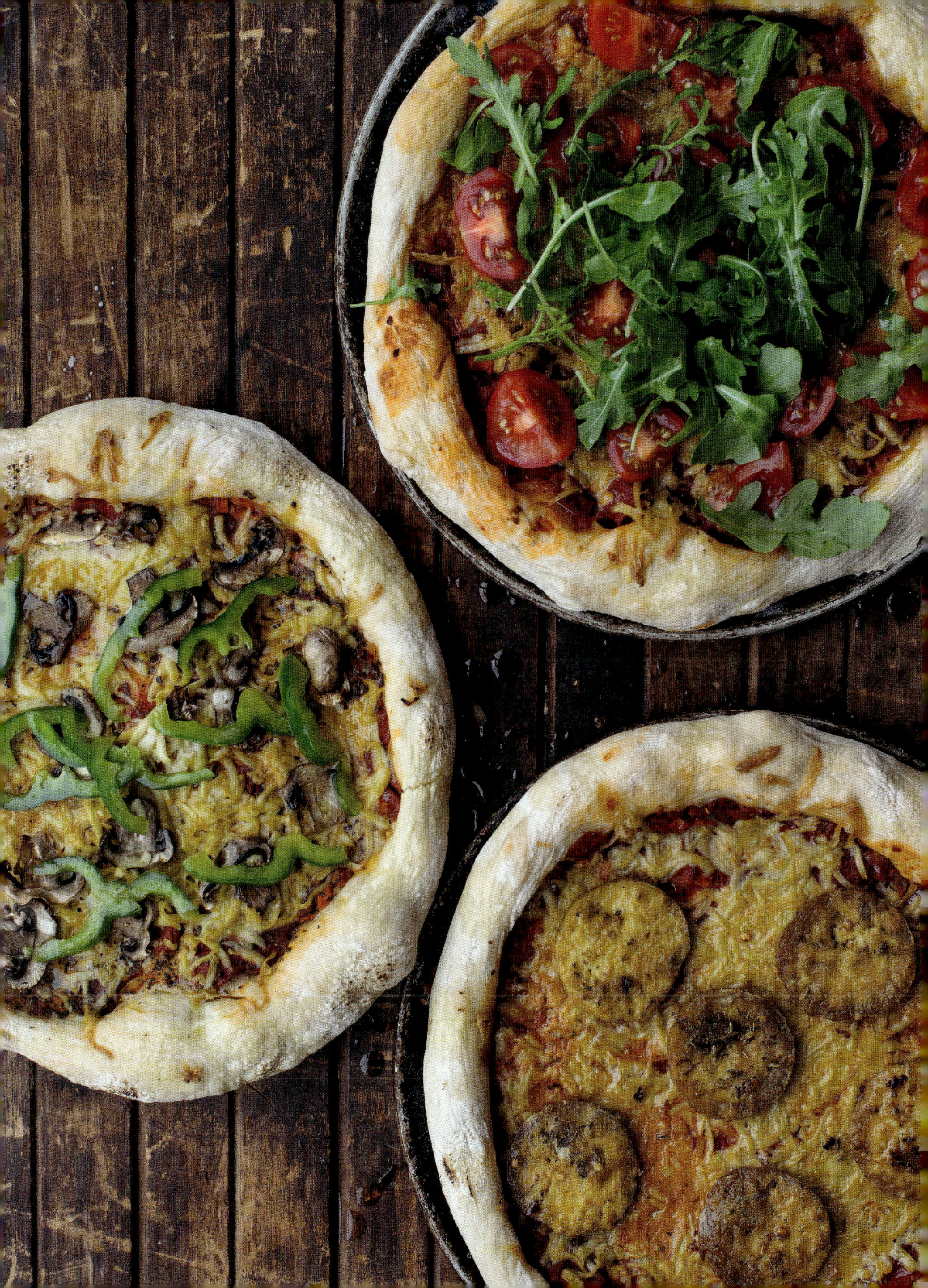

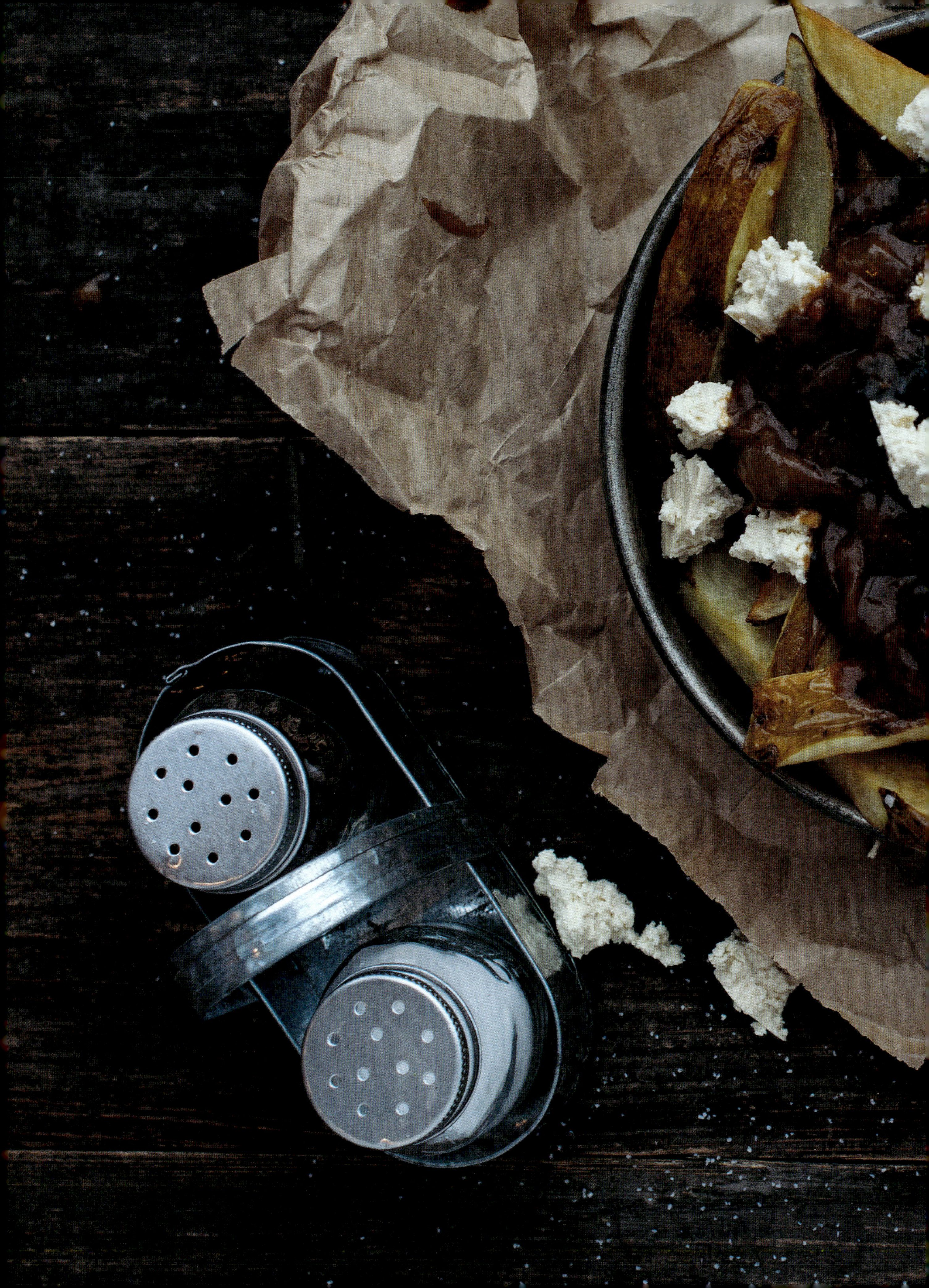

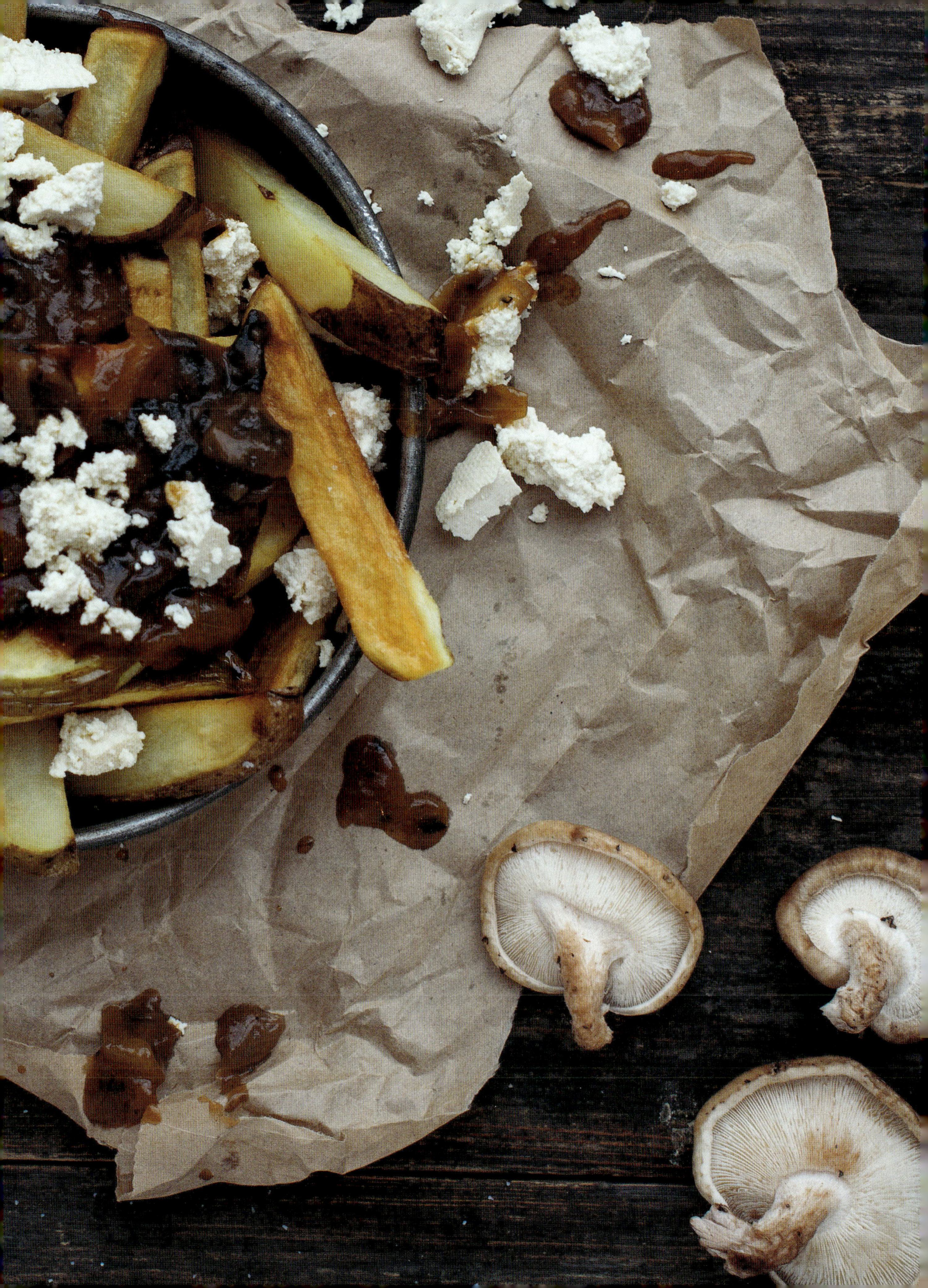

Poutine aux champignons

45 min / **2 PORTIONS**

25 min

30 min

SAUCE

1 oignon, émincé

4 c. à soupe (60 ml) huile végétale

2 tasses (150 g) champignons sauvages, émincés

¼ tasse (40 g) farine

2 tasses (500 ml) bouillon de légumes

2 c. à soupe (30 ml) miso

2 c. à soupe (30 ml) pâte de tomate

¼ c. à thé (1 ml) clou de girofle moulu

1 c. à soupe (15 ml) sirop d'érable

1 c. à soupe (15 ml) sauce soya

1 c. à thé (5 ml) vinaigre de cidre

Sel et poivre, au goût

Huile de truffe (facultatif)

PRÉPARER LA SAUCE

1. Dans une casserole, faire revenir l'oignon dans l'huile à feu moyen pendant 5 minutes. Ajouter les champignons et poursuivre la cuisson pendant 5 minutes.
2. Saupoudrer de la farine.
3. Incorporer le bouillon de légumes petit à petit en fouettant.
4. Ajouter le reste des ingrédients et poursuivre la cuisson pendant 5 minutes.
5. Rectifier l'assaisonnement. Réserver au chaud.

TOFU EN GRAINS

1 bloc (350 g) tofu ferme

1 c. à soupe (15 ml) jus de citron

3 c. à soupe (45 ml) vinaigre de cidre

1 c. à soupe (15 ml) sirop d'érable

½ c. à thé (2,5 ml) poudre d'oignon

½ c. à thé (2,5 ml) sel

FRITES

3 grosses pommes de terre Russet, pelées

Huile végétale, pour la friture

PRÉPARER LE TOFU EN GRAINS

1. Émietter le tofu et le plonger dans l'eau bouillante, puis faire bouillir pendant 2 minutes. Égoutter et réserver.
2. Dans un bol, mélanger le reste des ingrédients pour la marinade.
3. Ajouter le tofu, mélanger et laisser mariner pendant 30 minutes. Réserver.

PRÉPARER LES FRITES

1. Couper les pommes de terre en bâtonnets d'environ ¼ po (½ cm) d'épaisseur. Réserver les pommes de terre dans l'eau fraîche jusqu'au moment de la cuisson afin d'éviter qu'elles ne s'oxydent et ne brunissent.
2. Dans une friteuse, préchauffer l'huile à 325°F (160°C).
3. Égoutter les pommes de terre et bien les éponger avec un linge propre, puis les placer dans le panier de la friteuse. Plonger le panier dans l'huile chaude de la friteuse et cuire environ 3 minutes.
4. Retirer le panier de la friteuse et laisser reposer les frites.
5. Augmenter la température de l'huile de la friteuse à 350°F (180°C).
6. Remettre les pommes de terre dans la friteuse et cuire pendant 4 minutes, ou jusqu'à ce que les frites soient bien dorées. Retirer les frites de la friteuse et les laisser égoutter sur du papier absorbant. Saler et réserver au chaud, au besoin.

ASSEMBLER LA POUTINE

1. Répartir les frites dans deux assiettes, garnir du tofu en grains et napper de la sauce. Déguster.

Quinoa forestier

Sans gluten et reconnu pour sa valeur nutritive exceptionnelle, le quinoa est une excellente solution de rechange aux céréales traditionnelles. Et quoi de mieux que des champignons pour le mettre en valeur?

30 min / **2 PORTIONS**

20 à 25 min

1 tasse (180 g) quinoa, bien rincé

2 tasses (500 ml) bouillon de légumes ou eau

1 oignon, haché

2 ½ tasses (225 g) champignons sauvages, émincés

2 c. à soupe (30 ml) huile d'olive

1 c. à soupe (15 ml) vinaigre de cidre

2 c. à soupe (30 ml) sauce soya

1 c. à soupe (15 ml) sirop d'érable

1 c. à thé (5 ml) sambal oelek ou 1 pincée de piment rouge séché

½ tasse (75 g) petits pois surgelés

Sel et poivre, au goût

Quelques tranches d'avocat, pour garnir

Quelques amandes effilées, pour garnir

PRÉPARATION

1. Déposer le quinoa dans une casserole et ajouter le bouillon de légumes. Porter à ébullition, réduire le feu, couvrir et laisser mijoter pendant 12 minutes.
2. Retirer du feu et laisser reposer à couvert pendant 10 minutes. Réserver.
3. Dans une casserole, faire sauter l'oignon et les champignons dans l'huile à feu moyen-vif de 5 à 10 minutes.
4. Ajouter le quinoa cuit, le vinaigre de cidre, la sauce soja, le sirop d'érable, le sambal oelek et les petits pois.
5. Saler, poivrer et poursuivre la cuisson de 3 à 4 minutes afin de réchauffer la préparation. Servir le quinoa garni d'avocat et d'amandes effilées.

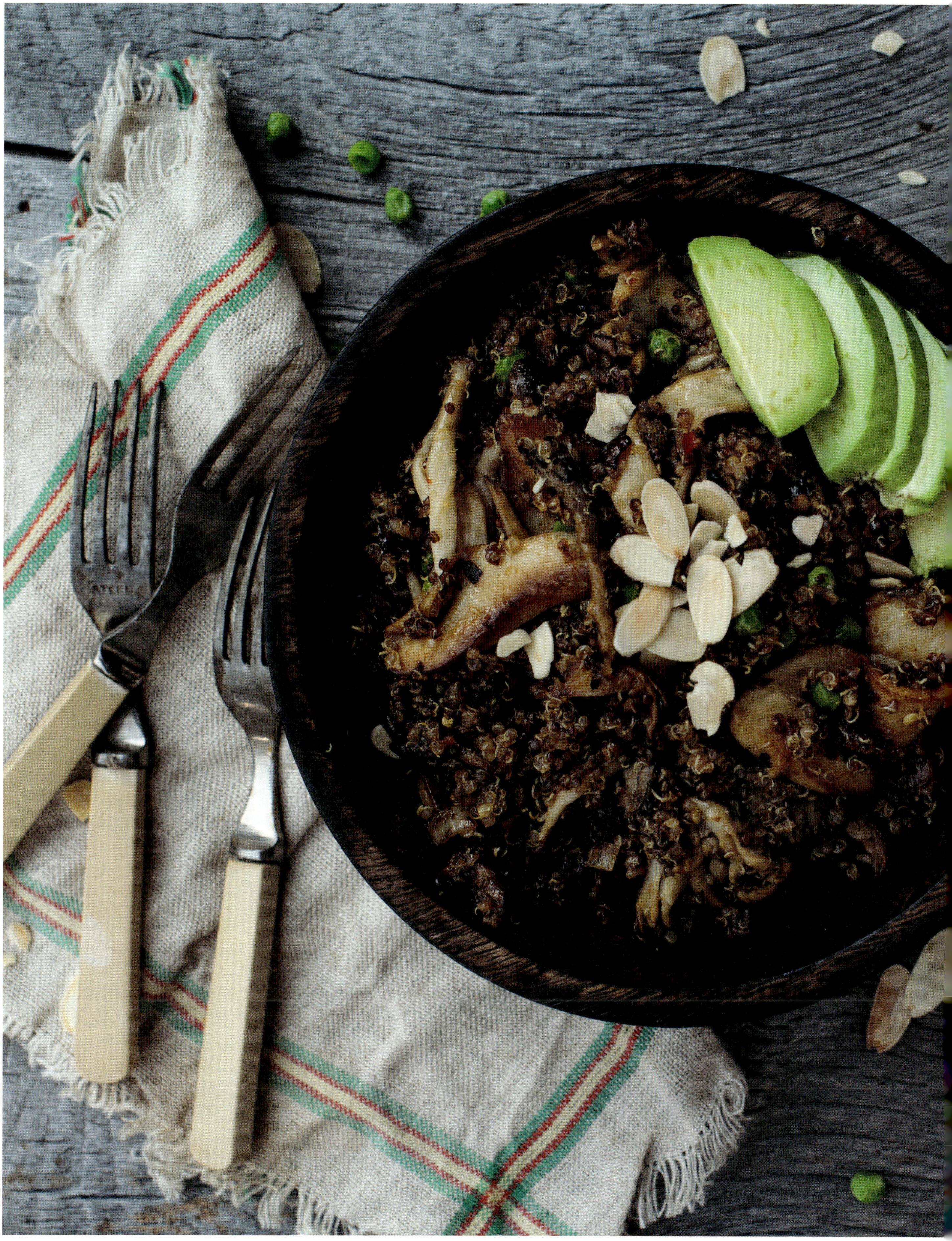

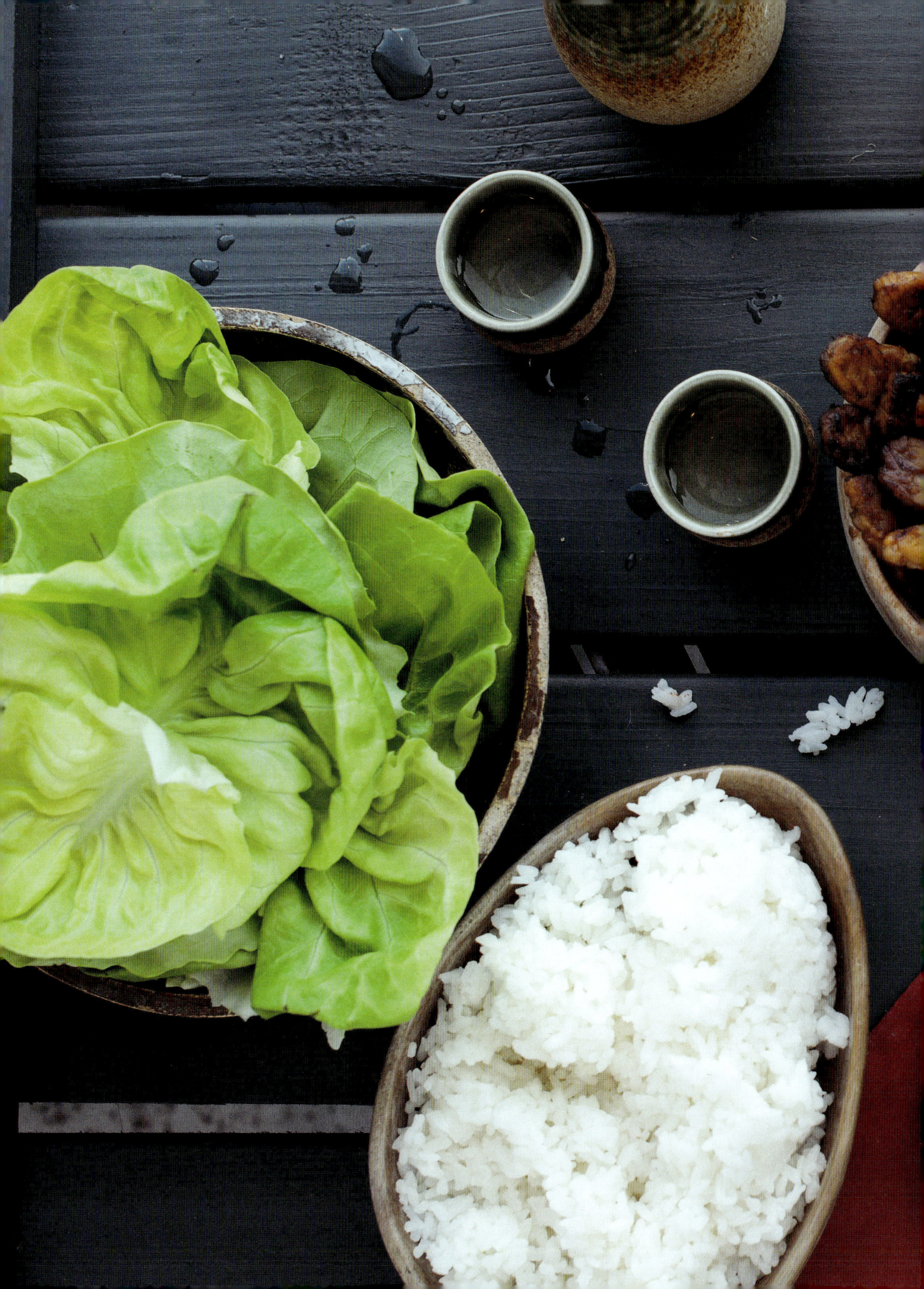

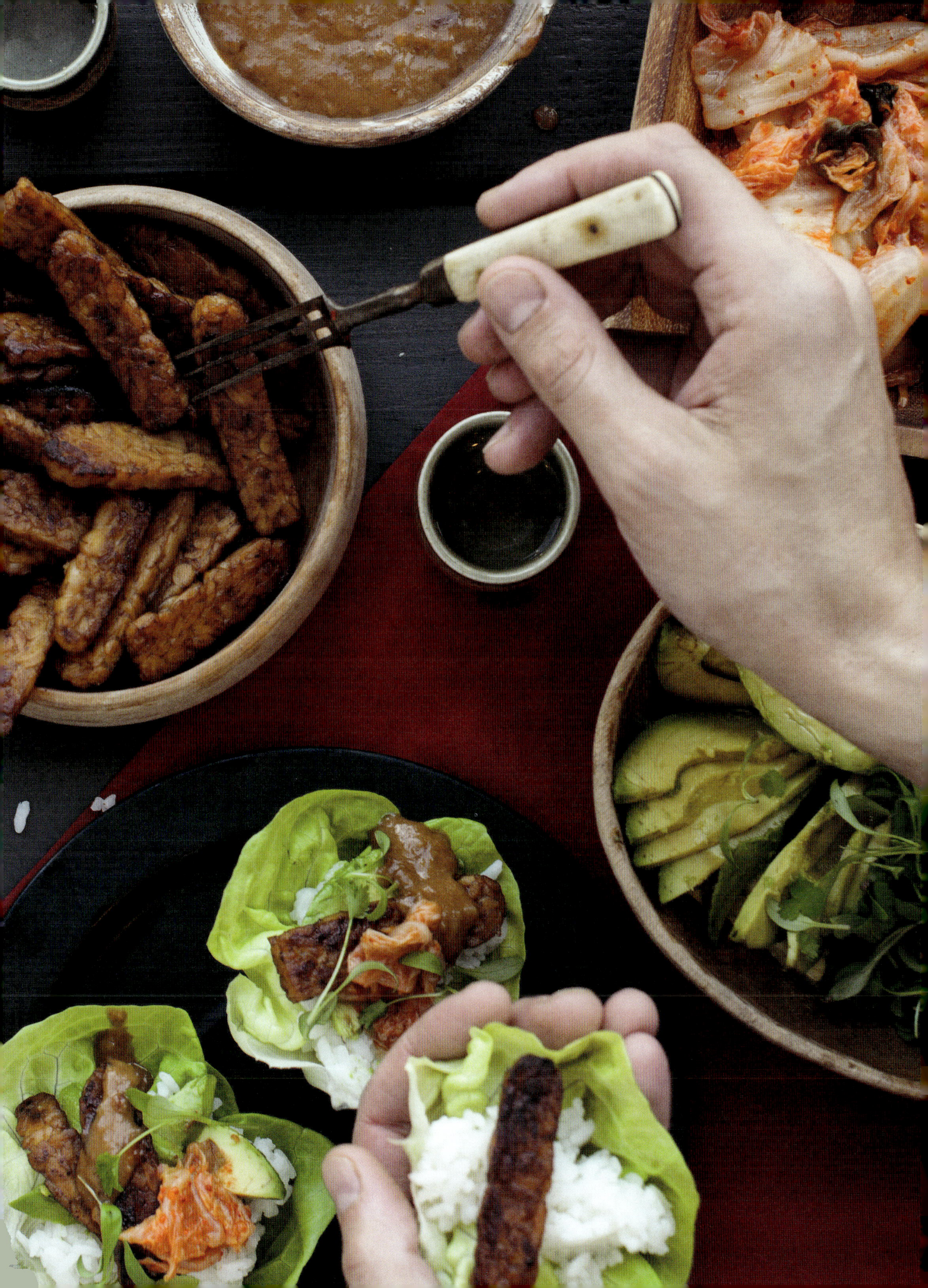

Ssams

Si vous aimez les sushis, vous adorerez ces pochettes. C'est comme la version coréenne d'un party où l'on fait ses propres sushis!

60 min / **4 PORTIONS**

40 min

26 h (kimchi) **+** 15 min (riz)

Temps de réfrigération 24 h (kimchi)

KIMCHI

1 chou chinois (napa) (environ 850 g)

3 c. à soupe (45 ml) sel

3 gousses d'ail, hachées

2 c. à soupe (30 ml) gingembre frais, haché

1 c. à soupe (15 ml) sucre de canne

½ tasse (50 g) poudre de chili coréenne

6 oignons verts, hachés

4 carottes, émincées (environ 200 g)

¼ tasse (60 ml) sauce soya

½ tasse (125 ml) eau

RIZ

1 tasse (225 g) riz à sushi

1 ½ tasse (375 ml) eau*

½ c. à thé (2,5 ml) sel

1 c. à soupe (15 ml) vinaigre de riz

1 c. à soupe (15 ml) sirop d'érable ou sirop d'agave

PRÉPARER LE KIMCHI

1. Couper le chou en morceaux de 1 ½ po (4 cm).
2. Déposer le chou dans un grand bol et ajouter le sel. Bien mélanger et laisser dégorger 2 heures.
3. Égoutter le chou et le rincer abondamment. Réserver.
4. Dans un mortier, broyer l'ail et le gingembre avec le sucre.
5. Transférer le mélange dans un grand cul-de-poule, ajouter le chou, la poudre de chili, les oignons verts, les carottes, la sauce soya et l'eau. Bien mélanger.
6. Déposer la préparation dans des pots en verre propres, mettre le couvercle et laisser fermenter, à la température ambiante dans un endroit sombre pendant 24 heures.
7. Transférer au réfrigérateur et poursuivre la fermentation pendant 24 heures. Se conserve jusqu'à 3 semaines au réfrigérateur.

FAIRE CUIRE LE RIZ

1. Rincer le riz à l'eau fraîche et le déposer dans une casserole. Ajouter l'eau, bien mélanger et porter à ébullition. Couvrir, réduire le feu au minimum et laisser frémir de 15 à 20 minutes, ou jusqu'à ce que toute l'eau soit absorbée.
2. Retirer du feu et laisser reposer, à couvert, pendant 15 minutes.
3. Ajouter le sel, le vinaigre de riz et le sirop d'érable. Bien mélanger et laisser refroidir.

* Suivre les indications de l'emballage et ajuster la quantité d'eau, au besoin.

TEMPEH

1 paquet (240 g) tempeh

2 c. à soupe (30 ml) huile de sésame grillé

2 c. à soupe (30 ml) sauce hoisin

1 tasse (250 ml) bouillon de légumes

SAUCE SATAY

2 gousses d'ail, hachées

1 c. à soupe (15 ml) huile végétale

2 c. à soupe (30 ml) sauce hoisin végane

¼ tasse (60 ml) bouillon de légumes

1 c. à soupe (15 ml) sirop d'érable

1 c. à thé (5 ml) sambal oelek

1 c. à soupe (15 ml) beurre d'arachide

8 à 12 feuilles de laitue

PRÉPARER LE TEMPEH

1. Trancher finement le tempeh et le déposer dans une poêle.
2. Dans un bol, mélanger l'huile de sésame, la sauce hoisin végane et le bouillon de légumes.
3. Verser la marinade sur les tranches de tempeh et porter à ébullition à feu vif.
4. Laisser bouillir jusqu'à ce que tout le liquide se soit évaporé, en retournant les tranches de tempeh à mi-cuisson. Réserver.

PRÉPARER LA SAUCE SATAY

1. Dans une poêle, faire revenir l'ail dans l'huile pendant 2 minutes.
2. Ajouter le reste des ingrédients, porter à ébullition et laisser réduire jusqu'à ce que la sauce ait épaissi. Réserver.

ASSEMBLER LES POCHETTES

1. Mettre une petite quantité de riz dans chaque feuille de laitue, puis garnir d'une tranche de tempeh, de la sauce et du kimchi. Replier la feuille de laitue sur la garniture et déguster.

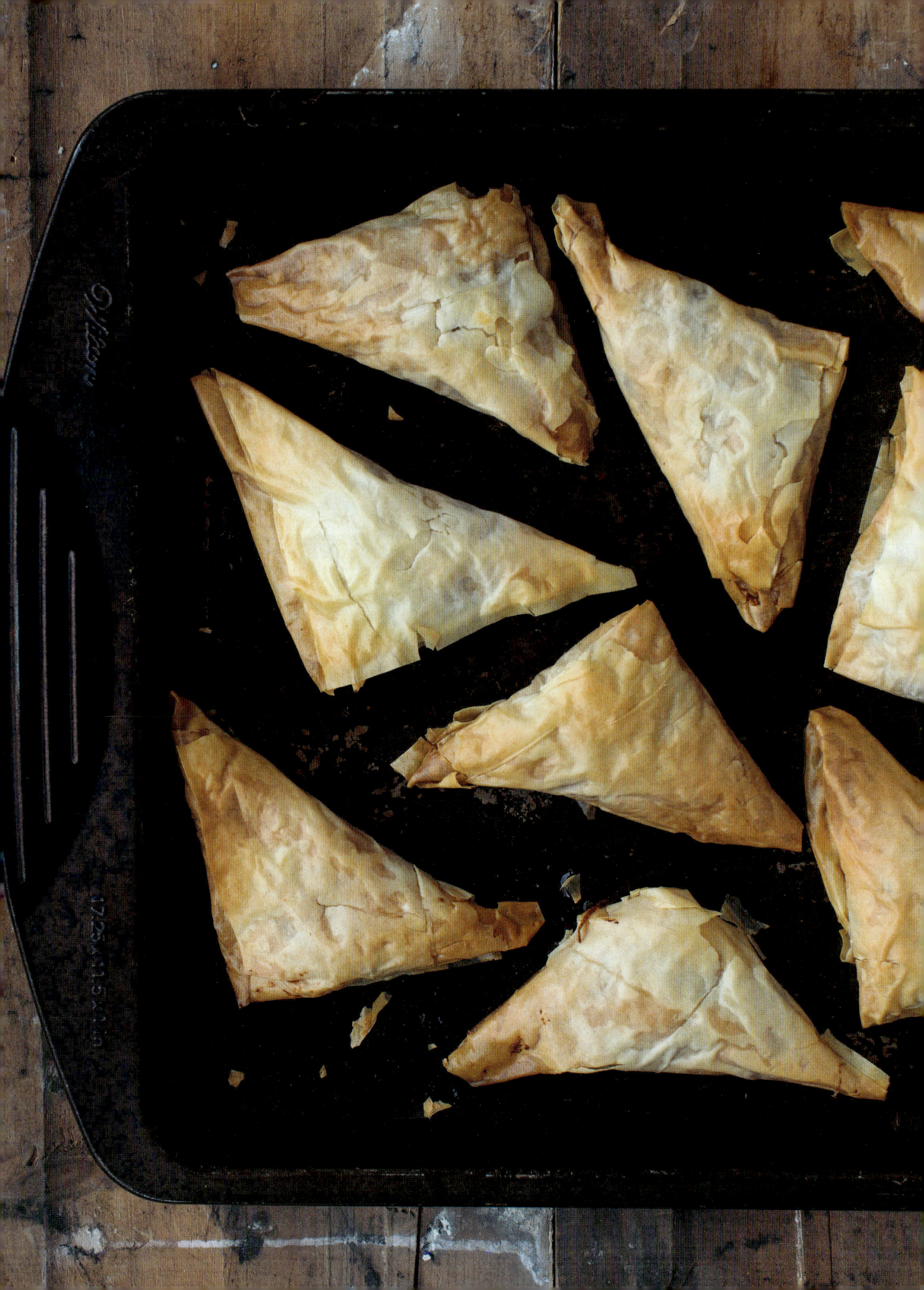

Champignons en pâte phyllo

30 min / **16 TRIANGLES**

30 min

INGRÉDIENTS

2 c. à soupe (30 ml) huile végétale (+ 3 c. à soupe/45 ml pour badigeonner la pâte phyllo)

4 tasses (227 g) champignons de Paris, émincés

1 ½ tasse (120 g) poireau, émincé

1 gousse d'ail, hachée

1 tasse (150 g) petits pois surgelés

¼ tasse (30 g) chapelure

1 tasse (250 ml) bouillon de légumes

1 c. à thé (5 ml) huile de truffe

Sel et poivre, au goût

8 feuilles de pâte phyllo

PRÉPARATION

1. Préchauffer le four à 375 °F (190 °C).
2. Dans une poêle à fond épais, faire chauffer l'huile à feu moyen.
3. Ajouter les champignons et le poireau, puis faire suer pendant 10 minutes.
4. Ajouter l'ail, les petits pois, la chapelure, le bouillon de légumes et l'huile de truffe. Saler et poivrer, puis mélanger et poursuivre la cuisson pendant 4 minutes. Réserver.
5. Sur un plan de travail, huiler légèrement une première feuille de pâte phyllo. Couvrir d'une deuxième feuille, puis badigeonner légèrement d'huile à nouveau.
6. Couper en quatre bandes égales dans le sens de la largeur. Déposer 1 c. à soupe comble (environ 20 ml) de garniture à la base de chaque bande de pâte phyllo.
7. Replier quatre fois les bandes de pâte avec la garniture de manière à former des triangles. Déposer les triangles sur une plaque à pâtisserie.
8. Répéter l'opération avec les autres feuilles de pâte phyllo et le reste de la garniture de manière à obtenir 16 triangles.
9. Huiler légèrement le dessus des triangles et cuire au four pendant 15 minutes. Laisser tiédir quelques minutes avant de déguster.

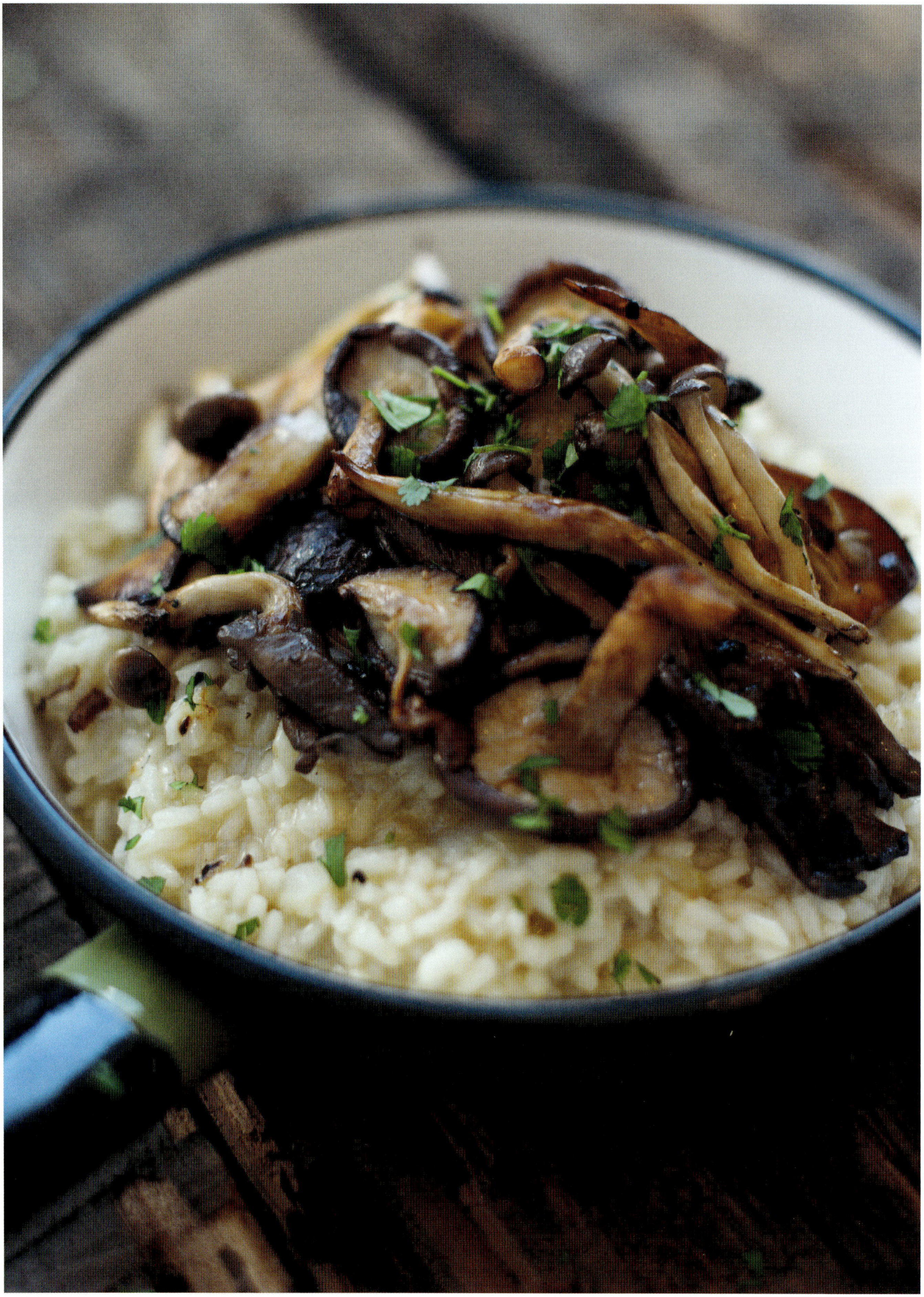

Risotto aux champignons sauvages

Un incontournable! J'ai préparé des centaines de risottos durant ma carrière et je me suis toujours demandé pourquoi certaines personnes sont encore intimidées devant ce classique de la cuisine italienne. Il suffit d'ajouter du bouillon chaud au riz, petit à petit, en mélangeant continuellement. Mais attention, il faut demeurer présent et attentif!

30 min / **4 PORTIONS**

30 min

RIZ

4 tasses (1 L) bouillon de légumes

1 oignon, haché

2 c. à soupe (30 ml) huile d'olive

1 ½ tasse (280 g) riz arborio

½ tasse (125 ml) vin blanc

⅓ tasse (25 g) levure alimentaire

1 c. à thé (5 ml) sel

½ c. à thé (2,5 ml) huile de truffe

CHAMPIGNONS

1 ½ tasse (100 g) shiitakes

1 ½ tasse (100 g) pleurotes

1 ½ tasse (100 g) champignons de Paris, hachés

¼ tasse (60 ml) huile d'olive

½ poireau, haché

½ c. à thé (2,5 ml) sel

2 c. à soupe (30 ml) sirop d'érable

½ c. à thé (2,5 ml) huile de truffe

PRÉPARER LE RIZ

1. Faire chauffer le bouillon de légumes. Réserver au chaud.
2. Dans une casserole, faire suer l'oignon dans l'huile à feu moyen pendant 4 minutes. Ajouter le riz et poursuivre la cuisson pendant 2 minutes en remuant.
3. Verser le vin blanc et laisser réduire pendant 2 minutes.
4. Ajouter 1 tasse (250 ml) du bouillon de légumes chaud, en remuant constamment.
5. Continuer à ajouter le bouillon de la même manière, 1 tasse (250 ml) à la fois, jusqu'à ce que tout le bouillon soit absorbé. À cette étape le risotto devrait avoir une consistance crémeuse.
6. Ajouter la levure alimentaire, le sel et l'huile de truffe, et mélanger.

PRÉPARER LES CHAMPIGNONS

1. Dans une casserole, faire revenir les champignons dans l'huile à feu vif, de 4 à 5 minutes, afin de permettre aux champignons de dorer. (Brasser le moins possible.) Ajouter de l'huile, au besoin.
2. Ajouter le poireau haché et poursuivre la cuisson de 2 à 3 minutes.
3. Incorporer le sirop d'érable et l'huile de truffe.
4. Au moment de servir, répartir le risotto dans des bols et garnir des champignons sautés.

Tourtières de millet

45 min / **2 GRANDES TOURTIÈRES OU 4 MOYENNES**

30 min (garniture) **+** 45 min (tourtière)

Temps de réfrigération 30 min (pâte à tarte)

PÂTE À TARTE

6 tasses (900 g) farine

1 c. à thé (5 ml) sel

2 tasses (380 g) beurre végétalien, coupé en dés

14 c. à soupe (210 ml) eau glacée

2 c. à soupe (30 ml) vinaigre blanc

GARNITURE DE MILLET

1 tasse (190 g) millet cru

2 c. à soupe (30 ml) huile végétale (+ ¼ tasse/60 ml, pour les légumes)

1 ½ tasse (375 ml) bouillon de légumes (+ ¾ tasse/180 ml, pour la garniture)

2 oignons, ciselés

4 tasses (227 g) champignons de Paris, émincés

1 tasse (120 g) céleri, haché

2 tasses (320 g) pomme de terre, coupée en dés

1 tasse (120 g) carotte, hachée

1 c. à soupe (15 ml) pâte de tomate

1 gousse d'ail, hachée

3 c. à soupe (45 ml) sauce soya

¼ c. à thé (1 ml) clou de girofle moulu

¼ c. à thé (1 ml) cannelle moulue

⅓ tasse (25 g) levure alimentaire (facultatif)

1 c. à soupe (15 ml) sirop d'érable

Sel et poivre, au goût

½ tasse (125 ml) lait végétal

½ tasse (65 g) chapelure

PRÉPARER LA PÂTE À TARTE

1. Dans un grand bol, mélanger la farine et le sel. À l'aide d'un coupe-pâte ou de deux couteaux, incorporer le beurre à la farine, jusqu'à l'obtention d'une texture granuleuse (avec des morceaux de beurre de la grosseur de petits pois).
2. Ajouter l'eau et le vinaigre et mélanger. (Il est important de ne pas trop travailler la pâte.)
3. Former une boule avec les mains et envelopper la pâte de pellicule plastique. Réfrigérer la pâte au moins 30 minutes.

PRÉPARER LA GARNITURE DE MILLET

1. Bien rincer le millet, puis l'égoutter.
2. Dans une casserole, faire revenir le millet dans 2 c. à soupe (30 ml) de l'huile pendant 2 minutes.
3. Ajouter 1 ½ tasse (375 ml) du bouillon de légumes. Porter à ébullition, réduire le feu, couvrir et laisser mijoter pendant 15 minutes. Retirer du feu et laisser reposer à couvert pendant 10 minutes.
4. Dans une autre casserole, faire tomber les oignons dans le reste de l'huile à feu moyen-vif pendant quelques minutes. Ajouter le reste des légumes et poursuivre la cuisson, en remuant de temps à autre, pendant 5 minutes.
5. Ajouter la pâte de tomate, l'ail, la sauce soya, le clou de girofle, la cannelle, la levure alimentaire, si désiré, le reste du bouillon de légumes, le millet cuit et le sirop d'érable. Saler et poivrer.
6. Poursuivre la cuisson pendant quelques minutes.
7. Retirer du feu, ajouter le lait végétal et la chapelure, puis mélanger. Laisser tiédir.

ASSEMBLER LA TOURTIÈRE

1. Préchauffer le four à 350 °F (180 °C).
2. Diviser la pâte à tarte selon le nombre de tourtières désiré.
3. À l'aide d'un rouleau à pâtisserie, abaisser la pâte à tarte en formant un disque de dimension environ deux fois plus grande que l'assiette à tarte.
4. Déposer l'abaisse dans l'assiette à tarte en laissant dépasser l'excédent de pâte. Répéter ces opérations avec le reste de la pâte à tarte pour les autres tourtières.
5. Répartir uniformément la garniture dans les abaisses. Replier l'excédent de pâte sur la garniture pour fermer les tourtières.
6. Cuire au four pendant 45 minutes, ou jusqu'à ce que les tourtières soient dorées. Servir bien chaud.

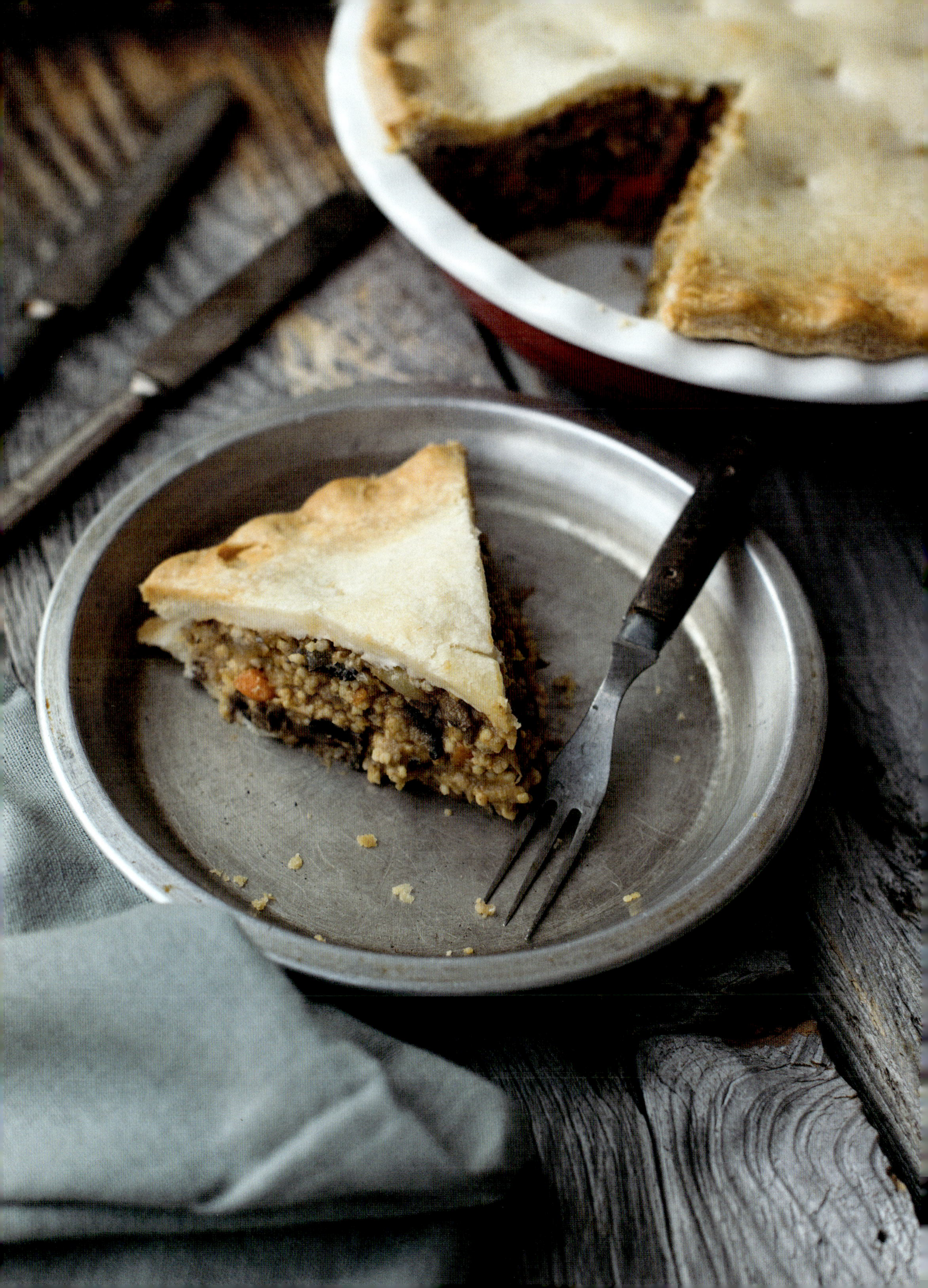

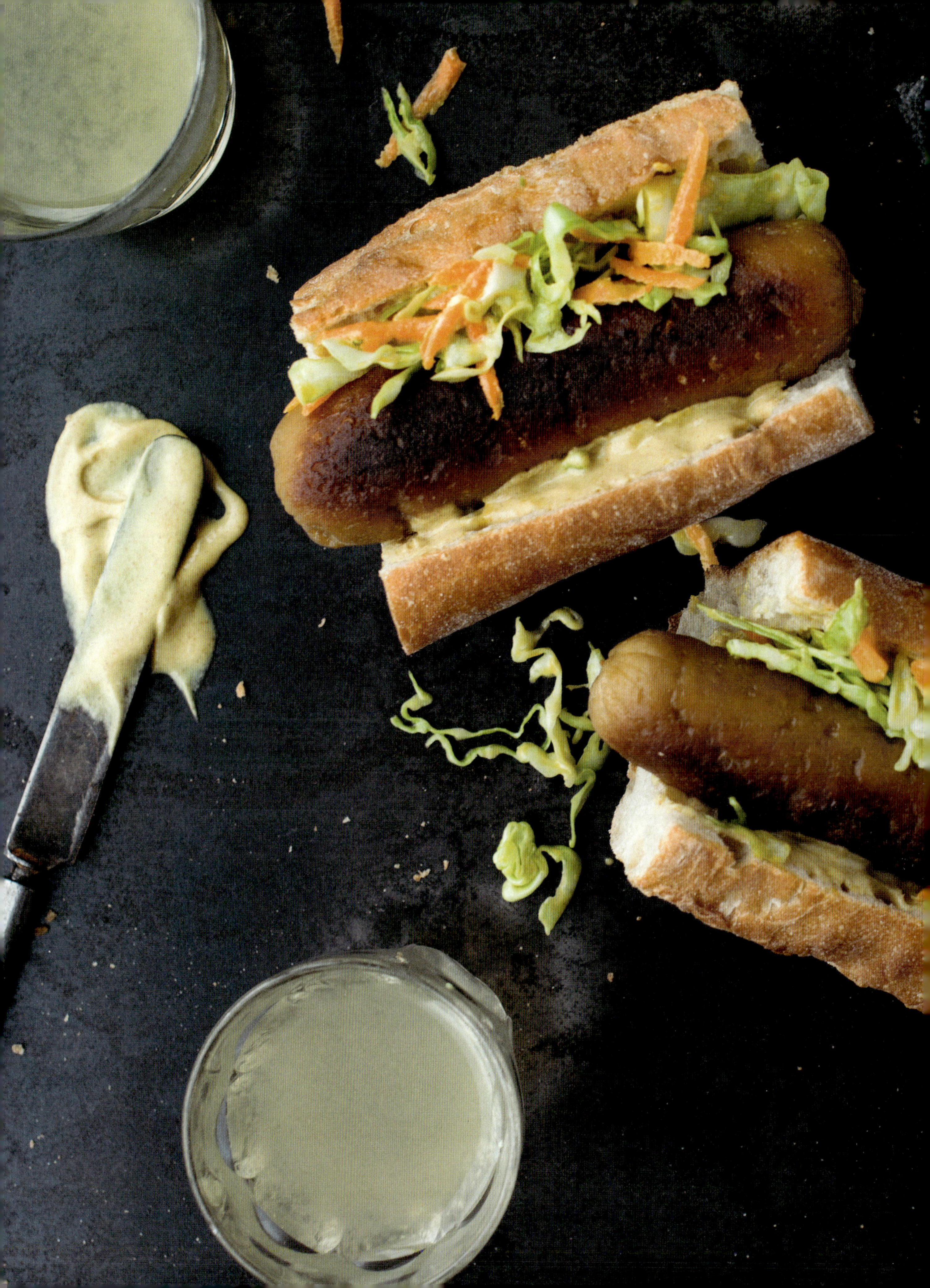

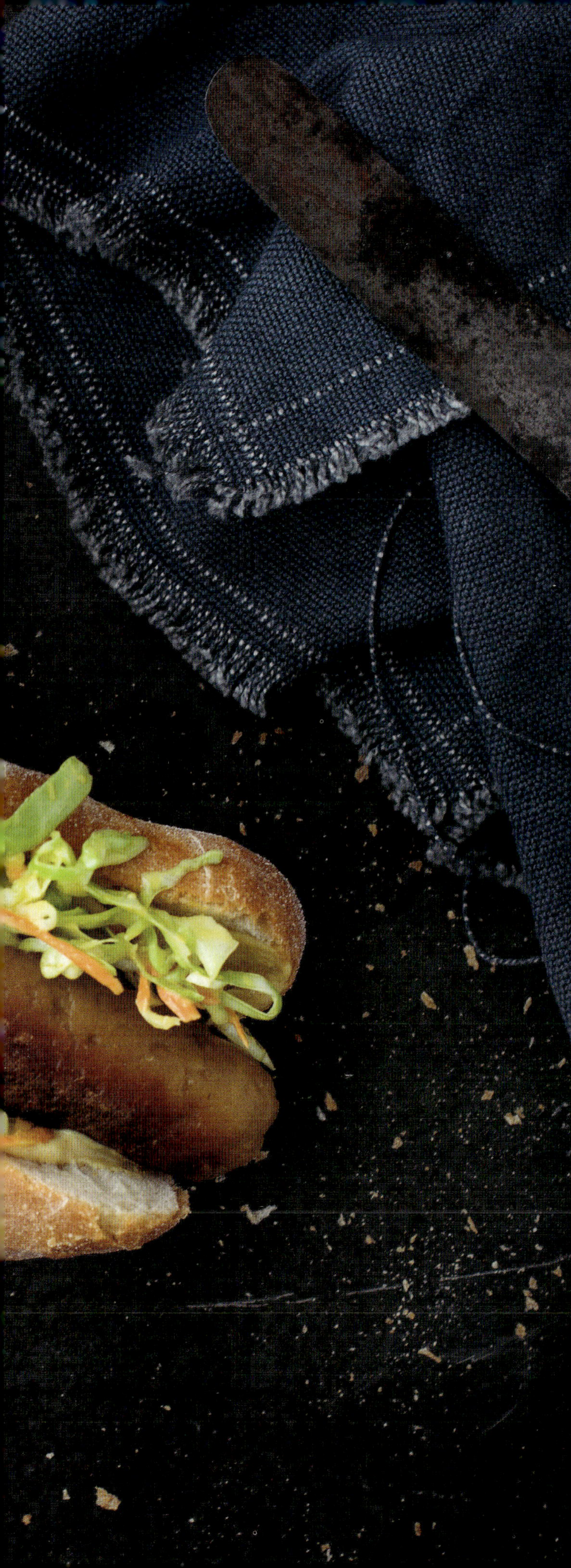

Saucisses

30 min / **ENVIRON 8 SAUCISSES**

70 min

INGRÉDIENTS

1 oignon, émincé

2 c. à soupe (30 ml) huile végétale

2 c. à soupe (30 ml) fumée liquide

1 c. à thé (5 ml) sirop d'érable

1 ½ tasse (375 ml) bouillon de légumes (+ 4 tasses / 1 L pour la cuisson)

2 tasses (260 g) farine de gluten

½ tasse (75 g) farine tout usage

1 c. à thé (5 ml) sel

1 c. à thé (5 ml) poudre d'ail

1 c. à thé (5 ml) poudre d'oignon

½ tasse (40 g) levure alimentaire

PRÉPARATION

1. Dans une poêle, faire revenir l'oignon dans l'huile à feu moyen pendant environ 10 minutes, ou jusqu'à ce qu'il soit légèrement caramélisé. Transvider dans un récipient.
2. Ajouter la fumée liquide, le sirop d'érable et 1 ½ tasse (375 ml) du bouillon de légumes. Broyer à l'aide d'un bras mélangeur.
3. Dans un grand bol, mélanger la farine de gluten, la farine tout usage, le sel, la poudre d'ail, la poudre d'oignon et la levure alimentaire.
4. Ajouter le mélange liquide aux ingrédients secs, bien mélanger et pétrir de 1 à 2 minutes.
5. Diviser la pâte en 8 portions égales, puis façonner chaque portion en saucisse.
6. Envelopper chaque saucisse dans une pellicule plastique ou dans du coton à fromage (étamine) et nouer les deux extrémités.
7. Dans une casserole, porter à ébullition le reste du bouillon. Plonger les saucisses dans le bouillon et les faire pocher pendant 60 minutes à feu doux.
8. Retirer les saucisses du bouillon et les laisser refroidir. Retirer la pellicule plastique. Réserver au réfrigérateur jusqu'au moment de servir.
9. Faire griller à la poêle ou sur le barbecue.

NOTE : Se conservent jusqu'à 5 jours au réfrigérateur, ou jusqu'à 8 semaines au congélateur.

Tofu au « beurre »

30 min / **4 PORTIONS**

20 min

INGRÉDIENTS

1 bloc (450 g) tofu ferme, coupé en dés

¼ tasse (35 g) fécule de maïs

3 c. à soupe (45 ml) beurre végétalien ou huile végétale

1 oignon, haché finement

2 gousses d'ail, hachées

½ c. à thé (2,5 ml) piment rouge broyé

¼ c. à thé (1 ml) curcuma

½ c. à thé (2,5 ml) graines de moutarde

1 c. à thé (5 ml) poudre de cari

2 c. à soupe (30 ml) levure alimentaire

3 c. à soupe (45 ml) pâte de tomate

1 c. à soupe (15 ml) sucre de canne ou sirop d'érable

1 c. à thé (5 ml) vinaigre de riz

1 conserve (400 ml) lait de coco

1 tasse (150 g) petits pois surgelés

Eau

Sel et poivre

Quelques micropousses au choix, pour garnir

PRÉPARATION

1. Dans un bol, mélanger le tofu avec la fécule de maïs pour bien l'enrober.
2. Dans une poêle, faire chauffer le beurre végétalien à feu moyen-vif. Ajouter la moitié des dés de tofu et les faire revenir, en les retournant de temps à autre, jusqu'à ce qu'ils soient bien dorés et croustillants.
3. Mettre le tofu sur un essuie-tout et laisser égoutter. Répéter l'opération avec le reste des dés de tofu. Ajouter du beurre ou de l'huile, au besoin. Réserver.
4. Dans la même poêle, faire revenir l'oignon dans l'huile pendant 4 minutes.
5. Ajouter l'ail, le piment rouge broyé, le curcuma, les graines de moutarde, la poudre de cari, la levure alimentaire, la pâte de tomate, le sucre et le vinaigre de riz. Poursuivre la cuisson pendant 2 minutes.
6. Ajouter le lait de coco et porter à ébullition.
7. Ajouter les petits pois et le tofu.
8. Laisser mijoter 5 minutes, ou jusqu'à ce que la sauce ait épaissi. Au moment de servir, garnir le tofu au beurre de quelques micropousses.

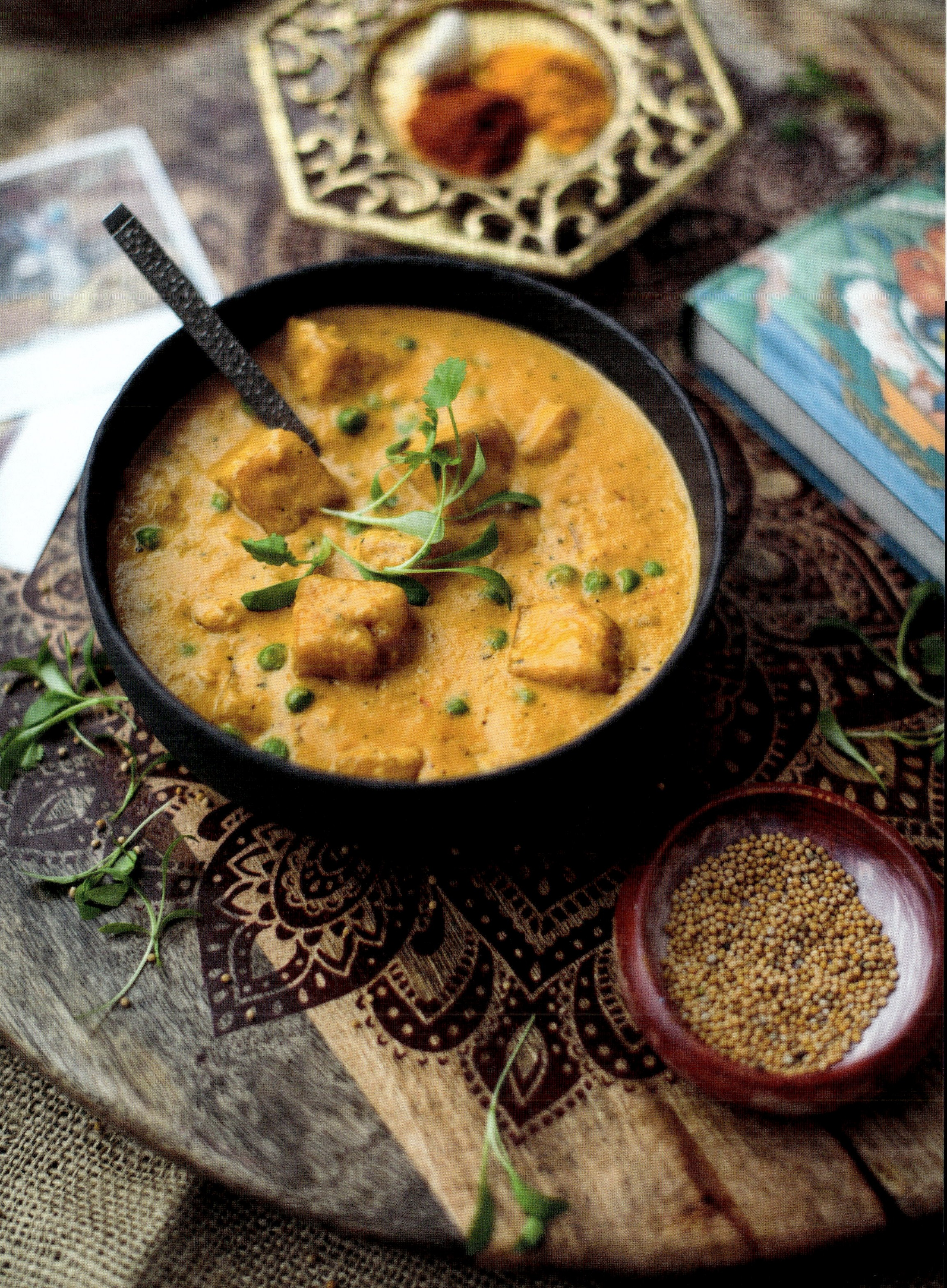

20 min / **4 PORTIONS**

10 min

INGRÉDIENTS

2 c. à soupe (30 ml) huile végétale

2 échalotes françaises, hachées

2 gousses d'ail, hachées

2 c. à soupe (30 ml) sauce soya

2 c. à soupe (30 ml) ketchup

¼ tasse (70 g) beurre d'arachide

1 c. à soupe (15 ml) sirop d'érable

1 tasse (250 ml) bouillon de légumes

½ c. à thé (2,5 ml) sauce sriracha

1 bloc (454 g) tofu ferme, coupé en dés

PRÉPARATION

1. Dans une casserole, faire chauffer l'huile à feu moyen-vif.
2. Ajouter les échalotes et l'ail. Faire revenir pendant 2 minutes.
3. Ajouter la sauce soya, le ketchup, le beurre d'arachide, le sirop d'érable, le bouillon de légumes et la sauce sriracha. Bien mélanger.
4. Ajouter le tofu, porter à ébullition et laisser réduire jusqu'à ce que la sauce soit onctueuse. Servir sur du riz et déguster.

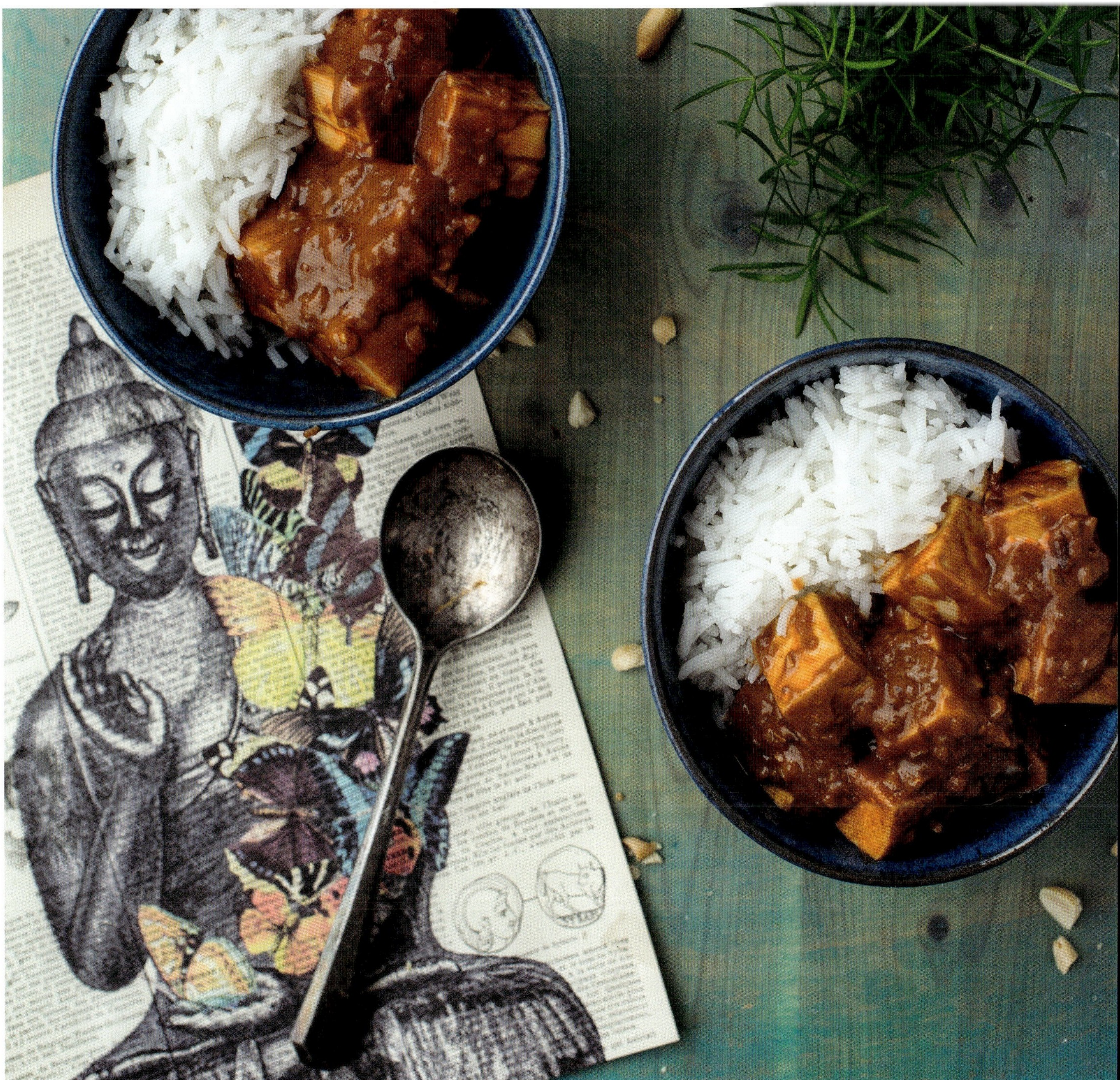

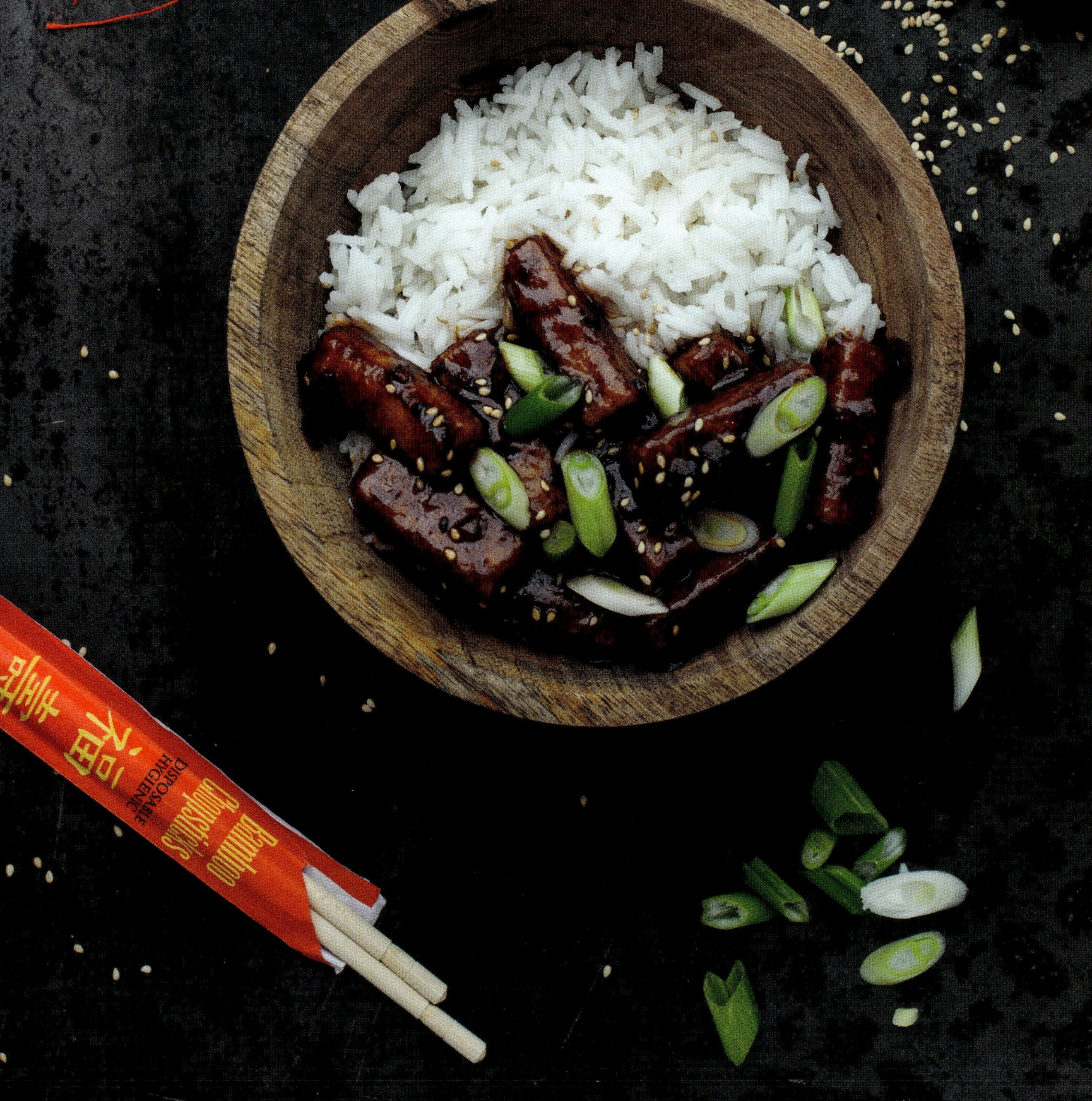
Bamboo Chopsticks
DISPOSABLE HYGIENIC

20 min / **4 PORTIONS**

15 min

INGRÉDIENTS

1 bloc (454 g) tofu ferme, coupé en dés

¼ tasse (35 g) fécule de maïs

3 c. à soupe (45 ml) huile végétale

2 gousses d'ail, hachées

1 c. à soupe (15 ml) gingembre frais, haché

2 c. à soupe (30 ml) sirop d'érable

2 c. à soupe (30 ml) sauce soya

2 c. à soupe (30 ml) ketchup

1 c. à thé (5 ml) sauce sriracha ou pâte de piment

3 oignons verts, émincés

¾ tasse (180 ml) bouillon de légumes

Oignons verts et graines de sésame, pour garnir

PRÉPARATION

1. Dans un bol, mélanger le tofu avec la fécule de maïs pour bien l'enrober.
2. Dans une casserole, faire chauffer l'huile à feu moyen-vif. Ajouter la moitié des dés de tofu et les faire revenir, en les retournant de temps à autre, jusqu'à ce qu'ils soient bien dorés et croustillants. Laisser égoutter le tofu sur un essuie-tout. Répéter l'opération avec le reste des dés de tofu. Ajouter de l'huile, au besoin.
3. Dans la même poêle, faire revenir l'ail et le gingembre pendant 1 minute. Ajouter de l'huile, au besoin.
4. Ajouter le sirop d'érable, la sauce soya, le ketchup, la sauce sriracha, les oignons verts et le bouillon de légumes. Laisser réduire quelques minutes et ajouter le tofu grillé pour le réchauffer. Servir sur du riz et garnir d'oignons verts émincés et de graines de sésame.

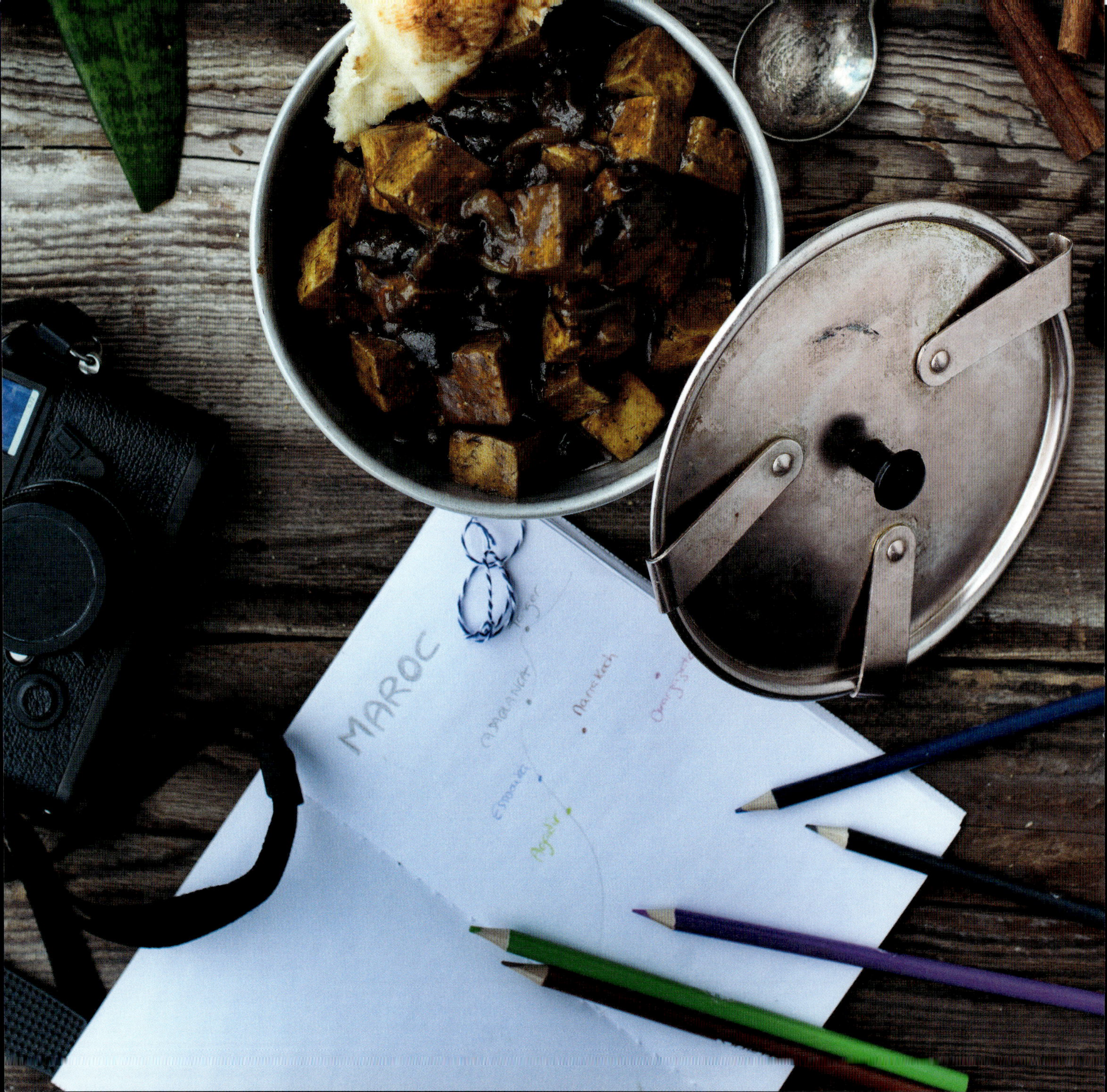
MAROC

20 min / **4 PORTIONS**

40 min

INGRÉDIENTS

2 c. à soupe (30 ml) huile végétale

1 oignon, émincé

1 bloc (454 g) tofu ferme, coupé en dés

8 pruneaux séchés, dénoyautés

½ c. à thé (2,5 ml) cannelle moulue

1 c. à soupe (15 ml) cari de Madras

¼ c. à thé (1 ml) clou de girofle moulu

1 c. à soupe (15 ml) sirop d'érable

¼ c. à thé (1 ml) piment rouge broyé

1 boîte (400 ml) lait de coco

2 c. à soupe (30 ml) pâte de tomate

½ c. à thé (2,5 ml) sel

Poivre, au goût

Pains naan

PRÉPARATION

1. Préchauffer le four à 350 °F (180 °C).
2. Dans une casserole, faire chauffer l'huile à feu moyen-vif. Ajouter l'oignon et le tofu. Faire revenir pendant 5 minutes.
3. Ajouter les pruneaux, la cannelle, le cari, le clou de girofle, le sirop d'érable et le piment rouge broyé. Poursuivre la cuisson pendant 3 minutes.
4. Ajouter le lait de coco et la pâte de tomate, puis mélanger. Saler et poivrer.
5. Transférer dans un plat allant au four.
6. Cuire au four pendant 30 minutes, ou jusqu'à ce que le tofu ait absorbé la moitié de la sauce. Servir avec des pains naan.

DESSERTS

20 min / **4 PORTIONS**

10 à 15 min

Temps de réfrigération 30 min

INGRÉDIENTS

⅔ tasse (160 ml) huile de coco (+ 2 c. à soupe/30 ml pour huiler les moules)

4 oz (115 g) chocolat végétalien à 85 % de cacao

1 ½ tasse (240 g) pois chiches en boîte, rincés et égouttés

1 tasse (250 ml) lait végétal

1 c. à thé (5 ml) sel

1 c. à thé (5 ml) poudre à pâte

½ c. à thé (2,5 ml) vanille

1 tasse (220 g) sucre de canne

½ tasse (75 g) farine (+ un peu pour enfariner les ramequins)

Sucre glace, pour garnir

PRÉPARATION

1. Préchauffer le four à 375 °F (190 °C).
2. En utilisant 2 c. à soupe (30 ml) de l'huile de coco, huiler 4 ramequins d'une capacité de ½ tasse (125 ml) chacun, puis les enfariner.
3. Dans une casserole, faire fondre à feu doux le chocolat et l'huile de coco. Réserver.
4. Déposer les pois chiches dans le récipient d'un mélangeur, ajouter le lait végétal, le sel, la poudre à pâte, la vanille et le sucre de canne, puis broyer.
5. Ajouter la farine et le mélange de chocolat fondu, puis mélanger jusqu'à l'obtention d'une pâte homogène.
6. Verser la pâte dans les ramequins et réfrigérer au moins 30 minutes.
7. Au moment de servir, cuire au four de 5 à 10 minutes, ou jusqu'à ce que le centre des gâteaux soit coulant, mais que l'extérieur soit cuit.
8. Démouler les fondants en les retournant sur des assiettes, puis saupoudrer de sucre glace. Servir chaud.

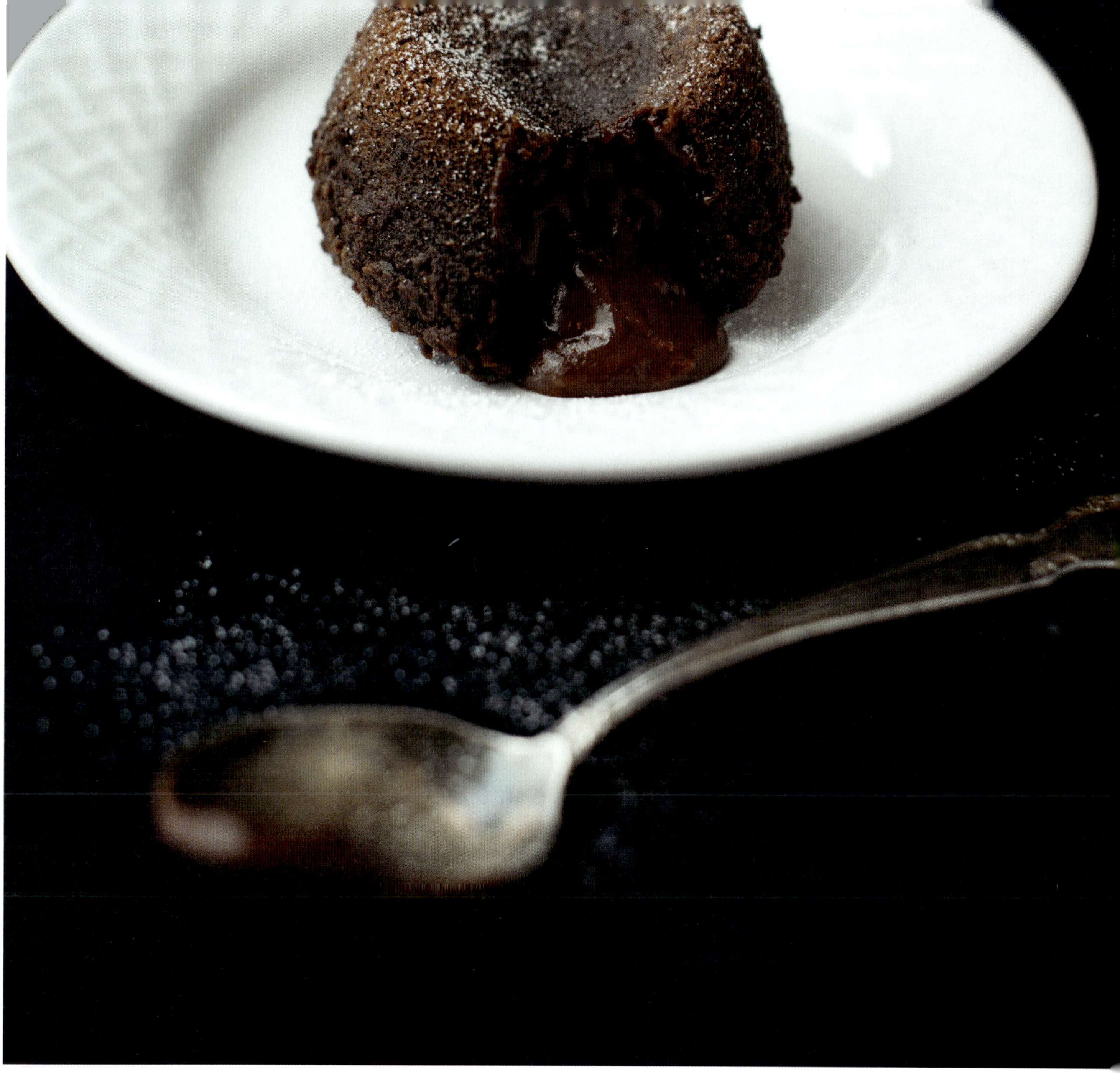

20 min / **8 PORTIONS**

35 min

SIROP

1 tasse (250 ml) sirop d'érable

½ tasse (125 ml) eau

1 c. à soupe (15 ml) jus de citron

¼ c. à thé (1 ml) cannelle

⅓ tasse (65 g) cassonade

FEUILLETÉ

1 tasse (120 g) pistaches

1 tasse (100 g) pacanes

¼ tasse (60 ml) huile végétale

5 feuilles de pâte phyllo

PRÉPARER LE SIROP

1. Dans une casserole, porter tous les ingrédients à ébullition. Laisser mijoter pendant 2 minutes, puis laisser tiédir à température ambiante. Réserver.

PRÉPARER LE FEUILLETÉ

1. Préchauffer le four à 325°F (160°C).
2. Au robot culinaire, hacher grossièrement les pistaches et les pacanes quelques secondes à la fois. Réserver.
3. Sur un plan de travail, huiler légèrement une première feuille de pâte phyllo.
4. Couvrir d'une deuxième feuille, puis badigeonner légèrement d'huile à nouveau. Répéter l'opération avec le reste de la pâte phyllo et de l'huile de manière à obtenir un feuilleté de 5 feuilles d'épaisseur.
5. Couper en deux le feuilleté ainsi obtenu et en déposer une moitié dans un moule de 13 po x 9 po (33 cm x 23 cm).
6. Saupoudrer des deux tiers des noix hachées.
7. Recouvrir de l'autre moitié de la pâte, saupoudrer du reste des noix hachées et couper en carrés égaux avant d'enfourner.
8. Cuire au four pendant 30 minutes, ou jusqu'à ce que le feuilleté soit bien doré.
9. Laisser refroidir. Si désiré, couper le feuilleté en deux, puis empiler les deux moitiés afin de doubler l'épaisseur du baklava. Napper de sirop et servir.

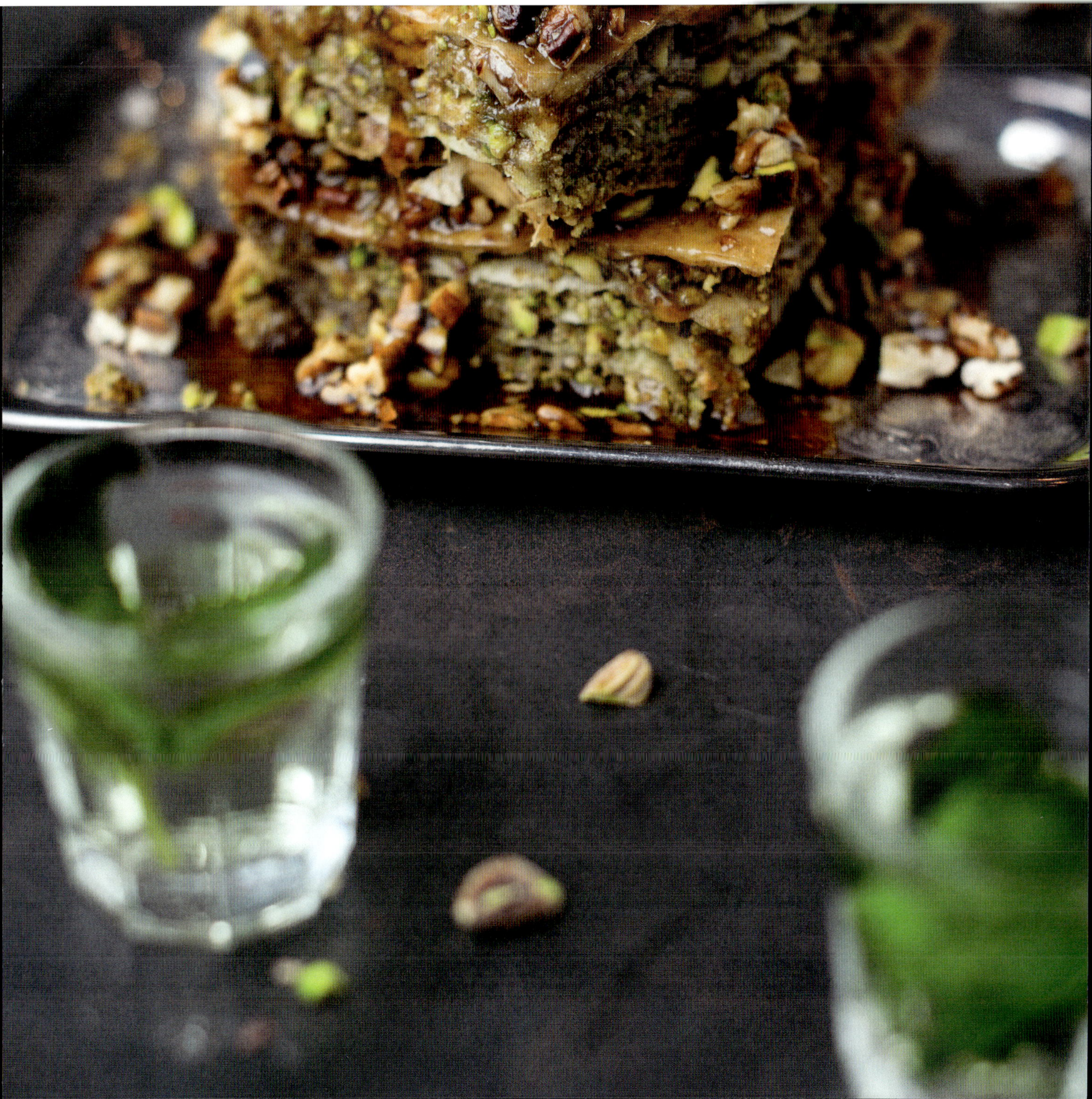

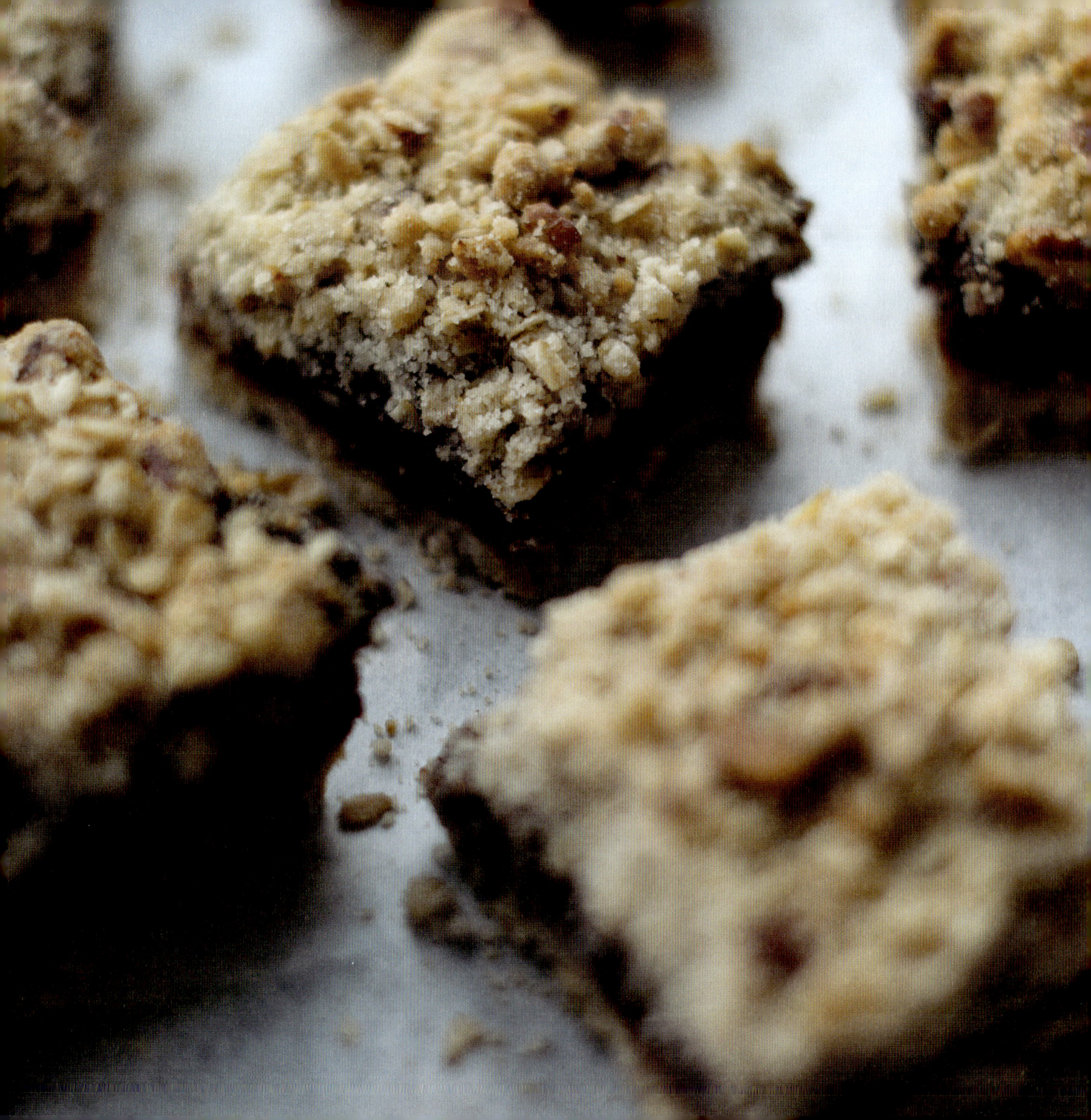

20 min / **12 PORTIONS**

45 à 60 min

INGRÉDIENTS

1 tasse (100 g) pacanes, hachées grossièrement

4 tasses (500 g) dattes dénoyautées, hachées

¼ tasse (60 ml) sirop d'érable

1 c. à soupe (15 ml) jus de citron

1 ⅔ tasse (410 ml) eau

1 ½ tasse (225 g) farine

1 tasse (100 g) flocons d'avoine

¼ tasse (50 g) sucre de canne

½ tasse (105 g) cassonade tassée

1 c. à thé (5 ml) sel

1 c. à thé (5 ml) bicarbonate de sodium

⅔ tasse (160 ml) beurre végétalien fondu

PRÉPARATION

1. Préchauffer le four à 350 °F (180 °C).
2. Déposer les pacanes sur une plaque à pâtisserie et les faire griller au four pendant 5 minutes. Réserver.
3. Dans une casserole, mettre les dattes, le sirop d'érable, le jus de citron et l'eau, porter à ébullition, puis réduire le feu et laisser cuire jusqu'à ce que tout le liquide soit absorbé. Réserver.
4. Dans un grand bol, mélanger les pacanes grillées, la farine, les flocons d'avoine, le sucre de canne, la cassonade, le sel et le bicarbonate de sodium, puis bien mélanger.
5. Ajouter le beurre fondu et mélanger jusqu'à ce qu'il soit bien incorporé.
6. Verser les deux tiers du mélange dans un moule de 9 po x 9 po (23 cm x 23 cm), beurré.
7. Ajouter la purée de dattes, bien égaliser et ajouter le reste du mélange à base de farine.
8. Cuire au four de 30 à 45 minutes, puis laisser refroidir quelques minutes.
9. Couper en carrés et déguster.

30 min / **1 GÂTEAU**

30 à 45 min

GÂTEAU

3 tasses (450 g) farine

1 ½ tasse (300 g) sucre

1 c. à thé (5 ml) sel

2 c. à thé (10 ml) bicarbonate de sodium

1 c. à thé (5 ml) poudre à pâte

¼ tasse (20 g) cacao en poudre

1 tasse (250 ml) huile végétale

1 ½ tasse (375 ml) lait végétal

¼ tasse (60 ml) vinaigre blanc

GLAÇAGE

2 c. à soupe (30 ml) huile de coco fondue

½ c. à thé (2,5 ml) vanille

2 tasses (230 g) sucre glace

¼ tasse (20 g) cacao en poudre

¼ tasse (60 ml) lait végétal

¼ tasse (35 g) noix de cajou, broyées

PRÉPARER LE GÂTEAU

1. Préchauffer le four à 350 °F (180 °C).
2. Huiler un moule à gâteau rond à charnières de 8 ½ po (22 cm) ou 9 po (23 cm) de diamètre. Réserver.
3. Dans un bol, mélanger la farine, le sucre, le sel, le bicarbonate de sodium, la poudre à pâte et le cacao.
4. Ajouter l'huile, le lait végétal et le vinaigre, puis battre pendant 1 minute, ou jusqu'à ce que le mélange soit homogène. (Ne pas trop mélanger.)
5. Verser la pâte dans le moule et cuire au four de 30 à 45 minutes, ou jusqu'à ce qu'un cure-dent inséré au centre du gâteau en ressorte propre.
6. Laisser refroidir le gâteau pendant 15 minutes. Démouler et laisser refroidir complètement sur une grille.

ENTRE-TEMPS, PRÉPARER LE GLAÇAGE

1. Dans un bol, mélanger l'huile de coco et la vanille. Incorporer le sucre glace, le cacao et le lait végétal, un ingrédient à la fois.
2. Battre jusqu'à ce que le mélange soit bien crémeux. (Pour un glaçage plus ferme, ajouter une plus grande quantité de sucre glace.)
3. Étendre le glaçage sur le gâteau refroidi, puis parsemer des noix de cajou avant de déguster.

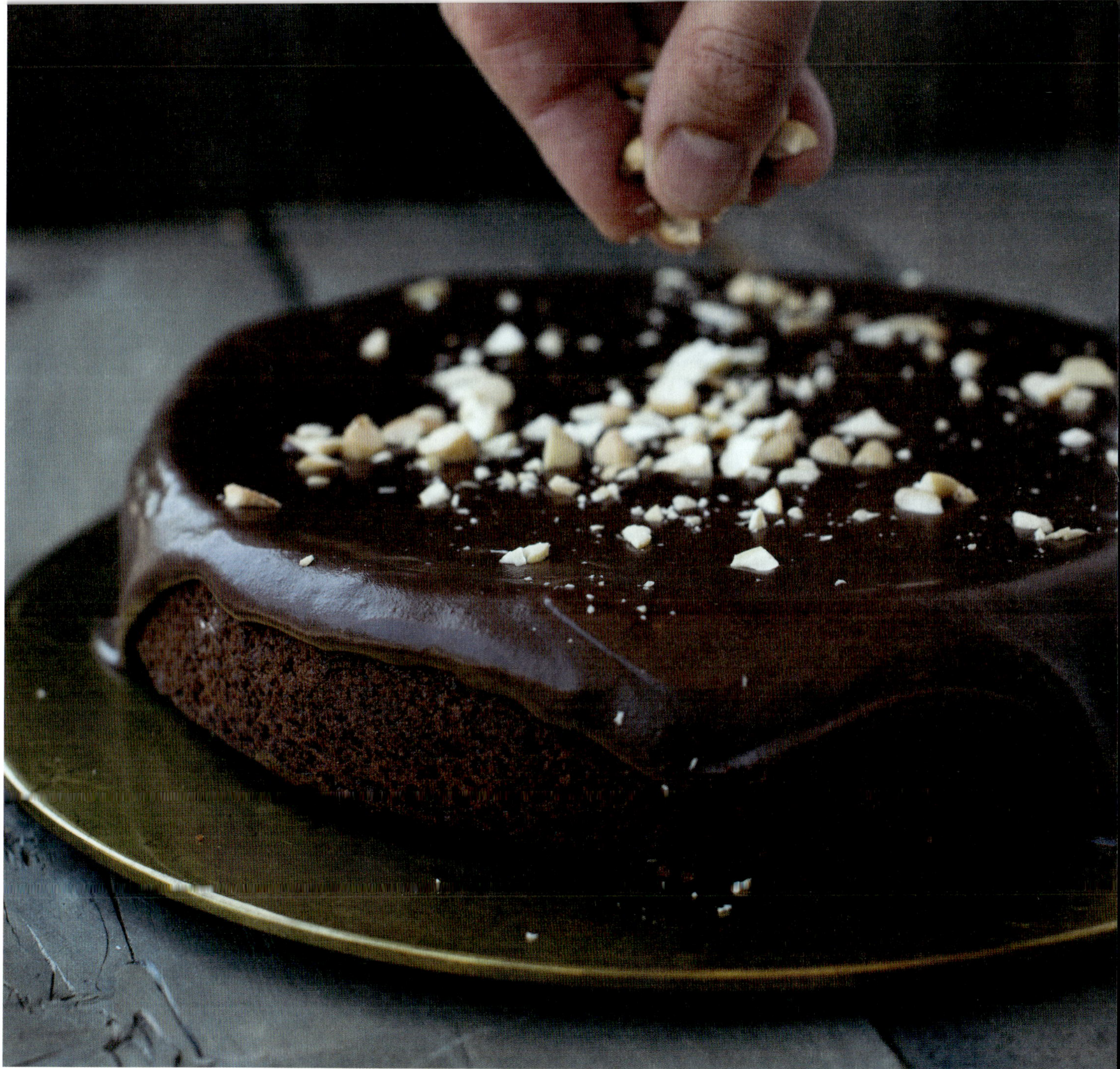

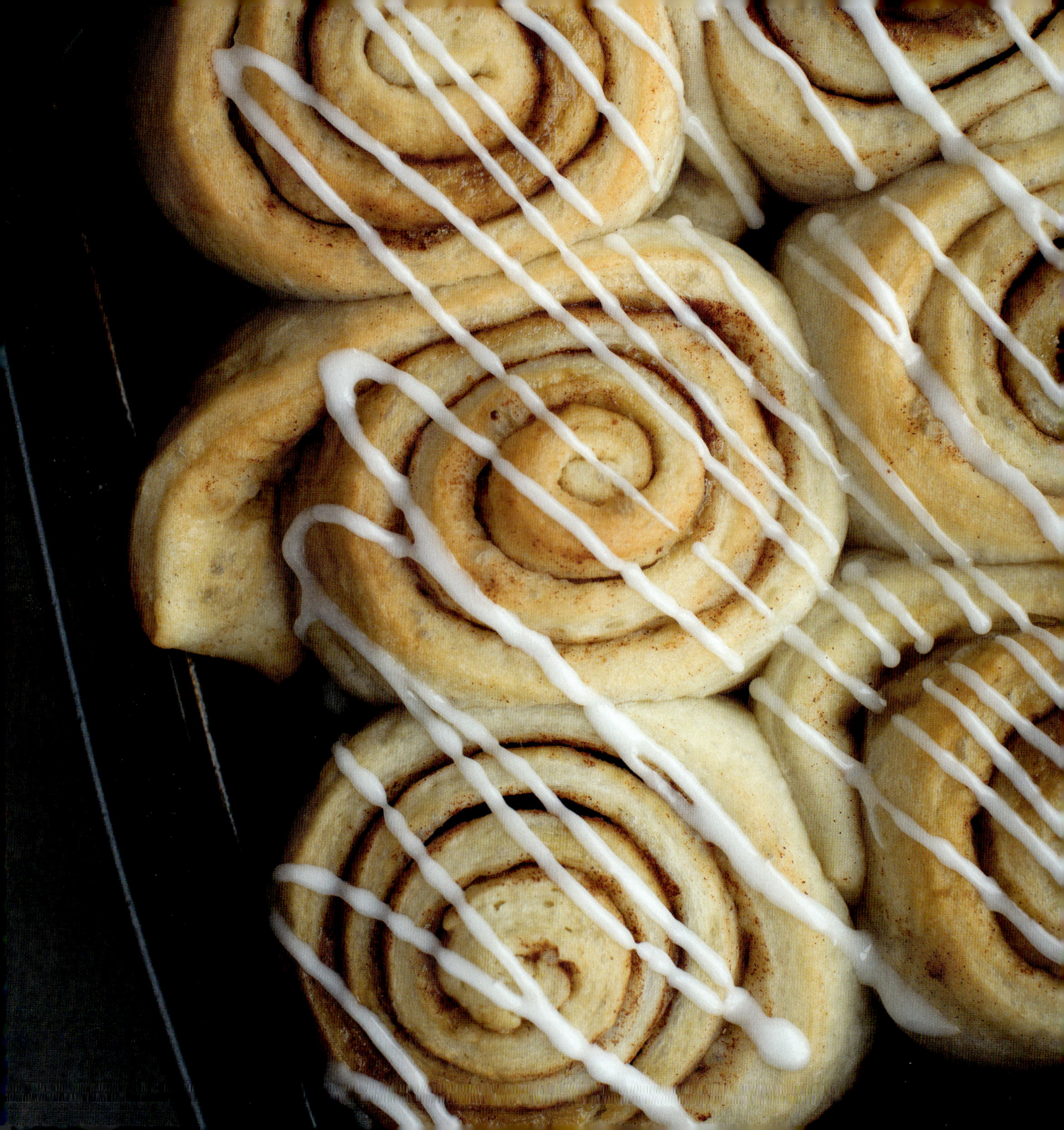

40 min / **9 BRIOCHES**

25 à 30 min

1 h 30 min

BRIOCHES

1 tasse (250 ml) lait végétal

1 c. à soupe (1 sachet de 8 g) levure sèche active

¼ tasse (50 g) sucre de canne

¼ tasse (60 ml) beurre végétalien fondu (+ ¼ tasse/60 ml, pour badigeonner la pâte)

1 c. à thé (5 ml) sel

2 ½ tasses (375 g) farine (+ un peu pour enfariner le plan de travail)

½ tasse (100 g) cassonade

1 ½ c. à thé (8 ml) cannelle

GLAÇAGE

2 c. à soupe (30 ml) huile de coco fondue

3 c. à soupe (45 ml) eau chaude

1 ¼ tasse (150 g) sucre glace

PRÉPARER LES BRIOCHES

1. Préchauffer le four à 350 °F (180 °C).
2. Faire chauffer le lait végétal au four à micro-ondes ou dans une poêle de 30 secondes à 1 minute, ou jusqu'à ce qu'il soit tiède.
3. Dans un grand bol, mélanger la levure et le lait végétal tiède.
4. Laisser reposer 5 minutes, jusqu'à la formation de bulles à la surface.
5. Ajouter le sucre, le beurre fondu et le sel. Bien mélanger.
6. Ajouter la farine et pétrir 1 minute, ou jusqu'à ce que le mélange forme une boule légèrement collante.
7. Recouvrir le bol d'un linge humide et laisser reposer pendant 1 heure à la température ambiante.
8. Déposer la pâte sur un plan de travail enfariné et abaisser avec un rouleau à pâte de façon à obtenir un rectangle de 12 po x 18 po (30 cm x 45 cm).
9. À l'aide d'un pinceau, badigeonner toute la surface de la pâte du reste du beurre.
10. Parsemer uniformément de la cassonade, puis saupoudrer de la cannelle.
11. Rouler le rectangle de pâte dans le sens de la longueur, puis couper le rouleau en 9 rondelles de même épaisseur.
12. Déposer les rondelles de pâte sur une plaque à pâtisserie beurrée ou tapissée de papier parchemin.
13. Laisser reposer 30 minutes supplémentaires afin de permettre aux brioches de gonfler.
14. Faire cuire au four de 20 à 30 minutes.

ENTRE-TEMPS, PRÉPARER LE GLAÇAGE

1. Dans une casserole, faire fondre l'huile de coco. Ajouter l'eau et le sucre glace, puis mélanger.
2. Retirer les brioches du four, puis les laisser refroidir quelques minutes. Arroser du glaçage avant de déguster.

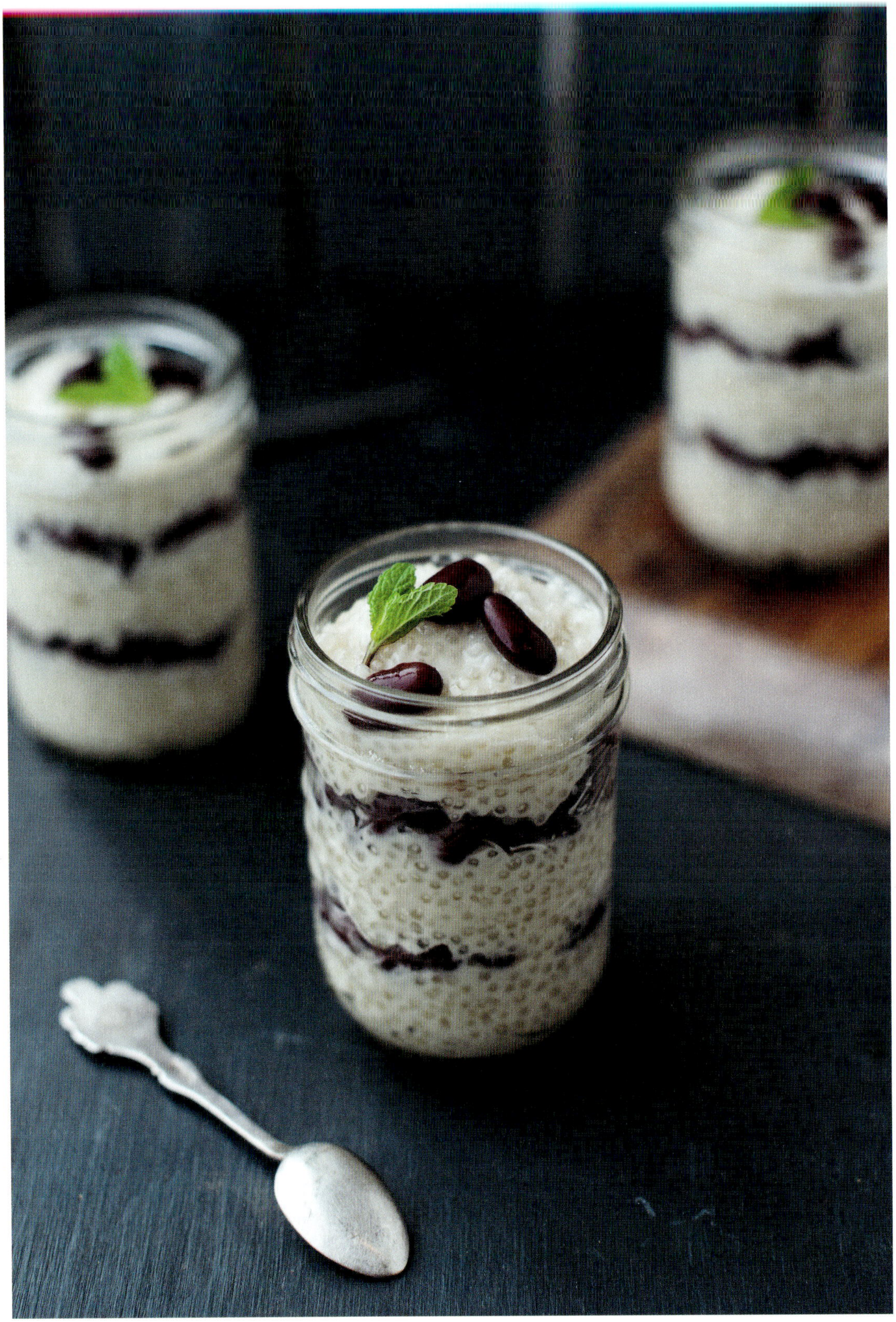

10 min / **4 PORTIONS**

30 min

Temps de réfrigération 2 h

INGRÉDIENTS

½ tasse (80 g) perles de tapioca, rincées et égouttées

1 ½ tasse (375 ml) lait végétal

1 boîte (400 ml) lait de coco

⅛ c. à thé (0,5 ml) sel

¼ tasse (60 ml) sirop d'érable

½ boîte (270 ml) haricots rouges, rincés et égouttés

PRÉPARATION

1. Dans une casserole, déposer tous les ingrédients, sauf les haricots rouges.
2. Porter à ébullition en remuant constamment, puis réduire le feu au minimum. Laisser mijoter doucement pendant 30 minutes en remuant fréquemment pour que le mélange ne colle pas.
3. Verser une couche du mélange de tapioca dans des ramequins, puis couvrir d'une couche de haricots rouges. Couvrir du reste du mélange de tapioca, puis réfrigérer pendant au moins 2 heures avant de déguster.

Tarte au citron meringuée

30 min / **1 TARTE**

35 min

Temps de réfrigération 1 h

MERINGUE VÉGÉTALE

1 tasse (250 ml) jus de pois chiches (le liquide de 1 boîte de 540 ml)

¼ tasse (30 g) sucre glace

⅛ c. à thé (0,5 ml) crème de tartre (facultatif)

CROÛTE

1 tasse (150 g) farine tout usage

1 tasse (130 g) poudre d'amande

⅓ tasse (70 g) sucre blanc

½ tasse (125 ml) huile de coco

¼ c. à thé (1 ml) sel

GARNITURE

½ tasse (70 g) fécule de maïs

¾ tasse (160 g) sucre blanc

½ c. à soupe (8 ml) agar agar en poudre

½ c. à thé (2,5 ml) curcuma

¼ c. à thé (1 ml) sel

⅓ tasse (80 ml) jus de citron

3 tasses (750 ml) lait de coco en conserve

Zeste de 2 citrons

PRÉPARER LA MERINGUE VÉGÉTALE

1. Dans une casserole, faire réduire le jus de pois chiches à feu doux pendant 10 à 15 minutes. (Le jus de pois chiches montera plus facilement ainsi.)
2. Transvider le jus réduit dans un bol et laisser refroidir pendant 5 minutes. Ajouter le sucre glace et la crème de tartre, puis battre pendant 5 minutes, ou jusqu'à ce que la meringue ait assez épaissi. Réserver au réfrigérateur.

PRÉPARER LA CROÛTE

1. Préchauffer le four à 350 °F (180 °C).
2. Dans un grand bol, mélanger la farine, la poudre d'amande, le sucre, l'huile de coco et le sel, jusqu'à l'obtention d'une texture granuleuse.
3. Du bout des doigts, presser la pâte dans le fond d'un moule à charnière de 10 po (25 cm) de diamètre.
4. Cuire au four pendant environ 20 minutes, ou jusqu'à ce que la croûte soit bien dorée. Laisser refroidir.

PRÉPARER LA GARNITURE

1. Dans une casserole, hors du feu, mélanger la fécule de maïs, le sucre, l'agar agar, le curcuma, le sel, le jus de citron, le lait de coco et le zeste de citron en remuant à l'aide d'un fouet.
2. Porter à ébullition en remuant. Laisser mijoter pendant 1 minute et retirer la casserole du feu.
3. Verser la garniture sur la croûte et laisser refroidir pendant au moins 1 heure au réfrigérateur. Garnir la tarte de la meringue avant de servir.

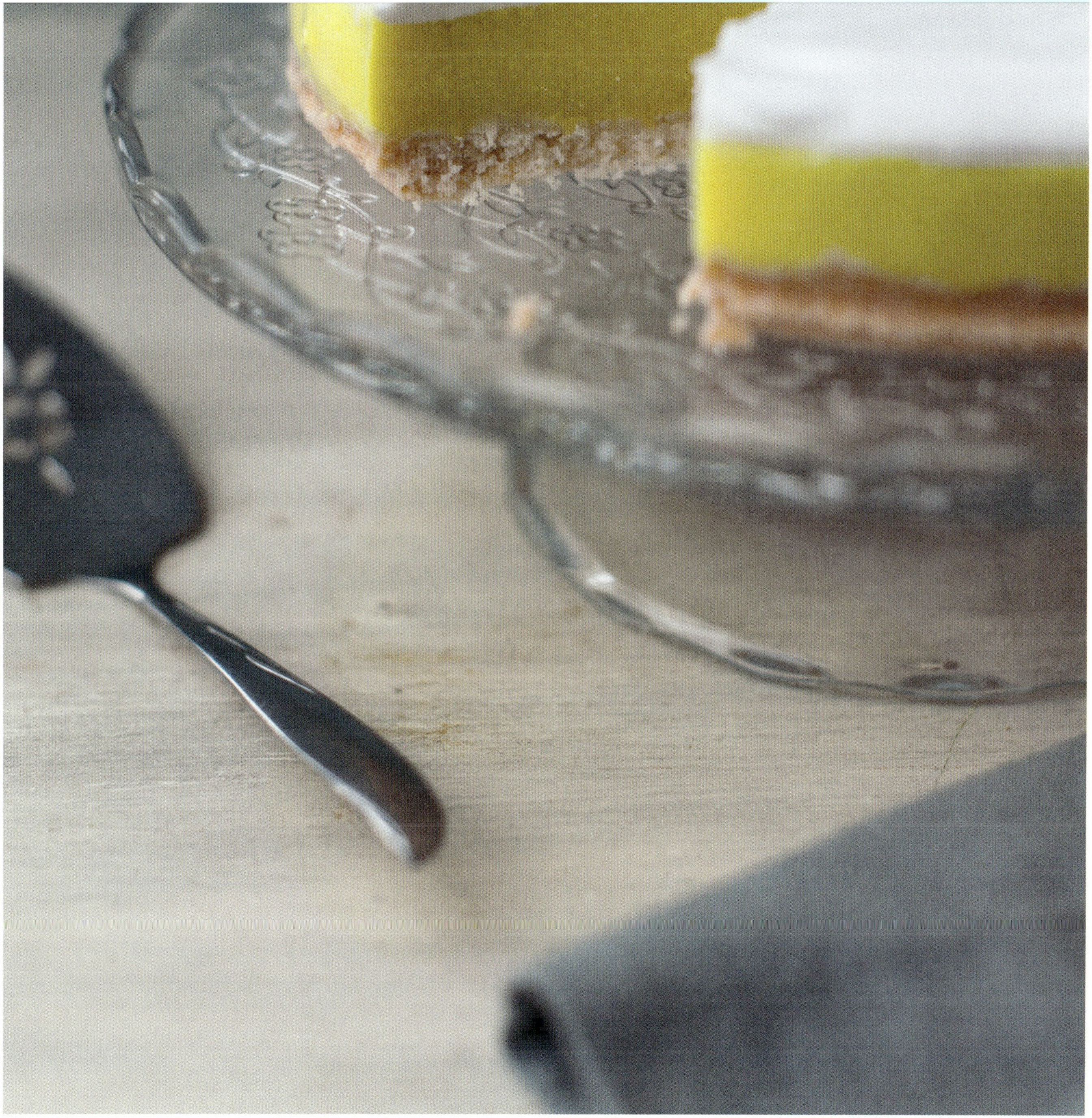

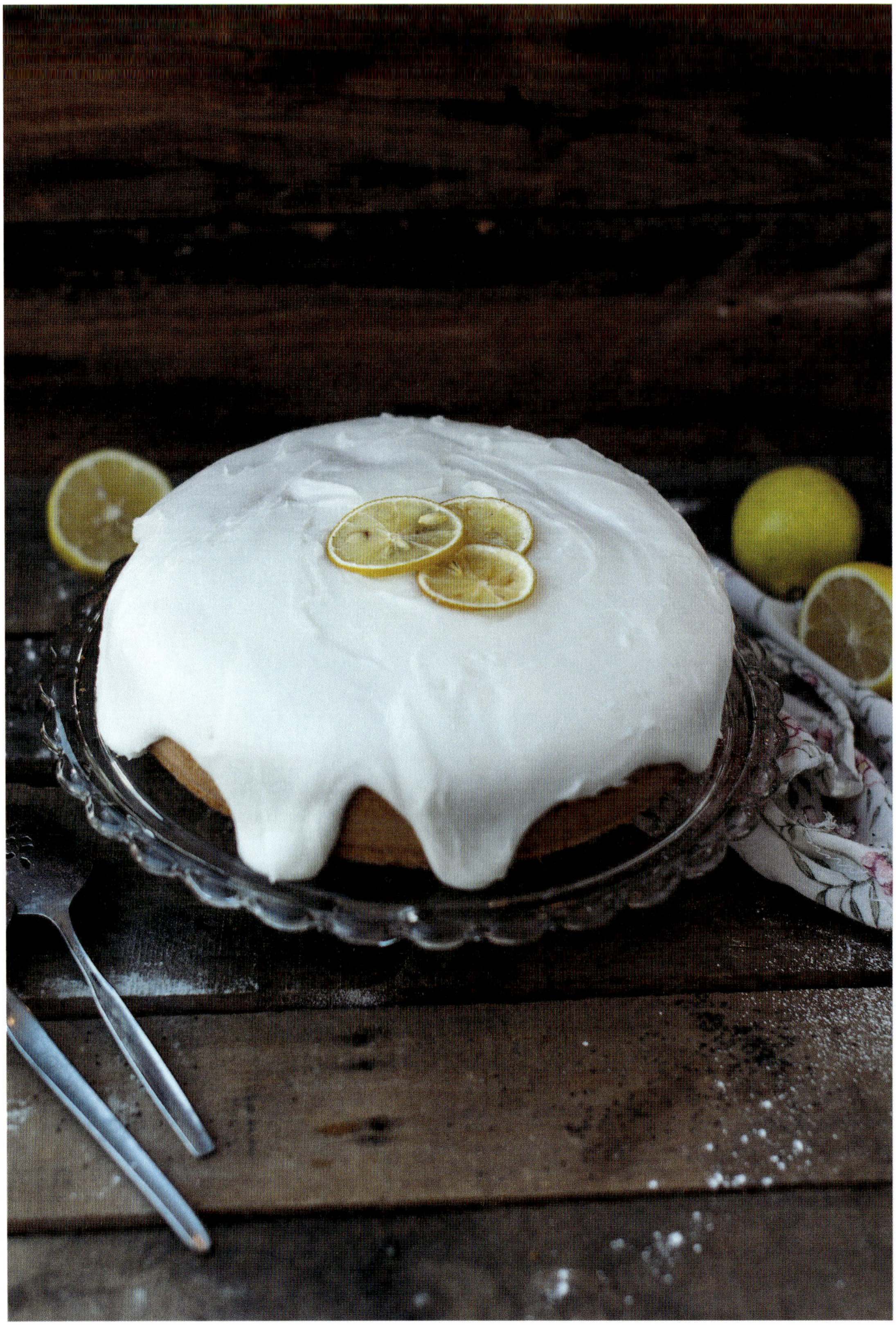

30 min / **1 GÂTEAU**

40 à 45 min

GÂTEAU

2 tasses (300 g) farine

1 tasse (100 g) poudre d'amande

1 tasse (200 g) sucre de canne

1 c. à thé (5 ml) sel

2 c. à thé (10 ml) poudre à pâte

½ tasse (125 ml) huile végétale

1 ¼ tasse (310 ml) lait végétal

Le zeste et le jus de 1 citron

¼ tasse (35 g) graines de pavot

GLAÇAGE

2 c. à soupe (30 ml) huile de coco fondue

2 c. à soupe (30 ml) jus de citron

1 ¼ tasse (145 g) sucre glace

Quelques tranches de citron, pour garnir

PRÉPARER LE GÂTEAU

1. Préchauffer le four à 350 °F (180 °C).
2. Huiler un moule carré de 8 po x 8 po (20 cm x 20 cm). Réserver.
3. Dans un bol, mélanger la farine, la poudre d'amande, le sucre, le sel et la poudre à pâte.
4. Ajouter l'huile végétale, le lait végétal, le zeste, le jus de citron et les graines de pavot, puis mélanger jusqu'à l'obtention d'une pâte lisse et homogène.
5. Verser la pâte dans le moule et cuire au four de 40 à 45 minutes, ou jusqu'à ce qu'un cure-dent inséré au centre du gâteau en ressorte propre.
6. Laisser refroidir le gâteau pendant 15 minutes. Démouler et laisser refroidir complètement sur une grille.

PRÉPARER LE GLAÇAGE

1. Dans un bol, bien mélanger l'huile de coco fondue, le jus de citron et le sucre glace.
2. Verser le glaçage sur le gâteau refroidi, garnir de quelques tranches de citron et laisser refroidir avant de servir.

BOISSONS

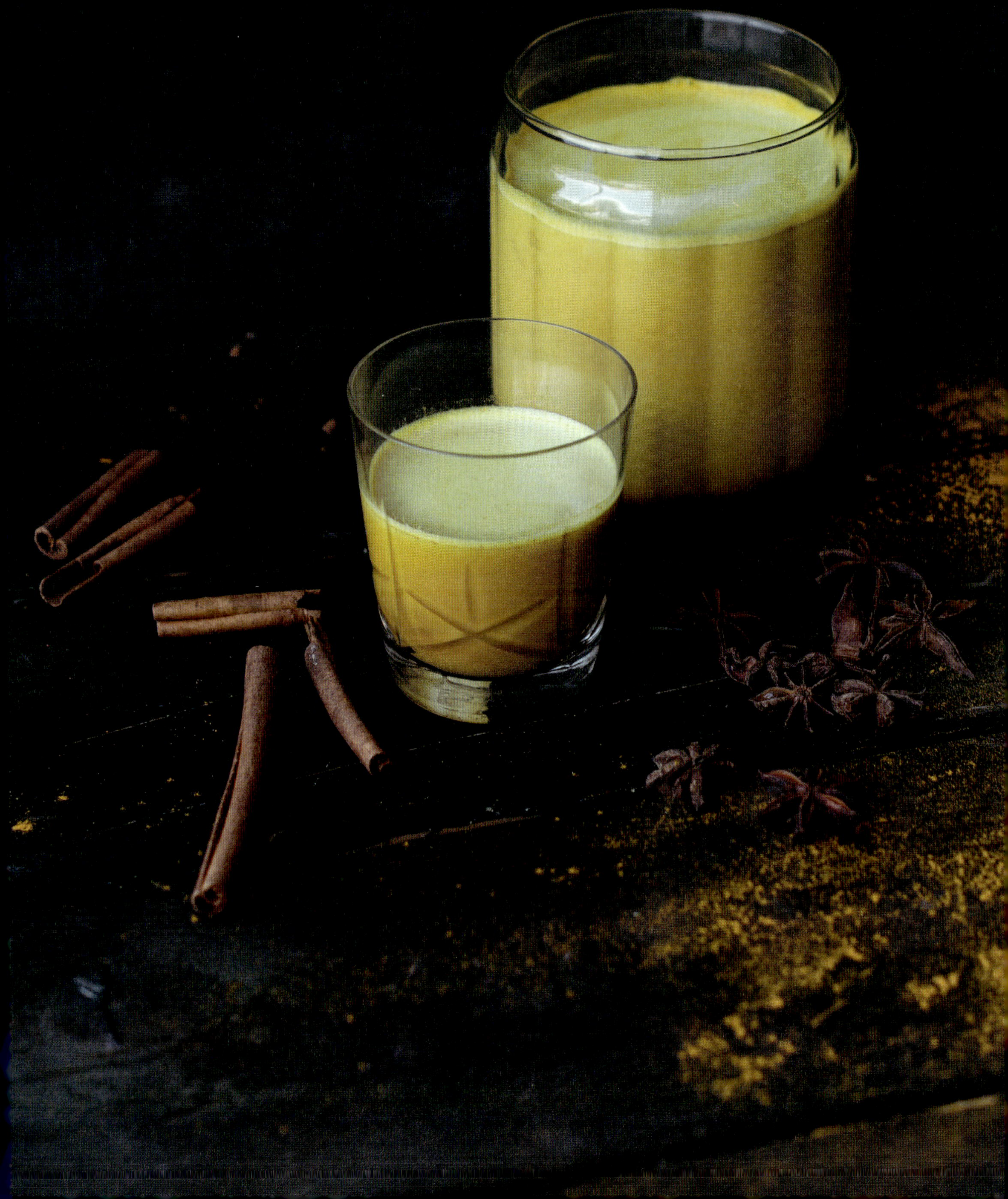

15 min / **1 PORTION**

INGRÉDIENTS

1 ½ tasse (375 ml) lait végétal

1 anis étoilé

½ c. à thé (2,5 ml) curcuma

1 pincée de sel

¼ c. à thé (1 ml) cardamome moulue

1 bâton de cannelle

2 c. à thé (10 ml) sirop d'érable

PRÉPARATION

1. Dans une casserole, porter tous les ingrédients à ébullition à feu moyen-vif, en remuant constamment. (Porter attention, car le lait aura tendance à déborder sitôt le point d'ébullition atteint.)
2. Retirer du feu et laisser reposer pendant 10 minutes.
3. Filtrer le lait et servir.

Bols de smoothie

15 min / **1 BOL PAR RECETTE**

RECETTE 1
INGRÉDIENTS

½ avocat

1 tasse (250 ml) mangues surgelées

2 c. à soupe (30 ml) sirop d'érable

1 c. à soupe (15 ml) jus de citron

2 c. à soupe (30 ml) lait végétal

Quelques amandes effilées, pour garnir

Quelques fruits (raisins, mûres, etc.), pour garnir

PRÉPARATION

1. Au robot culinaire, broyer l'avocat, la mangue, le sirop d'érable, le jus de citron et le lait végétal jusqu'à l'obtention d'une consistance homogène.
2. Verser le mélange dans un bol. Garnir d'amandes et de fruits. Servir bien frais.

RECETTE 2
INGRÉDIENTS

1 banane

½ tasse (70 g) mûres surgelées

¼ tasse (35 g) noix de cajou

¼ tasse (60 ml) lait végétal

Quelques fruits (banane, kiwis, etc.), pour garnir

Quelques pistaches concassées, pour garnir

Quelques graines de chia, pour garnir

PRÉPARATION

1. Au robot culinaire, broyer la banane, les mûres, les noix de cajou et le lait végétal jusqu'à l'obtention d'une consistance homogène.
2. Verser le mélange dans un bol. Garnir de fruits, de pistaches et de graines de chia. Servir bien frais.

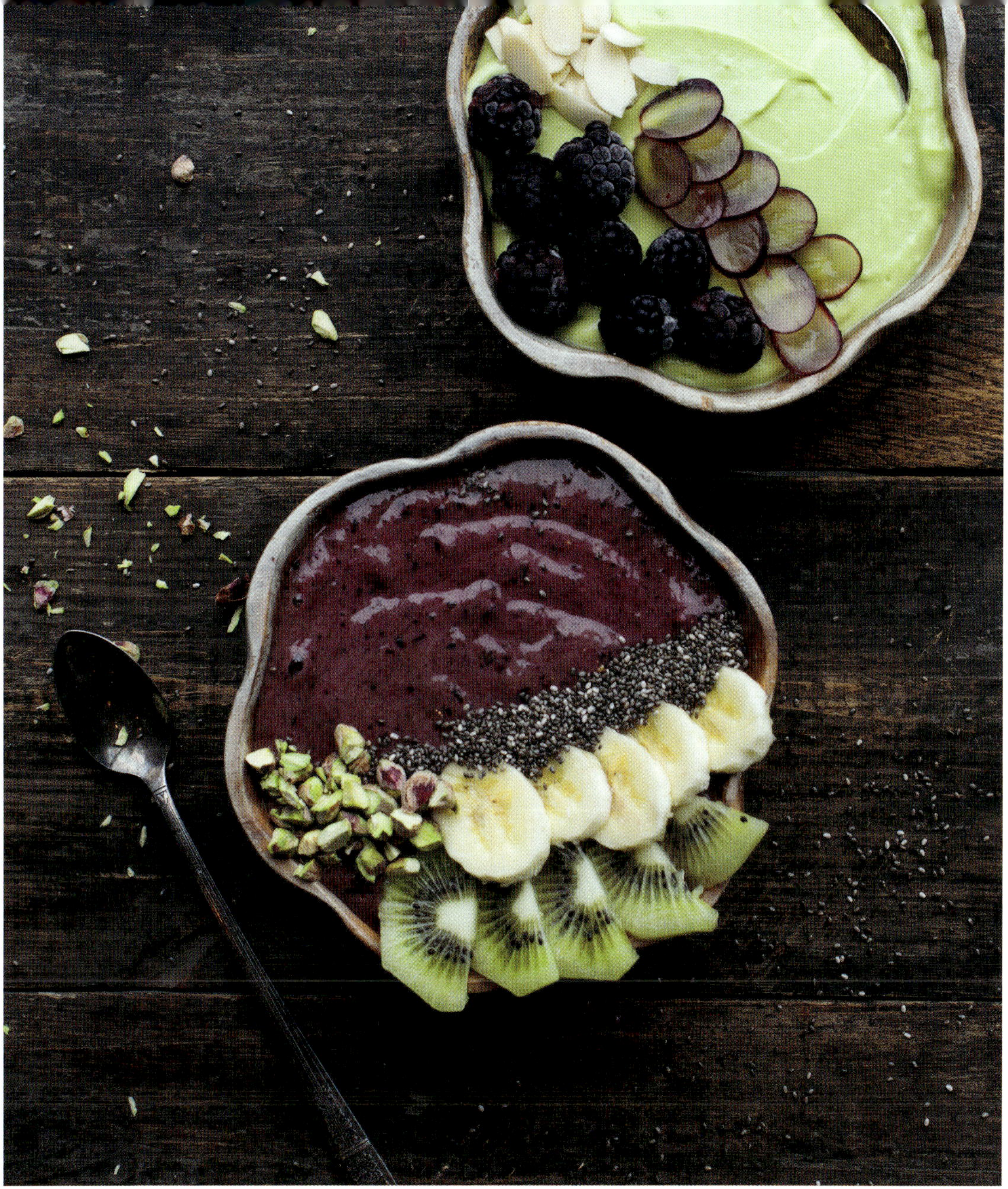

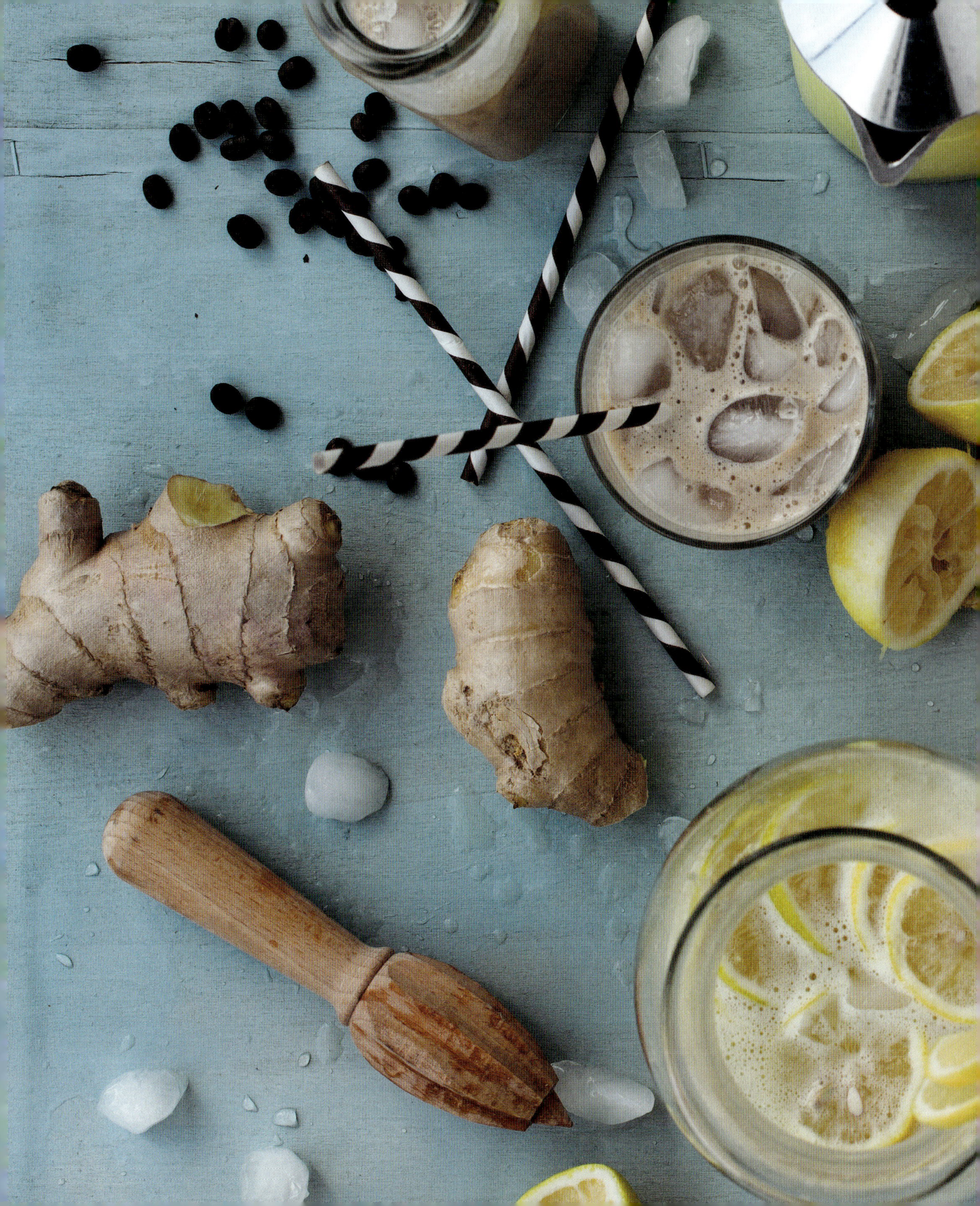

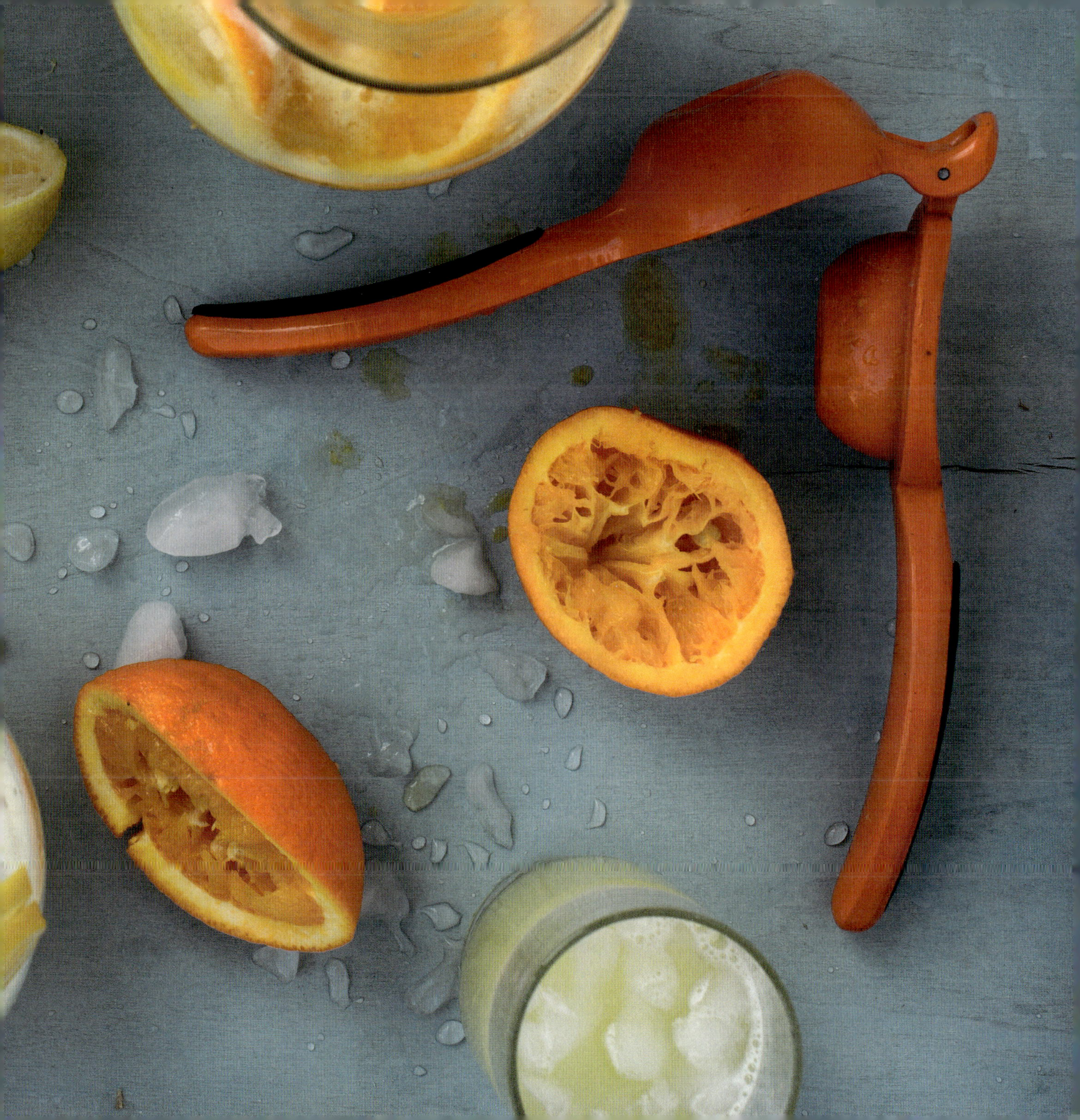

Café glacé infusé à froid

5 min / **1 PORTION**

45 min

Temps de réfrigération 2 à 12 h

INGRÉDIENTS

2 c. à soupe (30 ml) café moulu

½ c. à thé (2,5 ml) cacao en poudre

2 c. à soupe (30 ml) sirop d'érable

1 pincée de sel

1 ½ tasse (375 ml) lait végétal

Glaçons

PRÉPARATION

1. Dans une tasse, bien mélanger le café, le cacao, le sirop d'érable, le sel et le lait végétal.
2. Réfrigérer pendant 2 heures, ou jusqu'au lendemain. (Plus le café infusera longtemps plus son goût sera prononcé.)
3. Filtrer le mélange et servir sur des glaçons.

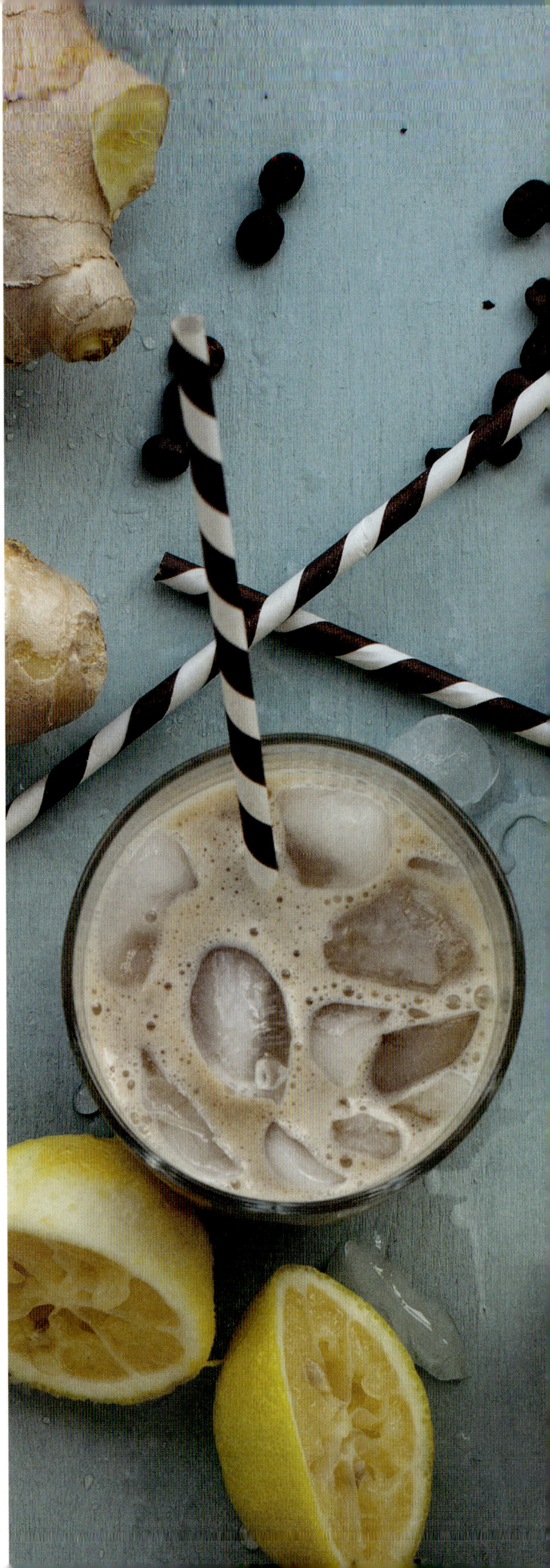

Limonade au gingembre

5 min / **1 PICHET**

INGRÉDIENTS

1 morceau de gingembre de 2 po (5 cm), épluché et coupé grossièrement

Le jus de 3 à 4 citrons

4 tasses (1 L) eau

⅓ tasse (80 ml) sirop d'érable

2 citrons, coupés en rondelles, pour garnir

Glaçons

PRÉPARATION

1. Dans le récipient d'un mélangeur, déposer le gingembre et verser le jus de citron.
2. Broyer.
3. Ajouter l'eau et le sirop d'érable. Bien mélanger.
4. Filtrer et servir sur des glaçons, avec une rondelle de citron.

Jus d'orange et d'ananas

5 min / **1 PICHET**

INGRÉDIENTS

4 oranges, pelées (les pépins enlevés, si possible)

2 tasses (300 g) ananas, coupé en dés

4 tasses (1 L) eau

Glaçons

PRÉPARATION

1. Dans le récipient d'un mélangeur, déposer les oranges, l'ananas et l'eau.
2. Broyer, filtrer et servir sur des glaçons.

COLLATIONS

Fauxmages de noix de macadam

20 min / **3 FAUXMAGES**
5 min
15 min
Temps de réfrigération 2 h

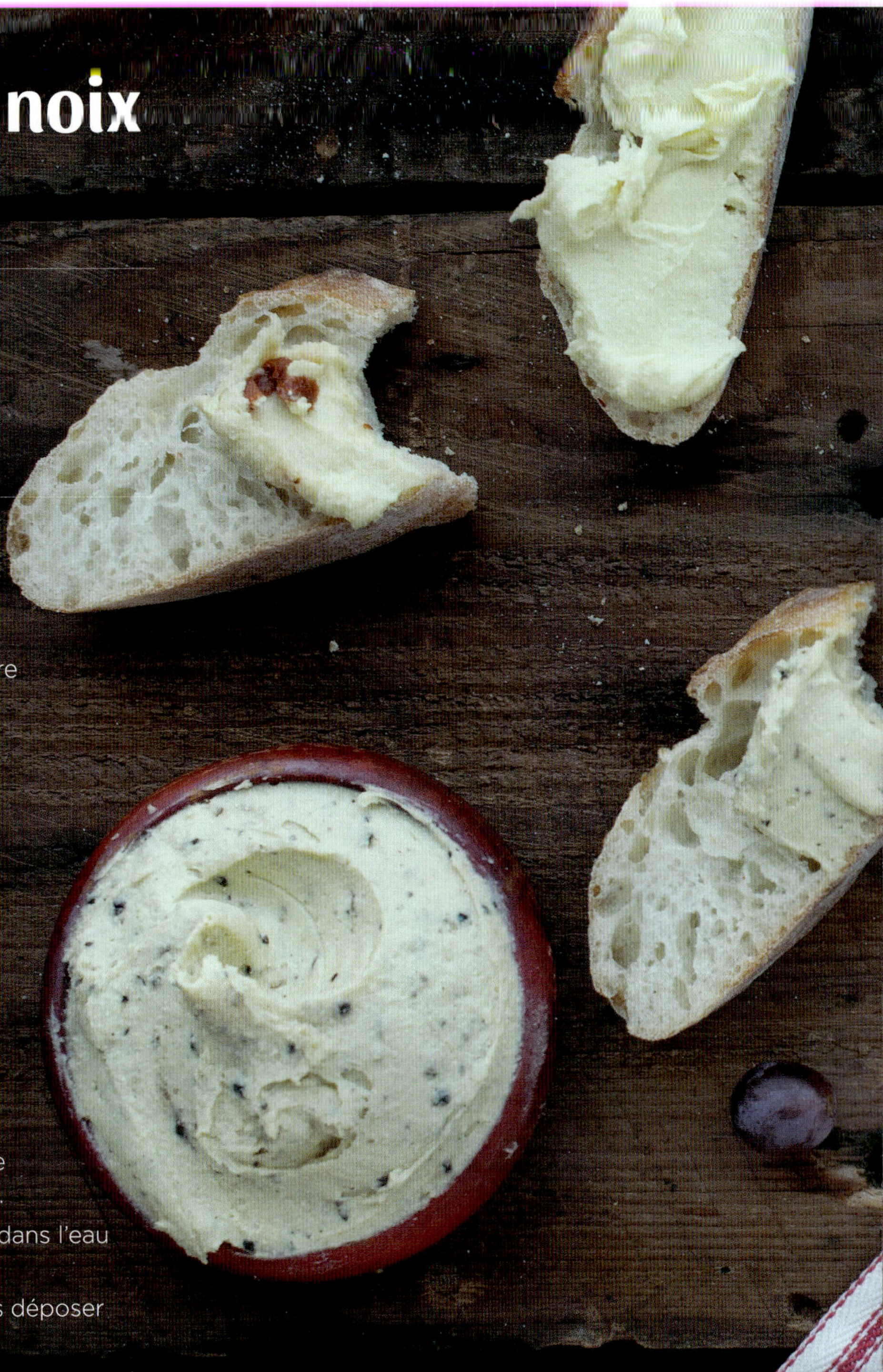

INGRÉDIENTS DE BASE

¼ tasse (35 g) noix de macadam
2 c. à soupe (30 ml) fécule de tapioca
1 c. à soupe (15 ml) agar agar en poudre
1 c. à thé (5 ml) jus de citron
1 c. à thé (5 ml) vinaigre de cidre
1 c. à thé (5 ml) sirop d'érable
¼ tasse (20 g) levure alimentaire
½ c. à thé (2,5 ml) poudre d'ail
⅓ tasse (70 g) huile de coco désodorisée solide
1 c. à thé (5 ml) sel
1 tasse (250 ml) eau

PRÉPARATION

1. Huiler légèrement 3 ramequins d'une capacité de ½ tasse (125 ml) chacun.
2. Faire tremper les noix de macadam dans l'eau bouillante pendant 15 minutes.
3. Égoutter les noix de macadam et les déposer dans le récipient d'un mélangeur.
4. Ajouter le reste des ingrédients et broyer jusqu'à l'obtention d'une texture homogène.
5. Verser la préparation dans une casserole et porter à ébullition à feu moyen-vif, en remuant constamment. Sitôt le point d'ébullition atteint, poursuivre la cuisson pendant 2 minutes et retirer du feu. (La préparation aura alors épaissi et sera prête à être versée dans les ramequins.)
6. Verser la préparation dans les ramequins, couvrir d'une pellicule plastique et réfrigérer pendant au moins 2 heures. Déguster.

FAUXMAGE AU POIVRE: recette de base + 1 c. à soupe (15 ml) poivre en grains moulus grossièrement, à ajouter en fin de cuisson.

FAUXMAGE À L'HUILE DE TRUFFE: recette de base + 1 c. à soupe (15 ml) huile de truffe, à ajouter en fin de cuisson.

FAUXMAGE AU PIMENT: recette de base + 1 c. à soupe (15 ml) piment jalapeño en boîte, haché, à ajouter en fin de cuisson.

NOTE: Se conservent jusqu'à 1 semaine au réfrigérateur.

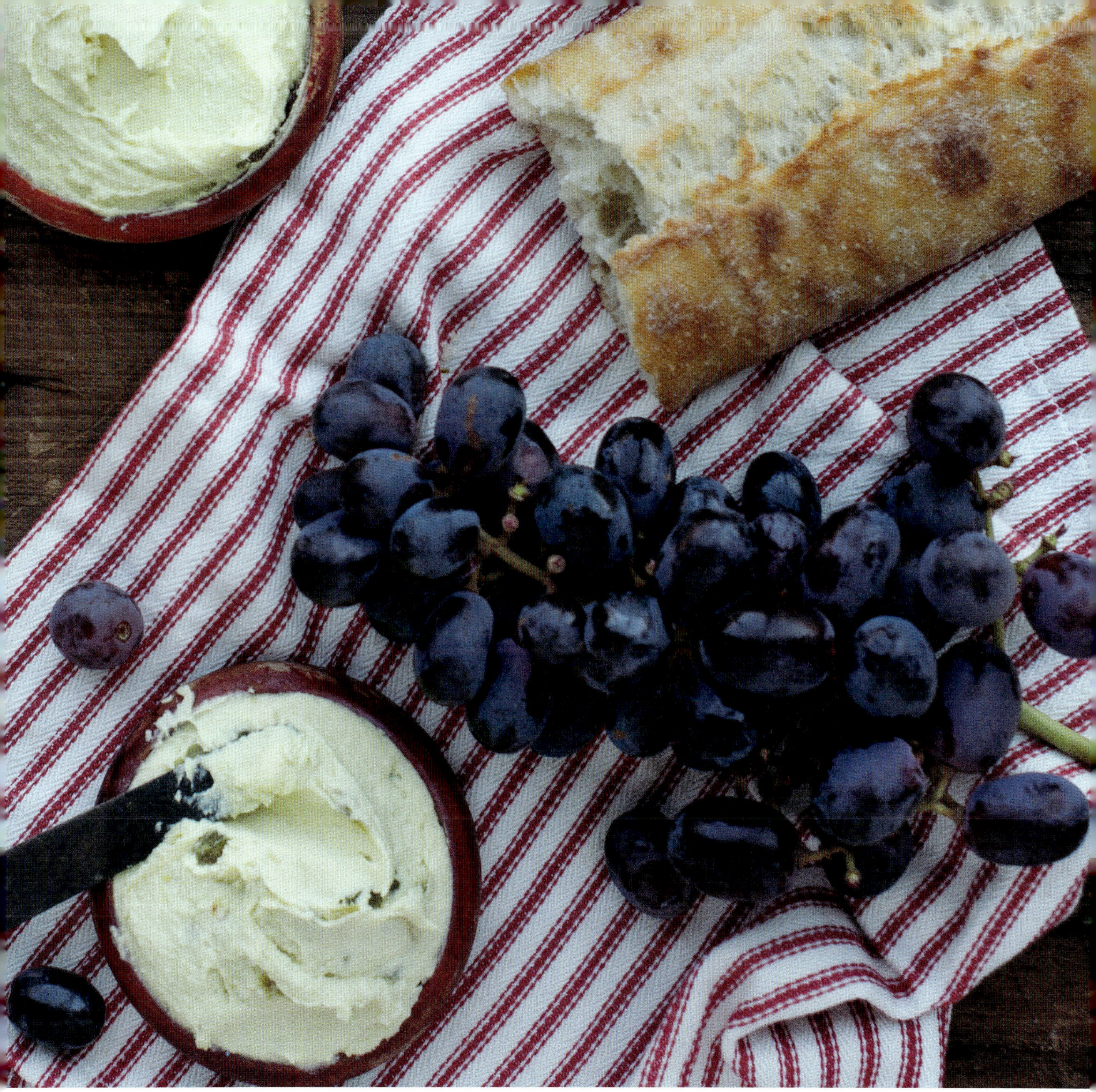

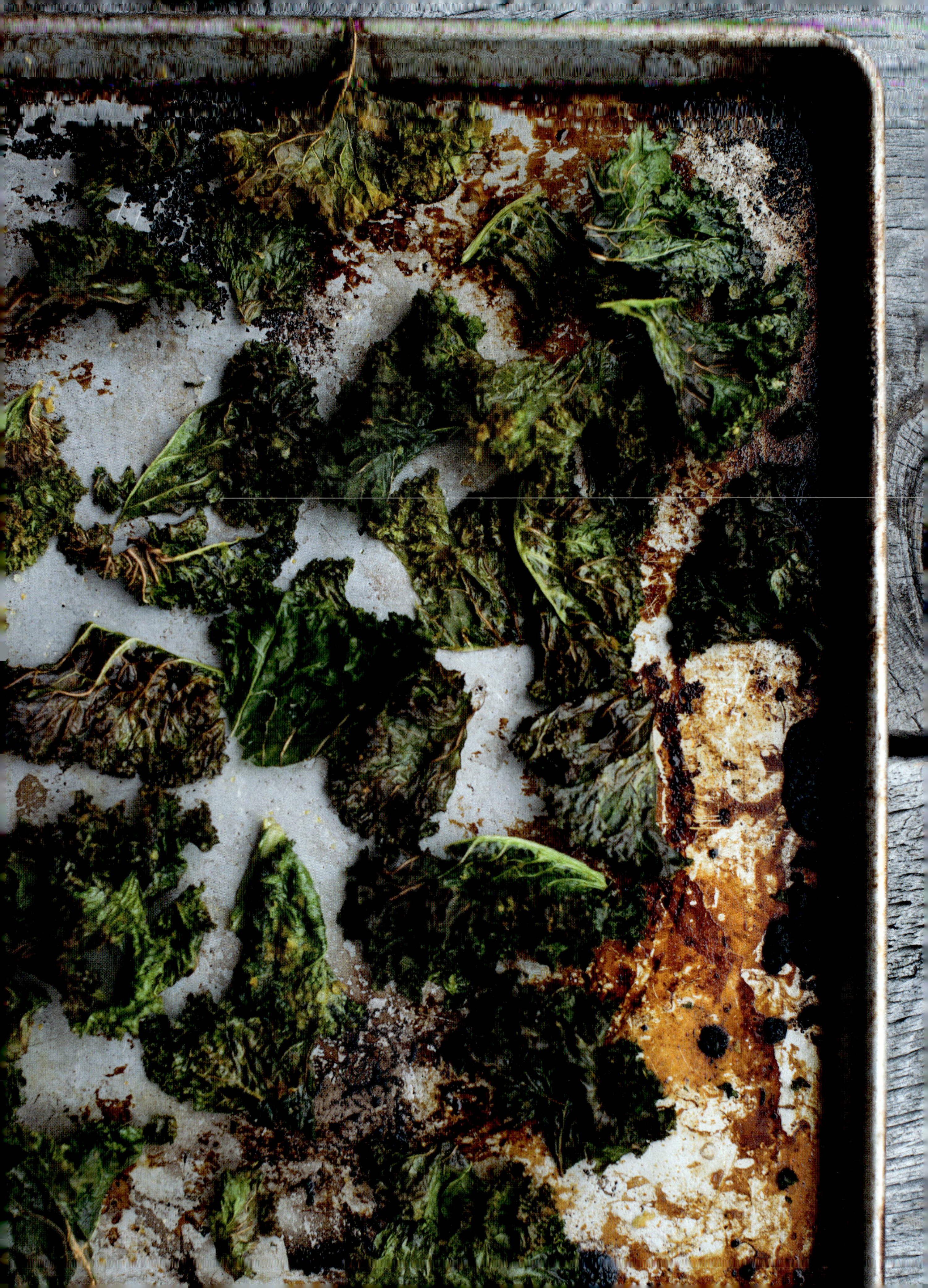

Le secret de cette recette est de bien essorer les feuilles de kale avant de les enrober.

15 min / **4 PORTIONS**

15 à 20 min

INGRÉDIENTS

1 botte (environ 150 g) chou frisé (kale)

2 c. à soupe (30 ml) huile d'olive

2 c. à soupe (30 ml) levure alimentaire

½ c. à thé (2,5 ml) fleur de sel

PRÉPARATION

1. Préchauffer le four à 325 °F (160 °C).
2. Débarrasser les feuilles de chou frisé de leur tige centrale en faisant glisser la lame d'un couteau de part et d'autre de la tige.
3. Déchirer les feuilles grossièrement.
4. Nettoyer les feuilles à l'eau et bien les essorer (idéalement, avec une essoreuse à salade).
5. Déposer les feuilles dans un grand bol.
6. Ajouter l'huile d'olive, la levure et la fleur de sel. Remuer pour bien enrober les feuilles.
7. Étendre les feuilles sur une plaque à pâtisserie.
8. Cuire au four de 15 à 20 minutes, ou jusqu'à ce que les chips soient bien croustillantes. Déguster.

Houmous

15 min / **ENVIRON 3 TASSES (750 ML)**

INGRÉDIENTS

1 boîte (540 ml) pois chiches, rincés et égouttés

3 c. à soupe (45 ml) tahini ou beurre d'arachide naturel

1 gousse d'ail, hachée

1 c. à thé (5 ml) cumin

⅛ c. à thé (0,5 ml) piment de Cayenne

2 c. à soupe (30 ml) huile d'olive extra vierge (+ 1 c. à soupe/15 ml pour la garniture)

⅓ tasse (80 ml) eau

Le jus de ½ citron

Sel, au goût

Paprika fumé, pour garnir

Pain pita

PRÉPARATION

1. Au robot culinaire, broyer les pois chiches avec le tahini, l'ail, le cumin, le piment de Cayenne, l'huile d'olive, l'eau, le jus de citron et le sel jusqu'à l'obtention d'une consistance homogène.
2. Transférer le houmous dans un plat de service. Garnir d'un filet d'huile d'olive et saupoudrer d'une pincée de paprika fumé. Déguster avec des pains pita, par exemple.

NOTE : Se conserve jusqu'à 4 jours au réfrigérateur.

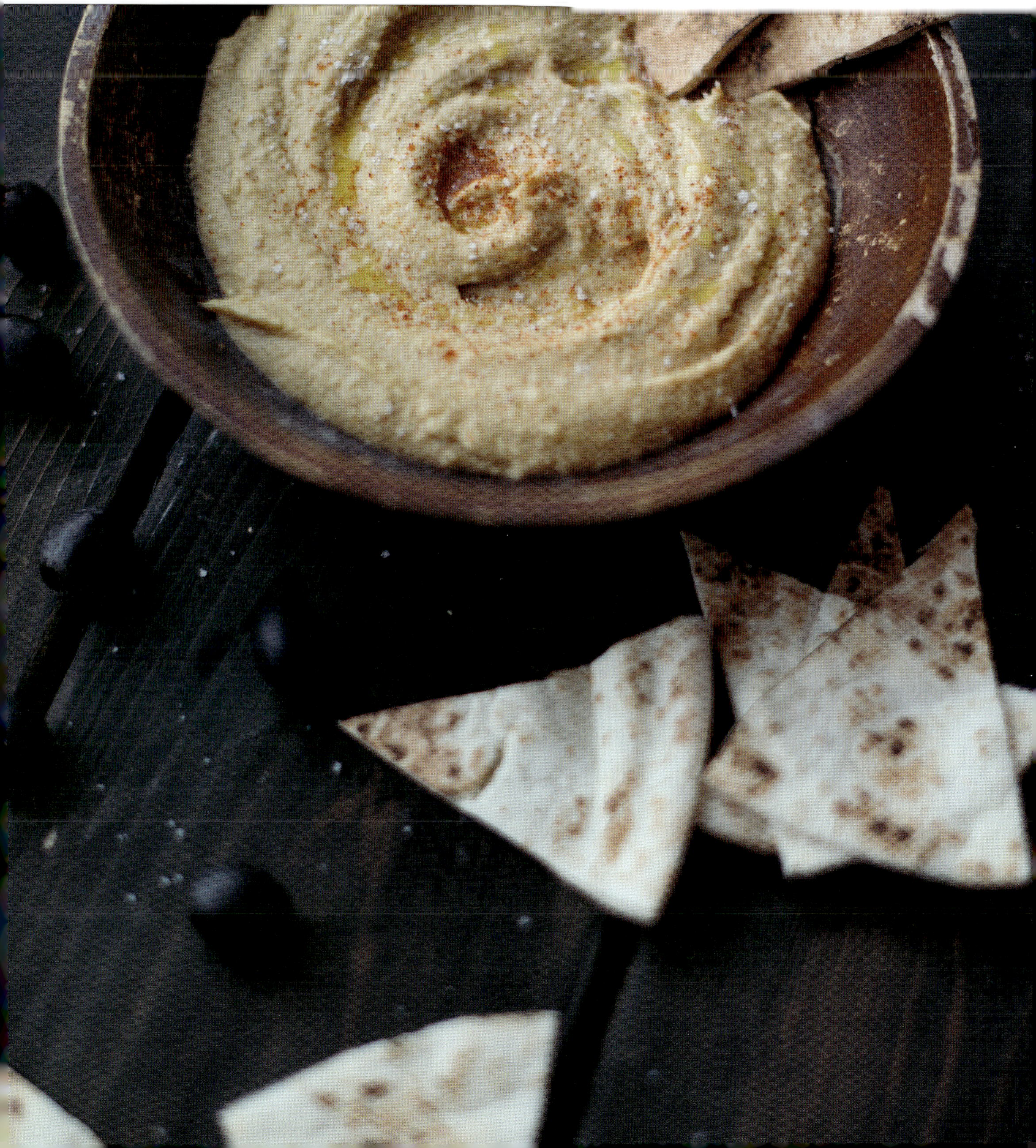

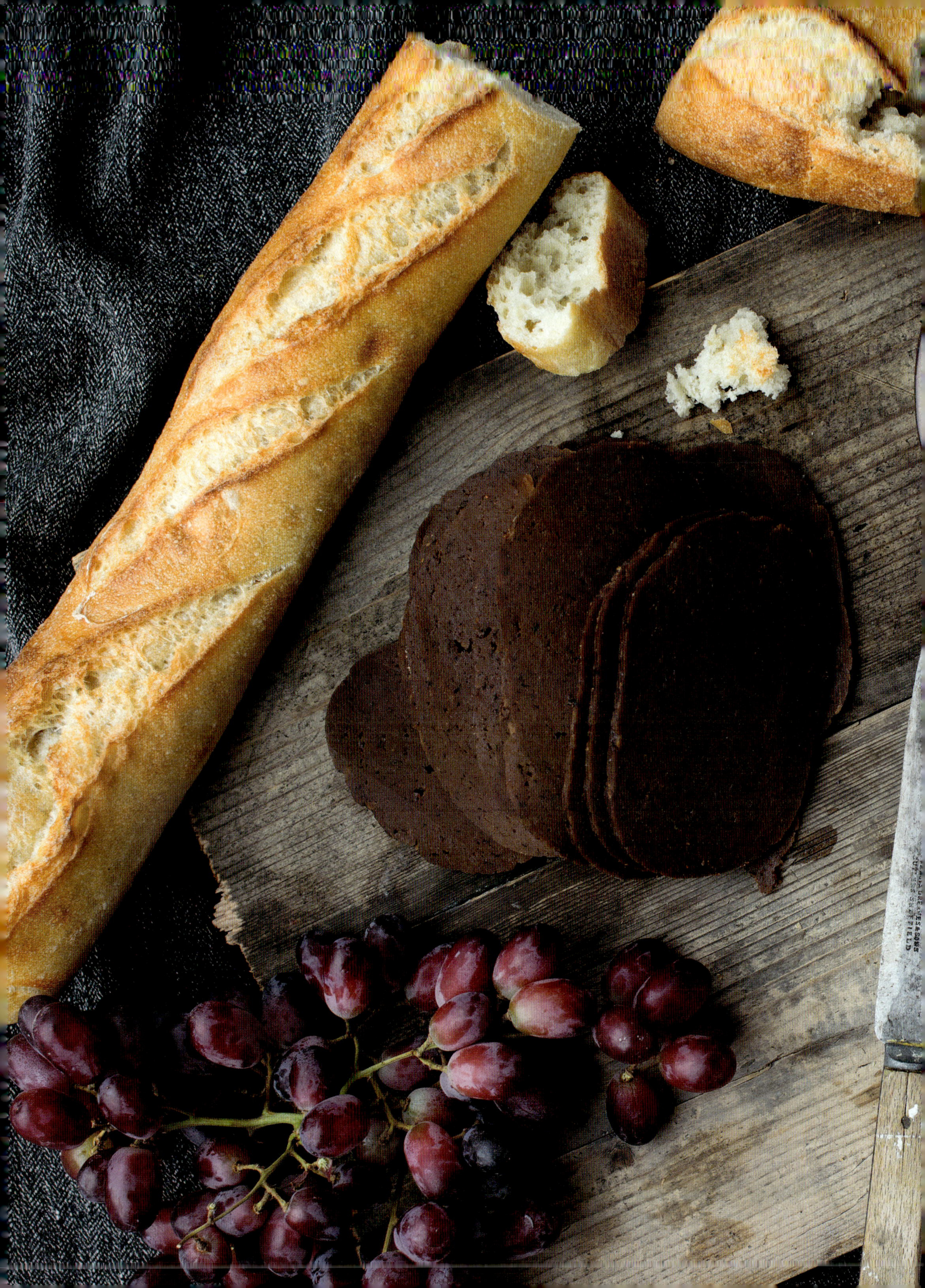

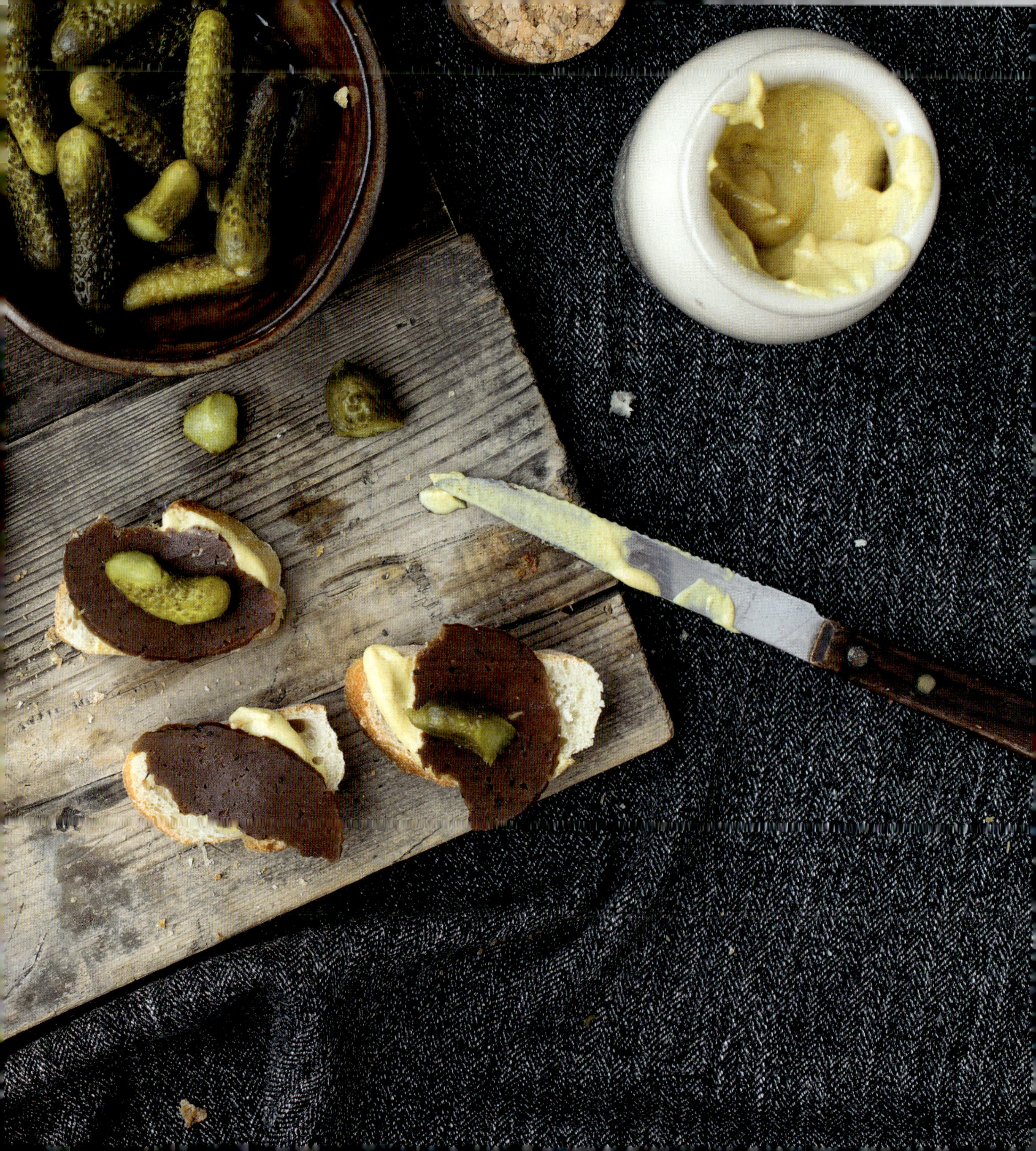

Seitan

Le seitan est un excellent succédané de viande dans tous les plats classiques. Il peut être cuit sur le gril, servi chaud ou froid, en sandwich ou en sauce. Il est moins gras que la viande ou le poisson, ne contient pas de cholestérol et il est plus riche en protéines.

30 min / **6 PORTIONS**

60 min

15 min

INGRÉDIENTS

2 tasses (260 g) farine de gluten

½ tasse (60 g) farine de pois chiches

½ tasse (40 g) levure alimentaire

1 c. à soupe (15 ml) paprika fumé

1 c. à soupe (15 ml) basilic séché

1 c. à soupe (15 ml) poudre d'oignon

1 c. à soupe (15 ml) ketchup

2 c. à soupe (30 ml) sauce Worcestershire végétalienne

½ tasse (125 ml) sauce soya

1 ½ tasse (375 ml) eau chaude

4 tasses (1 L) bouillon de légumes

PRÉPARATION

1. Dans un grand bol, bien mélanger la farine de gluten, la farine de pois chiches, la levure alimentaire, le paprika fumé, le basilic séché et la poudre d'oignon. Réserver.
2. Dans un autre bol, mélanger le ketchup, la sauce Worcestershire, la sauce soya et l'eau chaude.
3. Incorporer le mélange liquide aux ingrédients secs et bien mélanger.
4. Former une boule et pétrir de 2 à 3 minutes, en ajoutant de la farine de gluten, au besoin.
5. Envelopper le seitan dans une pellicule plastique ou dans un coton à fromage (étamine), puis nouer les deux extrémités.
6. Dans une casserole, porter à ébullition le bouillon de légumes et y plonger le seitan. Réduire le feu et faire pocher le seitan à feu doux pendant 1 heure, en le retournant de temps à autre.
7. Retirer du feu et laisser le seitan refroidir dans le bouillon pendant 15 minutes. Égoutter le seitan. Retirer la pellicule plastique.
8. Servir avec du pain et vos condiments préférés.

NOTE : Se conserve jusqu'à 5 jours au réfrigérateur ou 2 mois au congélateur.

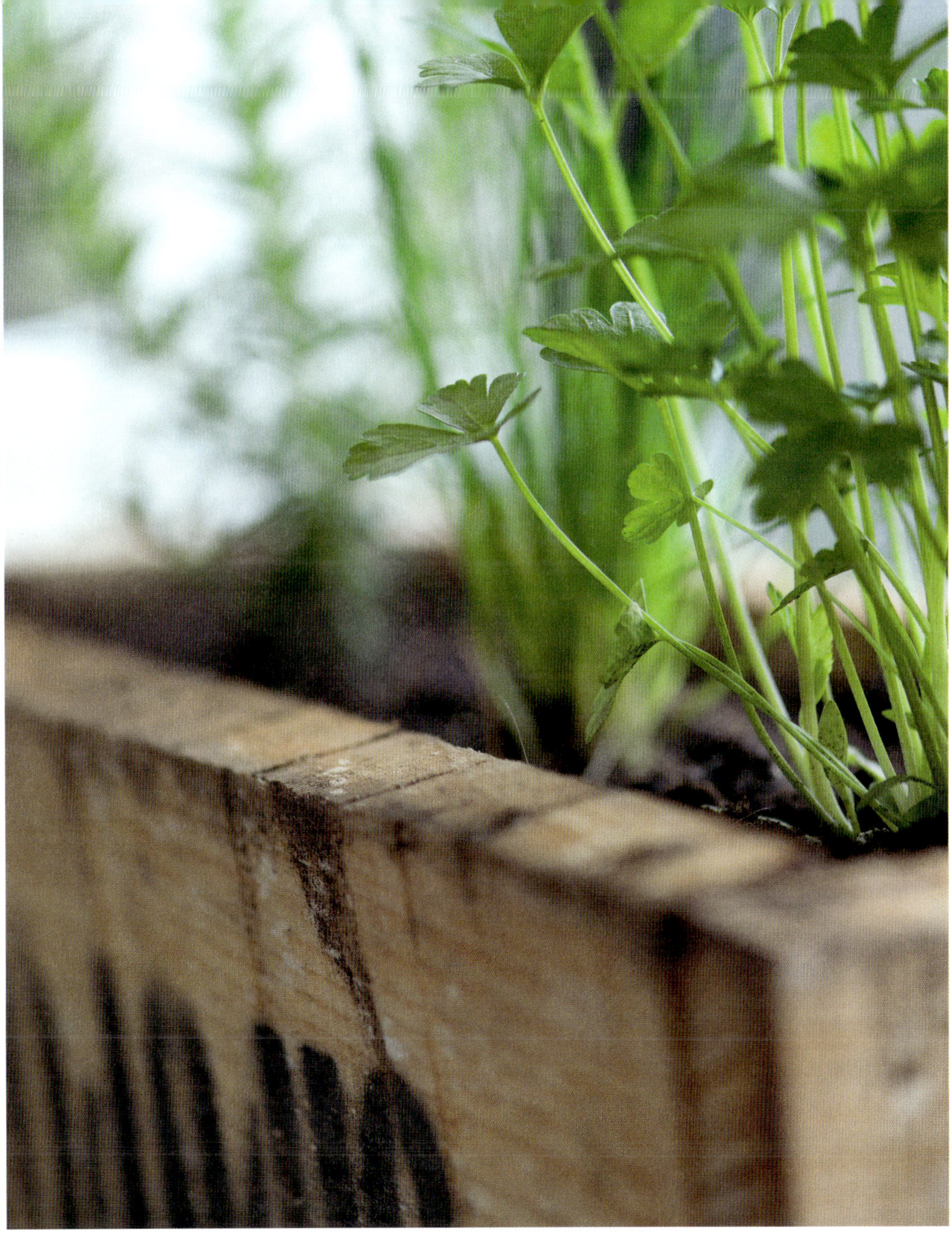

Pois chiches grillés

10 min / **2 PORTIONS**

30 à 45 min

INGRÉDIENTS

1 tasse (175 g) pois chiches en boîte, rincés et égouttés

2 c. à soupe (30 ml) huile végétale

1 c. à thé (5 ml) paprika

1 c. à thé (5 ml) coriandre moulue

1 c. à thé (5 ml) cumin moulu

1 c. à thé (5 ml) poudre d'ail

1 c. à thé (5 ml) sirop d'érable

⅛ c. à thé (0,5 ml) piment de Cayenne

Fleur de sel

PRÉPARATION

1. Préchauffer le four à 375 °F (190 °C).
2. Dans une poêle, faire revenir les pois chiches dans l'huile à feu vif pendant 2 minutes.
3. Ajouter le reste des ingrédients et bien mélanger.
4. Transférer sur une plaque à pâtisserie.
5. Cuire au four de 30 à 45 minutes. Laisser refroidir et déguster.

NOTE : Se conservent jusqu'à 10 jours à température ambiante.

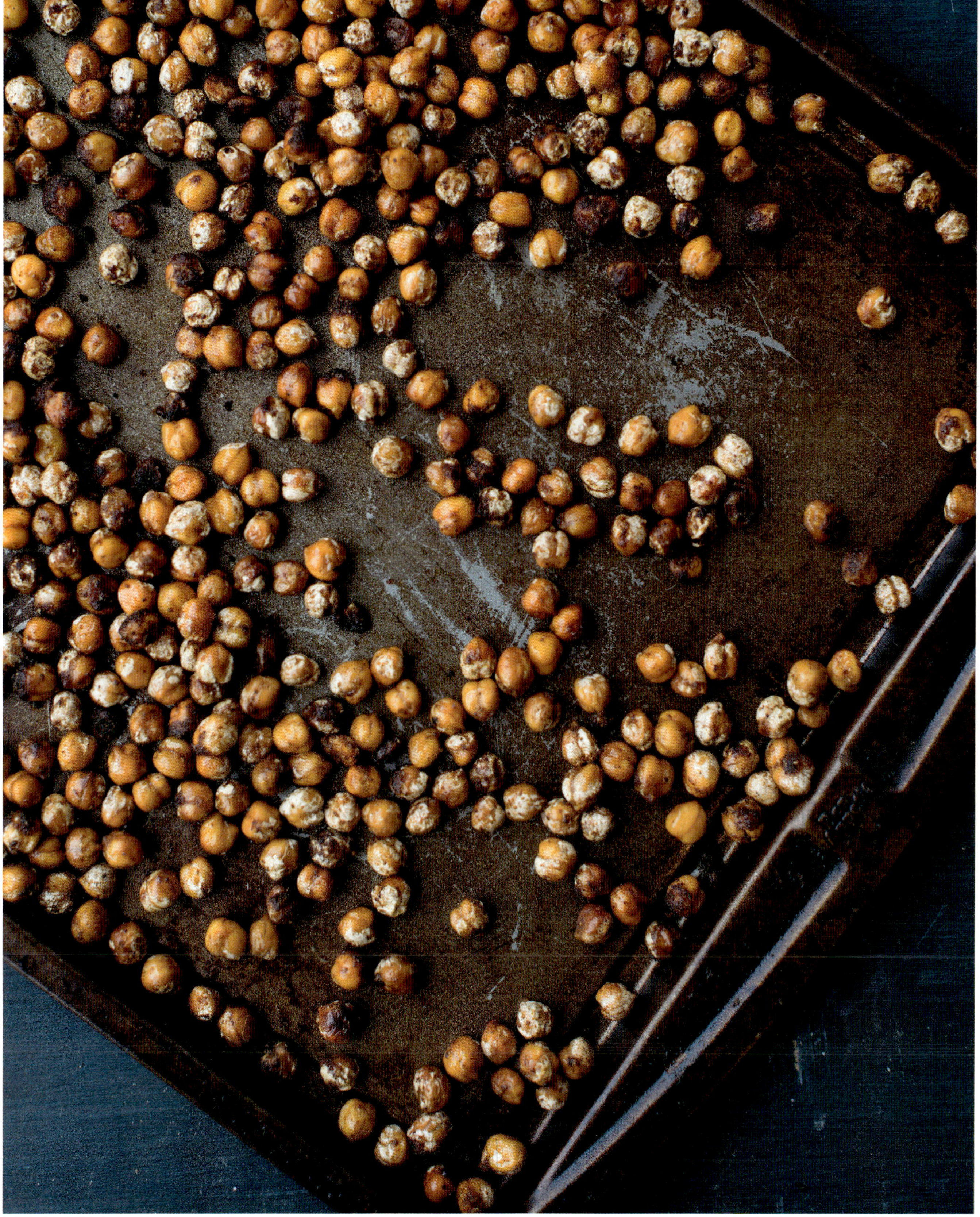

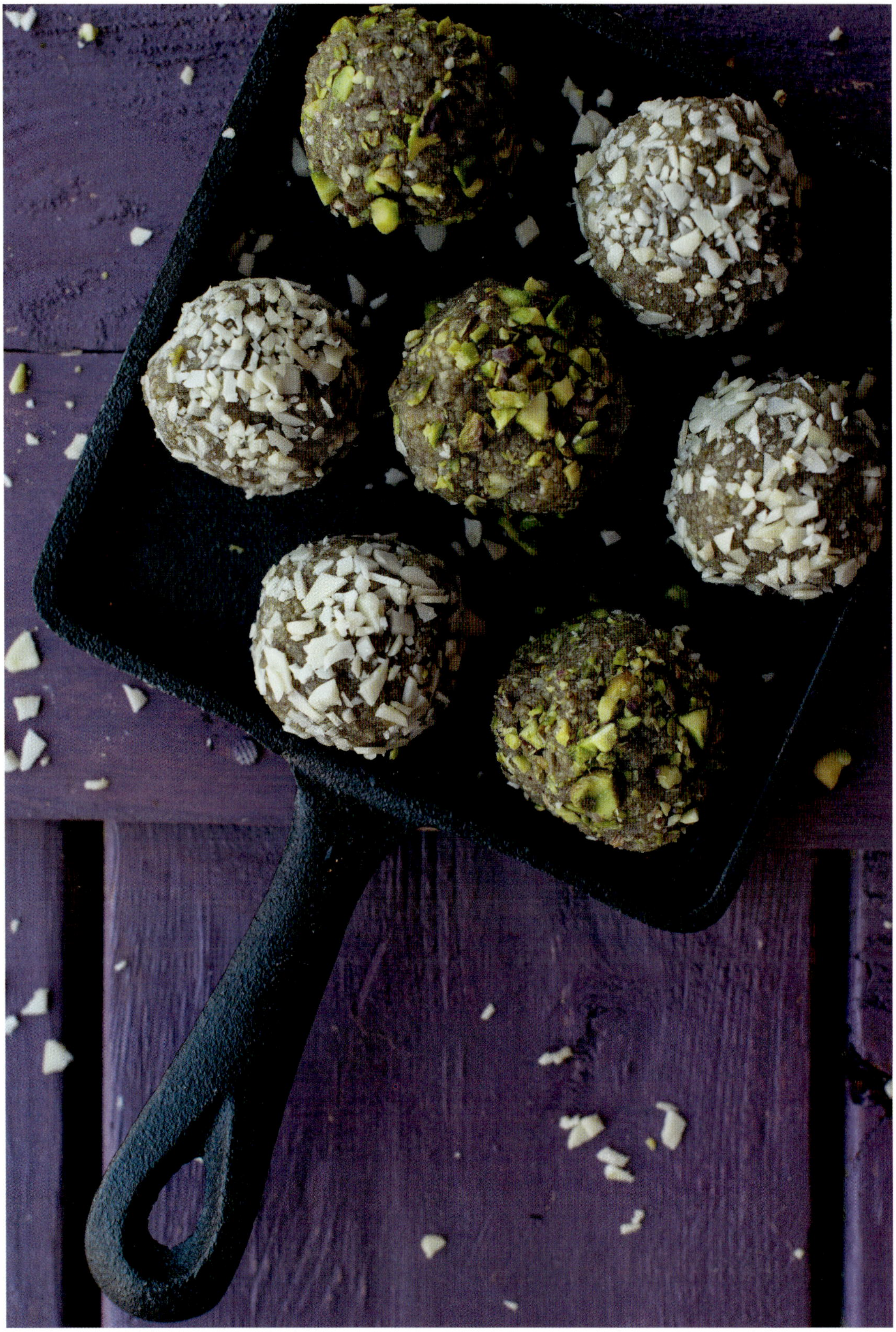

Boules d'énergie à la noix de coco et au matcha

15 min / **24 BOULES**

12 h

INGRÉDIENTS

½ tasse (65 g) noix de cajou

2 c. à thé (10 ml) matcha

2 tasses (250 g) petites dattes dénoyautées

2 c. à soupe (30 ml) huile de coco

2 tasses (160 g) noix de coco râpée non sucrée (+ un peu pour garnir)

1 pincée de sel

Quelques pistaches concassées, pour garnir

PRÉPARATION

1. Faire tremper les dattes dans de l'eau bouillante pendant 10 minutes. Égoutter.
2. Au robot culinaire, mélanger les noix de cajou, le matcha, les dattes, l'huile de coco, la noix de coco et le sel.
3. Former de petites boules et les rouler dans les pistaches et/ou un peu de noix de coco.
4. Réfrigérer jusqu'au lendemain, puis déguster à la température ambiante*.

NOTE : Se conservent jusqu'à 1 semaine au réfrigérateur et peuvent également être congelées.

Biscuits au beurre d'arachide

15 min / **12 BISCUITS**

10 à 12 min

INGRÉDIENTS

1 ⅔ tasse (250 g) farine

1 c. à thé (5 ml) sel

1 c. à thé (5 ml) bicarbonate de sodium

⅔ tasse (140 g) huile de coco solide

⅓ tasse (70 g) sucre de canne

⅓ tasse (70 g) cassonade tassée

¾ tasse (210 g) beurre d'arachide naturel*

1 c. à thé (5 ml) vanille

⅓ tasse (80 ml) lait végétal

PRÉPARATION

1. Préchauffer le four à 375 °F (190 °C).
2. Dans un grand bol, mélanger la farine, le sel et le bicarbonate de sodium. Réserver.
3. Dans un autre bol, battre le reste des ingrédients de 1 à 2 minutes.
4. Incorporer les ingrédients secs aux ingrédients liquides.
5. Former des boules à l'aide d'une cuillère à crème glacée et les déposer sur une plaque à pâtisserie tapissée de papier parchemin ou d'un tapis de cuisson en silicone.
6. Aplatir les biscuits avec une fourchette.
7. Cuire au four de 10 à 12 minutes, puis laisser refroidir sur la plaque avant de déguster.

* Il est impératif d'utiliser du beurre d'arachide naturel. Par ailleurs, prendre soin de retirer l'excédent d'huile qui pourrait s'être formé à la surface du pot.

Biscuits double chocolat

15 min / **12 BISCUITS**

10 min

INGRÉDIENTS

2 tasses (280 g) farine

1 tasse (100 g) poudre d'amande

1 c. à thé (5 ml) sel

1 c. à thé (5 ml) bicarbonate de sodium

¼ tasse (20 g) cacao en poudre

1 tasse (200 g) beurre végétalien

1 tasse (195 g) sucre de canne

½ tasse (105 g) cassonade tassée

1 c. à thé (5 ml) vanille

⅔ tasse (100 g) chocolat mi-amer végétalien, grossièrement haché

⅓ tasse (80 ml) lait végétal

PRÉPARATION

1. Préchauffer le four à 375 °F (190 °C).
2. Dans un grand bol, mélanger la farine, la poudre d'amande, le sel, le bicarbonate de sodium et le cacao. Réserver.
3. Dans un autre bol, battre le beurre, le sucre, la cassonade et la vanille pendant environ 5 minutes, ou jusqu'à l'obtention d'une consistance aérée.
4. Incorporer les ingrédients secs aux ingrédients liquides.
5. Ajouter les morceaux de chocolat et le lait végétal, puis bien mélanger.
6. Former des boules à l'aide d'une cuillère à crème glacée et les déposer sur une plaque à pâtisserie tapissée de papier parchemin ou d'un tapis de cuisson en silicone.
7. Aplatir les boules de pâte avec une fourchette.
8. Cuire au four pendant 10 minutes, puis laisser refroidir sur la plaque avant de déguster.

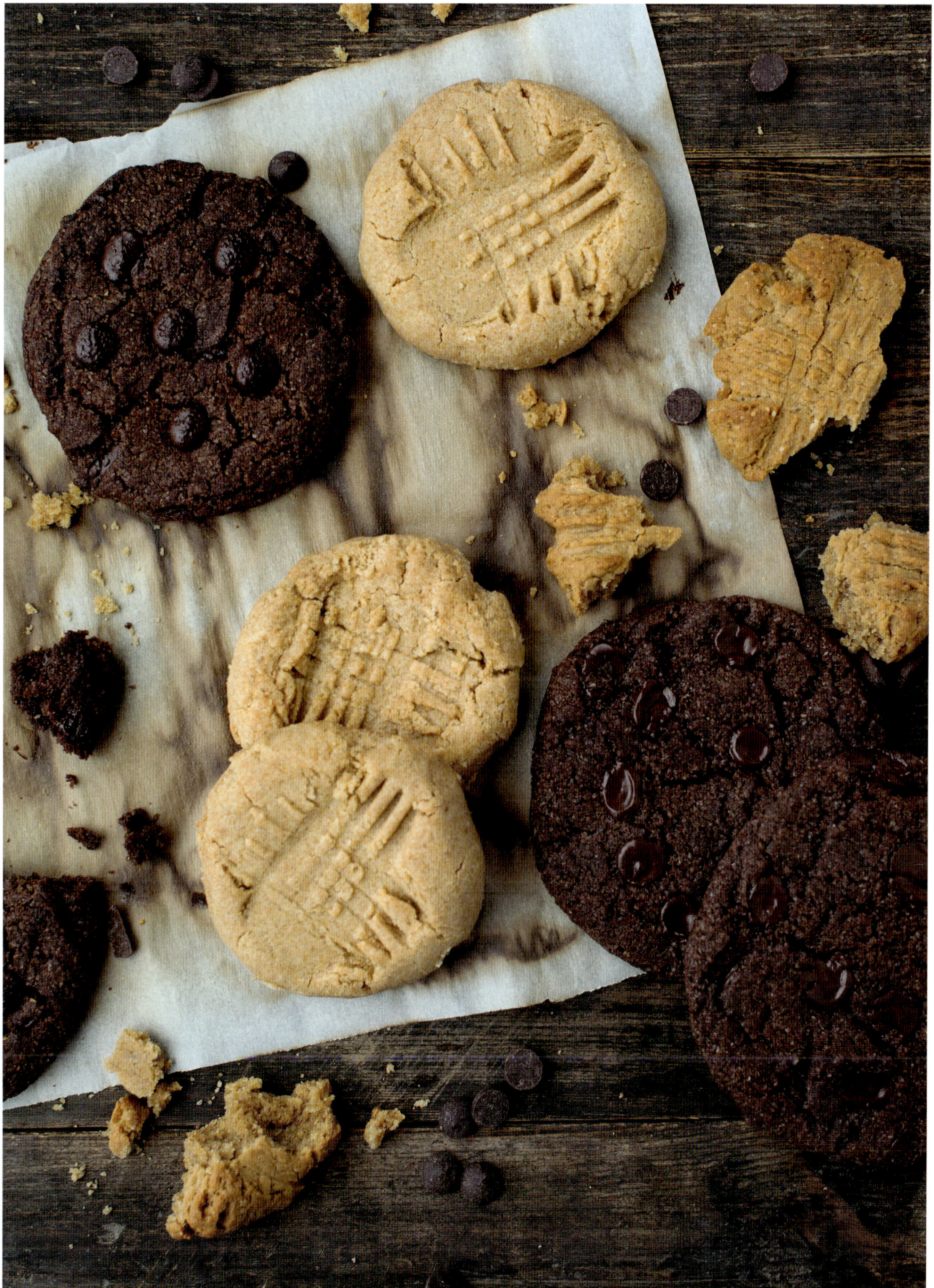

GARNITURES

Oignons rouges marinés

5 min / **ENVIRON 1 TASSE (150 G)**

INGRÉDIENTS

½ tasse (125 ml) vinaigre blanc

½ tasse (125 ml) eau

2 c. à soupe (30 ml) sucre de canne

1 pincée de sel

1 oignon rouge, émincé finement

PRÉPARATION

1. Dans une petite casserole, mélanger le vinaigre, l'eau, le sucre et le sel. Porter à ébullition, puis ajouter l'oignon. Faire bouillir de 1 à 2 minutes.
2. Retirer du feu et égoutter. Réserver.

NOTE : Se conservent jusqu'à 4 jours dans la saumure au réfrigérateur.

Parmesan de cajou

5 min / **ENVIRON ⅔ TASSE (80 G)**

INGRÉDIENTS

1 gousse d'ail, hachée

⅓ tasse (45 g) noix de cajou

⅓ tasse (30 g) levure alimentaire

½ c. à thé (2,5 ml) fleur de sel

PRÉPARATION

1. Au robot culinaire, broyer grossièrement tous les ingrédients.

NOTE : Se conserve jusqu'à 10 jours au réfrigérateur.

Pepperoni de tofu

15 min / **ENVIRON 1½ TASSE (200 G)**

15 à 20 min

15 min

INGRÉDIENTS

1 tasse (180 g) tofu ferme

¼ tasse (25 g) levure alimentaire

2 c. à soupe (30 ml) huile d'olive

1 c. à thé (5 ml) sirop d'érable

½ c. à thé (2,5 ml) sel

½ c. à thé (2,5 ml) graines de fenouil

½ c. à thé (2,5 ml) origan séché

¼ c. à thé (1 ml) piment rouge broyé

PRÉPARATION

1. Préchauffer le four à 375 °F (190 °C).
2. Trancher le tofu finement.
3. Avec un emporte-pièce, découper des rondelles de tofu du format désiré.
4. Dans un grand bol, bien mélanger le reste des ingrédients. Ajouter le tofu et remuer délicatement pour bien l'enrober. Laisser reposer de 15 minutes à quelques heures.
5. Huiler une plaque à pâtisserie et y déposer les rondelles de tofu.
6. Cuire au four pendant 10 minutes.

NOTE : Se conserve jusqu'à 5 jours au réfrigérateur.

Mayonnaise végétale

10 min / **ENVIRON ¾ TASSE (180 ML)**

INGRÉDIENTS

¼ tasse (60 ml) lait végétal non sucré

1 c. à thé (5 ml) moutarde de Dijon

1 c. à thé (5 ml) sirop d'érable

¼ c. à thé (5 ml) sel

½ tasse (125 ml) huile végétale

1 c. à thé (5 ml) jus de citron

1 c. à thé (5 ml) vinaigre de cidre

PRÉPARATION

1. Dans un récipient, mettre le lait végétal, la moutarde de Dijon, le sirop d'érable et le sel.
2. Mélanger avec un pied mélangeur, en versant très lentement l'huile en filet, jusqu'à ce que la mayonnaise prenne.
3. Aussitôt que la mayonnaise commence à prendre, ajouter le jus de citron et le vinaigre de cidre. Bien mélanger quelques secondes à la fois.

NOTE : Se conserve jusqu'à 5 jours au réfrigérateur.

Index des ingrédients

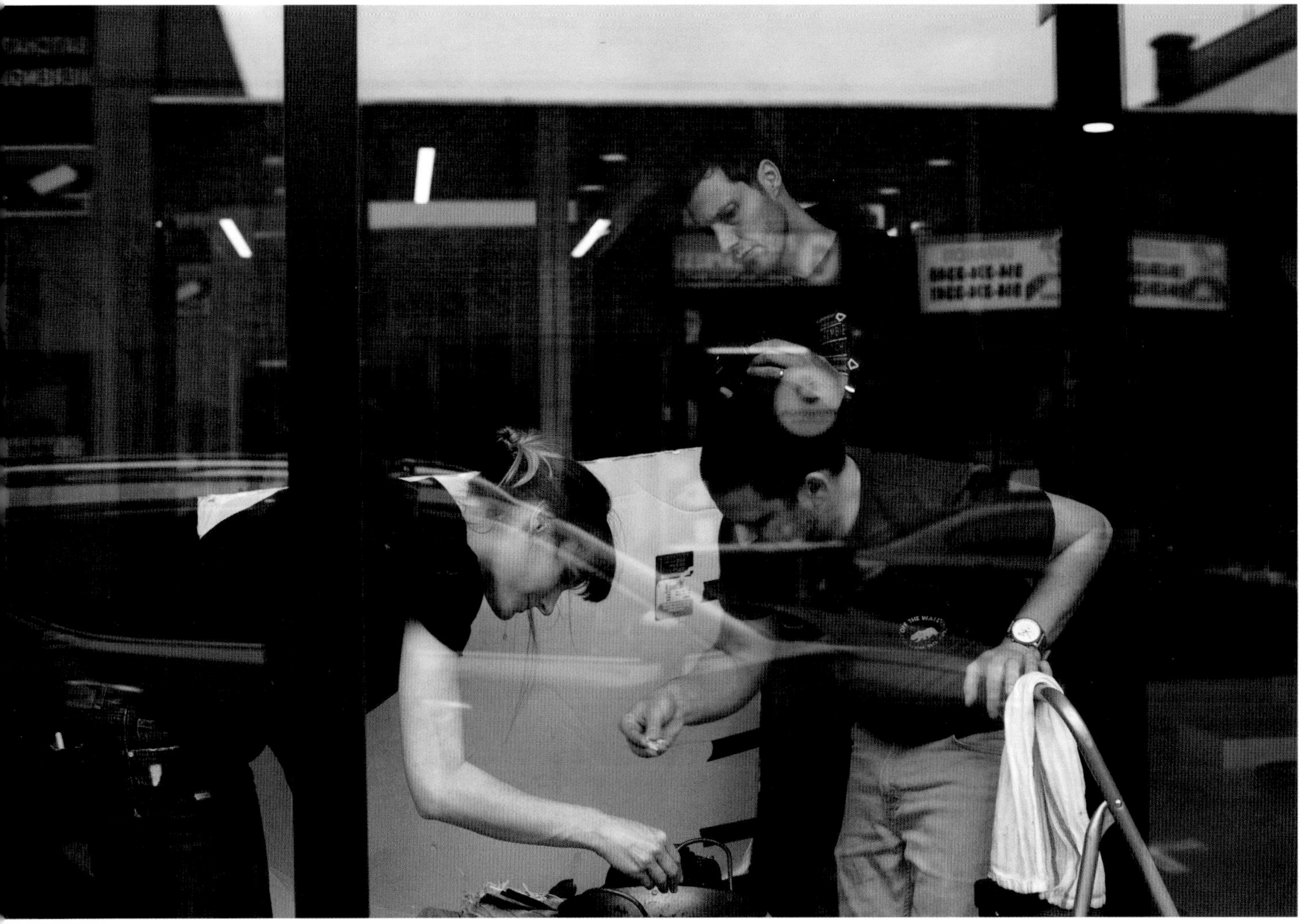

Remerciements

Je tiens tout d'abord à remercier ma femme, Amélie, sans qui ce projet n'aurait jamais vu le jour. Ses encouragements, son soutien et ses critiques plus-que-constructives auront été et seront toujours d'une valeur inestimable à mes yeux. Merci à Samuel Joubert pour son incroyable talent de photographe et de boute-en-train, merci à Noémie Graugnard pour son sens inné de l'esthétique et sa gentillesse. Merci à Emilie Villeneuve, l'instigatrice de ce beau projet, pour son appui. Merci à Marie Guarnera, pour sa patience. Merci à Antoine Ross Trempe de m'avoir permis de réaliser ce livre avec une maison d'édition aussi réputée que Cardinal. Merci à ma mère d'avoir fait naître en moi ce plaisir de cuisiner à l'âge où j'avais encore besoin de monter sur une chaise pour atteindre le comptoir. Merci à Natalie Collins d'avoir testé pratiquement toutes mes recettes. Je tiens aussi à remercier sincèrement les milliers de personnes qui me suivent sur les réseaux sociaux, qui partagent mes recettes, qui prennent le temps de commenter mes publications et qui m'écrivent en privé. Vos commentaires me font toujours chaud au cœur.

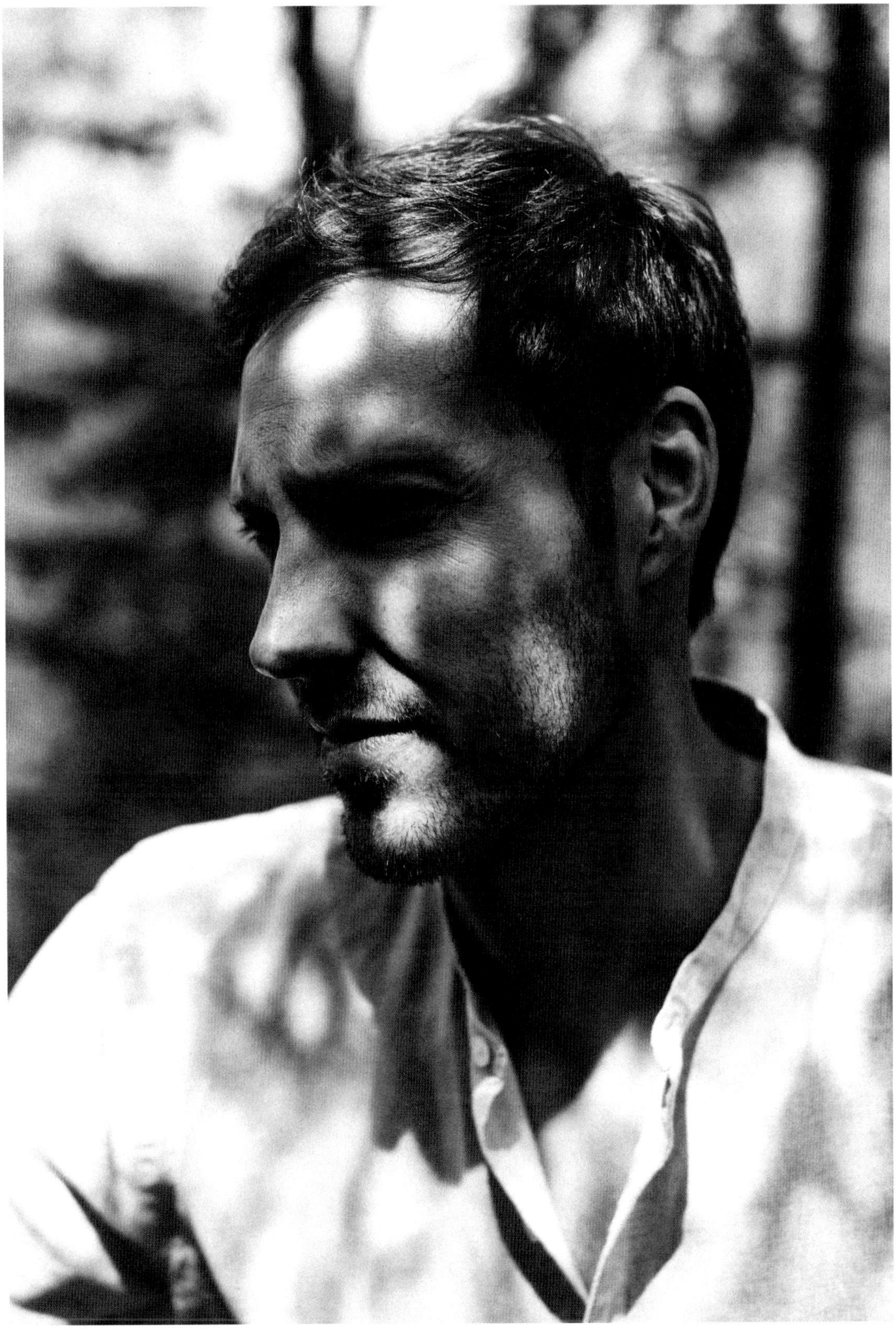

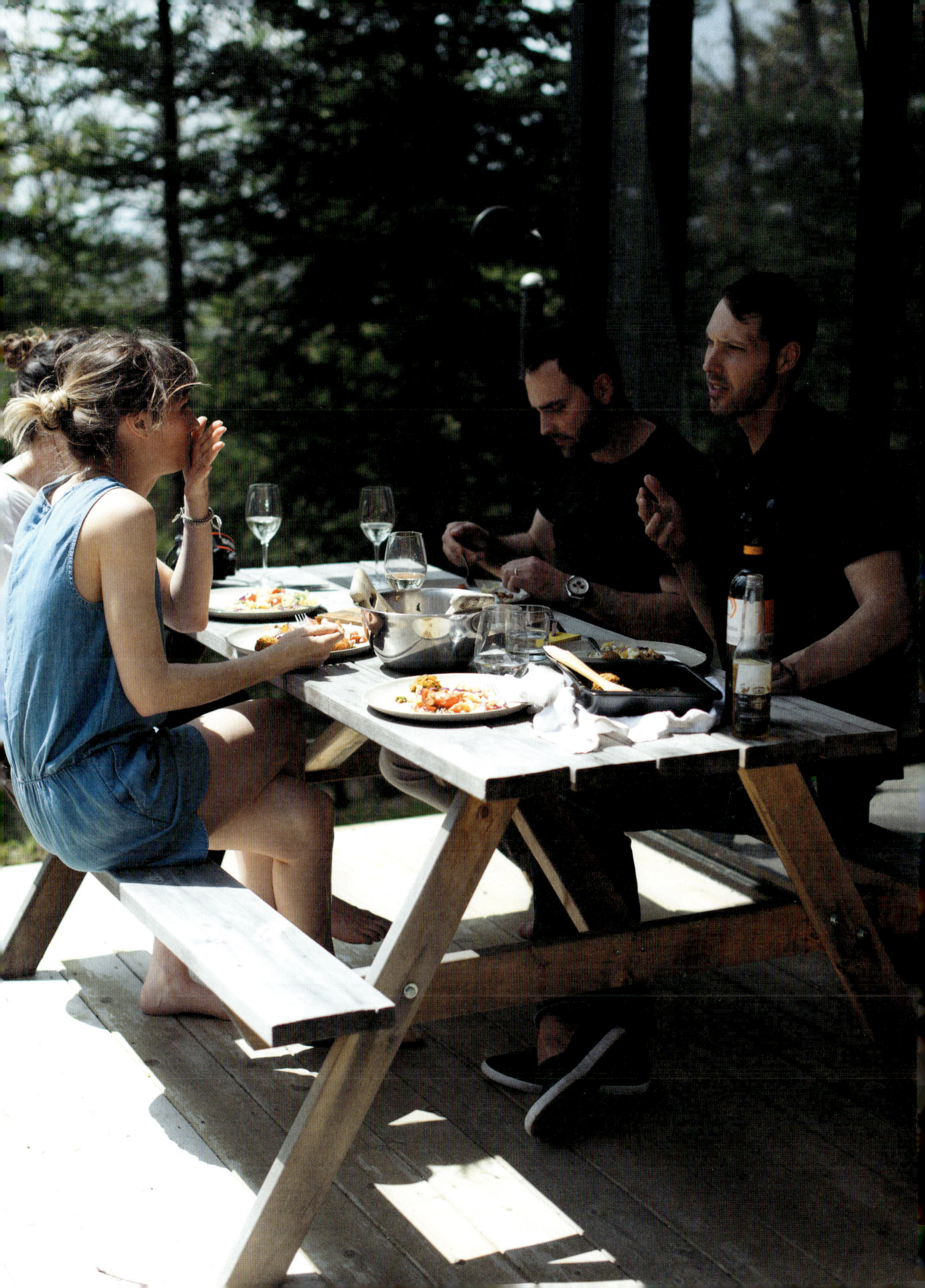